WITHDRAWN

Landmark Essays

Landmark Essays

on
Rhetorical Criticism

Edited by Thomas W. Benson

Hermagoras Press
1993

Landmark Essays Volume Five

Published 1993 by Hermagoras Press,
P.O. Box 1555, Davis, CA 95617

Cover design by Kathi Zamminer

Typesetting and Camera-ready Production
by Graphic Gold, Davis, California
Manufactured in the United States of America
by KNI Inc., Anaheim, California

ISBN 1-880393-08-5

2 3 4 5 6 7 8 9 0

Acknowledgments

I am grateful to Martin Medhurst, who read and commented on the introductory essay to this collection, to my colleagues in the Department of Speech Communication at Pennsylvania State University, and especially to my present and former colleagues in the rhetoric faculty—Richard Gregg, Gerard Hauser, Carroll Arnold, Stephen Browne, Herman Cohen, Eugene White, and Christopher Johnstone—to undergraduate and graduate students who have taught me so much about rhetoric over the years, and to department head Dennis Gouran. And to Margaret, whose professorial schedule and whose dinner table were often inconvenienced by the preparation of the manuscript.

About the Editor

Thomas W. Benson is Edwin Erle Sparks Professor of Rhetoric at Pennsylvania State University. He is coauthor of *Reality Fictions: The Films of Frederick Wiseman* (with Carolyn Anderson); *Documentary Dilemmas: Frederick Wiseman's "Titicut Follies"* (with Carolyn Anderson); *Nonverbal Communication* (with Kenneth Frandsen); coeditor of *Rhetorical Dimensions in Media* (with Martin Medhurst); *Readings in Classical Rhetoric* (with Michael Prosser) and *Readings in Medieval Rhetoric* (with Joseph Miller and Michael Prosser); and editor of *American Rhetoric: Context and Criticism* and *Speech Communication in the Twentieth Century*. He has served as editor of *Communication Quarterly* and *The Quarterly Journal of Speech*.

Table of Contents

Introduction

Essays

Introduction

"Beacons and Boundary-Markers: Landmarks in Rhetorical Criticism"

by Thomas W. Benson

This book is an anthology of "landmark" essays in rhetorical criticism. In historical usage, a landmark marks a path or a boundary; as a metaphor in social and intellectual history, "landmark" signifies some act or event that marks a significant achievement or turning point in the progress or decline of human effort. Hence, what may count as a landmark for one sojourner or one generation may fade from memory and be replaced by the next. In the history of Western law, it was considered a crime to remove or efface a physical landmark. In academic writing, on the other hand, there are rewards for some measure of originality. In the history of an academic discipline, we seem to mix the historically established senses of "landmark" together, jostling to set out and protect the turfmarkers of academic specialization; aligning footnotes to signify the beacons that have guided our thought (and that establish our affiliations); and, against these "conservative" tendencies, attempting to contribute fresh insights that tempt others along new trails. I have tried to choose essays for this collection that give some sense of the history of rhetorical criticism in this century, especially as it has been practiced in the discipline of speech communication, and have especially tried to emphasize materials that may illustrate where the discipline conceives itself to be going—how it has marked its boundaries; how it has established beacons to invite us to safety or warn us from the rocks; how it has sought to preserve a tradition by subjecting it to constant revision and struggle.

We might as well admit at the outset that what is defined as "rhetoric" and what passes as meeting the requirements of "criticism" are themselves contested issues. The contests over these issues, I hope, will form part of the pleasure a reader may take in looking over the essays in this volume.

In the hope of providing some coherence, I have limited the scope of this collection—with many misgivings—to rhetorical criticism as it has been practiced and understood within the discipline of speech communication in North America in this century.[1] I do this partly against the voice of my own

---

[1] Kenneth Burke, who is represented in this volume by his essay on Hitler's Mein Kampf, was not formally a member of the discipline of speech communication, though the discipline cannot fairly be represented without noting his tremendous influence. Burke was a member of the editorial board of the *Quarterly Journal of Speech*, 1987-1989. For decades, rhetorical criticism has been seen as one of

conscience and my own habits as a rhetorical critic, but out of the constraints of trying to fashion a volume limited in size—and price. Even so, in limiting itself to rhetorical criticism as seen from speech communication, a collection of this size cannot hope to represent a century's activities in a discipline so diverse. Worse yet, our limits, though necessary, leave out much that is immediately and organically relevant, since rhetorical criticism is a thriving interdisciplinary practice in literary and cultural studies generally, and one that cuts across the boundaries of institutional compartments. For these limitations, I offer the usual apologies, and promise to provide some hints along the way about parallel and divergent developments. But what remains, limits or no, is of considerable interest, and *it* requires no apologies. The essays collected here are landmarks but are not intended merely as a basement full of plaster monuments or a showcase of blue-ribbon-award-winners. Singly and together, these essays help us to mark where we have been and to move our inquiries forward—they are intended not simply to be admired but to be used.

I have chosen essays that, taken together, represent some of the major features of rhetorical criticism as it has unfolded since the establishment of the first speech departments in this century. But I have avoided arranging the essays to illustrate an array of brand-name methodologies of criticism, since such a venture seems to me self-defeating, though perhaps consoling. At its best, criticism is driven by a fascination with the particular, though it struggles to articulate the particularity of a given case in terms of larger concerns—interpretive, historical, technical, theoretical, and philosophical. Rhetorical criticism typically starts from the observation that rhetorical acts— say, a parliamentary speech or a Puritan sermon or a prosecutor's summa-tion—are the responses of fallible human beings to situations in which certain truth is unattainable and the assent of the audience is unpredictable. Facing these uncertainties, and given a vast variety of possible things to say, the speaker utters a speech. The speech may be more or less wise, more or less ethical, more or less effective, but there will never be a perfect speech with which to compare it. Rhetorical critics delight in this set of difficulties, taking moral and intellectual pleasure from trying to discern in a systematic way the meaning and significance of the unpredictable—but now actualized—speech. They do this by drawing upon the same body and lore of tradition available to speakers, a great intellectual grab-bag called rhetoric.

Rhetoric is variously understood as the study of techniques for fashioning discourses and more generally as an element of all symbolic, social actions—

---

three subfields of rhetorical studies in speech communication—rhetorical theory, rhetorical criticism, and public address. The three divisions, however, are not exhaustive of the field of rhetoric nor discrete categories in relation to each other. The present anthology, for reasons of space, omits rhetorical critiques of film, literature, and several other media and genres actively studied by rhetorical critics. For a sample of such works see, for example, Martin J. Medhurst and Thomas W. Benson, eds., *Rhetorical Dimensions in Media: A Critical Casebook*, 2nd ed. (Dubuque, IA: Kendall/Hunt, 1991).

since all human action depends on meaning-making, and all making of meanings is contingent and persuasive. In this sense, rhetoric is central to the crafting and communication of human knowledge; to the construction of self, the other, and society; to the inducement of cooperation and conflict. Rhetorical criticism has traditionally inquired, on a case-by-case basis, into how these symbolic functions are produced in and by texts, typically by close textual analysis and a variety of explorations of the historical and cultural context of those texts.

Speakers and rhetorical critics inevitably work within a situation in which it is possible to do better or worse but not possible to do perfectly—despite the always aggravating circumstance that symbolic forms seem to suggest the possibility of perfection. It follows that rhetorical action, and rhetorical theory and criticism, can never be codified and completed. Though this does not make rhetorical action, theory, and criticism pointless, it should prompt us to some humility. Rhetorical criticism, much like Aristotle's notion of rhetoric itself, is a cultivated faculty of discerning and attempting to bring into being in the individual case the technical moves and ethical possibilities of a civic culture.

The story of the development of rhetorical criticism in speech communication has been sketched in a number of places. As the story has been told in recent years, it is a tale of blighted and timid beginnings, of confusion and deferral, as a bold and sprawling but not very scholarly cluster of communication disciplines broke off from departments of English in the period 1909-1915, created a curriculum of skills courses for undergraduates, which they defended with a narrow reliance on a watered-down Aristotelianism, and—take your choice—either matured into a vibrant intellectual enterprise at the heart of the contemporary humanities and human sciences or—the gloomier version—became bogged down in grand theorizing, cookie-cutter criticism, second rate and derivative scholarship, and a cowardly, self-imposed enslavement to the basic service course.[2] Academics in all fields are terrible worriers, particularly about the health of their own resumes, departments, and

---

[2] For a contextualized sketch of rhetorical criticism in Greek and Roman antiquity, see D. A. Russell, *Criticism in Antiquity* (London: Duckworth, 1981), 114-127; for recent studies of rhetorical criticism in the field of speech communication, see Richard B. Gregg, "The Criticism of Symbolic Inducement: A Critical-Theoretical Connection," in Thomas W. Benson, ed., *Speech Communication in the 20th Century* (Carbondale: Southern Illinois University Press, 1985), 41-62; David Zarefsky, "The State of the Art in Public Address Scholarship," in Michael C. Leff and Fred Kauffeld, *Texts in Context* (Davis, CA: Hermagoras Press, 1989), 13-28; Martin J. Medhurst, "Public Address and Significant Scholarship: Four Challenges to the Rhetorical Renaissance," in Leff & Kauffeld, eds., *Texts in Context*, 29-42; Dilip Parameshwar Gaonkar, "The Oratorical Text: The Enigma of Arrival," in Leff & Kauffeld, *Texts in Context*, 255-275; Thomas W. Benson, "History, Criticism, and Theory in the Study of American Rhetoric," in Thomas W. Benson, ed., *American Rhetoric: Context and Criticism* (Carbondale: Southern Illinois University Press, 1989), 1-17; Martin J. Medhurst, "The Academic Study of Public Address: A Tradition in Transition," in Martin J. Medhurst, ed., *Landmark Essays in Public Address* (Davis: Hermagoras Press, 1993); Martin J. Medhurst and Thomas W. Benson, "Rhetorical Studies in a Media Age," in Martin J. Medhurst and Thomas W. Benson, eds., *Rhetorical Dimensions in Media*, 2d ed. (Dubuque: Kendall/Hunt, 1991), ix-xxiii.

disciplines, and, to be sure, there is some truth in the gloomier version of rhetorical scholarship in speech communication. But there is, on the whole, probably more to be said for a celebratory version. Journals in communication studies are thriving, and have probably never been more intellectually vibrant and far-reaching. University presses are publishing rhetorical criticism written by scholars from speech communication, English, and virtually every other field in the humanities and social sciences. Graduate programs in rhetoric (usually combined with communication studies in general) are active in most of the best universities in the country, and especially in the great public universities. The small sample of studies gathered here (and the enormous number for which there was no space) testify, it seems to me, to an energetic intellectual conversation—full of wonderful voices, a constantly refreshed enthusiasm for the experiment of democratic rhetoric, an ironic puzzlement at the persistence of the often scandalous abuses of truth and power in rhetoric-in-practice; and, always, delightful surprises.

The essays gathered in this volume illustrate something of the development and range of rhetorical criticism. Each of them contributes, often in multiple and complex ways, to what have emerged as central themes for critical inquiry—rhetoric as a situated, prudential action; rhetoric as an appeal to judgment; rhetoric as constitutive of identity; rhetoric as rooted in underlying, often invisible forms.

Rhetoric as Situated, Prudential Action

Whether considered fairly narrowly as the theory governing public oratory, or more broadly as the study of human symbol-using generally, rhetorical theory—and especially rhetorical criticism—has been interested in the ways in which rhetoric acts in the world, always seeing rhetoric as an action with potential consequences, and as meaningful because of its context. The founders of the American schools of rhetoric in the twentieth century were pragmatists—they saw rhetoric as a way of *doing*. For those who define rhetoric as debate in the public sphere, this is particularly evident. A central principle announced by Herbert Wichelns in his essay on "The Literary Criticism of Oratory" is that rhetorical criticism "is not concerned with permanence, nor yet with beauty. It is concerned with effect. It regards a speech as a communication to a specific audience, and holds its business to be the analysis and appreciation of the orator's method of imparting his ideas to his hearers."[3]

Wichelns's essay both stimulated and inhibited the flowering of rhetorical criticism in speech communication. On the one hand, Wichelns pointed clearly to the speeches of practical people in the public sphere as the proper

---

[3] Herbert Wichelns, "The Literary Criticism of Oratory." Unless otherwise noted, quotations in this introductory essay are from the essay by the cited author collected in this volume, and will appear without further citation.

object of study for rhetorical critics. But though his essay is full of the making of distinctions, it is full, too, of a sense of the instability of those distinctions. The inhibiting effects of his essay resulted partly, it seems to me, from a logical double-bind that was set in motion by the claim that rhetorical criticism "is concerned with effect." One reading sees "effect" as implying a search for "causes," which, in the climate of research for several decades, presumed invariant, psychological "effects" that could be achieved by the right combination of stimuli drawn from the armamentarium of traditional rhetoric. In the assumptions taken for granted by this view, psychological causation was a universal phenomenon, and the audience a mere respondent to irresistible discursive forces. Hence, criticism was a sort of case-by-case search for contributions to a grand social-scientific theory of rhetorical causation. This path, based on a misreading of Wichelns, who specifically denied the likelihood of finding "permanent" rules of effect, became a conceptual dead end, but its influence still lingers in a spirited discourse about the role of theory on the one hand and history on the other in rhetorical criticism—theory aspiring to stable generalities and history appealing to the claim that communication cannot be understood apart from its material, contingent, and highly particular situation.

At its best, rhetorical criticism focusing on effect has always conceded the peculiar ambiguities of its own categories, as in the observation of Carroll C. Arnold, writing of Lord Thomas Erskine: "Immediate influence, not beauty or profundity, was Lord Erskine's goal in the courtroom; in consequence, he achieved all three. In the process, he left his mark on Anglo-American law, advanced the general cause of political liberty, and at so unlikely a place as the counsel's bench, he enlarged the store of imaginative literature in the English language."

Another way of reading Wichelns is to understand him as concerned with the broadly pragmatic goals of an orator operating in an immediate situation, whose very immediacy and particularity make it impossible to derive fixed and predictive rules of rhetorical effect, though "effect" is still an operating goal of the speaker. After all these years, it also seems more intellectually respectful to Wichelns to regard his formulation as a site of conversation rather than as an attempt at a fixed rule. Indeed, in the years since Wichelns, virtually every major term in his proposition has been contested: the communicating agent is not assumed to be male; the notion of an autonomous, intending agent is dismissed by some as an untenable romantic humanism; the influence of rhetoric, though perhaps not permanent, may last beyond an immediate occasion; "beauty" is not simply an attribute of a poetic artifact but itself a situated communicative effect, hence perhaps "rhetorical"; "effect" should not be taken to presume involuntary submission on the part of an audience, who may better be conceived of as co-active participants; the oration is not the only symbolic form that may be rhetorical; in our day, "literary criticism" is no longer concerned solely with permanence and beauty, but also interrogates issues of authorship, situation, culture, and ideology; the communicator may be doing something other than "imparting ideas." And so on. My own personal recollection of Wichelns as a teacher is that though he might have disagreed with any of these contestations, he would have welcomed their discussion, and would have been particularly delighted with the ways in which the critics collected in this volume stretch our understanding of rhetoric in their readings of particular rhetorical actions.

Marie Hochmuth Nichols's celebrated essay on Abraham Lincoln's First Inaugural Address sets forth an extended description of the historical moment in which Lincoln came to speak, attempting to place the contemporary reader sufficiently into the situation to appreciate Lincoln's rhetorical achievement. Other critics, such as Michael Calvin McGee, have come to question what it means to speak of the "situatedness" of rhetoric. McGee claims that the analysis and explanation needed for rhetorical histories "must be distinct from traditional critical studies in public address, . . . for there must be a consistent emphasis on *situation* at the expense of focus on speaker, the speech, or the audience. Rather than study 'context' or 'occasion' only for analysis of the interrelationships among speaker, speech, and audience, in other words, one must look to speaker/speech/audience relationships for evidence of *situation*, proof of the shape and character of the rhetorical force in history in one time-setting."[4]

Critical studies of the role of situation in rhetoric have sometimes been a source of confusion, which makes this area a promising site for refreshed understandings and continuing inquiry. "Situation," in rhetoric, is used, sometimes equivocally, in several different senses. For Lloyd Bitzer, the "rhetorical situation" is stipulated philosophically as a set of pre-conditions and relations that define what is to count as rhetoric: "Rhetorical situation may be defined as a complex of persons, events, objects, and relations presenting an actual or potential exigence which can be completely or partially removed if discourse, introduced into the situation, can so constrain human decision or action as to bring about the significant modification of the exigence."[5]

A competing sense of situation that critics sometimes appeal to implicitly is the notion that the motive and meaning of any discourse for its participants are strongly influenced by the relevant "situation," "context," or, borrowing Kenneth Burke's terminology, the "scene." One result of these different usages is that critics sometimes find themselves equivocating amongst three theoretical agendas, often without clearly distinguishing them.

One way of following Bitzer's formulation for the practical critic is to regard situation as a philosophically transcendent ideal, and to determine the extent to which a given case meets the standards of that ideal. Another track turns the Wichelns doctrine that rhetoric is situated in immediacy and therefore concerned with "effect" into a demand that critics try to account for

---

[4] Michael C. McGee, "The Fall of Wellington: A Case Study of the Relationship between Theory, Practice, and Rhetoric in History," *Quarterly Journal of Speech* 63 (1977): 41-42.
[5] Lloyd Bitzer, "The Rhetorical Situation," *Philosophy and Rhetoric* 1 (1968): 6.

effect in some general sense, that is, to contribute to a general, stable, social-scientific account of what accounts for the success of discourse in the given case—the answer, by implication, usually being in some pre-existing and universal psychological response mechanism which it is the duty of criticism eventually to discover. In some of its worst moments in the development of the discipline, such criticism implicitly reduced the rhetorical situation to a sort of Skinner box. Both of these usages of the situation-effect relation, one that I have called philosophical and the other that I have called social-scientific, regard the truth, of which the critic strives to reveal a part, as always and already existing, waiting to be discovered. In practice, they are often combined with each other, sometimes fruitfully, sometimes with confusing results.

Still a third response to the notion of situation emphasizes the particularity that is implied by situation, regarding both "rhetoric" as a discipline and a traditional practice, and the particular rhetorical event as themselves the product of human action in a set of contingent circumstances—that is, as historically situated rather than as transcendently pre-existent. For these critics, an understanding of the dynamics of a particular text, revealed by close reading, or a detailed study of the relation of the text to its context, themselves justify the production of continued case studies—with or without resort to larger theoretical appeals—though "theory," in some sense, can never be entirely absent, even if it is merely implicit.

These three general understandings of the significance of "situation," each of them in turn understood in various ways by their adherents, each of them usually immanent in every work of rhetorical criticism, form part of the "situation" in which rhetorical criticism takes place as a disciplinary practice, both stimulating ongoing debate and occasionally—in less fortunate ways—providing the grounds for ongoing institutional gatekeeping, boundary-maintenance, and equivocation. In my own view, since this and other major issues are unlikely ever to be finally resolved, both institutional success and intellectual achievement are more likely to be stimulated by a pluralistic welcoming of divergent approaches than by any attempt to arrive at a single, final paradigm. Hence, in part, the pluralism—some might even say the eclecticism—of this collection.

Appeal to Judgment: Rhetoric and Social Knowledge

Rhetorical acts are always in some important sense about ideas, which they may either simply advocate or actually bring into being, and about which they ask listeners to make judgments. A central issue in contemporary rhetorical criticism is to understand the ways in which knowledge is not simply conveyed but constituted in the rhetorical act. Many of the critics in this volume are concerned with the communicator's ideas and with what it means to advocate those ideas.

Robert L. Scott employs a case study of Arthur Larson to undermine our confidence in "an orderly statement of facts" as "an ideal in standard discussions of rhetorical theory and practice." Scott argues that in ordinary human discourse, facts are not merely reported, but selected and even created, and should be understood as part of "human choice and design in all discourse."

John Angus Campbell, in a long series of articles on Charles Darwin, has shown the extent to which Darwin's work was rhetorical, not only in the sense that Darwin engaged in a persuasive campaign to promote his science, but in the stronger sense that rhetorical proofs were inseparable from the very formation of Darwin's theories. Campbell's essay on "The Rhetorical Ancestry of an Idea," reprinted in this anthology, is an early instance of a highly promising line of inquiry into the rhetoric of science or, as it is sometimes called, the rhetoric of inquiry.

In rhetorical criticism in general, the past two decades have witnessed a remarkable growth in studies of how we may understand the functions of rhetoric as a way of *knowing*. For centuries, rhetoricians have asked whether a rhetorical figure, such as metaphor, is best understood as a decoration, an inducement, or a proof. Or, some have asked, is metaphor itself a form of knowledge? Some have pressed further to argue that metaphor—or rhetoric generally—is the very substance of all knowledge. Similarly, rhetoricians have speculated about whether rhetoric as a whole is best considered as a specialized mode of persuasion, as persuasion in general, as the mode of knowing at play in the contingent world of political life, or as the mode of communicating or constituting knowledge of any sort.[6]

Persistence of Forms: Genre and Myth

Rhetoricians have long been fascinated by the persuasive power of traditional forms in the hands of a master speaker or artist. Some rhetorical theorists and critics go further and argue that traditional forms, such as genre, myth, tropes, and stories are themselves the fundamental material of our thinking, and govern our ideas without our awareness—hence they appear in human discourses not merely as devices of persuasion but as the underlying forms that make thought possible, sometimes with the risk of distortions and confusions. We might think of mythic and generic rhetorical criticism as emphasizing the constitutive force of the *arts* of rhetoric—rhetoric as a way of *making*. But each of the critics collected here raises at least implicitly the possibility that genre and myth are embedded in rhetorical texts not simply as

---

[6] Robert Scott initiated a re-examination of rhetoric as a way of knowing in his "On Viewing Rhetoric as Epistemic," *Central States Speech Journal* 38 (1967): 9-17. More recently, rhetorical critics and theorists have also debated this notion under the headings of rhetoric of science and rhetoric of inquiry. See, for example, Herbert W. Simons, ed., *The Rhetorical Turn: Invention and Persuasion in the Conduct of Inquiry* (Chicago: University of Chicago Press, 1990); John S. Nelson, Allan Megill, and Donald N. McCloskey, eds., *The Rhetoric of the Human Sciences: Language and Argument in Scholarship and Public Affairs* (Madison: University of Wisconsin Press, 1987).

ways of constituting the text or appealing to the listener, but that, at a more fundamental level, the very basis of our thoughts is in important ways socially and culturally pre-figured.

In "The Rhetoric of Hitler's 'Battle,'" Kenneth Burke argues that Hitler bases part of his demagogic effectiveness upon a rhetoric that is "a bastardization of fundamentally religious patterns of thought"—patterns that so shape social consciousness that their distortion by Hitler, in the circumstances of Nazi Germany, were insidiously powerful.

Stephen E. Lucas considers the persistence of generic patterns that might have influenced George Washington's first inaugural address, concluding that Washington's speech "was shaped above all by his personal beliefs and by his view of the rhetorical situation as he assumed the presidency. His response to that situation, however, appears to have been modulated by a set of generic constraints derived from the rhetoric of office-taking, from the inaugural speeches of Virginia's colonial governors, and, perhaps, from the accession speeches of eighteenth-century British monarchs."[7]

Constitution of Identity: Speaker, Audience, Other

In assessing the instruments available to prove a persuasive case, Aristotle argued that "character," as it is established in the speech, "is almost, so to speak, the controlling factor in persuasion."[8] Other writers on rhetoric have argued that, in important respects, the identities of the speaker, the listener, and other persons referred to in a speech or other rhetorical text are actually *created* by the message, constituting social roles and personae that would not exist otherwise. In this sense, rhetoric is a way of *being/becoming*. Several of the essays in this collection center on the constitution of identity.

In its consideration of the nature and relations of speaking-listening subjects, rhetorical criticism can be seen to work through—sometimes implicitly—various versions of a theory of selfhood and social identity. Some rhetorical critics, loyal to the Aristotelian and Ciceronian ideal of rhetoric as civic action, have a strong attachment to a notion of the autonomous, humanistic subject, engaged in purposeful speaking and judicious listening. Others, explicitly or implicitly, appear to be drawn by rhetoric's longstanding interest in technique to a notion of the listening subject as a less than

---

[7] For other studies of genre in rhetorical studies, see, for example, Karlyn Kohrs Campbell and Kathleen Hall Jamieson, *Deeds Done in Words: Presidential Rhetoric and the Genres of Governance* (Chicago: University of Chicago Press, 1990); and Herbert Simons and Aram Aghazarian, eds., *Form, Genre, and the Study of Political Discourse* (Columbia: University of South Carolina Press, 1986). On the rhetorical study of myth, see Janice Hocker Rushing, "The Rhetoric of the American Western Myth," *Communication Monographs* 50 (1983): 14-32; Janice Hocker Rushing, "Evolution of 'The New Frontier' in *Alien* and *Aliens*: Patriarchal Co-optation of the Feminine Archetype," *Quarterly Journal of Speech* 75 (1989): 1-24; Farrel Corcoran, "The Bear in the Back Yard: Myth, Ideology, and Victimage Ritual in Soviet Funerals," *Communication Monographs* 50 (1983): 305-320.

[8] Aristotle, *On Rhetoric*, trans. George A. Kennedy (New York: Oxford University Press, 1991), 38.

autonomous respondent, the clearest version in our century being the behaviorist's picture of listener as an unreflective element in a stimulus-response mechanism. Still other critics and theorists, stimulated by postmodernist theory and by rhetoric's long attachment to textual analysis, are drawn to the theory of the de-centered subject, of the self as a textually constituted entity, conceived as a nexus of textual, symbolic formations in an unending network of semiosis.

Literary critic Wayne C. Booth brought the theme of identity as a rhetorical accomplishment strongly to the critical agenda in 1961 with his *The Rhetoric of Fiction*, in which he describes the role of the "implied author," which he distinguishes from the "real" author of a novel. The implied author is a construction of the "real" author, construed by the reader in the process of reading, and revealed in the text, rather than from the consultation of external, biographical facts. Booth's book set off an active line of technical inquiry that quickly complicated his notion of the implied author.[9]

Among rhetorical critics in speech communication, one of the first major respondents to Booth's work was Edwin Black, a former student of Herbert Wichelns who had in 1965 upset the applecart of instrumental, "neo-Aristotelean" rhetorical criticism with the publication of his *Rhetorical Criticism: A Study in Method*.[10] In "The Second Persona," Black explores the counterpart of Booth's "implied author"—the implied audience, or second persona. "We have learned," says Black, "to keep continuously before us the possibility, and in some cases the probability, that the author implied by the discourse is an artificial creation: a persona, but not necessarily a person. . . . What equally well solicits our attention is that there is a second persona also implied by a discourse, and that persona is its implied auditor." In concluding his essay, Black remarks that "in all rhetorical discourse, we can find enticements not simply to believe something, but to *be* something."

As Black concedes, he was not the first to notice the implied auditor in discourse; similarly, others before and since Black have noted how populated is our discourse with speakers, auditors, and others, all of them in part constituted by discourse—which is in turn constrained by the immediate and larger situations and forms of culture. As with other essays in this volume, Black's essay both charted a theoretical path that other critics might follow and, equally important, helped clear a space for wide-ranging inquiry into the existential, ideological, and ethical dimensions of discourse.

Maurice Charland's essay on "constitutive rhetoric" argues that, radical as Black's position was, it was not radical enough, in that it appears to accept the pre-existence of a "person" who then identifies with a persona offered by a text. Charland points out that, if we accept the full implications of "the radical edge of Kenneth Burke's identificatory principle, . . . we cannot accept the 'givenness' of 'audience,' 'person,' or 'subject,' but must consider their

[9] Wayne C. Booth, *The Rhetoric of Fiction* (Chicago: The University of Chicago Press, 1961).
[10] Edwin Black, *Rhetorical Criticism: A Study in Method* (New York: Macmillan, 1965).

very textuality, their very constitution in rhetoric as a structured articulation
of signs. We must, in other words, consider the textual nature of social
being." In other words, the subject is "always already" textually constituted.
For many practicing critics, Charland's essay helped to open a still larger
space for critical inquiry or an opportunity for emancipatory social action; for
others, it appeared to open an existential abyss.

An increasingly productive line of investigation in rhetorical scholarship
inquires into the constraints of identity concerning gender, class, race, and
culture. Feminist rhetorical criticism has been particularly stimulated by the
pioneering criticism of Karlyn Kohrs Campbell, represented in this collection
by her study of Elizabeth Cady Stanton's "The Solitude of Self." Campbell
argues that the speech both advocates and, by adopting an unusual, lyric
mode, enacts its thesis about the solitude, individualism, and responsibility of
each person. "To encounter the speech," writes Campbell, "is to experience
the magnitude of human solitude."[11]

Rhetorical Criticism as an Academic Practice

Our consideration of the essays collected in this volume has clustered
them so as to emphasize certain emergent and enduring themes in rhetorical
criticism. And yet it is part of the genius of criticism as an intellectual
practice that seldom are these themes considered separately from one another
by the practicing critic. Rather, these themes—and others—are spun together
in new patterns, depending on the particulars of the case under consideration
and the interests of the critic. Virtually every one of the essays collected here
considers issues of situated practical action *and* socially constructed
knowledge *and* symbolically constituted identities *and* the constraints and
resources of persisting rhetorical forms. Similarly, each of the essays has its
own contribution to make to the theory and philosophy of rhetoric, typically
a contribution made not by offering a single theoretical proposition for which
the case study is offered as evidence but by considering the intersection of
practical, theoretical, and philosophical issues in the untidy, contradictory
materiality of social practice.

Rhetorical criticism, some claim, is a form of argument, but from its
beginnings, criticism has been a form of counter-theoretical practice and not
simply a mode of argument used to support a claim. Even for those critics
who do employ a case study as a way of testing a theoretical claim, there is

[11]For other rhetorical inquiries on the constitution of identity, see, for example, Kenneth Burke, "Antony on Behalf of the Play," in *The Philosophy of Literary Form*, 3d edition (Berkeley: University of California Press, 1973), 329-43; Richard B. Gregg, "The Ego-Function of the Rhetoric of Protest," *Philosophy and Rhetoric* 4 (1971): 71-91; Michael C. McGee, "In Search of 'The People': A Rhetorical Alternative," *The Quarterly Journal of Speech* 61 (1975): 235-49; Walter J. Ong, "The Writer's Audience Is Always a Fiction," in *Interfaces of the Word* (Ithaca: Cornell University Press, 1977), 53-81; Thomas W. Benson, "Rhetoric as a Way of Being," in T. Benson, ed., *American Rhetoric: Context and Criticism* (Carbondale: Southern Illinois University Press, 1989), 293-322.

often a sense that there is more in the event under study than the theory can comfortably account for, and we see the critic struggling to tame, or perhaps to celebrate, this sense of excess. In a sense, criticism is thus theoretically responsible and principled but not merely theoretical. Criticism is a form of interrogation, of performed response, of appreciation, interpretation, explanation, and judgment, always seeking clarity but never easily reducible to a paraphrase. At least, that is what the critics collected here, and the many others to whom I hope these landmark essays will lead the reader, seem to claim.

The Literary Criticism of Oratory

by Herbert A. Wichelns

I

Samuel Johnson once projected a history of criticism "as it relates to judging of authors." Had the great eighteenth-century critic ever carried out his intention, he would have included some interesting comments on the orators and their judges. Histories of criticism, in whole or in part, we now have, and histories of orators. But that section of the history of criticism which deals with judging of orators is still unwritten. Yet the problem is an interesting one, and one which involves some important conceptions. Oratory—the waning influence of which is often discussed in current periodicals—has definitely lost the established place in literature that it once had. Demosthenes and Cicero, Bossuet and Burke, all hold their places in literary histories. But Webster inspires more than one modern critic to ponder the question whether oratory is literature; and if we may judge by the emphasis of literary historians generally, both in England and in America, oratory is either an outcast or a poor relation. What are the reasons for this change? It is a question not easily answered. Involved in it is some shift in the conception of oratory or of literature, or of both; nor can these conceptions have changed except in response to the life of which oratory, as well as literature, is part.

This essay, it should be said, is merely an attempt to spy out the land, to see what some critics have said of some orators, to discover what their mode of criticism has been. The discussion is limited in the main to Burke and a few nineteenth-century figures—Webster, Lincoln, Gladstone, Bright, Cobden—and to the verdicts on these found in the surveys of literary history, in critical essays, in histories of oratory, and in biographies.

Of course, we are not here concerned with the disparagement of oratory. With that, John Morley once dealt in a phrase: "Yet, after all, to disparage eloquence is to depreciate mankind."[1] Nor is the praise of eloquence of moment here. What interests us is the method of the critic: his standards, his categories of judgment, what he regards as important. These will show, not so much what he thinks of a great and ancient literary type, as how he thinks

Reprinted from *Studies in Rhetoric and Public Speaking in Honor of James Albert Winans.* Edited by A.M. Drummond. (New York: The Century Co., 1925).
[1] *Life of William Ewart Gladstone*, New York, 1903, II, 593.

in dealing with that type. The chief aim is to know how critics have spoken of orators.

We have not much serious criticism of oratory. The reasons are patent. Oratory is intimately associated with statecraft; it is bound up with the things of the moment; its occasion, its terms, its background, can often be understood only by the careful student of history. Again, the publication of orations as pamphlets leaves us free to regard any speech merely as an essay, as a literary effort deposited at the shrine of the muses in hope of being blessed with immortality. This view is encouraged by the difficulty of reconstructing the conditions under which the speech was delivered; by the doubt, often, whether the printed text of the speech represents what was actually said, or what the orator elaborated afterwards. Burke's corrections are said to have been the despair of his printers.[2] Some of Chatham's speeches, by a paradox of fate, have been reported to us by Samuel Johnson, whose style is as remote as possible from that of the Great Commoner, and who wrote without even having heard the speeches pronounced.[3] Only in comparatively recent times has parliamentary reporting pretended to give full records of what was actually said; and even now speeches are published for literary or political purposes which justify the corrector's pencil in changes both great and small. Under such conditions the historical study of speech making is far from easy.

Yet the conditions of democracy necessitate both the making of speeches and the study of the art. It is true that other ways of influencing opinion have long been practised, that oratory is no longer the chief means of communicating ideas to the masses. And the change is emphasized by the fact that the newer methods are now beginning to be investigated, sometimes from the point of view of the political student, sometimes from that of the "publicity expert." But, human nature being what it is, there is no likelihood that face to face persuasion will cease to be a principal mode of exerting influence, whether in courts, in senate-houses, or on the platform. It follows that the critical study of oratorical method is the study, not of a mode outworn, but of a permanent and important human activity.

Upon the great figures of the past who have used the art of public address, countless judgments have been given. These judgments have varied with the bias and preoccupation of the critics, who have been historians, biographers, or literary men, and have written accordingly. The context in which we find criticism of speeches, we must, for the purposes of this essay at least, both note and set aside. For though the aim of the critic conditions his approach to our more limited problem—the method of dealing with oratory—still we find that an historian may view an orator in the same light as does a biographer or an essayist. The literary form in which criticism of

---

[2] *Select Works*, ed. E. J. Payne, Oxford, 1892, I, xxxviii.
[3] Basil Williams, *Life of William Pitt*, New York, 1913, II, 335-337.

oratory is set does not afford a classification of the critics.

"There are," says a critic of literary critics, "three definite points, on one of which, or all of which, criticism must base itself. There is the date, and the author, and the work."[4] The points on which writers base their judgments of orators do afford a classification. The man, his work, his times, are the necessary common topics of criticism; no one of them can be wholly disregarded by any critic. But mere difference in emphasis on one or another of them is important enough to suggest a rough grouping. The writers with whom this essay deals give but a subordinate position to the date; they are interested chiefly in the man or in his works. Accordingly, we have as the first type of criticism that which is predominantly personal or biographical, is occupied with the character and the mind of the orator, goes behind the work to the man. The second type attempts to hold the scales even between the biographical and the literary interest. The third is occupied with the work and tends to ignore the man. These three classes, then, seem to represent the practice of modern writers in dealing with orators. Each merits a more detailed examination.

II

We may begin with that type of critic whose interest is in personality, who seeks the man behind the work. Critics of this type furnish forth the appreciative essays and the occasional addresses on the orators. They are as the sands of the sea. Lord Rosebery's two speeches on Burke, Whitelaw Reid's on Lincoln and on Burke, may stand as examples of the character sketch.[5] The second part of Birrell's essay on Burke will serve for the mental character sketch (the first half of the essay is biographical); other examples are Sir Walter Raleigh's essay on Burke and that by Robert Lynd.[6] All these emphasize the concrete nature of Burke's thought, the realism of his imagination, his peculiar combination of breadth of vision with intensity; they pass to the guiding principles of his thought: his hatred of abstraction, his love of order and of settled ways. But they do not occupy themselves with Burke as a speaker, nor even with him as a writer; their first and their last concern is with the man rather than with his works; and their method is to fuse into a single impression whatever of knowledge or opinion they may have of the orator's life and works. These critics, in dealing with the public speaker, think of him as something other than a speaker. Since this type of writing makes but an indirect contribution to our judgment of the orator, there is no need of a more extended account of the method, except as we find it combined with a discussion of the orator's works.

---

[4] D. Nichol Smith, *Functions of Criticism,* Oxford, 1909, p. 15.
[5] See Rosebery, *Appreciations and Addresses,* London, 1899, and Whitelaw Reid, *American and English Studies,* New York, 1913, II.
[6] See Augustine Birrell, *Obiter Dicta,* New York, 1887, II; Walter Raleigh, *Some Authors,* Oxford, 1923; Robert Lynd, *Books and Authors,* London, 1922.

III

Embedded in biographies and histories of literature, we find another type of criticism, that which combines the sketch of mind and character with some discussion of style. Of the general interest of such essays there can be no doubt. Nine tenths of so-called literary criticism deals with the lives and personalities of authors, and for the obvious reason, that every one is interested in them, whereas few will follow a technical study, however broadly based. At its best, the type of study that starts with the orator's mind and character is justified by the fact that nothing can better illuminate his work as a persuader of men. But when not at its best, the description of a man's general cast of mind stands utterly unrelated to his art: the critic fails to fuse his comment on the individual with his comment on the artist; and as a result we get some statements about the man, and some statements about the orator, but neither casts light on the other. Almost any of the literary histories will supply examples of the gulf that may yawn between a stylistic study and a study of personality.

The best example of the successful combination of the two strains is Grierson's essay on Burke in the *Cambridge History of English Literature.* In this, Burke's style, though in largest outline only, is seen to emerge from the essential nature of the man. Yet of this essay, too, it must be said that the analysis of the orator is incomplete, being overshadowed by the treatment of Burke as a writer, though, as we shall see, the passages on style have the rare virtue of keeping to the high road of criticism. The majority of critics who use the mixed method, however, do not make their study of personality fruitful for a study of style, do not separate literary style from oratorical style even to the extent that Grierson does, and do conceive of literary style as a matter of details. In fact, most of the critics of this group tend to supply a discussion of style by jotting down what has occurred to them about the author's management of words; and in the main, they notice the lesser strokes of literary art, but not its broader aspects. They have an eye for tactics, but not for strategy. This is the more strange, as these same writers habitually take large views of the orator himself, considered as a personality, and because they often remark the speaker's great themes and his leading ideas. The management of ideas—what the Romans called invention and disposition—the critics do not observe; their practice is the *salto mortale* from the largest to the smallest considerations. And it needs no mention that a critic who does not observe the management of ideas even from the point of view of structure and arrangement can have nothing to say of the adaptation of ideas to the orator's audience.

It is thus with Professor McLaughlin in his chapter in the *Cambridge History of American Literature* on Clay and Calhoun and some lesser lights. The pages are covered with such expressions as diffuse, florid, diction restrained and strong, neatly phrased, power of attack, invective, gracious persuasiveness. Of the structure of the speeches by which Clay and Calhoun exercised their influence—nothing. The drive of ideas is not represented. The background of habitual feeling which the orators at times appealed to and at times modified, is hinted at in a passage about Clay's awakening the spirit of nationalism, and in another passage contrasting the full-blooded oratory of Benton with the more polished speech of Quincy and Everett; but these are the merest hints. In the main, style for McLaughlin is neither the expression of personality nor the order and movement given to thought, but a thing of shreds and patches. It is thus, too, with Morley's pages on Burke's style in his life of the orator, and with Lodge's treatment of Webster in his life of the great American. A rather better analysis, though on the same plane of detail, may be used as an example. Oliver Elton says of Burke:

> He embodies, more powerfully than any one, the mental tendencies and changes that are seen gathering force through the eighteenth century. A volume of positive knowledge, critically sifted and ascertained: a constructive vision of the past and its institutions; the imagination, under this guidance, everywhere at play; all these elements unite in Burke. His main field is political philosophy. . . . His favorite form is oratory, uttered or written. His medium is prose, and the work of his later years, alone, outweighs all contemporary prose in power. . . . His whole body of production has the unity of some large cathedral, whose successive accretions reveal the natural growth of a single mind, without any change or essential break. . . .
>
> Already [in the *Thoughts* and in the *Observations*] the characteristics of Burke's thought and style appear, as well as his profound conversance with constitutional history, finance, and affairs. There is a constant reference to general principles, as in the famous defence of Party. The maxims that come into play go far beyond the occasion. There is a perpetual ground-swell of passion, embanked and held in check, but ever breaking out into sombre irony and sometimes into figure: but metaphors and other tropes are not yet very frequent. . . .
>
> In the art of unfolding and amplifying, Burke is the rival of the ancients. . . .
>
> In the speech on Conciliation the [oft-repeated] key-word is peace. . . .This iteration makes us see the stubborn faces on the opposite benches. There is contempt in it; their ears must be dinned, they must remember the word peace through the long intricate survey that is to follow. . . .
>
> Often he has a turn that would have aroused the fervor of the great appreciator known to us by the name of Longinus. In his speech on Economical Reform (1780) Burke risks an appeal, in the face of the Commons, to the example of the enemy. He has described. . .the reforms of the French revenue. He says: "The French have imitated us; let us, through them, imitate ourselves, ourselves in our better and happier days." A speaker who was willing to offend

for the sake of startling, and to defeat his purpose, would simply have said, "The French have imitated us: let us imitate them." Burke comes to the verge of this imprudence, but he sees the outcry on the lips of the adversary, and silences them by the word *ourselves;* and then, seizing the moment of bewilderment, repeats it and explains it by the noble past; he does not say when those days were; the days of Elizabeth or of Cromwell? Let the House choose! This is true oratory, honest diplomacy.[7]

Here, in some twenty pages, we have but two hints that Burke had to put his ideas in a form adapted to his audience: only the reiterated *peace* in all Burke's writings reminds the critic of Burke's hearers: only one stroke of tact draws his attention. Most of his account is devoted to Burke's style in the limited use of the term: to his power of amplification—his conduct of the paragraph, his use of clauses now long, now short—to his figures, comparisons, and metaphors, to his management of the sentence pattern, and to his rhythms. For Professor Elton, evidently, Burke was a man, and a mind, and an artist in prose; but he was not an orator. Interest in the minutae of style has kept Elton from bringing his view of Burke the man to bear on his view of Burke's writings. The fusing point evidently is in the strategic purpose of the works, in their function as speeches. By holding steadily to the conception of Burke as a public man, one could make the analysis of mind and the analysis of art more illuminating for each other than Elton does.

It cannot be said that in all respects Stephenson's chapter on Lincoln in the *Cambridge History of American Literature* is more successful than Elton's treatment of Burke; but it is a better interweaving of the biographical and the literary strands of interest. Stephenson's study of the personality of Lincoln is directly and persistently used in the study of Lincoln's style.

Is it fanciful to find a connection between the way in which his mysticism develops—its atmospheric, non-dogmatic pervasiveness—and the way in which his style develops? Certainly the literary part of him works into all the portions of his utterance with the gradualness of daylight through a shadowy wood. . . . And it is to be noted that the literary quality . . . is of the whole, not of the detail. It does not appear as a gift of phrases. Rather it is the slow unfolding of those two original characteristics, taste and rhythm. What is growing is the degree of both things. The man is becoming deeper, and as he does so he imposes himself, in this atmospheric way, more steadily on his language.[8]

The psychology of mystical experience may appear a poor support for the study of style. It is but one factor of many, and Stephenson may justly be

---

[7] Oliver Elton, *Survey of English Literature, 1780-1830,* I, 234-53, published by The Macmillan Company.
[8] *Cambridge History of American Literature,* New York, 1921, III, 374-5.

reproached for leaning too heavily upon it. Compared to Grierson's subtler analysis of Burke's mind and art, the essay of Stephenson seems forced and one-sided. Yet he illuminates his subject more than many of the writers so far mentioned, because he begins with a vigorous effort to bring his knowledge of the man to bear upon his interpretation of the work. But though we find in Stephenson's pages a suggestive study of Lincoln as literary man, we find no special regard for Lincoln as orator. The qualities of style that Stephenson mentions are the qualities of prose generally:

> At last he has his second manner, a manner quite his own. It is not his final manner, the one that was to give him his assured place in literature. However, In a wonderful blend of simplicity, directness, candor, joined with a clearness beyond praise. and a delightful cadence, it has outstripped every other politician of the hour. And back of its words, subtly affecting its phrases, . . . is that brooding sadness which was to be with him to the end.[9]

The final manner, it appears, is a sublimation of the qualities of the earlier, which was "keen, powerful, full of character, melodious, impressive";[10] and it is a sublimation which has the power to awaken the imagination by its flexibility, directness, pregnancy, wealth.

In this we have nothing new, unless it be the choice of stylistic categories that emphasize the larger pattern of ideas rather than the minute pattern of grammatical units, such as we have found in Elton and to some extent shall find in Saintsbury; it must be granted, too. that Stephenson has dispensed with detail and gained his larger view at the cost of no little vagueness. "Two things," says Stephenson of the Lincoln of 1849-1858, "grew upon him. The first was his understanding of men, the generality of men. . . . The other thing that grew upon him was his power to reach and influence them through words."[11] We have here the text for any study of Lincoln as orator; but the study itself this critic does not give us.

Elton's characterization of Burke's style stands out from the usual run of superficial comment by the closeness of its analysis and its regard for the architectonic element. Stephenson's characterization of Lincoln's style is distinguished by a vigorous if forced effort to unite the study of the man and of the work. With both we may contrast a better essay, by a critic of greater insight. Grierson says of Burke:

> What Burke has of the deeper spirit of that movement [the romantic revival] is seen not so much in the poetic imagery of his finest prose as in the philosophical imagination which informs his conception of the state, in virtue of which he transcends the

---

[9] *Cambridge History of American Literature*, III, 378.
[10] *Ibid.*, pp. 381-2.
[11] *Ibid.*, p. 377.

rationalism of the century. . . . This temper of Burke's mind is reflected in his prose. . . . To the direct, conversational prose of Dryden
and Swift, changed social circumstances and the influence of Johnson
had given a more oratorical cast, more dignity and weight, but, also,
more of heaviness and conventional elegance. From the latter faults,
Burke is saved by his passionate temperament, his ardent imagination, and the fact that he was a speaker conscious always of his audience. . . . [Burke] could delight, astound, and convince an audience.
He did not easily conciliate and win them over. He lacked the first
essential and index of the conciliatory speaker, *lenitas vocis;* his
voice was harsh and unmusical, his gesture un-gainly. . . . And, even
in the text of his speeches there is a strain of irony and scorn which
is not well fitted to conciliate. . . . We have evidence that he could do
both things on which Cicero lays stress—move his audience to tears
and delight them by his wit. . . . Yet, neither pathos nor humor is
Burke's *forte*. . . . Burke's unique power as an orator lies in the
peculiar interpenetration of thought and passion. Like the poet and
the prophet, he thinks most profoundly when he thinks most
passionately. When he is not deeply moved, his oratory verges
toward the turgid; when he indulges feeling for his own sake, as in
parts of *Letters on a Regicide Peace,* it becomes hysterical. But, in
his greatest speeches and pamphlets, the passion of Burke's mind
shows itself in the luminous thoughts which it emits, in the imagery
which at once moves *and* teaches, throwing a flood of light not only
on the point in question, but on the whole neighboring sphere of
man's moral and political nature.[12]

The most notable feature of these passages is not their recognition that
Burke was a speaker, but their recognition that his being a speaker condi-
tioned his style, and that he is to be judged in part at least as one who
attempted to influence men by the spoken word. Grierson, like Elton, attends
to the element of structure and has something to say of the nature of Burke's
prose; but, unlike Elton, he distinguishes this from the description of Burke's
oratory—although without maintaining the distinction: he illustrates Burke's
peculiar oratorical power from a pamphlet as readily as from a speech. His
categories seem less mechanical than those of Elton, who is more concerned
with the development of the paragraph than with the general cast of Burke's
style: nor is his judgment warped, as is Stephenson's, by having a theory to
market. Each has suffered from the necessity of compression. Yet, all told,
Grierson realizes better than the others that Burke's task was not merely to
express his thoughts and his feelings in distinguished prose, but to communicate his thoughts and his feelings effectively. It is hardly true, however,

---

[12]From H.J.C. Grierson in *Cambridge History of English Literature,* Xl, 30-35 by Cambridge University
Press (1914). Abridgements by permission of the publisher.

that Grierson has in mind the actual audience of Burke; the audience of Grierson's vision seems to be universalized, to consist of the judicious listeners or readers of any age. Those judicious listeners have no practical interest in the situation; they have only a philosophical and aesthetic interest.

Of Taine in his description of Burke it cannot be said that he descends to the minutiae of style. He deals with his author's character and ideas, as do all the critics of this group, but his comments on style are simply a single impression, vivid and picturesque:

> Burke had one of those fertile and precise imaginations which believe that finished knowledge is an inner view, which never quits a subject without having clothed it in its colors and forms. . . .To all these powers of mind, which constitute a man of system, he added all those energies of heart which constitute an enthusiast. . . . He brought to politics a horror of crime, a vivacity and sincerity of conscience, a sensibility, which seem suitable only to a young man.
> . . .The vast amount of his works rolls impetuously in a current of eloquence. Sometimes a spoken or written discourse needs a whole volume to unfold the train of his multiplied proofs and courageous anger. It is either the exposé of a ministry, or the whole history of British India, or the complete theory of revolutions . . . which comes down like a vast overflowing stream . . . Doubtless there is foam on its eddies, mud in its bed; thousands of strange creatures sport wildly on its surface: he does not select, he lavishes. . . . Nothing strikes him as in excess. . . . He continues half a barbarian, battening in exaggeration and violence: but his fire is so sustained, his conviction so strong, his emotion so warm and abundant, that we suffer him to go on, forget our repugnance, see in his irregularities and his trespasses only the outpourings of a great heart and a deep mind. too open and too full.[13]

This is brilliant writing, unencumbered by the subaltern's interest in tactics, but it is strategy as described by a war-correspondent, not by a general. We get from it little light on how Burke solved the problem that confronts every orator: so to present ideas as to bring them into the consciousness of his hearers.

Where the critic divides his interest between the man and the work, without allowing either interest to predominate, he is often compelled to consider the work *in toto,* and we get only observations so generalized as not to include consideration of the form of the work. The speech is not thought of as essentially a means of influence; it is regarded as a specimen of prose, or as an example of philosophic thought. The date, the historical interest, the orator's own intention, are often lost from view; and criticism suffers in consequence.

---

[13]H. A. Taine, *History of English Literature,* tr. H. Van Laun, London, 1878, II, 81-3.

IV

We have seen that the critic who is occupied chiefly with the orator as a man can contribute, although indirectly, to the study of the orator as such, and that the critic who divides his attention between the man and the work must effect a fusion of the two interests if he is to help materially in the understanding of the orator. We come now to critics more distinctly literary in aim. Within this group several classes may be discriminated: the first comprises the judicial critics; the second includes the interpretative critics who take the point of view of literary style generally, regarding the speech as an essay, or as a specimen of prose; the third and last group is composed of the writers who tend to regard the speech as a special literary form.

The type of criticism that attempts a judicial evaluation of the literary merits of the work—of the orator's "literary remains"—tends to center the inquiry on the question: Is this literature? The futility of the question appears equally in the affirmative and in the negative replies to it. The fault is less with the query. however, than with the hastiness of the answers generally given. For the most part, the critics who raise this problem are not disposed really to consider it: they formulate no conception either of literature or of oratory; they will not consider their own literary standards critically and comprehensively. In short, the question is employed as a way to dispose briefly of the subject of a lecture or of a short essay in a survey of a national literature.

Thus Phelps, in his treatment of Webster and Lincoln in *Some Makers of American Literature,*[14] tells us that they have a place in literature by virtue of their style, gives us some excerpts from Lincoln and some comments on Webster's politics, but offers no reasoned criticism. St. Peter swings wide the gates of the literary heaven, but does not explain his action. We may suspect that the solemn award of a "place in literature" sometimes conceals the absence of any real principle of judgment.

Professor Trent is less easily satisfied that Webster deserves a "place in literature." He grants Webster's power to stimulate patriotism, his sonorous dignity and massiveness, his clearness and strength of style, his powers of dramatic description. But he finds only occasional splendor of imagination, discovers no soaring quality of intelligence, and is not dazzled by his philosophy or his grasp of history. Mr. Trent would like more vivacity and humor and color in Webster's style.[15] This mode of deciding Webster's place in or out of literature is important to us only as it reveals the critic's method of judging. Trent looks for clearness and strength, imagination, philosophic grasp, vivacity, humor, color in style. This is excellent so far as it goes, but

---

[14]Boston, 1923.
[15]W. P. Trent, *History of American Literature, 1607-1865,* New York, 1917, pp. 576-7.

goes no further than to suggest some qualities which are to be sought in any and all works of literary art: in dramas, in essays, in lyric poems, as well as in speeches.

Let us take a third judge. Gosse will not allow Burke to be a complete master of English prose: "Notwithstanding all its magnificence, it appears to me that the prose of Burke lacks the variety, the delicacy, the modulated music of the very finest writers."[16] Gosse adds that Burke lacks flexibility, humor, and pathos. As critical method, this is one with that of Trent.

Gosse, with his question about mastery of prose, does not directly ask, "is this literature?" Henry Cabot Lodge does, and his treatment of Webster (in the *Cambridge History of American Literature*) is curious. Lodge is concerned to show that Webster belongs to literature, and to explain the quality in his work that gives him a place among the best makers of literature. The test applied is permanence: Is Webster still read? The answer is, yes, for he is part of every schoolboy's education, and is the most quoted author in Congress. The sight of a literary critic resigning the judicial bench to the schoolmaster and the Congressman is an enjoyable one; as enjoyable as Mr. H. L. Mencken's reaction to it would be; but one could wish for grounds more relative than this. Mr. Lodge goes on to account for Webster's permanence: it lies in his power to impart to rhetoric the literary touch. The distinction between rhetoric and literature is not explained, but apparently the matter lies thus: rhetorical verse may be poetry; Byron is an example. Rhetorical prose is not literature until there is added the literary touch. We get a clue as to how the literary touch may be added: put in something imaginative, something that strikes the hearer at once. The example chosen by Lodge is a passage from Webster in which the imaginative or literary touch is given by the single word "mildew."[17] This method of criticism, too, we may reduce to that of Trent, with the exception that only one quality— imagination—is requisite for admission to the literary Valhalla.

Whether the critic's standards be imagination, or this together with other qualities such as intelligence, vivacity, humor, or whether it be merely "style," undefined and unexplained, the point of view is always that of the printed page. The oration is lost from view, and becomes an exercise in prose, musical, colorful, varied, and delicate, but, so far as the critic is concerned, formless and purposeless. Distinctions of literary type or kind are erased; the architectonic element is neglected: and the speech is regarded as a musical meditation might be regarded: as a kind of harmonious musing that drifts pleasantly along, with little of inner form and nothing of objective purpose. This, it should be recognized, is not the result of judicial criticism so much as the result of the attempt to decide too hastily whether a given

---

[16]Edmund Gosse, *History of Eighteenth Century English Literature, 1660-1780*, London, 1889, pp. 365-6.

[17]*Cambridge History of American Literature*, New York, 1918, II, 101.

work is to be admitted into the canon of literature.

V

It is, perhaps, natural for the historian of literature to reduce all literary production to one standard, and thus to discuss only the common elements in all prose. One can understand also that the biographer, when in the course of his task he must turn literary critic, finds himself often inadequately equipped and his judgment of little value, except on the scale of literature generally rather than of oratory or of any given type. More is to be expected, however, of those who set up as literary critics in the first instance: those who deal directly with Webster's style, or with Lincoln as man of letters. We shall find such critics as Whipple, Hazlitt, and Saintsbury devoting themselves to the description of literary style in the orators whom they discuss. Like the summary judicial critics we have mentioned, their center of interest is the work; but they are less hurried than Gosse and Lodge and Phelps and Trent; and their aim is not judgment so much as understanding. Yet their interpretations, in the main, take the point of view of the printed page, of the prose essay. Only to a slight degree is there a shift to another point of view, that of the orator in relation to the audience on whom he exerts his influence; the immediate public begins to loom a little larger; the essential nature of the oration as a type begins to be suggested.

Saintsbury has a procedure which much resembles that of Elton, though we must note the fact that the former omits consideration of Burke as a personality and centers attention on his work. We saw that Elton, in his passages on Burke's style, attends both to the larger elements of structure and to such relatively minute points as the management of the sentence and the clause. In Saintsbury the range of considerations is the same. At times, indeed, the juxtaposition of large and small ideas is ludicrous, as when one sentence ends by awarding to Burke literary immortality, and the next describes the sentences of an early work as "short and crisp, arranged with succinct antithetic parallels, which seldom exceed a single pair of clauses."[18] The award of immortality is not, it should be said, based entirely on the shortness of Burke's sentences in his earliest works. Indeed much of Saintsbury's comment is of decided interest:

> The style of Burke is necessarily to be considered throughout as conditioned by oratory. . . . In other words, he was first of all a rhetorician. and probably the greatest that modern times have ever produced. But his rhetoric always inclined much more to the written than to the spoken form, with results annoying perhaps to him at the time, but even to him satisfactory afterwards. and an inestimable gain to the world. . . .
> The most important of these properties of Burke's style, in so far

---

[18]G. E. B. Saintsbury, *Short History of English Literature,* New York, 1915, p. 630.

as it is possible to enumerate them here, are as follows. First of all, and most distinctive, so much so as to have escaped no competent critic, is a very curious and, until his example made it imitable, nearly unique faculty of building up an argument or a picture by a succession of complementary strokes, not added at haphazard but growing out of and onto one another. No one has ever been such a master of the best and grandest kind of the figure called . . . Amplification, and this . . . is the direct implement by which he achieves his greatest effects.

    . . . The piece [*Present Discontents*] may be said to consist of a certain number of specially labored paragraphs in which the arguments or pictures just spoken of are put as forcibly as the author can put them, and as a rule in a succession of shortish sentences, built up and glued together with the strength and flexibility of a newly fashioned fishing-rod. In the intervals the texts thus given are turned about, commented on justified, or discussed in detail, in a rhetoric for the most part, though not always, rather less serried, less evidently burnished, and in less full dress. And this general arrangement proceeds through the rest of his works.[19]

After a number of comments on Burke's skill in handling various kinds of ornament, such as humor, epigram, simile, Saintsbury returns to the idea that Burke's special and definite weapon was "imaginative argument, and the marshalling of vast masses of complicated detail into properly rhetorical battalions or (to alter the image) mosaic pictures of enduring beauty."[20] Saintsbury's attitude toward the communicative, impulsive nature of the orator's task is indicated in a passage on the well-known description of Windsor Castle. This description the critic terms "at once . . . a perfect harmonic chord, a complete visual picture, and a forcible argument."[21] It is significant that he adds, "The minor rhetoric, the suasive purpose [presumably the argumentative intent] must be kept in view; if it be left out the thing loses"; and holds Burke "far below Browne, who had no need of purpose."[22] It is less important that a critic think well of the suasive purpose than that he reckon with it, and of Saintsbury at least it must be said that he recognizes it, although grudgingly; but it cannot be said that Saintsbury has a clear conception of rhetoric as the art of communication: sometimes it means the art of prose, sometimes that of suasion.

    Hazlitt's method of dealing with Burke resembles Taine's as Saintsbury's resembles that of Elton. In Hazlitt we have a critic who deals with style in the large; details of rhythm, of sentence pattern, of imagery, are ignored. His

---

[19]*Ibid.*, pp. 629-30.
[20]*Ibid.*, p. 631.
[21]*Ibid.*
[22]*Ibid.*

principal criticism of Burke as orator is contained in the well-known contrast with Chatham, really a contrast of mind and temperament in relation to oratorical style. He follows this with some excellent comment on Burke's prose style; nothing more is said of his oratory; only in a few passages do we get a flash of light on the relation of Burke to his audience, as in the remark about his eagerness to impress his reader, and in the description of his conversational quality. It is notable too that Hazlitt finds those works which never had the form of speeches the most significant and most typical of Burke's style.

> Burke was so far from being a gaudy or flowery writer, that he was one of the severest writers we have. His words are the most like things: his style is the most strictly limited to the subject. He unites every extreme and every variety of composition: the lowest and the meanest words and descriptions with the highest. . . . He had no other object but to produce the strongest impression on his reader, by giving the truest, the most characteristic, the fullest, and most forcible description of things. trusting to the power of his own mind to mold them into grace and beauty. . . . Burke most frequently produced an effect by the remoteness and novelty of his combinations, by the force of contrast, by the striking manner in which the most opposite and unpromising materials were harmoniously blended together; not by laying his hands on all the fine things he could think of, but by bringing together those things which he knew would blaze out into glorious light by their collision.[23]

Twelve years after writing the essay from which we have quoted, Hazlitt had occasion to revise his estimate of Burke as a statesman; but his sketch of Burke's style is essentially unaltered.[24] In Hazlitt we find a sense of style as an instrument of communication; that sense is no stronger in dealing with Burke's speeches than in dealing with his pamphlets, but it gives to Hazlitt's criticisms a reality not often found. What is lacking is a clear sense of Burke's communicative impulse, of his persuasive purpose, as operating in a concrete situation. Hazlitt does not suggest the background of Burke's speeches, ignores the events that called them forth. He views his subject, in a sense, as Grierson does: as speaking to the judicious but disinterested hearer of any age other than Burke's own. But the problem of the speaker, as well as of the pamphleteer, is to interest men here and now; the understanding of that problem requires, on the part of the critic, a strong historical sense for the ideas and attitudes of the people (not merely of their leaders), and a full knowledge of the public opinion of the times in which the orator spoke. This

---

[23] *Sketches and Essays,* ed. W. C. Hazlitt, London, 1872, II, 420-1.
[24] *Political Essays with Sketches of Public Characters,* London, 1819, pp. 264-79.

we do not find in Hazlitt.

Two recent writers on Lincoln commit the opposite error: they devote themselves so completely to description of the situation in which Lincoln wrote as to leave no room for criticism. L. E. Robinson's *Lincoln as Man of Letters*[25] is a biography rewritten around Lincoln's writings. It is nothing more. Instead of giving us a criticism, Professor Robinson has furnished us with some of the materials of the critic; his own judgments are too largely laudatory to cast much light. The book, therefore, is not all that its title implies. A single chapter of accurate summary and evaluation would do much to increase our understanding of Lincoln as man of letters, even though it said nothing of Lincoln as speaker. A chapter or two on Lincoln's work in various kinds—letters. state papers, speeches—would help us to a finer discrimination than Professor Robinson's book offers. Again, the proper estimate of style in any satisfactory sense requires us to do more than to weigh the soundness of an author's thought and to notice the isolated beauties of his expression. Something should be said of structure, something of adaptation to the immediate audience, whose convictions and habits of thought, whose literary usages, and whose general cultural background all condition the work both of writer and speaker. Mr. Robinson has given us the political situation as a problem in controlling political forces, with little regard to the force even of public opinion, and with almost none to the cultural background. Lincoln's works, therefore, emerge as items in a political sequence, but not as resultants of the life of his time.

Some of the deficiencies of Robinson's volume are supplied by Dodge's essay, *Lincoln as Master of Words*.[26] Dodge considers, more definitely than Robinson, the types in which Lincoln worked: he separates messages from campaign speeches, letters from occasional addresses. He has an eye on Lincoln's relation to his audience, but this manifests itself chiefly in an account of the immediate reception of a work. Reports of newspaper comments on the speeches may be a notable addition to Lincolniana; supported by more political information and more insight than Mr. Dodge's short book reveals, they might become an aid to the critical evaluation of the speeches. But in themselves they are neither a criticism nor an interpretation of Lincoln's mastery of words.

Robinson and Dodge, then, stand at opposite poles to Saintsbury and Hazlitt. The date is put in opposition to the work as a center of critical interest. If the two writers on Lincoln lack a full perception of their author's background, they do not lack a sense of its importance. If the critics of Burke do not produce a complete and rounded criticism, neither do they lose themselves in preparatory studies. Each method is incomplete; each should

---

[25]New York, 1923.
[26]New York, 1924.

supplement the other.

We turn now to a critic who neglects the contribution of history to the study of oratory, but who has two compensating merits: the merit of recognizing the types in which his subject worked, and the merit of remembering that an orator has as his audience, not posterity, but certain classes of his own contemporaries. Whipple's essay on Webster is open to attack from various directions: It is padded, it "dates," it is overlaudatory, it is overpatriotic, it lacks distinction of style. But there is wheat in the chaff. Scattered through the customary discussion of Webster's choice of words, his power of epithet, his compactness of statement, his images, the development of his style, are definite suggestions of a new point of view. It is the point of view of the actual audience. To Whipple, at times at least, Webster was not a writer, but a speaker: the critic tries to imagine the man, and also his hearers: he thinks of the speech as a communication to a certain body of auditors. A phrase often betrays a mental attitude; Whipple alone of the critics we have mentioned would have written of "the eloquence, the moral power, he infused into his reasoning, so as to make the dullest citation of legal authority *tell* on the minds he addressed."[27] Nor would any other writer of this group have attempted to distinguish the types of audience Webster met. That Whipple's effort is a rambling and incoherent one, is not here in point. Nor is it pertinent that the critic goes completely astray in explaining why Webster's speeches have the nature of "organic formations, or at least of skilful engineering or architectural constructions"; though to say that the art of giving objective reality to a speech consists only of "a happy collocation and combination of words"[28] is certainly as far as possible from explaining Webster's sense of structure. What is significant in Whipple's essay is the occasional indication of a point of view that includes the audience. Such an indication is the passage in which the critic explains the source of Webster's influence:

> What gave Webster his immense influence over the opinion of the people of New England, was first, his power of so "putting things" that everybody could understand his statements; secondly, his power of so framing his arguments that all the steps, from one point to another, in a logical series, could be clearly apprehended by every intelligent farmer or mechanic who had a thoughtful interest in the affairs of the country: and thirdly, his power of inflaming the sentiment of patriotism In all honest and well-intentioned men by overwhelming appeals to that sentiment, so that after convincing their understandings, he clinched the matter by sweeping away their wills.
>
> Perhaps to these sources of influence may be added . . . a genuine respect for the intellect, as well as for the manhood, of average men.[29]

---

[27]E. P. Whipple, "Daniel Webster as a Master of English Style," in *American Literature,* Boston, 1887, p. 157.
[28]*Ibid.,* p. 208.
[29]*Ibid.,* p. 144.

In various ways the descriptive critics recognize the orator's function. In some, that recognition takes the form of a regard to the background of the speeches; in others, it takes the form of a regard to the effectiveness of the work, though that effectiveness is often construed as for the reader rather than for the listener. The "minor rhetoric, the suasive purpose" is beginning to be felt, though not always recognized and never fully taken into account.

VI

The distinction involved in the presence of a persuasive purpose is clearly recognized by some of those who have written on oratory, and by some biographers and historians. The writers now to be mentioned are aware, more keenly than any of those we have so far met, of the speech as a literary form—or if not as a literary form, then as a form of power: they tend accordingly to deal with the orator's work as limited by the conditions of the platform and the occasion, and to summon history to the aid of criticism.

The method of approach of the critics of oratory as oratory is well put by Lord Curzon at the beginning of his essay, *Modern Parliamentary Eloquence:*

> In dealing with the Parliamentary speakers of our time I shall, accordingly, confine myself to those whom I have myself heard, or for whom I can quote the testimony of others who heard them; and I shall not regard them as prose writers or literary men, still less as purveyors of instruction to their own or to future generations, but as men who produced, by the exercise of certain talents of speech, a definite impression upon contemporary audiences, and whose reputation for eloquence must be judged by that test, and that test alone.[30]

The last phrase, "that test alone," would be scanned; the judgment of orators is not solely to be determined by the impression of contemporary audiences. For the present it will be enough to note the topics touched in Curzon's anecdotes and reminiscences—his lecture is far from a systematic or searching inquiry into the subject, and is of interest rather for its method of approach than for any considered study of an orator or of a period. We value him for his promises rather than for his performance. Curzon deals with the relative rank of speakers, with the comparative value of various speeches by a single man, with the orator's appearance and demeanor, with his mode of preparation and of delivery, with his mastery of epigram or image. Skill in seizing upon the dominant characteristics of each of his subjects saves the author from the worst triviality of reminiscence. Throughout, the point of view is that of the man experienced in public life discussing the eloquence of other public men, most of whom he had known and actually

---

[30]London, 1914, p. 7.

heard. That this is not the point of view of criticism in any strict sense, is of course true; but the *naïveté* and directness of this observer correct forcibly some of the extravagances we have been examining.

The lecture on Chatham as an orator by H. M. Butler exemplifies a very different method arising from a different subject and purpose. The lecturer is thinking, he tells us, "of Oratory partly as an art, partly as a branch of literature, partly as a power of making history."[31] His method is first to touch lightly upon Chatham's early training and upon his mode of preparing and delivering his speeches; next, to present some of the general judgments upon the Great Commoner, whether of contemporaries or of later historians; then to re-create a few of the most important speeches, partly by picturing the historical setting, partly by quotation, partly by the comments of contemporary writers. The purpose of the essay is "to reawaken, however faintly, some echoes of the kingly voice of a genuine Patriot, of whom his country is still justly proud."[32] The patriotic purpose we may ignore, but the wish to reconstruct the *mise en scène* of Chatham's speeches, to put the modern Oxford audience at the point of view of those who listened to the voice of Pitt, saw the flash of his eye and felt the force of his noble bearing. This is a purpose different from that of the critics whom we have examined. It may be objected that Butler's lecture has the defects of its method: the amenities observed by a Cambridge don delivering a formal lecture at Oxford keep us from getting on with the subject; the brevity of the discourse prevents anything like a full treatment; the aim, revivification of the past, must be very broadly interpreted if it is to be really critical. Let us admit these things; it still is true that in a few pages the essential features of Pitt's eloquence are brought vividly before us, and that this is accomplished by thinking of the speech as originally delivered to its first audience rather than as read by the modern reader.

The same sense of the speaker in his relation to his audience appears in Lecky's account of Burke. This account, too, is marked by the use of contemporary witnesses, and of comparisons with Burke's great rivals. But let Lecky's method speak in part for itself:

> He spoke too often, too vehemently, and much too long; and his eloquence, though in the highest degree intellectual, powerful, various, and original, was not well adapted to a popular audience. He had little or nothing of that fire and majesty of declamation with which Chatham thrilled his hearers, and often almost overawed opposition; and as a parliamentary debater he was far inferior to Charles Fox. . . . Burke was not inferior to Fox in readiness, and in the power of clear and cogent reasoning. His wit, though not of the highest order, was only equalled by that of Townshend, Sheridan, and

---

[31] *Lord Chatham as an Orator*, Oxford, 1912, p. 5.
[32] *Ibid.*, pp. 39-40.

perhaps North, and it rarely failed in its effect upon the House. He far surpassed every other speaker in the copiousness and correctness of his diction, in the range of knowledge he brought to bear on every subject of debate, in the richness and variety of his imagination, in the gorgeous beauty of his descriptive passages. In the depth of the philosophical reflections and the felicity of the personal sketches which he delighted in scattering over his speeches. But these gifts were frequently marred by a strange want of judgment, measure. and self-control. His speeches were full of episodes and digressions, of excessive ornamentation and illustration, of dissertations on general principles of politics, which were invaluable in themselves, but very unpalatable to a tired or excited House waiting eagerly for a division.[33]

These sentences suggest, and the pages from which they are excerpted show, that historical imagination has led Lecky to regard Burke as primarily a speaker, both limited and formed by the conditions of his platform; and they exemplify, too, a happier use of stylistic categories than do the essays of Curzon and Butler. The requirements of the historian's art have fused the character sketch and the literary criticism; the fusing agent has been the conception of Burke as a public man, and of his work as public address. Both Lecky's biographical interpretation and his literary criticism are less subtle than that of Grierson; but Lecky is more definitely guided in his treatment of Burke by the conception of oratory as a special form of the literature of power and as a form molded always by the pressure of the time.

The merits of Lecky are contained, in ampler form, in Morley's biography of Gladstone. The long and varied career of the great parliamentarian makes a general summary and final judgment difficult and perhaps inadvisable; Morley does not attempt them. But his running account of Gladstone as orator, if assembled from his thousand pages, is an admirable example of what can be done by one who has the point of view of the public man, sympathy with his subject, and understanding of the speaker's art. Morley gives us much contemporary reporting: the descriptions and judgments of journalists at various stages in Gladstone's career, the impression made by the speeches upon delivery, comparison with other speakers of the time. Here history is contemporary: the biographer was himself the witness of much that he describes, and has the experienced parliamentarian's flair for the scene and the situation. Gladstone's temperament and physical equipment for the platform, his training in the art of speaking, the nature of his chief appeals, the factor of character and personality, these are some of the topics repeatedly touched. There is added a sense for the permanent results of Gladstone's speaking: not the votes in the House merely but the changed

---

[33]W. E. H. Lecky, *History of England in the Eighteenth Century,* New York, 1888, III, 203-4.

state of public opinion brought about by the speeches.

> Mr. Gladstone conquered the House, because he was saturated with a subject and its arguments; because he could state and enforce his case; because he plainly believed every word he said, and earnestly wished to press the same belief into the minds of his hearers; finally because he was from the first an eager and a powerful athlete. . . . Yet with this inborn readiness for combat, nobody was less addicted to aggression or provocation. . . .

> In finance, the most important of all the many fields of his activity, Mr. Gladstone had the signal distinction of creating the public opinion by which he worked, and warming the climate in which his projects throve. . . . Nobody denies that he was often declamatory and discursive, that he often overargued and overrefined; [but] he nowhere exerted greater influence than in that department of affairs where words out of relation to fact are most surely exposed. If he often carried the proper rhetorical arts of amplification and develop-ment to excess, yet the basis of fact was both sound and clear. . . . Just as Macaulay made thousands read history, who before had turned from it as dry and repulsive, so Mr. Gladstone made thou-sands eager to follow the public balance-sheet, and the whole nation became his audience. . . .

> [In the Midlothian campaign] it was the orator of concrete detail, of inductive instances, of energetic and immediate object; the orator confidently and by sure touch startling into watchfulness the whole spirit of civil duty in man; elastic and supple, pressing fact and figure with a fervid insistence that was known from his career and character to be neither forced nor feigned but to be himself. In a word, it was a man—a man impressing himself upon the kindled throngs by the breadth of his survey of great affairs of life and nations, by the depth of his vision, by the power of his stroke.[34]

Objections may be made to Morley's method chiefly on the ground of omissions. Though much is done to re-create the scene, though ample use is made of the date and the man, there is little formal analysis of the work. It is as if one had come from the House of Commons after hearing the speeches, stirred to enthusiasm but a little confused by the wealth of argument; not as if one came from a calm study of the speeches; not even as if one had corrected personal impressions by such a study. Of the structure of the speeches, little is said; but a few perorations are quoted; the details of style, one feels, although noticed at too great length by some critics, might well receive a modicum of attention here.

Although these deficiencies of Morley's treatment are not supplied by

---

[34]*Life of William Ewart Gladstone,* I, 193-4: II, 54-5, 593.

Bryce in his short and popular sketch of Gladstone, there is a summary which well supplements the running account offered by Morley. It has the merit of dealing explicitly with the orator as orator, and it offers more analysis and an adequate judgment by a qualified critic.

> Twenty years hence Mr. Gladstone's [speeches] will not be read, except of course by historians. They are too long, too diffuse, too minute in their handling of details, too elaborately qualified in their enunciation of general principles. They contain few epigrams and few...weighty thoughts put into telling phrases. ....The style, in short, is not sufficiently rich or finished to give a perpetual interest to matters whose practical importance has vanished. ...
>
> If, on the other hand, Mr. Gladstone be judged by the impression he made on his own time, his place will be high in the front rank. ... His oratory had many conspicuous merits. There was a lively imagination, which enabled him to relieve even dull matter by pleasing figures, together with a large command of quotations and illustrations. ....There was admirable lucidity and accuracy in exposition. There was great skill in the disposition and marshalling of his arguments and finally...there was a wonderful variety and grace of appropriate gesture. But above and beyond everything else which enthralled the listener, there were four qualities, two specially conspicuous in the substance of his eloquence—inventiveness and elevation: two not less remarkable in his manner—force in the delivery, expressive modulation in the voice.[35]

One is tempted to say that Morley has provided the historical setting, Bryce the critical verdict. The statement would be only partially true, for Morley does much more than set the scene. He enacts the drama; and thus he conveys his judgment—not, it is true, in the form of a critical estimate, but in the course of his narrative. The difference between these two excellent accounts is a difference in emphasis. The one lays stress on the setting: the other takes it for granted. The one tries to suggest his judgment by description; the other employs the formal categories of criticism.

Less full and rounded than either of these descriptions of an orator's style is Trevelyan's estimate of Bright. Yet in a few pages the biographer has indicated clearly the two distinguishing features of Bright's eloquence—the moral weight he carried with his audience, the persuasiveness of his visible earnestness and of his reputation for integrity, and his "sense for the value of words and for the rhythm of words and sentences";[36] has drawn a contrast between Bright and Gladstone; and has added a description of Bright's mode of work, together with some comments on the performance of the speeches

[35] *Gladstone, his Characteristics as Man and Statesman,* New York, 1898, pp. 41-4.
[36] G. M. Trevelyan, *Life of John Bright,* Boston, 1913, p. 384.

and various examples of details of his style. Only the mass and weight of that style are not represented.

If we leave the biographers and return to those who, like Curzon and Butler, have written directly upon eloquence, we find little of importance. Of the two general histories of oratory that we have in English, Hardwicke's[37] is so ill organized and so ill written as to be negligible; that by Sears[38] may deserve mention. It is uneven and inaccurate. It is rather a popular handbook which strings together the great names than a history: the author does not seriously consider the evolution of oratory. His sketches are of unequal merit; some give way to the interest in mere anecdote; some yield too large a place to biographical detail; others are given over to moralizing. Sears touches most of the topics of rhetorical criticism without making the point of view of public address dominant; his work is too episodic for that. And any given criticism shows marked defects in execution. It would not be fair to compare Sears's show-piece, his chapter on Webster with Morley or Bryce on Gladstone; but compare it with Trevelyan's few pages on Bright. With far greater economy, Trevelyan tells us more of Bright as a speaker than Sears can of Webster. The *History of Oratory* gives us little more than hints and suggestions of a good method.

With a single exception, the collections of eloquence have no critical significance. The exception is *Select British Eloquence*,[39] edited by Chauncey A. Goodrich, who prefaced the works of each of his orators with a sketch partly biographical and partly critical. The criticisms of Goodrich, like those of Sears, are of unequal value; some are slight, yet none descends to mere anecdote, and at his best, as in the characterizations of the eloquence of Chatham, Fox, and Burke, Goodrich reveals a more powerful grasp and a more comprehensive view of his problem than does Sears, as well as a more consistent view of his subject as a speaker. Sears at times takes the point of view of the printed page; Goodrich consistently thinks of the speeches he discusses as intended for oral delivery.

Goodrich's topics of criticism are: the orator's training, mode of work personal [physical] qualifications character as known to his audience, range of powers, dominant traits as a speaker. He deals too, of course, with those topics to which certain of the critics we have noticed confine themselves: illustration, ornament, gift of phrase, diction, wit, imagination, arrangement. But these he does not over-emphasize, nor view as independent of their effect upon an audience. Thus he can say of Chatham's sentence structure: "The sentences are not rounded or balanced periods, but are made up of short clauses, which flash themselves upon the mind with all the vividness of distinct ideas, and yet are closely connected together as tending to the same

[37]Henry Hardwicke, *History of Oratory and Orators*, New York, 1896.
[38]Lorenzo Sears, *History of Oratory*, Chicago, 1896.
[39]New York, 1852.

point and uniting to form larger masses of thought."[40] Perhaps the best brief indication of Goodrich's quality is his statement of Fox's "leading peculiarities."[41] According to Goodrich, Fox had a luminous simplicity, which combined unity of impression with irregular arrangement; he took everything in the concrete; he struck instantly at the heart of his subject, going to the issue at once; he did not amplify, he repeated; he rarely employed pre-conceived order of argument; reasoning was his *forte,* but it was the reasoning of the debater; he abounded in *hits*—abrupt and startling turns of thought—and in sideblows delivered in passing; he was often dramatic; he had astonishing skill in turning the course of debate to his own advantage. Here is the point of view of public address expressed as clearly as in Morley or in Curzon, though in a different idiom and without the biographer's fulness of treatment.

But probably the best single specimen of the kind of criticism now under discussion is Morley's chapter on Cobden as an agitator. This is as admirable a summary sketch as the same writer's account of Gladstone is a detailed historical picture. Bryce's brief essay on Gladstone is inferior to it both in the range of its technical criticisms and in the extent to which the critic realizes the situation in which his subject was an actor. In a few pages Morley has drawn the physical characteristics of his subject, his bent of mind, tempera-ment, idiosyncrasies; has compared and contrasted Cobden with his great associate, Bright; has given us contemporary judgments; has sketched out the dominant quality of his style, its variety and range; has noted Cobden's attitude to his hearers, his view of human nature; and has dealt with the impression given by Cobden's printed speeches and the total impression of his personality on the platform. The method, the angle of approach, the categories of description or of criticism, are the same as those employed in the great life of Gladstone; but we find them here condensed into twenty pages. It will be worth while to present the most interesting parts of Morley's criticism, if only for comparison with some of the passages already given:

> I have asked many scores of those who knew him, Conservatives as well as Liberals, what this secret [of his oratorical success] was, and in no single case did my interlocutor fail to begin, and in nearly every case he ended as he had begun, with the word *persuasiveness.* Cobden made his way to men's hearts by the union which they saw in him of simplicity, earnestness, and conviction, with a singular facility of exposition. This facility consisted in a remarkable power of apt and homely illustration, and a curious ingenuity in framing the argument that happened to be wanted. Besides his skill in thus hitting on the right argument, Cobden had the oratorical art of presenting it in the way that made its admission to the understanding of a listener

---

[40]P. 75.
[41]P. 461.

easy and undenied. He always seemed to have made exactly the right degree of allowance for the difficulty with which men follow a speech, as compared with the ease of following the same argument on a printed page. . . .

Though he abounded in matter, Cobden can hardly be described as copious. He is neat and pointed, nor is his argument ever left unclinched; but he permits himself no large excursions. What he was thinking of was the matter immediately in hand, the audience before his eyes, the point that would tell best then and there, and would be most likely to remain in men's recollections. . . . What is remarkable is, that while he kept close to the matter and substance of his case, and resorted comparatively little to sarcasm, humor, invective, pathos, or the other elements that are catalogued in manuals of rhetoric, yet no speaker was ever further removed from prosiness, or came into more real and sympathetic contact with his audience. . . .

After all, it is not tropes and perorations that make the popular speaker; it is the whole impression of his personality. We who only read them can discern certain admirable qualities in Cobden's speeches; aptness in choosing topics, lucidity in presenting them, buoyant confidence in pressing them home. But those who listened to them felt much more than all this. They were delighted by mingled vivacity and ease, by directness, by spontaneousness and reality, by the charm . . . of personal friendliness and undisguised cordiality.[42]

These passages are written in the spirit of the critic of public speaking. They have the point of view that is but faintly suggested in Elton and Grierson, that Saintsbury recognizes but does not use, and Hazlitt uses but does not recognize, and that Whipple, however irregularly, both understands and employs. But such critics as Curzon and Butler, Sears and Goodrich, Trevelyan and Bryce, think differently of their problem; they take the point of view of public address consistently and without question Morley's superiority is not in conception, but in execution, in all the writers of this group, whether historians, biographers, or professed students of oratory, there is a consciousness that oratory is partly an art, partly a power of making history, and occasionally a branch of literature. Style is less considered for its own sake than for its effect in a given situation. The question of literary immortality is regarded as beside the mark, or else, as in Bryce, as a separate question requiring separate consideration. There are, of course, differences of emphasis. Some of the biographers may be thought to deal too lightly with style. Sears perhaps thinks too little of the time, of the drama of the situation and, too much of style. But we have arrived at a different attitude towards the orator; his function is recognized for what it is: the art of influencing men in some concrete situation. Neither the personal nor the literary

---

[42] *Life of Richard Cobden,* Boston, 1881, pp. 130-2.

evaluation is the primary object. The critic speaks of the orator as a public man whose function it is to exert his influence by speech.

VII

Any attempt to sum up the results of this casual survey of what some writers have said of some public speakers must deal with the differences between literary criticism as represented by Gosse and Trent, by Elton and Grierson, and rhetorical criticism as represented by Curzon, Morley, Bryce, and Trevelyan. The literary critics seem at first to have no common point of view and no agreement as to the categories of judgment or description. But by reading between their lines and searching for the main endeavor of these critics, one can discover at least a unity of purpose. Different in method as are Gosse, Elton, Saintsbury, Whipple, Hazlitt, the ends they have in view are not different.

Coupled with almost every decription of the excellences of prose and with every attempt to describe the man in connection with his work is the same effort as we find clearly and even arbitrarily expressed by those whom we have termed judicial critics. All the literary critics unite in the attempt to interpret the permanent value that they find in the work under consideration. That permanent value is not precisely indicated by the term beauty, but the two strands of aesthetic excellence and permanence are clearly found not only in the avowed judicial criticism but in those writers who emphasize description rather than judgment. Thus Grierson says of Burke:

> His preoccupation at every juncture with the fundamental issues of wise government, and the splendor of the eloquence in which he set forth these principles, an eloquence in which the wisdom of his thought and the felicity of his language and imagery seem insep-arable from one another...have made his speeches and pamphlets a source of perennial freshness and interest.[43]

Perhaps a critic of temper different from Grierson's—Saintsbury, for ex-ample—would turn from the wisdom of Burke's thought to the felicity of his language and imagery. But aways there is implicit in the critic's mind the absolute standard of a timeless world: the wisdom of Burke's thought (found in the principles to which his mind always gravitates rather than in his decisions on points of policy) and the felicity of his language are not considered as of an age, but for all time. Whether the critic considers the technical excellence merely, or both technique and substance, his preoccu-pation is with that which age cannot wither nor custom stale. (From this point of view, the distinction between the speech and the pamphlet is of no moment, and Elton wisely speaks of Burke's favorite form as "oratory,

---

[43] *Cambridge History of English Literature,* New York, 1914, XI, 8.

uttered or written",[44] for a speech cannot be the subject of a permanent evaluation unless it is preserved in print.)

This is the implied attitude of all the literary critics. On this common ground their differences disappear or become merely differences of method or of competence. They are all, in various ways, interpreters of the permanent and universal values they find in the works of which they treat. Nor can there be any quarrel with this attitude—unless all standards be swept away. The impressionist and the historian of the evolution of literature as a self-contained activity may deny the utility or the possibility of a truly judicial criticism. But the human mind insists upon judgment *sub specie aeternitatis*. The motive often appears as a merely practical one: the reader wishes to be apprised of the best that has been said and thought in all ages; he is less concerned with the descent of literary species or with the critic's adventures among masterpieces than with the perennial freshness and interest those masterpieces may hold for him. There is, of course, much more than a practical motive to justify the interest in permanent values; but this is not the place to raise a moot question of general critical theory. We wished only to note the common ground of literary criticism in its preoccupation with the thought and the eloquence which is permanent.

If now we turn to rhetorical criticism as we found it exemplified in the preceding section, we find that its point of view is patently single. It is not concerned with permanence, nor yet with beauty. It is concerned with effect. It regards a speech as a communication to a specific audience, and holds its business to be the analysis and appreciation of the orator's method of imparting his ideas to his hearers.

Rhetoric, however, is a word that requires explanation; its use in connection with criticism is neither general nor consistent. The merely depreciatory sense in which it is often applied to bombast or false ornament need not delay us. The limited meaning which confines the term to the devices of a correct and even of an elegant prose style—in the sense of manner of writing and speaking—may also be eliminated, as likewise the broad interpretation which makes rhetoric inclusive of all style whether in prose or in poetry. There remain some definitions which have greater promise. We may mention first that of Aristotle: "the faculty of observing in any given case the available means of persuasion";[45] this readily turns into the art of persuasion as the editors of the *New English Dictionary* recognize when they define rhetoric as "the art of using language so as to persuade or influence others." The gloss on "persuade" afforded by the additional term "influence" is worthy of note. Jebb achieves the same result by defining rhetoric as "the art of using language in such a way as to produce a desired impression upon the hearer or reader."[46] There is yet a fourth definition, one which serves to

---

[44]Oliver Elton, *Survey of English Literature, 1780-1830,* London, 1912, I, 234.
[45]*Rhetoric,* ii, 2, tr. W. Rhys Roberts in *The Works of Aristotle,* XI, Oxford, 1924.
[46]Article "Rhetoric" in the *Encyclopaedia Britannica,* 9th and 11th editions.

illuminate the others as well as to emphasize their essential agreement: "taken broadly [rhetoric is] the science and art of communication in language";[47] the framers of this definition add that to throw the emphasis on communication is to emphasize prose, poetry being regarded as more distinctly expressive than communicative. A German writer has made a similar distinction between poetic as the art of poetry and rhetoric as the art of prose, but rather on the basis that prose is of the intellect, poetry of the imagination.[48] Wackernagel's basis for the distinction will hardly stand in face of the attitude of modern psychology to the "faculties"; yet the distinction itself is suggestive, and it does not contravene the more significant opposition of expression and communication. That opposition has been well stated, though with some exaggeration, by Professor Hudson:

> The writer in pure literature has his eye on his subject; his subject has filled his mind and engaged his interest and he must tell about it; his task is expression; his form and style are organic with his subject. The writer of rhetorical discourse has his eye upon the audience and occasion; his task is persuasion; his form and style are organic with the occasion.[49]

The element of the author's personality should not be lost from sight in the case of the writer of pure literature; nor may the critic think of the audience and the occasion as alone conditioning the work of the composer of rhetorical discourse, unless indeed he include in the occasion both the personality of the speaker and the subject. The distinction is better put by Professor Baldwin:

> Rhetoric meant to the ancient world the art of instructing and moving men in their affairs; poetic the art of sharpening and expanding their vision. . . . The one is composition of ideas; the other, composition of images. In the one field life is discussed; in the other it is presented. The type of the one is a public address, moving us to assent and action; the type of the other is a play, showing us [an] action moving to an end of character. The one argues and urges; the other represents. Though both appeal to imagination, the method of rhetoric is logical; the method of poetic, as well as its detail, is imaginative.[50]

It is noteworthy that in this passage there is nothing to oppose poetry, in its common acceptation of verse, to prose. Indeed, in discussing the four forms of discourse usually treated in textbooks. Baldwin explicitly classes exposition and argument under rhetoric, leaving narrative and description to

[47]J. L. Gerig and F. N. Scott, article "Rhetoric" in the *New International Encyclopaedia.*
[48]K. H. W. Wackernagel, *Poetik, Rhetorik und Stilistik,* ed. L. Sieber, Halle, 1873, p. II.
[49]H. H. Hudson, "The Field of Rhetoric," *Quarterly Journal of Speech Education,* IX (1923), 177. See also the same writer's "Rhetoric and Poetry," *ibid.,* X (1924), 143 ff.
[50]C. S. Baldwin, *Ancient Rhetoric and Poetic,* New York, 1924, p. 134.

the other field. But rhetoric has been applied to the art of prose by some who include under the term even nonmetrical works of fiction. This is the attitude of Wackernagel, already mentioned, and of Saintsbury, who observes that Aristotle's *Rhetoric* holds, "if not intentionally, yet actually, something of the same position towards Prose as that which the *Poetics* holds towards verse."[51] In Saintsbury's view, the *Rhetoric* achieves this position in virtue of its third book, that on style and arrangement: the frst two books contain "a great deal of matter which has either the faintest connection with literary criticism or else no connection with it at all."[52] Saintsbury finds it objectionable in Aristotle that to him, "prose as prose is merely and avowedly a secondary consideration: it is always in the main, and sometimes wholly, a mere necessary instrument of divers practical purposes,"[53] and that "he does not *wish* to consider a piece of prose as a work of art destined, first of all, if not finally, to fulfil its own laws on the one hand, and to give pleasure on the other."[54] The distinction between verse and prose has often troubled the writers of criticism. The explanation is probably that the outer form of a work is more easily understood and more constantly present to the mind than is the real form. Yet it is strange that those who find the distinction between verse and prose important should parallel this with a distinction between imagination and intellect, as if a novel had more affinities with a speech than with an epic. It is strange, too, that Saintsbury's own phrase about the right way to consider a "piece of prose"—as a work of art destined "to fulfil its own laws"—did not suggest to him the fundamental importance of a distinction between what he terms the minor or suasive rhetoric on the one hand and on the other poetic, whether or not in verse. For poetry always is free to fulfil its own law, but the writer of rhetorical discourse is, in a sense, perpetually in bondage to the occasion and the audience; and in that fact we find the line of cleavage between rhetoric and poetic.

The distinction between rhetoric as theory of public address and poetic as theory of pure literature, says Professor Baldwin, "seems not to have controlled any consecutive movement of modern criticism."[55] That it has not controlled the procedure of critics in dealing with orators is indicated in the foregoing pages; yet we have found, too, many suggestions of a better method, and some few critical performances against which the only charge is overcondensation.

Rhetorical criticism is necessarily analytical. The scheme of a rhetorical study includes the element of the speaker's personality as a conditioning factor; it includes also the public character of the man—not what he was but

---

[51]G. E. B. Saintsbury, *History of Criticism and Literary Taste in Europe,* New York, 1900, I, 39.
[52]*Ibid.,* p. 42.
[53]*History of Criticism and Literary Taste in Europe,* p. 48.
[54]*Ibid.,* p. 52.
[55]*Op. cit.,* p. 4.

what he was thought to be. It requires a description of the speaker's audience, and of the leading ideas with which he plied his hearers—his topics the motives to which he appealed the nature of the proofs he offered. These will reveal his own judgment of human nature in his audiences, and also his judgment on the questions which he discussed. Attention must be paid, too, to the relation of the surviving texts to what was actually uttered: in case the nature of the changes is known there may be occasion to consider adaptation to two audiences—that which heard and that which read. Nor can rhetorical criticism omit the speaker's mode of arrangement and his mode of expression, nor his habit of preparation and his manner of delivery from the platform; though the last two are perhaps less significant. "Style"—in the sense which corresponds to diction and sentence movement—must receive attention, but only as one among various means that secure for the speaker ready access to the minds of his auditors. Finally, the effect of the discourse on its immediate hearers is not to be ignored, either in the testimony of witnesses, nor in the record of events. And throughout such a study one must conceive of the public man as influencing the men of his own times by the power of his discourse.

VIII

What is the relation of rhetorical criticism, so understood, to literary criticism? The latter is at once broader and more limited than rhetorical criticism. It is broader because of its concern with permanent values: because it takes no account of special purpose nor of immediate effect; because it views a literary work as the voice of a human spirit addressing itself to men of all ages and times; because the critic speaks as the spectator of all time and all existence. But this universalizing of attitude brings its own limits with it: the influence of the period is necessarily relegated to the background; interpretation in the light of the writer's intention and of his situation may be ignored or slighted; and the speaker who directed his words to a definite and limited group of hearers may be made to address a universal audience. The result can only be confusion. In short, the point of view of literary criticism is proper only to its own objects, the permanent works. Upon such as are found to lie without the pale, the verdict of literary criticism is of negative value merely, and its interpretation is false and misleading because it proceeds upon a wrong assumption. If Henry Clay and Charles Fox are to be dealt with at all, it must not be on the assumption that their works, in respect of wisdom and eloquence, are or ought to be sources of perennial freshness and interest. Morley has put the matter well:

> The statesman who makes or dominates a crisis, who has to rouse and mold the mind of senate or nation, has something else to think about than the production of literary masterpieces. The great political speech, which for that matter is a sort of drama, is not made by passages for elegant extract or anthologies, but by personality,

movement, climax, spectacle, and the action of the time.[56]

But we cannot always divorce rhetorical criticism from literary. In the case of Fox or Clay or Cobden, as opposed to Fielding or Addison or De Quincey, it is proper to do so; the fact that language is a common medium to the writer of rhetorical discourse and to the writer in pure literature will give to the critics of each a common vocabulary of stylistic terms, but not a common standard. In the case of Burke the relation of the two points of view is more complex. Burke belongs to literature: but in all his important works he was a practitioner of public address written or uttered. Since his approach to *belles-lettres* was through rhetoric, it follows that rhetorical criticism is at least a preliminary to literary criticism, for it will erect the factual basis for the understanding of the works: will not merely explain allusions and establish dates, but recall the setting, reconstruct the author's own intention, and analyze his method. But the rhetorical inquiry is more than a mere preliminary; it permeates and governs all subsequent interpretation and criticism. For the statesman in letters is a statesman still: compare Burke to Charles Lamb, or even to Montaigne, and it is clear that the public man is in a sense inseparable from his audience. A statesman's wisdom and eloquence are not to be read without some share of his own sense of the body politic, and of the body politic not merely as a construct of thought, but as a living human society. A speech, like a satire, like a comedy of manners, grows directly out of a social situation; it is a man's response to a condition in human affairs. However broadly typical the situation may be when its essential elements are laid bare, it never appears without its coverings. On no plane of thought—philosophical, literary, political—is Burke to be understood without reference to the great events in America, India, France, which evoked his eloquence; nor is he to be understood without reference to the state of English society. (It is this last that is lacking in Grierson's essay: the page of comment on Burke's qualities in actual debate wants its supplement in some account of the House of Commons and the national life it represented. Perhaps the latter is the more needful to a full understanding of the abiding excellence in Burke's pages.) Something of the spirit of Morley's chapter on Cobden, and more of the spirit of the social historian (which Morley has in other parts of the biography) is necessary to the literary critic in dealing with the statesman who is also a man of letters.

In the case of Burke, then, one of the functions of rhetorical criticism is as a preliminary, but an essential and governing, preliminary, to the literary criticism which occupies itself with the permanent values of wisdom and of eloquence, of thought and of beauty, that are found in the works of the orator.

Rhetorical criticism may also be regarded as an end in itself. Even Burke may be studied from that point of view alone. Fox and Cobden and the

---

[56]*Life of William Ewart Gladstone,* II, 589-90.

majority of public speakers are not to be regarded from any other. No one will offer Cobden's works a place in pure literature. Yet the method of the great agitator has a place in the history of his times. That place is not in the history of *belles-lettres;* nor is it in the literary history which is a "survey of the life of a people as expressed in their writings." The idea of "writings" is a merely mechanical one; it does not really provide a point of view or a method; it is a book-maker's cloak for many and diverse points of view. Such a compilation as the *Cambridge History of American Literature,* for example, in spite of the excellence of single essays, may not unjustly be characterized as an uneven commentary on the literary life of the country and as a still more uneven commentary on its social and political life. It may be questioned whether the scant treatment of public men in such a compilation throws light either on the creators of pure literature, or on the makers of rhetorical discourse, or on the life of the times.

Rhetorical criticism lies at the boundary of politics (in the broadest sense) and literature; its atmosphere is that of the public life,[57] its tools are those of literature, its concern is with the ideas of the people as influenced by their leaders. The effective wielder of public discourse, like the military man, belongs to social and political history because he is one of its makers. Like the soldier, he has an art of his own which is the source of his power; but the soldier's art is distinct from the life which his conquests affect. The rhetorician's art represents a natural and normal process within that life. It includes the work of the speaker, of the pamphleteer, of the writer of editorials, and of the sermon maker. It is to be thought of as the art of popularization. Its practitioners are the Huxleys, not the Darwins, of science; the Jeffersons, not the Lockes and the Rousseaus, of politics.

Of late years the art of popularization has received a degree of attention: propaganda and publicity have been words much used; the influence of the press has been discussed; there have been some studies of public opinion. Professor Robinson's *Humanizing of Knowledge*[58] is a cogent statement of the need for popularization by the instructed element in the state, and of the need for a technique in doing so. But the book indicates, too, how little is known of the methods its author so earnestly desires to see put to use. Yet ever since Homer's day men have woven the web of words and counsel in the face of all. And ever since Aristotle's day there has been a mode of analysis of public address. Perhaps the preoccupation of literary criticism with "style" rather than with composition in the large has diverted interest from the more significant problem. Perhaps the conventional categories of historical thought have helped to obscure the problem: the history of thought, for example, is generally interpreted as the history of invention and discovery, both physical and intellectual. Yet the history of the thought of the people is at least as

---

[57] For a popular but suggestive presentation of the background of rhetorical discourse, see J. A. Spender, *The Public Life,* New York, 1925.
[58] New York, 1923.

potent a factor in the progress of the race. True, the popular thought may often represent a resisting force, and we need not marvel that the many movements of a poet's mind more readily capture the critic's attention than the few and uncertain movements of that Leviathan, the public mind. Nor is it surprising that the historians tend to be occupied with the acts and the motives of leaders. But those historians who find the spirit of an age in the total mass of its literary productions, as well as all who would tame Leviathan to the end that he shall not threaten civilization, must examine more thoroughly than they as yet have done the interactions of the inventive genius, the popularizing talent, and the public mind.

The Rhetoric
of Hitler's "Battle"

by Kenneth Burke

The appearance of *Mein Kampf* in unexpurgated translation has called forth far too many vandalistic comments. There are other ways of burning books than on the pyre—and the favorite method of the hasty reviewer is to deprive himself and his readers by inattention. I maintain that it is thoroughly vandalistic for the reviewer to content himself with the mere inflicting of a few symbolic wounds upon this book and its author, of an intensity varying with the resources of the reviewer and the time at his disposal. Hitler's "Battle" is exasperating, even nauseating; yet the fact remains: If the reviewer but knocks off a few adverse attitudinizings and calls it a day, with a guaranty in advance that his article will have a favorable reception among the decent members of our population, he is contributing more to our gratification than to our enlightenment.

Here is the testament of a man who swung a great people into his wake. Let us watch it carefully; and let us watch it, not merely to discover some grounds for prophesying what political move is to follow Munich, and what move to follow that move, etc.; let us try also to discover what kind of "medicine" this medicine-man has concocted, that we may know, with greater accuracy, exactly what to guard against, if we are to forestall the concocting of similar medicine in America.

Already, in many quarters of our country, we are "beyond" the stage where we are being saved from Nazism by our *virtues*. And fascist integration is being staved off, rather, by the *conflicts among our vices*. Our vices cannot get together in a grand united front of prejudices; and the result of this frustration, if or until they succeed in surmounting it, speaks, as the Bible might say, "in the name of" democracy. Hitler found a panacea, a "cure for what ails you," a "snakeoil," that made such sinister unifying possible within his own nation. And he was helpful enough to put his cards face up on the table, that we might examine his hands. Let us, then, for God's sake, examine them. This book is the well of Nazi magic; crude magic, but effective. A people trained in pragmatism should want to inspect this magic.

Reprinted from *The Philosophy of Literary Form* (Berkeley: University of California Press, 1973). Used by permission of the University of California Press.

1

Every movement that would recruit its followers from among many discordant and divergent bands, must have some spot towards which all roads lead. Each man may get there in his own way, but it must be the one unifying center of reference for all. Hitler considered this matter carefully, and decided that this center must be not merely a centralizing hub of *ideas*, but a mecca geographically located, towards which all eyes could turn at the appointed hours of prayer (or, in this case, the appointed hours of prayer-in-reverse, the hours of vituperation). So he selected Munich, as the *materialization* of his unifying panacea. As he puts it:

> The geo-political importance of a center of a movement cannot be overrated. Only the presence of such a center and of a place, bathed in the magic of a Mecca or a Rome, can at length give a movement that force which is rooted in the inner unity and in the recognition of a hand that represents this unity.

If a movement must have its Rome, it must also have its devil. For as Russell pointed out years ago, an important ingredient of unity in the Middle Ages (an ingredient that long did its unifying work despite the many factors driving towards disunity) was the symbol of a *common enemy*, the Prince of Evil himself. Men who can unite on nothing else can unite on the basis of a foe shared by all. Hitler himself states the case very succinctly:

> As a whole, and at all times, the efficiency of the truly national leader consists primarily in preventing the division of the attention of a people, and always in concentrating it on a single enemy. The more uniformly the fighting will of a people is put into action, the greater will be the magnetic force of the movement and the more powerful the impetus of the blow. It is part of the genius of a great leader to make adversaries of different fields appear as always belonging to one category only, because to weak and unstable characters the knowledge that there are various enemies will lead only too easily to incipient doubts as to their own cause.
>
> As soon as the wavering masses find themselves confronted with too many enemies, objectivity at once steps in, and the question is raised whether actually all the others are wrong and their own nation or their own movement alone is right.
>
> Also with this comes the first paralysis of their own strength. Therefore, a number of essentially different enemies must always be regarded as one in such a way that in the opinion of the mass of one's own adherents the war is being waged against one enemy alone. This strengthens the belief in one's own cause and increases one's bitterness against the attacker.

As everyone knows, this policy was exemplified in his selection of an "international" devil, the "international Jew" (the Prince was international, universal, "catholic"). This *materialization* of a religious pattern is, I think, one terrifically effective weapon of propaganda in a period where religion has been progressively weakened by many centuries of capitalist materialism. You need but go back to the sermonizing of centuries to be reminded that religion had a powerful enemy long before organized atheism came upon the scene. Religion is based upon the "prosperity of poverty," upon the use of ways for converting our sufferings and handicaps into a good—but capitalism is based upon the prosperity of acquisitions, the only scheme of value, in fact, by which its proliferating store of gadgets could be sold, assuming for the moment that capitalism had not got so drastically in its own way that it can't sell its gadgets even after it has trained people to feel that human dignity, the "higher standard of living," could be attained only by their vast private accumulation.

So, we have, as unifying step No. 1, the international devil materialized, in the visible, point-to-able form of people with a certain kind of "blood," a burlesque of contemporary neo-positivism's ideal of meaning, which insists upon a *material* reference.

Once Hitler has thus essentialized his enemy, all "proof" henceforth is automatic. If you point out the enormous amount of evidence to show that the Jewish worker is at odds with the "international Jew stock exchange capitalist," Hitler replies with one hundred per cent regularity: That is one more indication of the cunning with which the "Jewish plot" is being engineered. Or would you point to "Aryans" who do the same as his conspiratorial Jews? Very well; that is proof that the "Aryan" has been "seduced" by the Jew.

The sexual symbolism that runs through Hitler's book, lying in wait to draw upon the responses of contemporary sexual values, is easily characterized: Germany in dispersion is the "dehorned Siegfried." The masses are "feminine." As such, they desire to be led by a dominating male. This male, as orator, woos them—and, when he has won them, he commands them. The rival male, the villainous Jew, would on the contrary "seduce" them. If he succeeds, he poisons their blood by intermingling with them. Whereupon, by purely associative connections of ideas, we are moved into attacks upon syphilis, prostitution, incest, and other similar misfortunes, which are introduced as a kind of "musical" argument when he is on the subject of "blood-poisoning" by intermarriage or, in its "spiritual" equivalent, by the infection of "Jewish" ideas, such as democracy.[1]

The "medicinal" appeal of the Jew as scapegoat operates from another angle. The middle class contains, within the mind of each member, a duality: its members simultaneously have a cult of money and a detestation of this cult. When capitalism is going well, this conflict is left more or less in

---

[1] Hitler also strongly insists upon the total identification between leader and people. Thus, in wooing the people, he would in a roundabout way be wooing himself. The thought might suggest how the Führer, dominating the feminine masses by his diction, would have an incentive to remain unmarried.

abeyance. But when capitalism is balked, it comes to the fore. Hence, there is "medicine" for the "Aryan" members of the middle class in the projective device of the scapegoat, whereby the "bad" features can be allocated to the "devil," and one can "respect himself" by a distinction between "good" capitalism and "bad" capitalism, with those of a different lodge being the vessels of the "bad" capitalism. It is doubtless the "relief" of this solution that spared Hitler the necessity of explaining just how the "Jewish plot" was to work out. Nowhere does this book, which is so full of war plans, make the slightest attempt to explain the steps whereby the triumph of "Jewish Bolshevism," which destroys *all* finance, will be the triumph of "*Jewish*" finance. Hitler well knows the point at which his "elucidations" should rely upon the lurid alone.

The question arises, in those trying to gauge Hitler: Was his selection of the Jew, as his unifying devil-function, a purely calculating act? Despite the quotation I have already given, I believe that it was *not*. The vigor with which he utilized it, I think, derives from a much more complex state of affairs. It seems that, when Hitler went to Vienna, in a state close to total poverty, he genuinely suffered. He lived among the impoverished; and he describes his misery at the spectacle. He was *sensitive* to it; and his way of manifesting this sensitiveness impresses me that he is, at this point, wholly genuine, as with his wincing at the broken family relationships caused by alcoholism, which he in turn relates to impoverishment. During this time he began his attempts at political theorizing; and his disturbance was considerably increased by the skill with which Marxists tied him into knots. One passage in particular gives you reason, reading between the lines, to believe that the dialecticians of the class struggle, in their skill at blasting his muddled speculations, put him into a state of uncertainty that was finally "solved" by rage:

> The more I argued with them, the more I got to know their dialectics. First they counted on the ignorance of their adversary; then, when there was no way out, they themselves pretended stupidity. If all this was of no avail, they refused to understand or they changed the subject when driven into a corner; they brought up truisms, but they immediately transferred their acceptance to quite different subjects, and, if attacked again, they gave way and pretended to know nothing exactly. Wherever one attacked one of these prophets, one's hands seized slimy jelly; it slipped through one's fingers only to collect again in the next moment. If one smote one of them so thoroughly that, with the bystanders watching, he could but agree, and if one thus thought he had advanced at least one step, one was greatly astonished the following day. The Jew did not in the least remember the day before, he continued to talk in the same old strain as if nothing had happened, and if indignantly confronted, he pretended to be astonished and could not remember anything except that his assertions had already been proved true the day before.

> Often I was stunned.
> One did not know what to admire more: their glibness of tongue
> or their skill in lying.
> I gradually began to hate them.

At this point, I think, he is tracing the *spontaneous* rise of his anti-Semitism. He tells how, once he had discovered the "cause" of the misery about him, he could *confront it*. Where he had had to avert his eyes, he could now *positively welcome* the scene. Here his drastic structure of *acceptance* was being formed. He tells of the "internal happiness" that descended upon him.

> This was the time in which the greatest change I was ever to
> experience took place in me.
> From a feeble cosmopolite I turned into a fanatical anti-Semite,

and thence we move, by one of those associational tricks which he brings forth at all strategic moments, into a vision of the end of the world—out of which in turn he emerges with his slogan: "I am acting in the sense of the Almighty Creator: *By warding off Jews I am fighting for the Lord's work*" (italics his).

He talks of this transition as a period of "double life," a struggle of "reason" and "reality" against his "heart."[2] It was as "bitter" as it was "blissful." And finally, it was "reason" that won! Which prompts us to note that those who attack Hitlerism as a cult of the irrational should emend their statements to this extent: irrational it is, but it is carried on under the *slogan* of "Reason." Similarly, his cult of war is developed "in the name of" humility, love, and peace. Judged on a quantitative basis, Hitler's book

---

[2] Other aspects of the career symbolism: Hitler's book begins: "Today I consider it my good fortune that Fate designated Braunau on the Inn as the place of my birth. For this small town is situated on the border between those two German States, the reunion of which seems, at least to us of the younger generation, a task to be furthered with every means our lives long," an indication of his "transitional" mind, what Wordsworth might have called the "borderer." He neglects to give the date of his birth, 1889, which is supplied by the editors. Again there is a certain "correctness" here, as Hitler was not "born" until many years later—but he does give the exact date of his war wounds, which were indeed formative. During his early years in Vienna and Munich, he foregoes protest, on the grounds that he is "nameless." And when his party is finally organized and effective, he stresses the fact that his "nameless" period is over (i.e., he has shaped himself an identity). When reading in an earlier passage of his book some generalizations to the effect that one should not crystallize his political views until he is thirty, I made a note: "See what Hitler does at thirty." I felt sure that, though such generalizations may be dubious as applied to people as a whole, they must, given the Hitler type of mind (with his complete identification between himself and his followers), be valid statements about himself. One *should* do what he *did*. The hunch was verified: about the age of thirty Hitler, in a group of seven, began working with the party that was to conquer Germany. I trace these steps particularly because I believe that the orator who has a strong sense of his own "rebirth" has this to draw upon when persuading his audiences that his is offering them the way to a "new life." However, I see no categorical objection to this attitude; its menace derives solely from the values in which it is exemplified. They may be wholesome or unwholesome. If they are unwholesome, but backed by conviction, the basic sincerity of the conviction acts as a sound virtue to reinforce a vice—and this combination is the most disastrous one that a people can encounter in a demagogue.

certainly falls under the classification of hate. Its venom is everywhere, its charity is sparse. But the rationalized family tree for this hate situates it in "Aryan love." Some deep-probing German poets, whose work adumbrated the Nazi movement, did gravitate towards thinking *in the name of* war, irrationality, and hate. But Hitler was not among them. After all, when it is so easy to draw a doctrine of war out of a doctrine of peace, why should the astute politician do otherwise, particularly when Hitler has slung together his doctrines, without the slightest effort at logical symmetry? Furthermore, Church thinking always got to its wars in Hitler's "sounder" manner; and the patterns of Hitler's thought are a bastardized or caricatured version of religious thought.

I spoke of Hitler's fury at the dialectics of those who opposed him when his structure was in the stage of scaffolding. From this we may move to another tremendously important aspect of his theory: his attack upon the *parliamentary.* For it is again, I submit, an important aspect of his medicine, in its function as medicine for him personally and as medicine for those who were later to identify themselves with him.

There is a "problem" in the parliament—and nowhere was this problem more acutely in evidence than in the pre-war Vienna that was to serve as Hitler's political schooling. For the parliament, at its best, is a "babel" of voices. There is the wrangle of men representing interests lying awkwardly on the bias across one another, sometimes opposing, sometimes vaguely divergent. Morton Prince's psychiatric study of "Miss Beauchamp," the case of a woman split into several sub-personalities at odds with one another, variously combining under hypnosis, and frequently in turmoil, is the allegory of a democracy fallen upon evil days. The parliament of the Habsburg Empire just prior to its collapse was an especially drastic instance of such disruption, such vocal diaspora, with movements that would reduce one to a disintegrated mass of fragments if he attempted to encompass the totality of its discordancies. So Hitler, suffering under the alienation of poverty and confusion, yearning for some integrative core, came to take this parliament as the basic symbol of all that he would move away from. He damned the tottering Habsburg Empire as a "State of Nationalities." The many conflicting voices of the spokesmen of the many political blocs arose from the fact that various separationist movements of a nationalistic sort had arisen within a Catholic imperial structure formed prior to the nationalistic emphasis and slowly breaking apart under its development. So, you had this Babel of voices; and, by the method of associative mergers, *using ideas as imagery,* it became tied up, in the Hitler rhetoric, with "Babylon," Vienna as the city of poverty, prostitution, immorality, coalitions, half-measures, incest, democracy (i.e., majority rule leading to "lack of personal responsibility"), death, internationalism, seduction, and anything else of thumbs-down sort the associative enterprise cared to add on this side of the balance.

Hitler's way of treating the parliamentary babel, I am sorry to say, was at one important point not much different from that of the customary editorial in our own newspapers. Every conflict among the parliamentary spokesmen represents a corresponding conflict among the material interests of the groups for whom they are speaking. But Hitler did not discuss the babel from this angle. He discussed it on a purely *symptomatic* basis. The strategy of our orthodox press, in thus ridiculing the cacophonous verbal output of Congress, is obvious: by thus centering attack upon the *symptoms* of business conflict, as they reveal themselves on the dial of political wrangling, and leaving the underlying cause, the business conflicts themselves, out of the case, they can gratify the very public they would otherwise alienate: namely, the businessmen who are the activating members of their reading public. Hitler, however, went them one better. For not only did he stress the purely *symptomatic* attack here. He proceeded to search for the "cause." And this "cause," of course, he derived from his medicine, his racial theory by which he could give a noneconomic interpretation of a phenomenon economically engendered.

Here again is where Hitler's corrupt use of religious patterns comes to the fore. Church thought, being primarily concerned with matters of the "personality," with problems of moral betterment, naturally, and I think rightly, stresses as a necessary feature, the act of will upon the part of the individual. Hence its resistance to a purely "environmental" account of human ills. Hence its emphasis upon the "person." Hence its proneness to seek a noneconomic explanation of economic phenomena. Hitler's proposal of a noneconomic "cause" for the disturbances thus had much to recommend it from this angle. And, as a matter of fact, it was Lueger's Christian-Social Party in Vienna that taught Hitler the tactics of tying up a program of social betterment with an anti-Semitic "unifier." The two parties that he carefully studied at that time were this Catholic faction and Schoenerer's Pan-German group. And his analysis of their attainments and shortcomings, from the standpoint of demagogic efficacy, is an extremely astute piece of work, revealing how carefully this man used the current situation in Vienna as an experimental laboratory for the maturing of his plans.

His unification device, we may summarize, had the following important features:

(1) Inborn dignity. In both religious and humanistic patterns of thought, a "natural born" dignity of man is stressed. And this categorical dignity is considered to be an attribute of *all* men, if they will but avail themselves of it, by right thinking and right living. But Hitler gives this ennobling attitude an ominous twist by his theories of race and nation, whereby the "Aryan" is elevated above all others by the innate endowment of his blood, while other "races," in particular Jews and Negroes, are innately inferior. This sinister secularized revision of Christian theology thus puts the sense of dignity upon a fighting basis, requiring the conquest of "inferior races." After the defeat of Germany in the World War, there were especially strong emotional needs that this compensatory doctrine of an *inborn* superiority could gratify.

(2) *Projection* device. The "curative" process that comes with the ability to hand over one's ills to a scapegoat, thereby getting purification by dissociation. This was especially medicinal, since the sense of frustration

leads to a self-questioning. Hence if one can hand over his infirmities to a vessel, or "cause," outside the self, one can battle an external enemy instead of battling an enemy within. And the greater one's internal inadequacies, the greater the amount of evils one can load upon the back of "the enemy." This device is furthermore given a semblance of reason because the individual properly realizes that he is not alone responsible for his condition. There *are* inimical factors in the scene itself. And he wants to have them "placed," preferably in a way that would require a minimum change in the ways of thinking to which he had been accustomed. This was especially appealing to the middle class, who were encouraged to feel that they could conduct their businesses without any basic change whatever, once the businessmen of a different "race" were eliminated.

(3) Symbolic rebirth. Another aspect of the two features already noted. The projective device of the scapegoat, coupled with the Hitlerite doctrine of inborn racial superiority, provides its followers with a "positive" view of life. They can again get the feel of *moving forward*, towards a *goal* (a promissory feature of which Hitler makes much). In Hitler, as the group's prophet, such rebirth involved a symbolic change of lineage. Here, above all, we see Hitler giving a malign twist to a benign aspect of Christian thought. For whereas the Pope, in the familistic pattern of thought basic to the Church, stated that the Hebrew prophets were the *spiritual ancestors* of Christianity, Hitler uses this same mode of thinking in reverse. He renounces this "ancestry" in a "materialistic" way by voting himself and the members of his lodge a different "blood stream" from that of the Jews.

(4) Commercial use. Hitler obviously here had something to sell—and it was but a question of time until he sold it (i.e., got financial backers for his movement). For it provided a *noneconomic interpretation of economic ills.* As such, it served with maximum efficiency in deflecting the attention from the economic factors involved in modern conflict; hence by attacking "Jew finance" instead of *finance*, it could stimulate an enthusiastic movement that left "Aryan" finance in control.

Never once, throughout his book, does Hitler deviate from the above formula. Invariably, he ends his diatribes against contemporary economic ills by a shift into an insistence that we must get to the "true" cause, which is centered in "race." The "Aryan" is "constructive"; the Jew is "destructive"; and the "Aryan," to continue his *construction*, must *destroy* the Jewish *destruction*. The Aryan, as the vessel of *love,* must *hate* the Jewish *hate.*

Perhaps the most enterprising use of his method is in his chapter "The Causes of the Collapse," where he refuses to consider Germany's plight as in any basic way connected with the consequences of war. Economic factors, he insists, are "only of second or even third importance," but "political, ethical-moral, as well as factors of blood and race, are of the first importance." His rhetorical steps are especially interesting here, in that he begins by seeming to flout the national susceptibilities: "The military defeat of the German people is not an undeserved catastrophe, but rather a deserved punishment by eternal retribution." He then proceeds to present the military collapse as but a "consequence of moral poisoning, visible to all, the consequence of a decrease in the instinct of self-preservation . . . which had already begun to undermine the foundations of the people and the Reich many years before." This moral decay derived from "a sin against the blood and the degradation of the race," so its innerness was an outerness after all: the Jew, who thereupon gets saddled with a vast amalgamation of evils, among them being capitalism, democracy, pacifism, journalism, poor housing, modernism, big cities, loss of religion, half measures, ill health, and weakness of the monarch.

2

Hitler had here another important psychological ingredient to play upon. If a State is in economic collapse (and his theories, tentatively taking shape in the pre-war Vienna, were but developed with greater efficiency in post-war Munich), you cannot possibly derive dignity from economic stability. Dignity must come first—and if you possess it, and implement it, from it may follow its economic counterpart. There is much justice to this line of reasoning, so far as it goes. A people in collapse, suffering under economic frustration and the defeat of nationalistic aspirations, with the very midrib of their integrative efforts (the army) in a state of dispersion, have little other than some "spiritual" basis to which they could refer their nationalistic dignity. Hence, the categorical dignity of superior race was a perfect recipe for the situation. It was "spiritual" in so far as it was "above" crude economic "interests," but it was "materialized" at the psychologically "right" spot in that "the enemy" was something you could *see*.

Furthermore, you had the desire for unity, such as a discussion of class conflict, on the basis of conflicting interests, could not satisfy. The yearning for unity is so great that people are always willing to meet you halfway if you will give it to them by fiat, by flat statement, regardless of the facts. Hence, Hitler consistently refused to consider internal political conflict on the basis of conflicting interests. Here again, he could draw upon a religious pattern, by insisting upon a *personal* statement of the relation between classes, the relation between leaders and followers, each group in its way fulfilling the same commonalty of interests, as the soldiers and captains of an army share a common interest in victory. People so dislike the idea of internal division that, where there is a real internal division, their dislike can easily be turned against the man or group who would so much as *name* it, let alone propose to act upon it. Their natural and justified resentment against internal division itself is turned against the diagnostician who states it as a *fact*. This diagnostician, it is felt, is the *cause* of the disunity he named.

Cutting in from another angle, therefore, we note how two sets of equations were built up, with Hitler combining or coalescing *ideas* the way a poet combines or coalesces *images*. On the one side, were the ideas, or images, of disunity, centering in the parliamentary wrangle of the Habsburg "State of Nationalities." This was offered as the antithesis of German nationality, which was presented in the curative imagery of unity, focused upon the glories of the Prussian Reich, with its mecca now moved to "folkish" Vienna. For though Hitler at first attacked the many "folkish" movements, with their hankerings after a kind of Wagnerian mythology of Germanic origins, he subsequently took "folkish" as a basic word by which to conjure. It was, after all, another noneconomic basis of reference. At first we find him objecting to "those who drift about with the word 'folkish' on their caps," and asserting that "such a Babel of opinions cannot serve as the basis of a political fighting movement." But later he seems to have realized, as he well should, that its vagueness was a major point in its favor. So it was incorporated in the grand coalition of his ideational imagery, or imagistic ideation; and Chapter XI ends with the vision of "a State which represents not a mechanism of economic considerations and interests, alien to the people, but a folkish organism."

So, as against the disunity equations, already listed briefly in our discussion of his attacks upon the parliamentary, we get a contrary purifying set; the wrangle of the parliamentary is to be stilled by the giving of *one* voice to the whole people, this to be the "inner voice" of Hitler, made uniform throughout the German boundaries, as leader and people were completely identified with each other. In sum: Hitler's inner voice equals leader-people identification, equals unity, equals Reich, equals the mecca of Munich, equals plow, equals sword, equals work, equals war, equals army as midrib, equals responsibility (the personal responsibility of the absolute ruler), equals sacrifice, equals the theory of "German democracy" (the free popular choice of the leader, who then accepts the responsibility, and demands absolute obedience in exchange for his sacrifice), equals love (with the masses as feminine), equals idealism, equals obedience to nature, equals race, nation.[3]

And, of course, the two keystones of these opposite equations were Aryan "heroism" and "sacrifice" vs. Jewish "cunning" and "arrogance." Here again we get an astounding caricature of religious thought. For Hitler presents the concept of "Aryan" superiority, of all ways, in terms of "Aryan humility." This "humility" is extracted by a very delicate process that requires, I am

---

[3] One could carry out the equations further, on both the disunity and unity side. In the aesthetic field, for instance, we have expressionism on the thumbs-down side, as against aesthetic hygiene on the thumbs-up side. This again is a particularly ironic moment in Hitler's strategy. For the expressionist movement was unquestionably a symptom of unhealthiness. It reflected the increasing alienation that went with the movement towards world war and the disorganization after the world war. It was "lost," vague in identity, a drastically accurate reflection of the response to material confusion, a pathetic attempt by sincere artists to make their wretchedness bearable at least to the extent that comes of giving it expression. And it attained its height during the period of wild inflation, when the capitalist world, which bases its morality of work and savings upon the soundness of its money structure, had this last prop of stability removed. The anguish, in short, reflected precisely the kind of disruption that made people *ripe* for a Hitler. It was the antecedent in a phrase of which Hitlerism was the consequent. But by thundering against this *symptom* he could gain persuasiveness, though attacking the very *foreshadowings of himself.*

afraid, considerable "good will" on the part of the reader who would follow it:

The Church, we may recall, had proclaimed an integral relationship between Divine Law and Natural Law. Natural Law was the expression of the Will of God. Thus, in the middle age, it was a result of natural law, working through tradition, that some people were serfs and other people nobles. And every good member of the Church was "obedient" to this law. Everybody resigned himself to it. Hence, the serf resigned himself to his poverty, and the noble resigned himself to his riches. The monarch resigned himself to his position as representative of the people. And at times the Churchmen resigned themselves to the need of trying to represent the people instead. And the pattern was made symmetrical by the consideration that each traditional "right" had its corresponding "obligations." Similarly, the Aryan doctrine is a doctrine of resignation, hence of humility. It is in accordance with the laws of nature that the "Aryan blood" is superior to all other bloods. Also, the "law of the survival of the fittest" is God's law, working through natural law. Hence, if the Aryan blood has been vested with the awful responsibility of its inborn superiority, the bearers of this "culture-creating" blood must resign themselves to struggle in behalf of its triumph. Otherwise, the laws of God have been disobeyed, with human decadence as a result. We must fight, he says, in order to "deserve to be alive." The Aryan "obeys" nature. It is only "Jewish arrogance" that thinks of "conquering" nature by democratic ideals of equality.

This picture has some nice distinctions worth following. The major virtue of the Aryan race was its instinct for self-preservation (in obedience to natural law). But the major vice of the Jew was his instinct for self-preservation; for, if he did not have this instinct to a maximum degree, he would not be the "perfect" enemy—that is, he wouldn't be strong enough to account for the ubiquitousness and omnipotence of his conspiracy in destroying the world to become its master.

How, then, are we to distinguish between the benign instinct of self-preservation at the roots of Aryanism, and the malign instinct of self-preservation at the roots of Semitism? We shall distinguish thus: The Aryan self-preservation is based upon *sacrifice*, the sacrifice of the individual to the group, hence, militarism, army discipline, and one big company union. But Jewish self-preservation is based upon individualism, which attains its cunning ends by the exploitation of peace. How, then, can such arrant individualists concoct the world-wide plot? By the help of their "herd instinct." By their sheer "herd instinct" individualists can band together for a common end. They have no real solidarity, but unite opportunistically to seduce the Aryan. Still, that brings up another technical problem. For we have been hearing much about the importance of the *person*. We have been told how, by the "law of the survival of the fittest," there is a sifting of people on the basis of their individual capacities. We even have a special chapter of pure Aryanism: "The Strong Man is Mightiest Alone." Hence, another distinction is necessary: The Jew represents individualism; the Aryan represents "super-individualism."

I had thought, when coming upon the "Strong Man is Mightiest Alone" chapter, that I was going to find Hitler at his weakest. Instead, I found him at his strongest. (I am not referring to *quality*, but to *demagogic effectiveness*.) For the chapter is not at all, as you might infer from the title, done in a "rise of Adolph Hitler" manner. Instead, it deals with the Nazis' gradual absorption of the many disrelated "folkish" groups. And it is managed throughout by means of a spontaneous identification between leader and people. Hence, the Strong Man's "aloneness" is presented as a *public* attribute, in terms of tactics for the struggle against the *Party's* dismemberment under the pressure of rival saviors. There is no explicit talk of Hitler at all. And it is simply *taken for granted* that *his* leadership is the norm, and all other leaderships the abnorm. There is no "philosophy of the superman," in Nietzschean cast. Instead, Hitler's blandishments so integrate leader and people, commingling them so inextricably, that the politician does not even present himself as candidate. Somehow, the battle is over already, the decision has been made. "German democracy" has chosen. And the deployments of politics are, you might say, the chartings of Hitler's private mind translated into the vocabulary of nationalistic events. He says *what he thought* in terms of *what parties did*.

Here, I think, we see the distinguishing quality of Hitler's method as an instrument of persuasion, with reference to the question whether Hitler is sincere or deliberate, whether his vision of the omnipotent conspirator has the drastic honesty of paranoia or the sheer shrewdness of a demagogue trained in *Realpolitik* of the Machiavellian sort.[4] Must we choose? Or may we not, rather, replace the "either—or" with a "both—and"? Have we not by now offered grounds enough for our contention that Hitler's sinister powers of persuasion derive from the fact that he spontaneously evolved his "cure-all" in response to inner necessities?

3

So much, then, was "spontaneous." It was further channelized into the anti-Semitic pattern by the incentives he derived from the Catholic Christian-

---

[4] I should not want to use the word "Machiavellian," however, without offering a kind of apology to Machiavelli. It seems to me that Machiavelli's *Prince* has more to be said in extenuation than is usually said of it. Machiavelli's strategy, as I see it, was something like this: He accepted the values of the Renaissance rule as a *fact*. That is: whether you like these values or not, they were there and operating, and it was useless to try persuading the ambitious ruler to adopt other values, such as those of the Church. These men believed in the cult of material power, and they had the power to implement their beliefs. With so much as "the given," could anything in the way of benefits for the people be salvaged? Machiavelli evolved a typical "Machiavellian" argument in favor of popular benefits, on the basis of the prince's own scheme of values. That is: the ruler, to attain the maximum strength, requires the backing of the populace. That this backing be as effective as possible, the populace should be made as strong as possible. And that the populace be as strong as possible, they should be well treated. Their gratitude would further repay itself in the form of increased loyalty.

It was Machiavelli's hope that, for this roundabout project, he would be rewarded with a well-paying office in the prince's administrative bureaucracy.

Social Party in Vienna itself. Add, now, the step into *criticism*. Not criticism in the "parliamentary" sense of doubt, of hearkening to the opposition and attempting to mature a policy in the light of counter-policies; but the "unified" kind of criticism that simply seeks for conscious ways of making one's position more "efficient," more thoroughly itself. This is the kind of criticism at which Hitler was an adept. As a result, he could *spontaneously* turn to a scapegoat mechanism, and he could, by conscious planning, perfect the symmetry of the solution towards which he had spontaneously turned.

This is the meaning of Hitler's diatribes against "objectivity." "Objectivity" is interference-criticism. What Hitler wanted was the kind of criticism that would be a pure and simple coefficient of power, enabling him to go most effectively in the direction he had chosen. And the "inner voice" of which he speaks would henceforth dictate to him the greatest amount of realism, as regards the tactics of efficiency. For instance, having decided that the masses required certainty, and simple certainty, quite as he did himself, he later worked out a 25-point program as the platform of his National Socialist German Workers Party. And he resolutely refused to change one single item in this program, even for purposes of "improvement." He felt that the *fixity* of the platform was more important for propagandistic purposes than any revision of his slogans could be, even though the revisions in themselves had much to be said in their favor. The astounding thing is that, although such an attitude gave good cause to doubt the Hitlerite promises, he could explicitly explain his tactics in his book and still employ them without loss of effectiveness.[5]

Hitler also tells of his technique in speaking, once the Nazi party had become effectively organized, and had its army of guards, or bouncers, to maltreat hecklers and throw them from the hall. He would, he recounts, fill his speech with *provocative* remarks, whereat his bouncers would promptly swoop down in flying formation, with swinging fists, upon anyone whom these provocative remarks provoked to answer. The efficiency of Hitlerism is the efficiency of the one voice, implemented throughout a total organization. The trinity of government which he finally offers is: *popularity* of the leader, *force* to back the popularity, and popularity and force maintained together long enough to become backed by a *tradition*. Is such thinking spontaneous

---

[5] On this point Hitler reasons as follows: "Here, too, one can learn from the Catholic Church. Although its structure of doctrines in many instances collides, quite unnecessarily, with exact science and research, yet it is unwilling to sacrifice even one little syllable of its dogmas. It has rightly recognized that its resistibility does not lie in a more or less great adjustment to the scientific results of the moment, which in reality are always changing, but rather in a strict adherence to dogmas, once laid down, which alone give the entire structure the character of creed. Today, therefore, the Catholic Church stands firmer than ever. One can prophesy that in the same measure in which the appearances flee, the Church itself, as the resting pole in the flight of appearances, will gain more and more blind adherence."

or deliberate—or is it not rather both?[6]

Freud has given us a succinct paragraph that bears upon the spontaneous aspect of Hitler's persecution mania. (A persecution mania, I should add, different from the pure product in that it was constructed of *public* materials; all the ingredients Hitler stirred into his brew were already rife, with spokesmen and bands of followers, before Hitler "took them over." Both the pre-war and post-war periods were dotted with saviors, of nationalistic and "folkish" cast. This proliferation was analogous to the swarm of barter schemes and currency-tinkering that burst loose upon the United States after the crash of 1929. Also, the commercial availability of Hitler's politics was, in a low sense of the term, a *public* qualification, removing it from the realm of "pure" paranoia, where the sufferer develops a wholly *private* structure of interpretations.)

I cite from *Totem and Taboo:*

Another trait in the attitude of primitive races towards their rulers recalls a mechanism which is universally present in mental disturbances, and is openly revealed in the so-called delusions of persecution. Here the importance of a particular person is extraordinarily heightened and his omnipotence is raised to the improbable in order to make it easier to attribute to him responsibility for everything painful which happens to the patient. Savages really do not act differently towards their rulers when they ascribe to them power over rain and shine, wind and weather, and then dethrone them or kill them because nature has disappointed their expectation of a good hunt or a ripe harvest. The prototype which the paranoiac reconstructs in his persecution mania is found in the relation of the child to its father. Such omnipotence is regularly attributed to the father in the imagination or the son, and distrust of the father has been shown to be intimately connected with the heightened esteem for him. When a paranoiac names a person of his acquaintance as his "persecutor," he thereby elevates him to the paternal succession and brings him under conditions which enable him to make him responsible for all the misfortune which he experiences.

---

[6] Hitler also paid great attention to the conditions under which political oratory is most effective. He sums up thus:

"All these cases involve encroachments upon man's freedom of will. This applies, of course, most of all to meetings to which people with a contrary orientation of will are coming, and who now have to be won for new intentions. It seems that in the morning and even during the day men's will power revolts with highest energy against an attempt at being forced under another's will and another's opinion. In the evening, however, they succumb more easily to the dominating force of a stronger will. For truly every such meeting presents a wrestling match between two opposed forces. The superior oratorical talent of a domineering apostolic nature will now succeed more easily in winning for the new will people who themselves have in turn experienced a weakening of their force of resistance in the most natural way, than people who still have full command of the energies of their minds and their will power.

"The same purpose serves also the artificially created and yet mysterious dusk of the Catholic churches, the burning candles, incense, censers, etc."

I have already proposed my modifications of this account when discussing the symbolic change of lineage connected with Hitler's project of a "new way of life." Hitler is symbolically changing from the "spiritual ancestry" of the Hebrew prophets to the "superior" ancestry of "Aryanism," and has given his story a kind of bastardized modernization, along the lines of naturalistic, materialistic "science," by his fiction of the special "blood-stream." He is voting himself a new identity (something contrary to the wrangles of the Habsburg Babylon, a soothing national unity); whereupon the vessels of the old identity become a "bad" father, i.e., the persecutor. It is not hard to see how, as his enmity becomes implemented by the backing of an organization, the rôle of "persecutor" is transformed into the rôle of persecuted, as he sets out with his like-minded band to "destroy the destroyer."

Were Hitler simply a poet, he might have written a work with an anti-Semitic turn, and let it go at that. But Hitler, who began as a student of painting, and later shifted to architecture, himself treats his political activities as an extension of his artistic ambitions. He remained, in his own eyes, an "architect," building a "folkish" State that was to match, in political materials, the "folkish" architecture of Munich.

We might consider the matter this way (still trying, that is, to make precise the relationship between the drastically sincere and the deliberately scheming): Do we not know of many authors who seem, as they turn from the role of citizen to the rôle of spokesman, to leave one room and enter another? Or who has not, on occasion, talked with a man in private conversation, and then been almost startled at the transformation this man undergoes when addressing a public audience? And I know persons today who shift between the writing of items in the class of academic, philosophic speculation to items of political pamphleteering, and whose entire style and method changes with this change of rôle. In their academic manner, they are cautious, painstaking, eager to present all significant aspects of the case they are considering; but when they turn to political pamphleteering, they hammer forth with vituperation, they systematically misrepresent the position of their opponent, they go into a kind of political trance, in which, during its throes, they throb like a locomotive; and behold, a moment later, the mediumistic state is abandoned, and they are the most moderate of men.

Now, one will find few pages in Hitler that one could call "moderate." But there are many pages in which he gauges resistances and opportunities with the "rationality" of a skilled advertising man planning a new sales campaign. Politics, he says, must be sold like soap—and soap is not sold in a trance. But he did have the experience of his trance, in the "exaltation" of his anti-Semitism. And later, as he became a successful orator (he insists that revolutions are made solely by the power of the spoken word), he had this "poetic" rôle to draw upon, plus the great relief it provided as a way of slipping from the burden of logical analysis into the pure "spirituality" of vituperative prophecy. What more natural, therefore, than that a man so insistent upon unification would integrate this mood with less ecstatic moments, particularly when he had found the followers and the backers that put a price, both spiritual and material, upon such unification?

Once this happy "unity" is under way, one has a "logic" for the development of a method. One knows when to "spiritualize" a material issue, and when to "materialize" a spiritual one. Thus, when it is a matter of materialistic interests that cause a conflict between employer and employee, Hitler here disdainfully shifts to a high moral plane. He is "above" such low concerns. Everything becomes a matter of "sacrifices" and "personality." It becomes crass to treat employers and employees as different *classes* with a corresponding difference in the classification of their interests. Instead, relations between employer and employee must be on the "personal" basis of leader and follower, and "whatever may have a divisive effect in national life should be given a unifying effect through the army." When talking of national rivalries, however, he makes a very shrewd materialistic gauging of Britain and France with relation to Germany. France, he says, desires the "Balkanization of Germany" (i.e., its breakup into separationist movements— the "disunity" theme again) in order to maintain commercial hegemony on the continent. But Britain desires the "Balkanization of *Europe*," hence would favor a fairly strong and unified Germany, to use as a counter-weight against French hegemony. *German* nationality, however, is unified by the *spiritual* quality of Aryanism (that would produce the national organization via the Party) while this in turn *is materialized* in the myth of the blood-stream.

What are we to learn from Hitler's book? For one thing, I believe that he has shown, to a very disturbing degree, the power of endless repetition. Every circular advertising a Nazi meeting had, at the bottom, two slogans: "Jews not admitted" and "War victims free." And the substance of Nazi propaganda was built about these two "complementary" themes. He describes the power of spectacle; insists that mass meetings are the fundamental way of giving the individual the sense of being protectively surrounded by a movement, the sense of "community." He also drops one wise hint that I wish the American authorities would take in treating Nazi gatherings. He says that the presence of a special Nazi guard, in Nazi uniforms, was of great importance in building up, among the followers, a tendency to place the center of authority in the Nazi party. I believe that we should take him at his word here, but use the advice in reverse, by insisting that, where Nazi meetings are to be permitted, they be policed by the authorities alone, and that uniformed Nazi guards to enforce the law be prohibited.

And is it possible that an equally important feature of appeal was not so much in the repetitiousness per se, but in the fact that, by means of it, Hitler provided a "world view" for people who had previously seen the world but piecemeal? Did not much of his lure derive, once more, from the *bad* filling of a *good* need? Are not those who insist upon a purely *planless* working of the market asking people to accept far too slovenly a scheme of human purpose, a slovenly scheme that can be accepted so long as it operates with a fair degree of satisfaction, but becomes abhorrent to the victims of its disarray? Are they not then psychologically ready for a rationale, *any* rationale, if it but offer them some specious "universal" explanation? Hence, I doubt whether the appeal was in the sloganizing element alone (particularly as even slogans can only be hammered home, in speech after speech, and two or three hours at a stretch, by endless variations on the themes). And Hitler himself somewhat justifies my interpretation by laying so much stress upon the *half-measures* of the middle-class politicians, and the contrasting *certainty* of his own methods. He was not offering people a *rival* world view; rather, he was offering a world view to people who had no other to pit against it.

As for the basic Nazi trick: the "curative" unification by a fictitious devil-function, gradually made convincing by the sloganizing repetitiousness of standard advertising technique—the opposition must be as unwearying in the attack upon it. It may well be that people, in their human frailty, require an enemy as well as a goal. Very well: Hitlerism itself has provided us with such an enemy—and the clear example of its operation is guaranty that we have, in him and all he stands for, no purely fictitious "devil-function" made to look like a world menace by rhetorical blandishments, but a reality whose ominousness is clarified by the record of its conduct to date. In selecting his brand of doctrine as our "scapegoat," and in tracking down its equivalents in America, we shall be at the very center of accuracy. The Nazis themselves have made the task of clarification easier. Add to them Japan and Italy, and you have *case histories* of fascism for those who might find it more difficult to approach an understanding of its imperialistic drives by a vigorously economic explanation.

But above all, I believe, we must make it apparent that Hitler appeals by relying upon a bastardization of fundamentally religious patterns of thought. In this, if properly presented, there is no slight to religion. There is nothing in religion proper that requires a fascist state. There is much in religion, when misused, that does lead to a fascist state. There is a Latin proverb, *Corruptio optimi pessima,* "the corruption of the best is the worst." And it is the corruptors of religion who are a major menace to the world today, in giving the profound patterns of religious thought a crude and sinister distortion.

Our job, then, our anti-Hitler Battle, is to find all available ways of making the Hitlerite distortions of religion apparent, in order that politicians of his kind in America be unable to perform a similar swindle. The desire for unity is genuine and admirable. The desire for national unity, in the present state of the world, is genuine and admirable. But this unity, if attained on a deceptive basis, by emotional trickeries that shift our criticism from the accurate locus of our trouble, is no unity at all. For, even if we are among those who happen to be "Aryans," we solve no problems even for ourselves by such solutions, since the factors pressing towards calamity remain. Thus, in Germany, after all the upheaval, we see nothing beyond a drive for ever more and more upheaval, precisely because the "new way of life" was no new way, but the dismally oldest way of sheer deception—hence, after all the "change," the factors driving towards unrest are left intact, and even strengthened. True, the Germans had the resentment of a lost war to increase their susceptibility to Hitler's rhetoric. But in a wider sense, it has repeatedly been observed, the whole world lost the War—and the accumulating ills of the capitalist order were but accelerated in their movements towards confusion. Hence, here too there are the resentments that go with frustration of men's ability to work and earn. At that point a certain kind of industrial or financial monopolist may, annoyed by the contrary voices of our parliament, wish for the momentary peace of one voice, amplified by social organizations, with all the others not merely quieted, but given the quietus. So he might, under Nazi promptings, be tempted to back a group of gangsters who, on becoming the political rulers of the state, would protect him against the necessary demands of the workers. His gangsters, then, would be his insurance against his workers. But who would be his insurance against his gangsters?

Lincoln's First Inaugural

by Marie Hochmuth Nichols

Part I

"Spring comes gently to Washington always," observed the poet-historian, Carl Sandburg. "In early March the green of the grass brightens, the magnolia softens. Elms and chestnuts burgeon. Redbud and lilac carry on preparations soon to bloom. The lovemaking and birthing in many sunny corners go on no matter what or who the blue-prints and personages behind the discreet bureau and departmental walls."[1] Spring of 1861 was little different from other springs in physical aspect. March 4th dawned as other March 4th's, no doubt, wavering between clearness and cloudiness. At daylight clouds hung dark and heavy in the sky. Early in the morning a few drops of rain fell, but scarcely enough to lay the dust. A northwest wind swept down the cross streets to Pennsylvania Avenue. The weather was cool and bracing, and on the whole, "favorable to the ceremonies of the day."[2] The sun had come out.

But if, on the whole, spring had come "gently" as usual, there was little else that bespoke the same rhythm. Out of the deep of winter had come the somewhat bewildered voice of President Buchanan asking, "Why is it . . . that discontent now so extensively prevails, and the union of the States, which is the source of all these blessings is threatened with destruction?"[3] Spiritually and morally, the city, indeed the nation, were out of tune, cacophonous, discordant.

Would there be a harmonizing voice today from the gaunt "orator of the West," about to take the helm of the nation? "Behind the cloud the sun is shining still," Abraham Lincoln had said three weeks before, as his train meandered across the Illinois prairies taking him on an "errand of national importance, attended . . . with considerable difficulties."[4] Trouble had not come suddenly to the nation, of course. Only a year previously the country had been "eminently prosperous in all its material interests."[5] Harvests had

---

Reprinted from *American Speeches*. Ed. Wayland Maxfield Parrish and Marie Hochmuth Nichols. (New York: David McKay, 1954). Pp. 60-100. Reprinted with permission.

[1] *Carl Sandburg*, Abraham Lincoln: The War Years (*Harcourt, Brace and Co., 1939*), I, 120.

[2] New York Times, *March 5, 1861, p. 1, col. 1.*

[3] *James Buchanan, "Fourth Annual Message, December 3, 1860,"* The Works of James Buchanan, collected and edited by John Bassett Moore *(Philadelphia: J. B. Lippincott Co., 1910), XI, 7.*

[4] *Speech at Tolono, Illinois, February 11, 1861, as reported in* New York Daily Tribune, *February 12, 1861, p. 5, col. 3.*

[5] *Buchanan,* loc. cit.

been abundant, and plenty smiled throughout the land. But for forty years
there had been an undercurrent of restlessness. As early as 1820, an
occasional voice had urged the necessity for secession. Again in 1850, with
somewhat greater vehemence, voices were raised as the distribution of newly
acquired Mexican territory took place. Then came the repeal of the Missouri
Compromise in 1854, the civil war in Kansas and the Sumner-Brooks combat
in the Senate in 1856, the Dred Scott decision in 1857, and the spectacular
John Brown's raid at Harper's Ferry in 1859, all giving rise to disorder,
unrest, and threats of secession as abolition sentiment mounted. Finally, came
the election of 1860, and the North appeared to have "capped the mighty
pyramid of unfraternal enormities by electing Abraham Lincoln to the Chief
Magistracy, on a platform and by a system which indicates nothing but the
subjugation of the South and the complete ruin of her social, political and
industrial institutions."[6] It was not merely that Lincoln had been elected
president, but the "majorities" by which he was elected were "more
significant and suggestive than anything else—more so than the election
itself—for they unmistakably indicate the hatred to the South which animates
and controls the masses of the numerically strongest section of the
Confederacy."[7] Senator Clingman of North Carolina found the election a
"great, remarkable and dangerous fact that has filled my section with alarm
and dread for the future," since Lincoln was elected *because he was known
to be a dangerous man,"* avowing the principle of the "irrepressible conflict."[8]
Richmond observers commented that a party "founded on the single
sentiment, the exclusive feeling of hatred of African slavery," was "now the
controlling power in this Confederacy," and noted that the question "What is
to be done . . . presses on every man."[9] In Charleston, South Carolina, the
news of Lincoln's election was met with great rejoicing and "long continued
cheering for a Southern Confederacy."[10]

Scarcely more than a month had passed when South Carolina led off in
the secession movement. Her two senators resigned their seats in the United
States Senate on November 10, 1860, and on December 20 an Ordinance of
Secession was adopted,[11] bringing in its wake secessionist demonstrations
throughout the South.[12] By the first of February of the new year, Mississippi,
Florida, Alabama, Louisiana, Texas, and Georgia had "repealed, rescinded,

[6] New Orleans Daily Crescent, *November 13, 1860, as quoted in* Southern Editorials on Secession,
edited by Dwight Lowell Dumond (New York and London: The Century Co., 1931), p. 237.
[7] New Orleans Daily Crescent, *November 12, 1860, as quoted in* Southern Editorials on Secession, *p.
228.*
[8] *Speech of Senator Thomas L. Clingman of North Carolina in the Senate, December 3, 1860,* The
Congressional Globe, *Second Session, 36th Congress, Vol. 30, p. 3.*
[9] Richmond Semi-Weekly Examiner, *November 9, 1860, as quoted in* Southern Editorials on Secession,
p. 223.
[10] The Daily Herald, *Wilmington, N. C., November 9, 1860, as quoted in* Southern Editorials on
Secession, *p. 226.*
[11] *Daniel Wait Howe*, Political History of Secession *(New York: G. P. Putnam's Sons, 1914), p. 449.*
[12] *J. G. Randall*, Lincoln the President *(New York: Dodd, Mead and Co., 1945), I, 215.*

and abrogated" their membership in the Union by adopting secession ordinances, standing "prepared to resist by force any attempt to maintain the supremacy of the Constitution of the United States."[13] The other slaveholding states held a position of "quasi neutrality," declaring that their adhesion to the Union could be secured only by affording guarantees against wrongs of which they complained, and dangers which they apprehended.[14] Already by the end of 1860, secessionists at Charleston were in possession of the post office, the federal courts, the customhouses, and forts Castle Pinckney and Moultrie.[15]

It was not without clamor and fanfare that senators took their leave from familiar places. When, on December 31, Senator Judah Benjamin of Louisiana reported that he would make a parting secession speech, "every corner was crowded"[16] in the Senate galleries. His closing declaration that "you can never subjugate us; you never can convert the free sons of the soil into vassals . . . never, never can degrade them to the level of an inferior and servile race. Never! Never!"[17] was greeted by the galleries with "disgraceful applause, screams and uproar."[18] As the galleries were cleared because of misbehavior, people murmured in departing, "Now we will have war," "D—n the Abolitionists," "Abe Lincoln will never come here."[19] Critics observing the national scene remarked, "The President . . . enters upon one of the most momentous and difficult duties ever devolved upon any man, in this country or any other. No one of his predecessors was ever called upon to confront dangers half as great, or to render a public service half as difficult, as those which will challenge his attention at the very outset of his Administration."[20]

January of 1861 came without hope, and with little possibility of the cessation of unrest. Occasionally the newspapers scoffed at the recommendation of the *Richmond Inquirer* that an armed force proceeding from Virginia or Maryland should invade the District of Columbia and prevent the peaceful inauguration of Abraham Lincoln, dismissing it as the "exaggeration of political rhetoric."[21] The capital of the nation was beset by rumor, clamor, occasional attempts at compromise, and general misbehavior. "I passed a part of last week in Washington," observed a Baltimore reporter, "and never, since the days of Jerico [sic], has there been such a blowing of rams' horns as may now be heard in that distracted city. If sound and clamor could overthrow the Constitution, one might well expect to see it go down before the windy suspirations of forced breath that shock and vibrate on all sides." Almost

---

[13]New York Times, *February 11, 1861, p. 4, col. 2.*
[14]Ibid.
[15]*Randall*, loc. cit.
[16]New York Times, *January 1, 1861, p. 1, col. 1.*
[17]Congressional Globe, *Second Session, 36th Congress, Vol. 30, p. 217.*
[18]New York Times, *January 1, 1861, p. 1, col. 1.*
[19]Ibid.
[20]New York Times, *February 11, 1861, p. 4, col. 2.*
[21]The National Intelligencer *(Washington), January 3, 1861, p. 3, col. 2.*

everywhere he met "intemperate and alarming disciples of discord and confusion." "War, secession, and disunion are on every lip; and no hope of compromise or adjustment is held out by any one. The prevailing sentiment in Washington is with the South."[22]

As secession went on apace in the South, Wendell Phillips declared in Boston's Music Hall that he hoped that all the slave states would leave the Union.[23] Horace Greeley, impatient after forty years of Southern threat, disclaimed a "union of force,—a union held together by bayonets," and would interpose "no obstacle to their peaceful withdrawal."[24] Meanwhile, however, a few held out for compromise. On December 18, Senator Crittenden of Kentucky introduced a series of compromises in the Senate,[25] but action seemed unlikely. And when, on January 7, Senator Toombs of Georgia made a "noisy and ranting secession speech, and at the close was greeted with a storm of hisses and applause, which was continued some time," Crittenden's "appeal to save the country," presented in "good taste," created "little or no additional favor for his compromise measure."[26] While Crittenden appealed in the Senate, a peace conference met in Washington at the invitation of Virginia, with its announced purpose "to afford to the people of the slaveholding States adequate guarantees for the security of their rights."[27] Although delegates assembled and conducted business, ultimately submitting to the Senate a series of resolutions, it appeared from the beginning that "no substantial results would be gained."[28] It was clear that the sympathies of the border states which had not yet seceded "were with those which had already done so."[29] Ultimately, the propositions were rejected by the Senate, just as were the Crittenden resolutions, in the closing days of the Congress. In all, it appeared to be an era of "much talk and small performance," a dreary season of debate, with "clouds of dusty and sheety showers of rhetoric," a nation trying to live by "prattle alone," a "miserably betalked nation."[30]

When Lincoln left Springfield, February 11, to wend his way toward Washington, another President, Jefferson Davis, elected on February 9 to head the newly organized Southern Confederacy, was traveling from Mississippi to the Montgomery Convention of slaveholding states to help complete the act of secession, his trip being "one continuous ovation."[31] "The time for

[22]New York Times, *January 15, 1861, p. 1, col. 5.*
[23]New York Times, *January 21, 1861, p. 1, col. 4; see also, complete text of speech in ibid., p. 8, cols. 5, 6 and p. 5, cols. 1, 2.*
[24]*Horace Greeley,* Recollections of a Busy Life *(New York: J. B. Ford and Co., 1868), p. 398.*
[25]Congressional Globe, *Second Session, 36th Congress, Part I, Vol. 30, pp. 112-14.*
[26]New York Times, *January 8, 1861, p. 1, col. 1; see also,* Congressional Globe, *Second Session, 36th Congress, Part I, Vol. 30, pp. 264-71.*
[27]*Howe, op. cit., p. 465.*
[28]Ibid., *p. 467.*
[29]Ibid., *p. 467.*
[30]New York Daily Tribune, *March 13, 1861, p. 4, col. 4.*
[31]New York Daily Tribune, *February 18, 1861, p. 5, col. 6.*

compromise is past," observed Davis, as he paused at the depot at Montgomery to address the crowd, "and we are now determined to maintain our position, and make all who oppose us smell Southern powder, feel Southern steel."[32] Clearly, people could agree that Lincoln was to inherit "a thorny wilderness of perplexities."[33] Would he "coerce" the seceded states and ask for the restoration of federal properties in possession of the secessionists? Would he respond to pressure "from all sides" and from a "fraction of his own party" to consent to "extension" of slavery, particularly below the line 36° 30'? Would he listen to "compromise" Republicans in Congress and only "*seem*" to compromise, "so as not to appear obstinate or insensible to the complaints of the Slaveholders"?[34] Would he stand by the Chicago Republican platform, severe in its strictures on the incumbent Democratic administration's acceptance of the principle that the personal relation between master and slave involved "an unqualified property in persons"?[35] Would he stand by the part of the platform which pledged "the maintenance inviolate of the rights of the States, and especially the right of each State to order and control its own domestic institutions according to its own judgment exclusively"?[36] Was the belief that he had so often uttered representative of the true Lincoln: "A house divided against itself cannot stand"?[37]

On March 4 as the newspapers gave advance notice of what was to transpire during the day, there was a note of fear and uncertainty in regard to the safety of the President-elect, along with the general eagerness about the outlines of Lincoln's course of action to be announced in the Inaugural. "The great event to which so many have been looking forward with anxiety— which has excited the hopes and fears of the country to an extent unparalleled in its comparatively brief history—will take place today," observed the *New York Times.* "The occasion has drawn to the Federal Capital a greater crowd, probably, than has ever been assembled there on any similar occasion. . . . Whether the ceremonies will be marred by any untoward event is, of course, a matter of conjecture, though grave fears are expressed on the subject."[38] While visitors to Washington were seeking to get a glimpse of the tumultuous Senate in all-night session, General Scott and his advisers were together planning to take the "greatest precaution" for preventing "any attack upon the procession or demonstration against Mr. Lincoln's person."[39] Rumors of the

---

[32]Ibid., *p. 5, col. 6.*

[33]Ibid., *March 4, 1861, p. 4, col. 2.*

[34]New York Daily Tribune, *February 18, 1861, p. 6, col. 1.*

[35]*M. Halstead, A History of the National Political Conventions of the Current Presidential Campaign (Columbus, Ohio: Follett, Foster and Co., 1860), p. 138.*

[36]Ibid.

[37]*"A House Divided: Speech Delivered at Springfield, Illinois, at the Close of the Republican State Convention, June 16, 1858,"* in Abraham Lincoln: His Speeches and Writings, *edited with critical and analytical notes by Roy P. Basler (Cleveland, Ohio: The World Publishing Co., 1946), p. 372.*

[38]New York Times, *March 4, 1861, p. 4, col. 1.*

[39]New York Times, *March 4, 1861, p. 1, col. 2.*

presence of a "large gang of 'Plug Uglies' who are here from Baltimore,"[40] circulated freely. Whether they were in Washington to make an attack on the person of the President or to "create a disturbance, and plunder private persons"[41] was a matter for general speculation. Whatever the purpose, General Scott and his advisers had decided to leave nothing undone to secure the safety of the president-elect. Riflemen in squads were to be placed in hiding on the roofs commanding buildings along Pennsylvania Avenue. Orders were given to fire in the event of a threat to the presidential carriages. There were cavalry regulars to guard the side-street crossings, moving from one to another as the procession passed. From the windows of the Capitol wings riflemen were to watch the inauguration platform. General Scott would oversee the ceremonies from the top of a slope commanding the north entrance to the Capitol, ready to take personal charge of a battery of flying artillery stationed there. District militia in three ranks were to surround the platform to keep back the crowd. Armed detectives in citizen's clothing were to be scattered through the great audience.[42]

The occasion must have seemed strange to the man who had been accustomed to being carried on the shoulders of admirers on speaking occasions in his years as a stump orator in the West, and to being the idol of many a torchlight procession during the combats with the "Little Giant" in the tumultuous debates of 1858. Even the Capitol grounds where the crowds had begun to assemble had a strangely unfamiliar look in contrast to its fixity during his years as congressman in 1847 and 1848. "The old dome familiar to Congressman Lincoln in 1848 had been knocked loose and hauled down," noted Sandburg. "The iron-wrought material on the Capitol grounds, the hammers, jacks, screws, scaffolds, derricks, ladders, props, ropes, told that they were rebuilding, extending, embellishing the structure on March 4, 1861." "On the slope of lawn fronting the Capitol building stood a bronze statue of Liberty shaped as a massive, fertile woman holding a sword in one hand for power and a wreath of flowers in the other hand for glory. Not yet raised to her pedestal, she looked out of place. She was to be lifted and set on top of the Capitol dome, overlooking the Potomac Valley, when the dome itself should be prepared for her."[43] The carpenters had set up a temporary platform fronting the Senate wing for the occasion, with a small wooden canopy covering the speaker's table.[44] "The crowd swarmed about all the

---

[40] Ibid.
[41] Ibid.
[42] Ibid.; *see also, Sandburg,* The War Years, *I, 120-21; Randall,* Lincoln the President, *I, 293, 294; William E. Baringer,* A House Dividing *(Springfield, Ill.: Abraham Lincoln Association, 1945), pp. 331-34;* The Diary of a Public Man, *Prefatory notes by F. Lauriston Bullard, Foreword by Carl Sandburg (Chicago: Privately printed for Abraham Lincoln Book Shop, 1945), pp. 73, 74; Clark E. Carr,* Stephen A. Douglas, His Life and Public Services, Speeches and Patriotism *(Chicago: A. C. McClurg and Co., 1909), p. 123.*
[43] *Sandburg,* The War Years, *I, 120.*
[44] *Baringer, op. cit., p. 333.*

approaches leading to the capitol grounds," observed a witness, "while the spacious level extending from the east front of the capitol was one vast black sea of heads."[45] There were between 25,000 and 50,000 people there, waiting with expectancy.[46] "Every window in the north front of the Capitol was filled with ladies. Every tree top bore its burden of eager eyes. Every fence and staging, and pile of building material, for the Capitol extension was made a 'coyn of vantage' for its full complement of spectators."[47] It was noticeable that "scarce a Southern face is to be seen"[48] in the crowd, "judging from the lack of long-haired men."[49] While the crowd waited for the administration of the oath of the Vice-President, which took place in the Senate chambers, it was entertained with martial music, and "by the antics of a lunatic, who had climbed a tall tree in front of the capitol and made a long political speech, claiming to be the rightful President of the United States." Policemen were detached to bring him down, but he merely climbed higher and "stood rocking in the wind, and made another speech."[50] The ceremonies over indoors, the major figures of the occasion were seen emerging, Abraham Lincoln with James Buchanan by his side.

As Lincoln and Buchanan took places on the right side of the speaker's stand, Chief Justice Taney, who soon would administer the oath of office, took a seat upon the left. Many in the audience were seeing Lincoln for the first time. "Honest Abe Lincoln," the folks back home called him, or just "Old Abe" was the affectionate cry at the Chicago "Wigwam" as thousands cheered and shook the rafters "like the rush of a great wind, in the van of a storm,"[51] when he was nominated. Walt Whitman thought "four sorts of genius, four mighty and primal hands, will be needed to the complete limning of this man's future portrait—the eyes and brains and finger-touch of Plutarch and Eschylus and Michel Angelo, assisted by Rabelais."[52] "If any personal description of me is thought desirable," Lincoln had written two years before, "it may be said I am, in height, six feet four inches, nearly; lean in flesh, weighing on an average one hundred and eighty pounds; dark complexion, with coarse black hair and gray eyes. No other marks or brands recollected."[53] He was "not a pretty man," his, law partner, Herndon, thought, "nor was he an ugly one: he was a homely man, careless of his looks, plain looking and plain acting." But he had that "inner quality which distinguishes one person

---

[45]*Correspondence of the* Cincinnati Commercial, *as quoted in* The Chicago Daily Tribune, March 8, 1861, p. 2, col. 4.
[46]New York Daily Tribune, *March 5, 1861, p. 5, col. 4.*
[47]Chicago Daily Tribune, *March 9, 1861, p. 3, col. 2.*
[48]New York Times, *March 4, 1861, p. 1, col. 2.*
[49]Chicago Daily Tribune, *March 5, 1861, p. 1, col. 2.*
[50]*Correspondence of the* Cincinnati Commercial, *as quoted in* The Chicago Daily Tribune, *March 8, 1861, p. 2, col. 4.*
[51]*Halstead, op. cit., pp. 149-51.*
[52]The Complete Writings of Walt Whitman *(New York: G. P. Putnam's Sons, 1902), II, 244.*
[53]*Lincoln to J. W. Fell, Springfield, Illinois, December 20, 1859,* Complete Works of Abraham Lincoln, *edited by John G. Nicolay and John Hay (New York: The Tandy-Thomas Co., 1905), V, 288, 289.*

from another."[54] "I never saw a more thoughtful face," observed David Locke, "I never saw a more dignified face, I never saw so sad a face."[55] Emerson had found in him the "grandeur and strength of absolute simplicity," when, on occasion, he had heard him speak, seen his small gray eyes kindle, heard his voice ring, and observed his face shine and seem "to light up a whole assembly."[56] "Abraham Lincoln: one of nature's noblemen," he was some-times toasted.[57]

"It was unfortunate," says the noted Lincoln scholar, J. G. Randall, "that Lincoln was not better known, North and South, in March of 1861. Had people more fully understood his pondering on government, reverence for law, peaceful intent and complete lack of sectional bitterness, much tragedy might have been avoided."[58] "Gentle, and merciful and just!"[59] William Cullen Bryant was eventually to write. But now, in 1861, there was something unknown about Lincoln to many. It is true that after the Lincoln-Douglas debates he had gained recognition beyond the limits of his state. The Chicago *Democrat* called attention to the fact that "Mr. Lincoln's name has been used by newspapers and public meetings outside the State in connection with the Presidency and Vice Presidency, so that it is not only in his own State that Honest Old Abe is respected." "Even his opponents profess to love the man, though they hate his principles," it observed.[60] Again the *Illinois State Journal* took pride in reporting his growing fame. In "other states," it said, he had been found "not only . . . an unrivalled orator, strong in debate, keen in his logic and wit, with admirable powers of statement, and a fertility of resources which are equal to every occasion; but his truthfulness, his candor, his honesty of purpose, his magnanimity . . . have stamped him as a statesman whom the Republicans throughout the Union may be proud of."[61] In 1860, in New York, the "announcement that Hon. Abraham Lincoln, of Illinois would deliver an address in Cooper Institute . . . drew thither a large and enthusiastic assemblage," and William Cullen Bryant thought that he had only "to pronounce the name of Abraham Lincoln" who had previously been known "only by fame" in order to secure the "profoundest attention."[62] Lincoln had faced thousands of people along the way to Washington, at Indianapolis, Cleveland, Philadelphia, Albany, Harrisburg, and elsewhere, being greeted

---

[54] *Herndon MS fragment, quoted in Randall, op. cit., p. 28.*

[55] Remembrances of Abraham Lincoln by Distinguished Men of His Time, *collected and edited by Allen Thorndike Rice (8th ed.; New York: Published by the* North American Review, *1889), p. 442.*

[56] *John Wesley Hill,* Abraham Lincoln, Man of God *(4th ed.; New York: G. P. Putnam's Sons, 1930), p. 306.*

[57] *Carl Sandburg,* Abraham Lincoln, The Prairie Years *(New York: Harcourt, Brace and Co., 1926), 1, 199, 200.*

[58] New York Times Magazine, *February 6, 1949, p. 11.*

[59] "Abraham Lincoln," *in* The Poetical Works of William Cullen Bryant, *edited by Parke Godwin (New York: D. Appleton and Co., 1883), II, 151.*

[60] *Quoted in* Daily Illinois State Journal, *November 15, 1858, p. 1, col. 1.*

[61] Ibid., *November 12, 1858, p. 2, col. 1.*

[62] New York Times, *February 28, 1860, p. 1, col. 1.*

enthusiastically. Still, "in general," observes Randall, "it cannot be said that he had a 'good press' at the threshold of office. Showmanship failed to make capital of his rugged origin, and there faced the country a strange man from Illinois who was dubbed a 'simple Susan,' a 'baboon,' or a 'gorilla.' "[63] "Our Presidential Merryman," *Harper's Weekly* had labeled him,[64] later carrying a caricature recounting the fabricated story of his incognito entry into Washington. "He wore a Scotch plaid Cap and a very long Military Cloak, so that he was entirely unrecognizable," the caption read.[65] Men like Stanton thought of him as a "low, cunning clown."[66] And the Associated Press reporter, Henry Villard, remembered his "fondness for low talk," and could not have persuaded himself "that the man might possibly possess true greatness of mind and nobility of heart," admitting to a feeling of "disgust and humiliation that such a person should have been called upon to direct the destinies of a great nation."[67]

In the South, there had been little willingness to know the Lincoln they "should have known," the Lincoln who "intended to be fair to the Southern people, and, as he had said at the Cooper Union in February of 1860, 'do nothing through passion and ill-temper,' 'calmly consider their demands, and yield to them' where possible."[68] The South had made up its mind that whatever the North did to ingratiate Lincoln with them was done in deceit. "Since the election of Lincoln most of the leading Northern Abolition papers have essayed the herculean task of reconciling the Southern People to his Presidential rule," observed the *New Orleans Daily Crescent.* "Having succeeded to their heart's content in electing him—having vilified and maligned the South through a long canvass, without measure or excuse—they now tell us that Mr. Lincoln is a very good man, a very amiable man; that he is not at all violent in his prejudices or partialities; that, on the contrary, he is a moderate, kindly-tempered, conservative man, and if we will only submit to his administration for a time, we will ascertain that he will make one of the best Presidents the South or the country ever had! 'Will you walk into my parlor said the spider to the fly.' " "Mr. Lincoln may be all that these Abolition journals say he is. But, we do not believe a word they say," the *Crescent* continued. "We are clearly convinced that they are telling falsehoods to deceive the people of the South, in order to carry out their own selfish and unpatriotic purposes the more easily. They know that, although Lincoln is elected to the Presidency, he is not yet President of the United States, and they are shrewd enough to know that grave doubts exist whether he ever will

[63]*Randall*, op. cit., *I*, 292.
[64]*Vol. V (March 2, 1861), p. 144.*
[65]Ibid. *(March 9, 1861), p. 160.*
[66]The Diary of a Public Man, *pp. 48, 49.*
[67]Memoirs of Henry Villard *(Boston: Houghton, Mifflin Co., 1904), I, 144.*
[68]*J. G. Randall, "Lincoln's Greatest Declaration of Faith,"* New York Times Magazine, *February 6, 1949, p. 11.*

be. The chances are that he will not, unless the South is quieted. . . ."[69]

The South found it easier to view Lincoln as a stereotype, a "radical Abolitionist," an "Illinois ape," a "traitor to his country." Then, too, the escape through Baltimore by night could "not fail to excite a most mischievous feeling of contempt for the personal character of Mr. Lincoln throughout the country, especially at the South."[70]

Thus appeared Lincoln, who "without mock modesty" had described himself en route to Washington as "the humblest of all individuals that have ever been elevated to the presidency."[71]

Senator Baker of Oregon advanced to the platform and announced, "Fellow-Citizens: I introduce to you Abraham Lincoln, the President-elect of the United States of America."[72]

Mr. Lincoln had the crowd "matched"[73] in sartorial perfection. He was wearing a new tall hat, new black suit of clothes and black boots, expansive white shirt bosom. He carried an ebony cane with a gold head the size of a hen's egg. He arose, "walked deliberately and composedly to the table, and bent low in honor of the repeated and enthusiastic cheering of the countless host before him. Having put on his spectacles, he arranged his manuscript on the small table, keeping the paper thereon by the aid of his cane."[74] In a clear voice he began:[75]

> *Fellow-citizens of the United States:*
>
> *In compliance with a custom as old as the government itself, I appear before you to address you briefly, and to take, in your presence, the oath prescribed by the Constitution of the United States, to be taken by the President "before he enters on the execution of his office."*
>
> *I do not consider it necessary at present for me to discuss those matters of administration about which there is no special anxiety or excitement.*
>
> *Apprehension seems to exist among the people of the Southern States, that by the accession of a Republican Administration, their property, and their peace, and personal security, are to be endangered. There has never been any reasonable cause for such apprehension. Indeed, the most ample evidence to the contrary has all the while existed, and been open to their inspection. It is found in nearly all the published speeches of him who now addresses you. I do*

---

[69] Southern Editorials on Secession, *p. 229.*
[70] The Diary of a Public Man, *p. 46.*
[71] *"Address to the Legislature of New York, at Albany, February 18, 1861,"* in Complete Works of Abraham Lincoln, *VI, 140.*
[72] New York Times, *March 5, 1861, p. 1, col. 3.*
[73] *Sandburg,* The War Years, *I, 122.*
[74] New York Times, *March 5, 1861, p. 1, col. 3.*
[75] *The text of the Inaugural being used is that contained in* Abraham Lincoln: His Speeches and Writings, *edited by Roy P. Basler, pp. 579-90.*

but quote from one of those speeches when I declare that "I have no purpose, directly or indirectly, to interfere with the institution of slavery in the States where it exists. I believe I have no lawful right to do so, and I have no inclination to do so." Those who nominated and elected me did so with full knowledge that I had made this, and many similar declarations, and had never recanted them. And more than this, they placed in the platform, for my acceptance, and as a law to themselves, and to me, the clear and emphatic resolution which I now read:

"Resolved, That the maintenance inviolate of the rights of the States, and especially the right of each State to order and control its own domestic institutions according to its own judgment exclusively, is essential to that balance of power on which the perfection and endurance of our political fabric depend; and we denounce the lawless invasion by armed force of the soil of any State or Territory, no matter under what pretext, as among the gravest of crimes."

I now reiterate these sentiments: and in doing so, I only press upon the public attention the most conclusive evidence of which the case is susceptible, that the property, peace and security of no section are to be in any wise endangered by the now incoming Administration. I add too, that all the protection which, consistently with the Constitution and the laws, can be given, will be cheerfully given to all the States when lawfully demanded, for whatever cause—as cheerfully to one section as to another.

There is much controversy about the delivering up of fugitives from service or labor. The clause I now read is as plainly written in the Constitution as any other of its provisions:

"No person held to service or labor in one State, under the laws thereof, escaping into another, shall, in consequence of any law or regulation therein, be discharged from such service or labor, but shall be delivered up on claim of the party to whom such service or labor may be due."

It is scarcely questioned that this provision was intended by those who made it, for the reclaiming of what we call fugitive slaves; and the intention of the law-giver is the law. All members of Congress swear their support to the whole Constitution—to this provision as much as to any other. To the proposition, then, that slaves whose cases come within the terms of this clause, "shall be delivered up," their oaths are unanimous. Now, if they would make the effort in good temper, could they not, with nearly equal unanimity, frame and pass a law, by means of which to keep good that unanimous oath?

There is some difference of opinion whether this clause should be enforced by national or by state authority; but surely that difference is not a very material one. If the slave is to be surrendered, it can be of but little consequence to him, or to others, by which authority it is done. And should any one, in any case, be content that his oath shall go unkept, on a merely unsubstantial controversy as to how it shall be kept?

Again, in any law upon this subject, ought not all the safeguards of liberty known in civilized and humane jurisprudence to be introduced, so that a free man be not, in any case, surrendered as a slave? And might it not be well, at the same time to provide by law for the enforcements of that clause in the Constitution which guarantees that "the citizens of each State shall be entitled to all privileges and immunities of citizens in the several States"?

I take the official oath to-day, with no mental reservations, and with no purpose to construe the Constitution or laws, by any hyper-critical rules. And while I do not choose now to specify particular acts of Congress as proper to be enforced, I do suggest that it will be much safer for all, both in official and private stations, to conform to, and abide by, all those acts which stand unrepealed, than to violate any of them, trusting to find impunity in having them held to be unconstitutional.

It is seventy-two years since the first inauguration of a President under our national Constitution. During that period fifteen different and greatly distinguished citizens, have, in succession, administered the executive branch of the government. They have conducted it through many perils; and, generally, with great success. Yet, with all this scope for [of] precedent, I now enter upon the same task for the brief constitutional term of four years, under great and peculiar difficulty. A disruption of the Federal Union, heretofore only menaced, is now formidably attempted.

I hold, that in contemplation of universal law, and of the Constitution, the Union of these States is perpetual. Perpetuity is implied, if not expressed, in the fundamental law of all national governments. It is safe to assert that no government proper, ever had a provision in its organic law for its own termination. Continue to execute all the express provisions of our national Constitution, and the Union will endure forever—it being impossible to destroy it, except by some action not provided for in the instrument itself.

Again, if the United States be not a government proper, but an association of States in the nature of contract merely, can it, as a contract, be peaceably unmade, by less than all the parties who made it? One party to a contract may violate it—break it, so to speak; but does it not require all to lawfully rescind it?

Descending from these general principles, we find the proposition that, in legal contemplation, the Union is perpetual, confirmed by the history of the Union itself. The Union is much older than the Constitution. It was formed in fact, by the Articles of Association in 1774. It was matured and continued by the Declaration of Independence in 1776. It was further matured and the faith of all the then thirteen States expressly plighted and engaged that it should be perpetual, by the Articles of Confederation in 1778. And finally, in 1787, one of the declared objects for ordaining and establishing the Constitution, was "to form a more perfect Union."

But if [the] destruction of the Union, by one, or by a part only, of the States, be lawfully possible, the Union is less perfect than before the Constitution, having lost the vital element of perpetuity.

It follows from these views that no State, upon its own mere motion, can lawfully get out of the Union,—that resolves and ordinances to that effect are legally void, and that acts of violence, within any State or States, against the authority of the United States, are insurrectionary or revolutionary, according to the circumstances.

I therefore consider that in view of the Constitution and the laws, the Union is unbroken; and to the extent of my ability I shall take care, as the Constitution itself expressly enjoins upon me, that the laws of the Union be faithfully executed in all the States. Doing this I deem to be only a simple duty on my part; and I shall perform it, so far as practicable, unless my rightful masters, the American people, shall withhold the requisite means, or, in some authoritative manner, direct the contrary. I trust this will not be regarded as a menace, but only as the declared purpose of the Union that it will constitutionally defend and maintain itself.

In doing this there needs to be no bloodshed or violence; and there shall be none, unless it be forced upon the national authority. The power confided to me will be used to hold, occupy, and possess the property and places belonging to the government, and to collect the duties and imposts; but beyond what may be necessary for these objects, there will be no invasion—no using of force against or among the people anywhere. Where hostility to the United States, in any interior locality, shall be so great and so universal, as to prevent competent resident citizens from holding the Federal offices, there will be no attempt to force obnoxious strangers among the people for that object. While the strict legal right may exist in the government to enforce the exercise of these offices, the attempt to do so would be so irritating, and so nearly impracticable with all, that I deem it better to forego, for the time, the uses of such offices.

The mails, unless repelled, will continue to be furnished in all parts of the Union. So far as possible, the people everywhere shall have that sense of perfect security which is most favorable to calm thought and reflection. The course here indicated will be followed, unless current events and experience shall show a modification or change to be proper; and in every case and exigency my best discretion will be exercised according to circumstances actually existing, and with a view and a hope of a peaceful solution of the national troubles, and the restoration of fraternal sympathies and affections.

That there are persons in one section or another who seek to destroy the Union at all events, and are glad of any pretext to do it, I will neither affirm or deny; but if there be such, I need address no word to them. To those, however, who really love the Union, may I not speak?

Before entering upon so grave a matter as the destruction of our national fabric, with all its benefits, its memories and its hopes, would it not be wise to ascertain precisely why we do it? Will you hazard so desperate a step, while there is any possibility that any portion of the ills you fly from have no real existence? Will you, while the certain ills you fly to, are greater than all the real ones you fly from? Will you risk the commission of so fearful a mistake?

All profess to be content in the Union, if all constitutional rights can be maintained. Is it true, then, that any right, plainly written in the Constitution, has been denied? I think not. Happily the human mind is so constituted, that no party can reach to the audacity of doing this. Think, if you can, of a single instance in which a plainly written provision of the Constitution has ever been denied. If, by the mere force of numbers, a majority should deprive a minority of any clearly written constitutional right, it might, in a moral point of view, justify revolution—certainly would, if such a right were a vital one. But such is not our case. All the vital rights of minorities, and of individuals, are so plainly assured to them, by affirmations and negations, guarantees and prohibitions, in the Constitution, that controversies never arise concerning them. But no organic law can ever be framed with a provision specifically applicable to every question which may occur in practical administration. No foresight can anticipate, nor any document of reasonable length contain express provisions for all possible questions. Shall fugitives from labor be surrendered by national or by State authority? The Constitution does not expressly say. May Congress prohibit slavery in the territories? The Constitution does not expressly say. Must Congress protect slavery in the territories? The Constitution does not expressly say.

From questions of this class spring all our constitutional controversies, and we divide upon them into majorities and minorities. If the minority will not acquiesce, the majority must, or the government must cease. There is no other alternative; for continuing the government, is acquiescence on one side or the other. If a minority, in such case, will secede rather than acquiesce, they make a precedent which, in turn, will divide and ruin them; for a minority of their own will secede from them whenever a majority refuses to be controlled by such minority. For instance, why may not any portion of a new confederacy, a year or two hence, arbitrarily secede again, precisely as portions of the present Union now claim to secede from it? All who cherish disunion sentiments, are now being educated to the exact temper of doing this.

Is there such perfect identity of interests among the States to compose a new Union, as to produce harmony only, and prevent renewed secession?

Plainly, the central idea of secession, is the essence of anarchy. A majority, held in restraint by constitutional checks and limitations, and always changing easily with deliberate changes of popular opinions and sentiments is the only true sovereign of a free people. Whoever rejects it, does, of necessity, fly to anarchy or to despotism. Unanimity is impossible; the rule of a minority, as a permanent arrangement, is wholly inadmissible; so that, rejecting the majority principle, anarchy or despotism in some form is all that is left.

I do not forget the position assumed by some, that constitutional questions are to be decided by the Supreme Court; nor do I deny that such decisions must be binding in any case, upon the parties to a suit, as to the object of that suit, while they are also entitled to very high respect and consideration in all parallel cases by all other departments of the government. And while it is obviously possible that such decision may be erroneous in any given case, still the evil effect following it, being limited to that particular case, with the chance that it may be overruled, and never become a precedent for other cases, can better be borne than could the evils of a different practice. At the same time, the candid citizen must confess that if the policy of the government upon vital questions, affecting the whole people, is to be irrevocably fixed by decisions of the Supreme Court, the instant they are made, in ordinary litigation between parties, in personal actions, the people will have ceased to be their own rulers, having to that extent practically resigned their government into the hands of that eminent tribunal. Nor is there in this view any assault upon the court or the judges. It is a duty from which they may not shrink, to decide cases properly brought before them; and it is no fault of theirs if others seek to turn their decisions to political purposes.

One section of our country believes slavery is right, and ought to be extended, while the other believes it is wrong, and ought not to be extended. This is the only substantial dispute. The fugitive slave clause of the Constitution, and the law for the suppression of the foreign slave trade, are each as well enforced, perhaps, as any law can ever be in a community where the moral sense of the people imperfectly supports the law itself. The great body of the people abide by the dry legal obligation in both cases, and a few break over in each. This, I think, cannot be perfectly cured; and it would be worse in both cases after the separation of the sections, than before. The foreign slave trade, now imperfectly suppressed, would be ultimately revived without restriction, in one section; while fugitive slaves, now only partially surrendered, would not be surrendered at all, by the other.

Physically speaking, we cannot separate. We cannot remove our respective sections from each other, nor build an impassable wall *between them. A husband and wife may be divorced, and go out of the presence, and beyond the reach of each other; but the different parts of our country cannot do this. They cannot but remain face to face; and intercourse, either amicable or hostile, must continue between them. Is it possible, then, to make that intercourse more advantageous or more satisfactory,* after *separation than* before? *Can aliens make treaties easier than friends can make laws? Can treaties be more faithfully enforced between aliens than laws can among friends? Suppose you go to war, you cannot fight always; and when, after much loss on both sides, and no gain on either, you cease fighting, the identical old questions, as to terms of intercourse, are again upon you.*

This country, with its institutions, belongs to the people who inhabit it. Whenever they shall grow weary of the existing government, they can exercise their constitutional *right of amending it, or their* revolutionary *right to dismember or overthrow it. I cannot be ignorant of the fact that many worthy and patriotic citizens are desirous of having the national Constitution amended. While I make no recommendation of amendments, I fully recognize the rightful authority of the people over the whole subject to be exercised in either of the modes prescribed in the instrument itself; and I should under existing circumstances favor rather than oppose a fair opportunity being afforded the people to act upon it.*

I will venture to add that to me the Convention mode seems preferable, in that it allows amendments to originate with the people themselves, instead of only permitting them to take or reject propositions, originated by others, not especially chosen for the purpose, and which might not be precisely such as they would wish to either accept or refuse. I understand a proposed amendment to the Constitution, which amendment, however, I have not seen, has passed Congress, to the effect that the federal government shall never interfere with the domestic institutions of the States, including that of persons held to service. To avoid misconstruction of what I have said, I depart from my purpose not to speak of particular amendments, so far as to say that holding such a provision to now be implied constitutional law, I have no objection to its being made express and irrevocable.

The Chief Magistrate derives all his authority from the people, and they have conferred none upon him to fix terms for the separation of the States. The people themselves can do this also if they choose; but the executive, as such, has nothing to do with it. His duty is to administer the present government, as it came to his hands, and to transmit it, unimpaired by him, to his successor.

Why should there not be a patient confidence in the ultimate justice of the people? Is there any better or equal hope, in the world? In our present differences, is either party without faith of being in the right? If the Almighty Ruler of nations, with his eternal truth and justice, be on your side of the North or on yours of the South, that truth, and that justice, will surely prevail, by the judgment of this great tribunal, the American people.

By the frame of the government under which we live, this same people have wisely given their public servants but little power for mischief; and have, with equal wisdom, provided for the return of that little to their own hands at very short intervals.

While the people retain their virtue and vigilance, no administration, by any extreme of wickedness or folly, can very seriously injure the government in the short space of four years.

My countrymen, one and all, think calmly and well, *upon this whole subject. Nothing valuable can be lost by taking time. If there be an object to* hurry *any of you, in hot haste, to a step which you would never take deliberately, that object will be frustrated by taking time; but no good object can be frustrated by it. Such of you as are now dissatisfied, still have the old Constitution unimpaired, and, on the sensitive point, the laws of your own framing under it; while the new administration will have no immediate power, if it would, to change either. If it were admitted that you who are dissatisfied, hold the right side in the dispute, there still is no single good reason for precipitate action. Intelligence, patriotism, Christianity, and a firm reliance on Him, who has never yet forsaken this favored land, are still competent to adjust, in the best way, all our present difficulty.*

In your *hands, my dissatisfied fellow countrymen, and not in* mine, *is the momentous issue of civil war. The government will not assail you. You can have no conflict, without being yourselves the aggressors. You have no oath registered in Heaven to destroy the government, while I shall have the most solemn one to "preserve, protect and defend" it.*

I am loth to close. We are not enemies, but friends. We must not be enemies. Though passion may have strained, it must not break our bonds of affection. The mystic chords of memory, stretching from every battle-field, and patriot grave, to every living heart and hearthstone, all over this broad land, will yet swell the chorus of the Union, when again touched, as surely they will be, by the better angels of our nature.

With "more of Euclid than of Demosthenes"[76] in him, his delivery was not that of the spellbinder, agitator, or demagogue. His voice was a tenor that "carried song-tunes poorly but had clear and appealing modulations."[77]

---

[76]*Randall*, op. cit., *I, 49.*
[77]*Sandburg*, The Prairie Years, *I,* 305.

Habitually a little "scared"[78] when he spoke, he was "pale and very nervous"[79] on this occasion, but his "cheerfulness was marked."[80] "Compelled by nature, to speak slowly,"[81] his manner was "deliberate and impressive"[82] and his voice "remarkably clear and penetrating."[83] There was little evidence in his voice of the fear that might have come as the result of knowing that there were "heavy bets" about his safety.[84] Some of the spectators noted a "loud, and distinct voice, quite intelligible by at least ten thousand persons below him";[85] others found it a "clear, ringing voice, that was easily heard by those on the outer limits of the crowd";[86] still others noted his "firm tones of voice," his "great deliberation and precision of emphasis."[87] Sandburg might have remarked that it gave out "echoes and values."[88]

As Lincoln read on, the audience listened respectfully, with "intense interest, amid a stillness almost oppressive."[89] In the crowd behind the speaker sat Horace Greeley, momentarily expecting the crack of rifle fire.[90] At one point he thought it had come. The speaker stopped. But it was only a spectator crashing down through a tree.[91] Otherwise, the crowd in the grounds "behaved very well."[92] Buchanan sat listening, and "looking as straight as he could at the toe of his right boot."[93] Douglas, close by on Lincoln's right, listened "attentively," showing that he was "apparently satisfied" as he "exclaimed, *sotto voce*, 'Good,' 'That's so,' 'No coercion,' and 'Good again.'"[94] Chief Justice Taney "did not remove his eyes from Mr. Lincoln during the entire delivery."[95] Mr. Cameron stood with his back to the President, on the opposite side to Mr. Douglas, "peering off into the crowd."[96] Senator Seward and the other Cabinet officers-elect "kept themselves in the background."[97] Senator Wigfall of Texas, with folded arms "leaned

---

[78] [*W. H. Herndon and J. W. Weik*], Herndon's Life of Lincoln, *with an introduction and notes by Paul M. Angle (Cleveland: The World Publishing Co., 1949), p. 220.*

[79] The Diary of a Public Man, *p. 74.*

[80] *Correspondence of the* Cincinnati Commercial, *as quoted in* Chicago Daily Tribune, *March 8, 1861, p. 2, col. 4.*

[81] *Herndon and Weik, op. cit., p. 273.*

[82] New York Tribune, *March 5, 1861, p. 5, col. 4.*

[83] Ibid.

[84] New York Times, *March 4, 1861, p. 1, col. 2.*

[85] National Intelligencer, *March 5, 1861, p. 3, col. 3.*

[86] New York Times, *March 5, 1861, p. 1, col. 3.*

[87] *Correspondence of the* Cincinnati Commercial, *quoted in* Chicago Daily Tribune, *March 8, 1861, p. 2, col. 4.*

[88] *Sandburg,* The Prairie Years, *I, 306.*

[89] *Frederick W. Seward,* Seward at Washington, as Senator and Secretary of State *(New York: Derby and Miller, 1891), I, 516.*

[90] *Greeley, op. cit., p. 404.*

[91] Diary of a Public Man, *p. 74.*

[92] Ibid.

[93] New York Times, *March 5, 1861, p. 1, col. 3.*

[94] Ibid.

[95] Ibid.

[96] *Correspondence of the* Cincinnati Commercial, *as quoted in* Chicago Daily Tribune, *March 8, 1861, p. 2, col. 4.*

[97] Ibid.

conspicuously in a Capitol doorway," listening to the Inaugural, plainly wearing "contempt, defiance, derision, on his face, his pantomimic posture saying what he had said in the Senate, that the old Union was a corpse and the question was how to embalm it and conduct the funeral decently."[98] Thurlow Weed moved away from the crowd, reporting to General Scott at the top of the slope "The Inaugural is a success," as the old general exclaimed, "God be praised! God in his goodness be praised."[99] To a newspaper reporter surveying the scene, there was a "propriety and becoming interest which pervaded the vast assembly" and "impressed every spectator who had the opportunity of overlooking it."[100] The crowd "applauded repeatedly" and "at times, rapturously,"[101] particularly at points where he "announced his inflexible purpose to execute the laws and discharge his whole constitutional duty."[102] When Lincoln declared, "I hold that in the contemplation of international law, and of the Constitution, the Union of these States is perpetual," the "cheers were hearty and prolonged."[103] When he said, "I shall take care that the laws of the Union be faithfully executed in all the States," he was met with a "tremendous shout of approval."[104] But the "greatest impression of all was produced by the final appeal,"[105] noted one of the reporters. "With great solemnity of emphasis, using his gestures to add significance to his words," Lincoln remarked "You have no oath registered in Heaven to destroy this Government, while I shall have the most solemn one to preserve, protect and defend it," and the crowd responded with "round after round of cheering."[106] Finally, after Lincoln had addressed his "words of affection" to the audience, ending his address, "men waved their hats, and broke forth in the heartiest manifestations of delight. The extraordinary clearness [sic], straight-forwardness and lofty spirit of patriotism which pervaded the whole address, impressed every listener, while the evident earnestness, sincerity and manliness of Mr. Lincoln extorted the praise even of his enemies."[107] "The effect of the Inaugural on the country at large remains to be awaited and to be gathered from many sources," observed a reporter, "but it is conceded on all hands that its effect, already noticeable on the vast gathering here, upon the city, and the tone of feeling here is eminently happy, and the source of great gratulation on every side."[108]

Chief Justice Taney stepped forward, shrunken, old, his hands trembling with emotion, and held out an open Bible. Lincoln laid his left hand upon it,

[98]*Sandburg,* The War Years, *I, 123.*
[99]*Seward, op. cit., pp. 516, 517.*
[100]New York Daily Tribune, *March 5, 1861, p. 5, col. 4.*
[101]Chicago Daily Tribune, *March 8, 1861, p. 2, col. 4, quoted from* Cincincinati Commercial.
[102]New York Daily Tribune, *March 5, 1861, p. 5, col. 4.*
[103]Chicago Daily Tribune, *March 8, 1861, p. 2, col. 4, quoted from* Cincinnati Commercial.
[104]Chicago Daily Tribune, *March 8, 1861, p. 2, col. 4, quoted from* Cincinnati Commercial.
[105]Ibid.
[106]Ibid.
[107]Chicago Daily Tribune, *March 8, 1861, p. 2, col. 4, quoted from* Cincinnati Commercial.
[108]Chicago Daily Tribune, *March 9, 1861, p. 3, col. 2.*

raised his right hand, and repeated with a "firm but modest voice"[109] the oath: "I do solemnly swear that I will faithfully execute the office of President of the United States, and will, to the best of my ability, preserve, protect, and defend the Constitution of the United States." Lincoln was now president. Below, the crowd "tossed their hats, wiped their eyes, cheered at the tops of their voices, hurrahed themselves hoarse," and "had the crowd not been so very dense, they would have demonstrated in more lively ways, their joy, satisfaction and delight."[110] Over on the slope the artillery boomed a salute to the sixteenth president of the United States.[111] The crowd ebbed away, and Lincoln rode down Pennsylvania Avenue with Buchanan, bidding him good-bye at the Presidential mansion.[112]

The address had taken thirty-five minutes in delivery, and now it was all over, at least until the nation in general turned in its response. Lincoln had spent six weeks in preparing it—six weeks and many years of lonely thought, along with his active experience on the circuit and the stump. Like the "House Divided Speech" and the "Cooper Union Address" it was deliberately and cautiously prepared, undergoing revision up to the moment of delivery. "Late in January," he told his law partner, Herndon, that he was "ready to begin"[113] the preparation of the Inaugural. In a room over a store, across the street from the State House, cut off from all intrusion and outside communication, he began the preparation. He had told Herndon what works he wanted to consult and asked to be furnished "Henry Clay's great speech delivered in 1850; Andrew Jackson's proclamation against Nullification; and a copy of the Constitution." He "afterwards" called for a copy of Webster's reply to Hayne, a speech which he regarded as "the grandest specimen of American oratory."[114] "With these few 'volumes,' and no further sources of reference,"[115] he began his work on the address.

On February 2, 1861, he wrote a friend, George D. Prentice,[116] editor of the *Louisville Journal*, "I have the document blocked out; but in the now rapidly shifting scenes I shall have to hold it subject to revision up to the time of delivery."[117] He had an original draft printed by one of the proprietors of the *Illinois State Journal* to whom he entrusted the manuscript.[118] "No one else seems to have been taken into the confidence of Mr. Lincoln as to its contents until after he started for Washington on February 11."[119] Upon reaching Indianapolis, he presented a copy to O. H. Browning who had

---

[109] New York Times, *March 5, 1861, p. 1, col. 3.*
[110] Ibid.
[111] *Sandburg, The War Years, I, 122.*
[112] *Baringer, op. cit., p. 334.*
[113] *Herndon and Weik, op. cit., p. 386.*
[114] Ibid.
[115] Ibid.
[116] Lincoln Lore, *No. 308 (March 4, 1935).*
[117] *Louis A. Warren, "Original Draft of the First Inaugural," Lincoln Lore, No. 358 (February 17, 1936).*
[118] Ibid.
[119] Ibid.

accompanied him from Springfield. According to Browning, "before parting with Mr. Lincoln at Indianapolis, Tuesday, he gave me a copy of his inaugural address, and requested me to read it, and give him my opinion, which I did. I thought it able, well considered, and appropriate, and so informed him. It is, in my judgment, a very admirable document. He permitted me to retain a copy, under promise not to show it except to Mrs. Browning."[120]

Upon arriving in Washington, Lincoln submitted a copy to Secretary Seward with the same invitation to criticize it.[121] According to Louis A. Warren, "As far as we know these two men are the only ones who made any suggestions about certain revisions in the original copy,"[122] even though a few others may have seen it.[123]

Reporters showed an avid interest in the preparation of the Inaugural, sometimes reporting inaccurately on the various stages of its preparation. Recording the activities of the President on Saturday night, March 2, one reporter erroneously observed: "Mr. Lincoln sent for Senator Seward, and at 11½ o'clock that gentleman reached the hotel. Mr. Lincoln read to him the Inaugural for the first time, and then asked his advice. Senator Seward took it up section after section and concurred heartily in a great part of it. He suggested a few modifications, an occasional emendation and a few additional paragraphs, all of which were adopted by Mr. Lincoln, and the Inaugural was declared complete and perfect by Senator Seward, who then retired."[124] On Sunday, the reporter remarked, "Mr. Lincoln stated this evening that the Inaugural could not be printed, as some points might require modifying or extending, according to the action of the Senate to-night. His son is now writing copies of what is finished, one of which will be given to the Associated Press when he commences reading it.[125] On the same day there were "reports of efforts in high quarters to induce the president to tone down his inaugural, but it is not affirmed that they were successful."[126]

A final report on the preparation of the Inaugural records the activities on the morning of March 4th: "Mr. Lincoln rose at 5 o'clock. After an early breakfast, the Inaugural was read aloud to him by his son Robert, and the completing touches were added, including the beautiful and impassioned closing paragraph."[127]

---

[120]The Diary of Orville Hickman Browning, *edited with an introduction and notes by Theodore Calvin Pease and James G. Randall (Springfield, Ill.: Illinois State Historical Library, 1925), I, 1850-1864, 455, 456.*

[121]*Seward,* op. cit., *p. 512.*

[122]Lincoln Lore, *No. 358.*

[123]*John G. Nicolay and John Hay,* Abraham Lincoln, A History *(New York: The Century Co., 1914), III, 319. Nicolay and Hay observe that "Judge David Davis read it while in Springfield," and "Francis P. Blair, Sr., read it in Washington, and highly commended it, suggesting no changes."*

[124]New York Times, *March 4, 1861, p. 1, col. 1.*

[125]New York Times, *March 4, 1861, p. 1, col. 2.*

[126]New York Daily Tribune, *March 4, 1861, p. 5, col. 1.*

[127]New York Times, *March 5, 1861, p. 1, col. 1.*

As J. G. Randall has observed, "if one would justly appraise Lincoln's first presidential state paper, this inaugural of 1861 deserves to be read as delivered and to be set over against the alternative statements that Lincoln avoided or struck out in revision. Statements pledging maintenance of Federal authority were toned down and shorn of truculence, while promises of conciliation were emotionally underlined."[128] Mr. Browning advised "but one change," supposed by some authorities to be "the most important one in the entire document."[129] "Mr. Seward made thirty-three suggestions for improving the document and nineteen of them were adopted, eight were used after Mr. Lincoln had modified them, and six were discarded *in toto*."[130] Finally, Lincoln, "without suggestion from any one made sixteen changes in the original draft."[131]

And so, however much the country might criticize as it scanned the Inaugural, Lincoln could respond, as he did to the Douglas taunt in 1858 that the "House Divided Speech" had been "evidently well prepared and carefully written,"[132] "I admit that it was. I am not master of language; I have not a fine education; . . . I know what I meant and I will not leave this crowd in doubt. . . ."[133]

Lincoln did not have to wait long for a response from the country at large. As he delivered the address, little audiences unseen by the speaker dotted the land, clustering around newspaper offices and waiting for telegraphic reports of what was in the Inaugural. Between Washington and New York, the American Telegraph Company had placed at the disposal of the Associated Press three wires for the communication of the address.[134] Similar arrangements had been made with other key cities. The delivery of the Inaugural commenced at 1:30 p.m., Washington time, and the "telegraphers promptly to the minute" began its transmission. "The first words of the Message were received by the agents of the Press at 1:45, and the last about 3:30," observed the *New York Times*.[135] "Such rapidity in telegraphic communication has never before been reached in this country."[136] By four o'clock, "the entire document was furnished to the different newspapers,"[137] and special editions of the press were in the hands of readers

[128] *Randall*, op. cit., *I*, 309.
[129] *Warren*, loc. cit.
[130] Ibid.
[131] Ibid.
[132] *Speech of Senator Douglas, delivered in Chicago, July 9, 1858, in* The Political Debates between Abraham Lincoln and Stephen A. Douglas, *with an introduction by George Haven Putnam (New York: G. P. Putnam's Sons, 1913), p. 24.*
[133] *Speech in reply to Douglas at Chicago, Illinois, July 10, 1858, in* Abraham Lincoln, His Speeches and Writings, *edited by Roy P. Basler, p. 392.*
[134] New York Times, *March 5, 1861, p. 8, col. 5.*
[135] Ibid.
[136] Ibid.
[137] Ibid.

within an hour. "People of all parties in this city, as elsewhere, were on tip-toe all day to know what was going on at Washington, and especially to hear what President Lincoln would say in his Inaugural," observed the *New York Times*.[138] "At length it was announced that the procession had reached the Capitol, and then, while the President was delivering his speech and the reporters were transmitting it by telegraph, there was a long period of unalloyed expectancy. Meantime, men given to talking, in the many crowds, discussed all sorts of topics, connected with the questions of the day, before little groups of gaping listeners. There was many a prophet among them, not without honor, before the Message was received, who knew exactly what it was going to contain, and foretold with marvelous preciseness the points which Mr. Lincoln would dwell on.

"It was nearly 5 o'clock when the eloquence of these worthies was suddenly quenched as by a wet blanket, and the wet sheets of the latest edition, with the President's Inaugural in black and white, leaped forth from the presses into the hands of all who could get copies. Then there was wild scrambling around the counters in publication offices, a laying down of pennies and a rape of newspapers, and the crowds began to disperse, each man hastening to some place remote from public haunt, where he might peruse the document in peace. The newsboys rushed through the city crying with stentorian lungs 'The President's Message!' 'Lincoln's Speech!' 'Ex-tray Times!' 'Get Lincoln's Inau-gu-ra-a-a-il!' And an hour later everybody had read the Message and everybody was talking about it."[139]

Out in Mattoon, Illinois, a similar scene was being enacted. A roving reporter, heading south from Chicago to observe the reactions of the crowds, made a "tour of the town" and stopped at hotel lobbies, where the speech, fresh from the press, was being "read and re-read, silently and aloud, to groups of ardent listeners . . . As the reading in a crowd progresses, when the reader comes to the place where Mr. Lincoln 'puts his foot down,' down goes likewise every foot in the circle."[140]

The home folks whom Lincoln had bade an affectionate farewell three weeks before were among the most anxious of the unseen audiences. Whereas they spoke only for themselves at the time of the tearful departure, they were now ready to speak for the nation. "The Inaugural Address of our noble Chief Magistrate has electrified the whole country," they said. "It has satisfied people of all parties who love the Union and desire its preservation. In this city it gives almost universal satisfaction."[141] In Quincy, the scene of one of the debates of 1858, the address was received with "much enthusiasm," and the Republican Gun Squad fired thirty-four guns;[142] in Peoria, "so great was

---

[138]New York Times, *March 5, 1861, p. 8, cols. 4, 5.*
[139]Ibid.
[140]Chicago Daily Tribune, *March 8, 1861, p. 2, col. 3.*
[141]Illinois State Journal, *March 6, 1861, p. 2.*
[142]Chicago Daily Tribune, *March 6, 1861, p. 1, col. 3.*

the anxiety felt to see what Mr. Lincoln said, that people came forty miles to get copies of the message,"[143] reading it with "much enthusiasm."[144]

But occasionally there was a dissenting voice back home, particularly in the Democratic press, as there was generally throughout the North. While the *Chicago Daily Tribune* was "quite sure that no document can be found among American state papers embodying sounder wisdom and higher patriotism,— breathing kindlier feelings to all sections of the country,"[145] the Chicago *Times* denounced the Inaugural as "a loose, disjointed, rambling affair," concluding that the Union was now "lost beyond hope."[146] While the *New York Times* observed that "conservative people are in raptures over the Inaugural," and that "Its conciliatory tone, and frank, outspoken declaration of loyalty to the whole country, captured the hearts of many heretofore opposed to Mr. Lincoln,"[147] the New York *Herald* found that "the inaugural is not a crude performance—it abounds in traits of craft and cunning. It bears marks of indecision, and yet of strong coercion proclivities . . . It is neither candid nor statesmanlike; nor does it possess any essential dignity or patriotism. It would have caused a Washington to mourn, and would have inspired a Jefferson, Madison, or Jackson with contempt."[148] There were those in Maine who found it a "poor, weak, trashy affair, a standing disgrace to the country, and a fit commentary on the fanaticism and unreasonableness which made him President."[149] Some in Pennsylvania found it "one of the most awkwardly constructed official documents we have ever inspected," and "pitiably apologetical for the uprising of the Republican party, and his own election to the Presidency, by it."[150] And there were those in Ohio "who never expected to see a Black Republican peaceably inaugurated in this White Republican country . . . but now the Rubicon is passed," and the Inaugural, "like its distinguished author," is "flat-footed. It is more *magazinish* in *sound* than in *style*, smelling strongly of gunpowder, and is '*coercion*' *all over*, as the South understands that word."[151]

"It is an interesting study" said a Douglas journal, the Peoria *Daily Democratic Union*, on March 7th, "to look over the various journals that have come to our table since the delivery of President Lincoln's Inaugural Address, and notice the different manner in which they speak of it." "All of these criticisms of the Address cannot be correct, for they clash materially; and that fact demonstrates very plainly that some of them were either the offspring of prejudice, or were written by men incapable of judging of the merits of this

---

[143] Ibid.
[144] Ibid.
[145] Chicago Daily Tribune, *March 5, 1861, p. 1, col. 1.*
[146] *Quoted in Randall, op. cit., p. 306.*
[147] New York Times, *March 5, 1861, p. 1, col. 4.*
[148] *Quoted in the* New York Daily Tribune, *March 7, 1861, p. 6, col. 6.*
[149] The Bangor Union, *as quoted in* New York Daily Tribune, *March 8, 1861, p. 6, col. 5.*
[150] The Philadelphia Evening Journal, *as quoted in* New York Daily Tribune, *March 7, 1861, p. 7, col. 3.*
[151] Cleveland Plaindealer, *as quoted in* Chicago Daily Tribune, *March 9, 1861, p. 1, col. 3.*

first state paper of President Lincoln."[152]

Whereas there was difference of opinion in the North, much of it stopped short of vehement denunciation. However, the South saw little hope from Lincoln, and expressed itself accordingly. "Mr. Lincoln's Inaugural Address is before our readers," observed the *Richmond Enquirer,* "couched in the cool, unimpassioned, deliberate language of the fanatic, with the purpose of pursuing the promptings of fanaticism even to the dismemberment of the Government with the horrors of civil war . . . Civil war must now come. Sectional war, declared by Mr. Lincoln, awaits only the signal gun from the insulted Southern Confederacy, to light its horrid fires all along the borders of Virginia."[153] The *Richmond Dispatch* was equally strong: "The Inaugural Address of Abraham Lincoln inaugurates civil war, as we have predicted it would from the beginning . . . The sword is drawn and the scabbard thrown away . . . ere long Virginia may be engaged in a life and death struggle. . . ."[154] The *Baltimore Sun* observed, "The Inaugural, as a whole, breathes the spirit of mischief," and found "no Union spirit in the address."[155] "We presume nobody is astonished to hear that Secessionists regard the Inaugural as a 'declaration of war,'" noted one observer. "Before the Inaugural has been read in a single Southern State, it is denounced, through the telegraph, from every Southern point, as a declaration of war."[156] "I have heard but one construction of Mr. Lincoln's declaration of his intention to 'hold, occupy, and possess the property and places belonging to the Government, and to collect the duties and imposts,'" observed a special correspondent in Richmond. The Inaugural "is received with much disfavor," and "is regarded, if not as a declaration of war, as at least the expression of a determination to coerce the seceding States into compliance with the demands of the Federal Government."[157] Reporting from Charleston, South Carolina, another correspondent observed, "The part which, of course, attracted most attention and was read and re-read with deep interest, was that wherein Mr. Lincoln declares that to the best of his ability, he will take care, according to his oath and the Constitution, that 'the laws of the Union are faithfully executed in all the States,' and that he will use the power confided to him to 'hold, occupy and possess the property and places belonging to the Government, and to collect the duties and imposts.'" The verdict was, according to this correspondent, "that rebellion would not be treated tenderly by Mr. Lincoln, and that he was quite another sort of man from James Buchanan."[158]

---

[152] *Quoted in* Northern Editorials on Secession, *edited by Howard Cecil Perkins (New York: D. Appleton-Century Co., 1942), II, 643.*

[153] *Quoted in* New York Daily Tribune, *March 7, 1861, p. 7, col. 2. See also,* Southern Editorials on Secession, *pp. 474, 475.*

[154] Southern Editorials on Secession, *p. 475.*

[155] *Quoted in* New York Daily Tribune, *March 7, 1861, p. 7, col. 1.*

[156] New York Times, *March 7, 1861, p. 4, col. 2.*

[157] New York Daily Tribune, *March 9, 1861, p. 6, col. 2.*

[158] New York Daily Tribune, *March 9, 1861, p. 6, col. 1.*

At least a minority of the people of the South responded less vehemently. Occasionally a roving reporter, mingling among the crowds in Southern cities, reported less fury. From Montgomery came word that Alexander Stevens had found the Inaugural "the most *adroit* State paper ever published on the Continent," and "a great moral impression has been produced"[159] in both Charleston and Montgomery. In Savannah, Georgia, "Not a word have we yet heard uttered against its tone," observed a reporter, predicting "a powerful and sweeping effect at the South."[160] Now and then a reporter noticed "a pretty general disappointment that the document contained so little 'blood and thunder.'"[161] "That the document should be calm and dignified in tone and style, logical in its conclusions, and plain and kind in its treatment of the great topic of the day, was annoying to the Rebels, who hoped to find in the address a provocation for extreme action."[162]

While the country at large read the speech and responded both favorably and unfavorably, Senator Clingman of North Carolina and Stephen A. Douglas engaged in debate over its meaning in the United States Senate. "If I understand it aright, all that is direct in it, I mean, at least, that purpose which seems to stand out clearly and directly, is one which I think must lead to war—war against the confederate or seceding State"[163] remarked Clingman. Douglas, on the other hand, who had "read it carefully" could not "assent to the construction" of the senator from North Carolina, believing he could "demonstrate that there is no foundation for the apprehension which has been spread throughout the country, that this message is equivalent to a declaration of war."[164]

Just as the country searched the Inaugural for the sentiments it contained, it also examined and appraised the language and style in which it was couched. The Toronto *Leader* could not admire the "tawdry and corrupt schoolboy style," even as it gave "credit" for its "good sense."[165] An Albany, New York, observer found it "useless to criticize the style of the President's Inaugural when the policy it declares is fraught with consequences so momentous." Nevertheless, he paused to describe it as a "rambling, discursive, questioning, loose-jointed stump speech." It consisted of "feeble rhetorical stuff."[166] While papers unfriendly to Lincoln were finding it "inferior in point of elegance, perspicuity, vigor, talent, and all the graces of composition to any other paper of a like character which has ever emanated from a President of the Republic,"[167] papers that were friendly found the

---

[159] New York Daily Tribune, *March 12, 1861, p. 6, col. 1.*
[160] New York Daily Tribune, *March 11, 1861, p. 6, col. 2.*
[161] New York Daily Tribune, *March 9, 1861, p. 6, col. 1.*
[162] Ibid.
[163] Congressional Globe, *Second Session, 36th Congress, Vol. 30, Part II, p. 1436.*
[164] Ibid.
[165] *Quoted in* New York Daily Tribune, *March 7, 1861, p. 7, col. 3.*
[166] Albany Atlas and Argus, *as quoted in* Northern Editorials on Secession, *II, 628.*
[167] Jersey City American Standard, *as quoted in* Northern Editorials on Secession, *II, 625.*

contrary to be the case. "It is clear as a mountain brook," commented a Detroit reporter. "The depth and flow of it are apparent at a glance."[168] In Boston, the *Transcript* reporter commented at length: "The style of the Address is as characteristic as its temper. 'Right words in their right places'; this is the requirement of good rhetoric. Right words at the right times, should be the test by which we try the speech of statesmen; and this test Mr. Lincoln's address will bear. It has not one flaming expression in the whole course of its firm and explicit statements. The language is level to the popular mind,—the plain homespun language of a man accustomed to talk with 'the folks' and 'the neighbors,' the language of a man of vital common sense, whose words exactly fit his facts and thoughts."[169] Occasionally, the concluding paragraph was singled out for praise. In Indianapolis, the reporter of the *Daily Journal* remarked: "The closing sentence, the only attempt at rhetorical display in the whole address, is singularly and almost poetically beautiful."[170]

Part II

Given the circumstances that brought forth the Inaugural Address, and removed in time from the passions which agitated the country, what may one say of Lincoln's address on March 4, 1861? The historian has often examined it for its effects, and has concluded that "Though not fully appreciated then, this was one of the great American inaugurals."[171] And the literary critic has sometimes observed its final passage, finding in it poetic beauty and enduring worth. Unlike the historian, we are not concerned merely with the Inaugural as a force in the shaping of American culture; nor are we concerned with its enduring worth as literature. The Inaugural was a speech, "meant to be heard and intended to exert an influence of some kind on those who heard it,"[172] or those who read it. We must, therefore, be concerned with evaluating the Inaugural as a speech, a medium distinct from other media, and with methods peculiarly its own. We must be concerned with discovering in this particular case "the available means of persuasion" and with evaluating their worth.

Let us view the Inaugural as a communication, with a purpose, and a content presumably designed to aid in the accomplishment of that purpose, further supported by skillful composition in words, and ultimately unified by the character and manner of the person who presented it.

We must not casually assume that Lincoln's purpose is easily discernible

---

[168]Detroit Daily Tribune, *as quoted in* Northern Editorials on Secession, *II, 623.*

[169]*Quoted in* New York Daily Tribune, *March 7, 1861, p. 7, col. 1.*

[170]*Quoted in* Northern Editorials on Secession, *II, 619.*

[171]*J. G. Randall, "Lincoln's Great Declarations of Faith,"* New York Times Magazine, *February 6, 1949, p. 23.*

[172]*Wayland M. Parrish and Marie Hochmuth Nichols,* American Speeches *(New York: David McKay, 1954), p. 3.*

in the occasion itself. It is true, of course, that this was an inaugural ceremony, with a ritual fairly well established by fifteen predecessors, "Yet, with all this scope for [of] precedent," Lincoln was keenly aware that he entered upon the same task "under great and peculiar difficulty. A disruption of the Federal Union, heretofore only menaced, is now formidably attempted." If we are to discern the purpose that Lincoln had when he addressed the American people on March 4, 1861, we must recall the experiences of the nation between his election as president and the day of his inauguration. During that time, he had been made keenly aware of Southern resentment to a "sectional" president. The rapid movement of the Secessionists followed closely on the announcement of his election, and of the ascendancy of the Republican party to a position of power. The South viewed the Republican platform as an instrument for its "subjugation" and the "complete ruin of her social, political and industrial institutions."[173] By its acts of secession, and its establishment of a provisional government of its own, the lower South raised the very practical question: What is the authority of the federal government in regard to maintaining itself and in regard to reclaiming those federal properties possessed by retiring members?

Lincoln had also been made keenly aware of the doubts and skepticism that prevailed regarding his ability to lead his party and the nation. "I cannot but know what you all know," he had observed on his way to Washington, "that without a name, perhaps without a reason why I should have a name, there has fallen upon me a task such as did not rest even upon the Father of his Country. . . ."[174] In addition, he was keenly aware of both Northern and Southern distrust of his moral character and integrity. Even to members of his party, he was a "funny man," given to stories in bad taste, and an Illinois wag. And to the South, he was at best thought to be as radical as the most rabid of the left-wing Republicans, hence a "dangerous man."[175] That he was aware of the prevailing sentiments regarding him as a man is reflected in his casual remark en route to Washington when, for a moment, his address was misplaced. In a worried search, he described the Inaugural as "my certificate of moral character, written by myself."[176]

Although from the time of his election he was urged to state his views on the passing events, Lincoln had remained silent. That his silence was not due to a lack of anxiety is easily apparent. "Allusion has been made," he noted on his way to Washington, "to the interest felt in relation to the policy of the new administration. In this I have received from some a degree of credit for

[173] New Orleans Daily Crescent, *November 13, 1860, as quoted in* Southern Editorials on Secession, *p. 237.*
[174] *"Address to the Legislature of Ohio at Columbus, February 13, 1861,"* Complete Works, *VI, 121.*
[175] *Speech of Senator Clingman of North Carolina in the Senate, December 3, 1860,* The Congressional Globe, *Second Session, 36th Congress, Vol. 30, p. 3.*
[176] *Ward Hill Lamon,* Recollections of Abraham Lincoln, 1847-1865, *edited by Dorothy Lamon Teillard (Washington, D. C.: Published by the editor, 1911), p. 36.*

having kept silence, and from others some deprecation. I still think that I was right . . .

"In the varying and repeatedly shifting scenes of the present, and without a precedent which could enable me to judge by the past, it has seemed fitting that before speaking upon the difficulties of the country I should have gained a view of the whole field, being at liberty to modify and change the course of policy as future events may make a change necessary.

"I have not maintained silence from any want of real anxiety."[177]

What, then, was Lincoln's purpose? Clearly, he intended to take the occasion of the inauguration to declare the position of the Republican party in regard to the South, to announce his considered judgment in regard to the practical questions raised by the movement of secession, and, in all, to give what assurance he could of his personal integrity.

In evaluating the Inaugural, we must keep in mind its purpose, for the purpose of the speech controlled Lincoln's selection of materials, his arrangement, his style, and his manner.

Let us turn to the speech itself in order to note the materials and methods he employed to sustain his purpose. Considering the general predisposition of the South to view the incoming administration with suspicion, and considering the fact that Lincoln had not spoken for his own party since his nomination, he found it necessary to take a moment to "press upon the public attention the most conclusive evidence of which the case is susceptible," the idea of the integrity of the Republican party and his own integrity as its helmsman. Wise judgment could scarcely have dictated otherwise, for the lower South had gone out of the Union partly on the grounds that it expected no fair consideration from the newly born party, and the border states were contemplating similar measures. Lincoln attempted to conciliate his audience by assuring the country that "the property, peace and security of no section are to be in any wise endangered by the now incoming Administration." In order to do this he called attention to the fact that he was taking a solemn oath in "your presence"; he committed himself again to previously spoken words [178] that have "all the while existed, and been open to their inspection"; to the Republican platform pertaining to the "maintenance inviolate of the rights of the States, and especially the right of each State to order and control its own domestic institutions according to its own judgment exclusively";[179] and to the clause "plainly written in the Constitution," pertaining to delivering up "on claim of the party to whom such service or labor may be due"[180] the escaping fugitive. He concluded his opening remarks with a reiteration of the

---

[177] *"Address to the Legislature of Ohio at Columbus, February 13, 1861,"* Complete Works, VI, 121, 122.

[178] *"Mr. Lincoln's Reply," First Joint Debate, at Ottawa, August 21, 1858,* The Political Debates between Abraham Lincoln and Stephen A. Douglas, *p. 209.*

[179] *Halstead,* op. cit., *p. 138.*

[180] *Article IV, Sec. 2.*

avowal that he took the "official oath to-day, with no mental reservations, and with no purpose to construe the Constitution or laws, by any hypercritical rules." This was neither the material nor the method of a "deceitful" or "dangerous" man. By it, Lincoln was attempting to touch off those favorable responses that accrue to the appearance of honesty, straightforwardness, and obedience to the Constitution. One must remember that Lincoln's pledge of faith could not have given satisfaction to the Abolitionist group within his own party with whom he was constantly identified by the South; it did, however, serve to differentiate him from the radical element and hence to reassure the states yet within the Union. From the standpoint of persuasiveness Lincoln was undoubtedly wise in taking the advice of Seward to omit the two paragraphs immediately following his opening statement in the original draft of the Inaugural:

> *The more modern custom of electing a Chief Magistrate upon a previously declared platform of principles, supercedes, in a great measure, the necessity of restating those principles in an address of this sort. Upon the plainest grounds of good faith, one so elected is not at liberty to shift his position. It is necessarily implied, if not expressed, that, in his judgment, the platform which he thus accepts, binds him to nothing either unconstitutional or inexpedient.*
>
> *Having been so elected upon the Chicago Platform, and while I would repeat nothing in it, of aspersion or epithet or question of motive against any man or party, I hold myself bound by duty, as well as impelled by inclination to follow, within the executive sphere, the principles therein declared. By no other course could I meet the reasonable expectations of the country.[181]*

To have used the paragraphs would undoubtedly have incited anew the suspicion that he was merely a "sectional" President and an "abolitionist" or "party man."

Having spent time in an attempt to gain a fair hearing for the rest of his address, Lincoln next took up the question for which the whole country awaited an answer, namely, What is the duty and the policy of the Republican administration in regard to Secession? Without delay, he laid down the proposition, "I hold, that in contemplation of universal law, and of the Constitution, the Union of these States is perpetual. Perpetuity is implied, if not expressed, in the fundamental law of all national governments"; hence

---

[181] *For changes in the Inaugural, see MS of early printed version with secretarial reproductions of the changes, and accompanying letter of John Hay to Charles Eliot Norton, dated March 25, 1899, explaining the nature of the revisions, in Widener Library of Harvard University. See also, John G. Nicolay and John Hay,* Abraham Lincoln, *III, 327-344; Louis A. Warren, "Original Draft of the First Inaugural,"* Lincoln Lore, *No. 358 (February 17, 1936) and No. 359 (February 24, 1936). See,* The Robert Todd Lincoln Collection of the Papers of Abraham Lincoln, *Library of Congress. Microfilm in University of Illinois Library. This collection contains the most important source for the various working sheets of the Inaugural.*

"no State, upon its own mere motion, can lawfully get out of the Union,—
that *resolves* and *ordinances* to that effect are legally void, and that acts of
violence, within any State or States, against the authority of the United States,
are insurrectionary or revolutionary, according to circumstances." Furthermore, "if the United States be not a government proper, but an association of
States in the nature of contract merely, can it, as a contract, be peaceably
unmade, by less than all the parties who made it?"

To the North, the mere assertion of the principle of perpetuity would have
been sufficient; no further proof would have been necessary. But to the lower
South, already out of the Union, and to the border states and upper South
contemplating similar action, clearly assertion was not sufficient. Therefore,
Lincoln found his proposition "confirmed by the history of the Union itself."
The Union, he pointed out, was "much older than the Constitution"; it was
"formed in fact, by the Articles of Association in 1774"; it was "matured and
continued by the Declaration of Independence in 1776"; it was "further
matured and the faith of all the then thirteen States expressly plighted and
engaged that it should be perpetual, by the Articles of Confederation in
1778"; finally "in 1787, one of the declared objects for ordaining and
establishing the Constitution, was *'to form a more perfect Union.'*" Although
Lincoln's support of his proposition was factual, the facts themselves carried
with them the respect and loyalty that had always attached to the founding
fathers who were held in esteem for their vision and their wisdom.

Having stated the principle that guided him, Lincoln continued logically
with its application, holding that "to the extent of my ability I shall take care,
as the Constitution itself expressly enjoins upon me, that the laws of the
Union be faithfully executed in all the States." In discussing the policy of the
government in enforcing the laws of the Union, Lincoln does not speak as the
master or the mere advocate handing down a bloodless decision, but as a
servant performing a "simple duty," the "American people" being "my
rightful masters." As a skilled persuader, he was undoubtedly aware that lines
of argument will often meet with varied responses according to whether they
are put forward by those toward whom one feels sympathetic or antago-
nistic.[182] Nowhere in the Inaugural does Lincoln seek more earnestly to be
conciliating and mild. He was aware that legalism alone would not sustain his
purpose. He could have used the bold and confident assertion that appeared
in the original draft of the Inaugural:

> All the power at my disposal will be used to reclaim the public
> property and places which have fallen; to hold, occupy and possess
> these, and all other property and places belonging to the government
> and to collect the duties and imposts; but beyond what may be
> necessary for these objects, there will be no invasion of any State.

---

[182] *Robert K. Merton,* Mass Persuasion *(New York: Harper and Brothers, 1946), p. 109.*

Even in the original draft, Lincoln had avoided the use of the names of specific forts to which he had reference. Pickens and Sumter were in a precarious position and were peculiarly explosive topics of discussion. However, Lincoln yielded even further in tempering his remarks, accepting the suggestion of O. H. Browning, and finally choosing only to say:

> *The power confided to me will be used to hold, occupy, and possess the property and places belonging to the Government, and to collect the duties and imposts; but, beyond what may be necessary for these objects, there will be no invasion, no using of force against or among the people anywhere.*

Furthermore, "Where hostility to the United States, in any interior locality, shall be so great and so universal, as to prevent competent resident citizens from holding the Federal offices," he would make "no attempt to force obnoxious strangers among the people for that object," even though the "strict legal right may exist." And, the mails "unless repelled" would continue to be furnished. In doing this, "there needs to be no bloodshed or violence," he assured the country, and promised that "there shall be none, unless it be forced upon the national authority." Nowhere did Lincoln assert a power or a practice that he believed impossible of enforcement, or that he believed could be interpreted as "coercion" in its baldest and most belligerent form.

Having announced his specific policy, Lincoln turned to those "who really love the Union," neither affirming nor denying that there were those "who seek to destroy the Union at all events," being "glad of any pretext to do it." In his original draft, he had intended pointedly to observe "Before entering upon so grave a matter as the destruction of our national Union, would it not be wise to ascertain precisely why we do it?" In his final draft, however, he blotted out the word "Union" and substituted for it the unifying and figurative word "fabric," further inserting the words "with all its benefits, its memories and its hopes," thereby seeking to heighten feeling by suggesting appropriate attitudes.

Having passed the climax of his remarks, Lincoln moved, in the last half of the Inaugural, to a reasoned discussion of related topics. He denied that any right plainly written in the Constitution had been violated, observing that majorities and minorities arise as a result of that class of questions for which no specific constitutional answer has been provided. The alternative to accepting the "majority principle" was always either "anarchy or depotism." Not even the Supreme Court could serve as the final arbiter on questions "affecting the whole people," for unless it limited its activity to making decisions on specific "cases properly brought before them," the "people will have ceased to be their own rulers." He argued the impracticability of secession, contrasting it with the simple act of divorce between husband and wife who may remain "beyond the reach of each other," and concluded that "Physically speaking, we cannot separate." Not even war was a satisfactory solution to difficulties, for "you cannot fight always," and after much "loss on both sides, and no gain on either," the "identical old questions" are again to be settled. "This country, with its institutions, belongs to the people who inhabit it," he insisted, urging that when the whole people "shall grow weary of the existing government, they can exercise their *constitutional* right of amending it, or their *revolutionary* right to dismember or overthrow it."

Lincoln's appeal throughout was to the "patient confidence in the ultimate justice of the people." "Is there any better or equal hope, in the world?" he asked, even as he noted the human tendency of parties in dispute to insist with equal confidence on being in the "right." Rising to the position of impartial leader, he sought faith in a higher law, and in a disinterested Ruler: "If the Almighty Ruler of nations, with his eternal truth and justice, be on your side of the North or on yours of the South, that truth, and that justice, will surely prevail, by the judgment of this great tribunal, the American people."

Lincoln ended his address with both a challenge and a declaration of faith. "In *your* hands, my dissatisfied fellow countrymen, and not in *mine, is* the momentous issue of civil war. The government will not assail *you.*" He was just about to take an oath, and to him an oath was a solemn pledge, not only in word, but in truth. It was an avowal of morality, binding him not only to duty to the people but to God, "the Almighty Ruler of nations." "*You* have no oath registered in Heaven to destroy the government," he pleaded in an attempt to secure the cooperation of all those who could help him in fulfilling the pledge he was to take, "while *I* shall have the most solemn one to 'preserve, protect and defend' it." His final appeal was to feeling rather than to reason. He undoubtedly realized that when men cannot achieve common ground through reason, they may achieve it through the medium of feeling. "I am loth to close," he observed. "We are not enemies, but friends. We must not be enemies. Though passion may have strained, it must not break our bonds of affection." No longer the advocate, or even the president performing official duties, Lincoln, taking the advice of Seward, became the affectionate father, the benevolent and hopeful counselor, trusting not only in reason, but calling on "memory," the "patriot grave," the "heart and hearth-stone," "the better angels of our nature" to "swell the chorus of the Union."

Whereas the disgruntled may have "found too much argumentative discussion of the question at issue, as was to have been expected from a man whose whole career has been that of an advocate,"[183] obviously others could not have failed to notice that Lincoln sought valiantly to employ all the "available means of persuasion." He had sought to reach his audience not only through reason, but through feeling and through the force of his own ethical ideals.

Any fair-minded critic, removed from the passions of the times, must find himself much more in agreement with those observers of the day who believed the Inaugural met the "requirements of good rhetoric" by having

---

[183]The Diary of a Public Man, *p. 75.*

"right words in their right places" and "right words at the right times,"[184] than with those who labeled it "feeble rhetorical stuff," and found it "inferior in point of elegance, perspicuity, vigor, talent, and all the graces of composition to any other paper of a like character from a President of the Republic."[185] One who studies the revisions in phrase and word in the various drafts of the Inaugural must become aware that Lincoln was concerned not only with using the right argument, but with using words cautiously, and purposefully, to obtain a desired effect from his listeners and from his potential readers. To the rhetorician, style is not an aspect of language which can be viewed in isolation or judged merely by the well-attuned ear. Nor is it sufficient to apply such rubrics as clarity, vividness, elegance as absolute values, or as an adequate description of style. Words are an "available means of persuasion," and the only legitimate question is: Did Lincoln use words effectively to achieve his specific purpose?

Although Lincoln may have lamented that he did not have a "fine education" or that he was not a "master of language,"[186] he had a keen sensitiveness for language. He "studied to see the subject matter clearly," said an early teacher, "and to express it truly and strongly. I have known him to study for hours the best way of three to express an idea."[187] And when his partner, Herndon, attempted the grandiose in expression, Lincoln sometimes remarked, "Billy, don't shoot too high—aim lower and the common people will understand you. They are the ones you want to reach—at least they are the ones you ought to reach. The educated and refined people will understand you any way. If you aim too high, your ideas will go over the heads of the masses, and only hit those who need no hitting."[188] Lincoln had become adept at stump speaking, and knew how to use language to make himself clear and to make a point. That he knew the power of language to fire passions and to cloud understanding is amply demonstrated in his remarks at Indianapolis when he was en route to Washington. "Solomon says there is 'a time to keep silence,'" he observed, "and when men wrangle by the month with no certainty that they mean the same thing, while using the same word, it perhaps were as well if they would keep silence. The words 'coercion' and 'invasion' are much used in these days, and often with some temper and hot blood. Let us make sure, if we can, that we do not misunderstand the meaning of those who use them. Let us get exact definitions of these words, not from dictionaries, but from the men themselves, who certainly deprecate the things they would represent by the use of words."[189] Lincoln was keenly

[184]The Boston Transcript, *as quoted in* New York Daily Tribune, *March 7, 1861, p. 7, col. 1.*
[185]Jersey City Standard, *as quoted in* Northern Editorials on Secession, *II, 625.*
[186]*Speech in reply to Douglas at Chicago, Illinois, July 10, 1858, in* Abraham Lincoln: His Speeches and Writings, *edited by Roy P. Basler, p. 393.*
[187]*Herndon and Weik,* op. cit., *p. 99.*
[188]Ibid., *p. 262.*
[189]*"Address to the Legislature of Indiana at Indianapolis, February 12, 1861,"* Complete Works, *VI, 112, 113.*

aware that words themselves were often grounds for argument, systems of attitudes suggesting courses of action.[190] Then, too, Lincoln knew that his "friends feared" and "those who were not his friends hoped, that, forgetting the dignity of his position, and the occasion, he would descend to the practices of the story-teller, and fail to rise to the level of a statesman."[191]

The desire for clearness, the desire to subdue passion, the desire to manifest the integrity and dignity befitting a statesman in a responsible position—these are the factors that influenced Lincoln in his composition of the Inaugural, and to appraise his style without constant awareness of them is likely to lead the critic far afield. Let us consider Lincoln's style, then, as a system of symbols designed to evoke certain images favorable to the accomplishment of his purpose and, in so far as he could, to prevent certain other images from arising.

One of the most marked characteristics of Lincoln's style is its directness. By it he attempts to achieve the appearance of candor and honesty, traits that were eminently significant to the success of the Inaugural, considering the doubts and suspicions that were prevalent regarding his integrity. From the opening sentence to the conclusion one notes the unmistakable honesty and straightforwardness that reside in direct address. "I appear before you," he remarks, "to address you briefly, and to take, in your presence, the oath prescribed by the Constitution of the United States. . . ." Again, he observes, "I have no purpose, directly or indirectly, to interfere with the institution of slavery in the States where it exists"; "I now reiterate these sentiments"; "I take the official oath to-day, with no mental reservations"; "*You* have no oath registered in Heaven to destroy the government, while *I* shall have the most solemn one to 'preserve, protect and defend' it." Direct and forthright throughout, he could scarcely have used words to better advantage in emphasizing his honesty and integrity.

What doubts there were pertaining to inadequacies traceable to his humble origins and his lack of formal education must in some wise have been dispelled by his clearness, his accuracy, and his freedom from the awkward expression or the simple idiom of the Western stump speaker. Lincoln had felt his inadequacies when he addressed an Eastern audience of educated men at Cooper Union and was uncomfortable. In his Inaugural, prepared for an audience representative of the whole country, he had been cautious and careful to use language that was sustained in its dignity. Seward, sometimes known for his polished expression, had given him some aid in the choice of the proper word. Lincoln accepted advice in such word changes as "acquiesce" instead of "submit," "constituted" instead of "constructed," "void" instead of "nothing," "repelled" instead of "refused," and he also

---

[190] *Kenneth Burke, "Two Functions of Speech,"* The Language of Wisdom and Folly, *edited and with an introduction by Irving J. Lee (New York: Harper and Brothers, 1949), p. 40.*

[191] *L. E. Chittenden,* Recollections of President Lincoln and His Administration *(New York: Harper and Brothers, 1904), p. 88.*

accepted such a change of phrase as "imperfectly supports the law itself" for "is against the law itself." Although the changes are minor, they reflect Lincoln's desire for correctness and conciseness. On his own better judgment, he deleted the one extended metaphor that appeared in the original draft. "I am, rather for the old ship, and the chart of the old pilots," he had originally written, with some of the tang and flavor of his speech in addressing popular Western audiences. "If, however, the people desire a new, or an altered vessel, the matter is exclusively their own, and they can move in the premises, as well without as with an executive recommendation." The figure was not equal in elevation to the rest of his remarks. His final draft read simply, "I cannot be ignorant of the fact that many worthy and patriotic citizens are desirous of having the national Constitution amended. While I make no recommendation of amendments, I fully recognize the rightful authority of the people over the whole subject. . . ." Such phrasing, simple in its dignity, undoubtedly was more appropriate and suited to his needs.

That Lincoln sought to control the behavior of his audience and the reader through the appropriately affective word is apparent throughout his address. There are times when even the level of specificity and concreteness, usually thought to be virtues of style, is altered in favor of the more general word or allusion. For instance, Lincoln had originally intended to say, "why may not South Carolina, a year or two hence, arbitrarily, secede from a new Southern Confederacy . . . ?" Finally, however, he avoided being specific, altering his remarks to read "why may not any portion of a new confederacy, a year or two hence, arbitrarily secede again . . . ?" Again, the ridicule in his assertion, "The Union is less perfect than before, which contradicts the Constitution, and therefore is absurd," is eliminated and reason is substituted: "The Union is *less perfect* than before the Constitution, having lost the vital element of its perpetuity." Lincoln sometimes chose the longer statement in preference to the sharp, pointed word or phrase, if by a longer expression he could avoid truculence or the pointing of an accusing finger. Such a phrase as "be on your side of the North or on yours of the South," aided considerably in creating an image of impartiality, and was to be preferred for the shorter, but divisive phrase, "be on our side or yours." The changes that Lincoln made in the direction of fullness rather than compression were designed to aid in clearness, exactness, and completeness, for the country expected him to express himself fully on the disturbing problems of the time.

The close of Lincoln's address, often cited for its poetic beauty, reflects not only his aesthetic sense, but perhaps more importantly, his power of using words to evoke images conducive to controlling response. As is very well known, Lincoln was not merely trying to be eloquent when he closed the address. He achieved eloquence and cadenced beauty through his direct attempt to be "affectionate," Seward having reminded him that perhaps feeling should supplement reason, and having suggested a possible conclusion:

"I close. We are not we must not be aliens or enemies but

~~countrym~~ fellow countrymen and brethren. Although passion has strained our bonds of affection too hardly they must not ~~be broken~~ ~~they will not~~ I am sure they will not be broken. The mystic chords of memory which proceeding from ~~every ba~~ so many battle fields and ~~patriot~~ so many patriot graves ~~bi~~ pass through all the hearts and all the hearths in this broad continent of ours will yet ~~harmo~~ again harmonize in their ancient music when ~~touched as they surely~~ breathed upon ~~again~~ by the ~~better anger~~ guardian angel of the nation."[192]

An image of great-heartedness, great humility, and great faith resulted when Lincoln rephrased Seward's suggestion in his own style. It was his final declaration of faith and had in it the emotional intensity that often accompanies the hoped-for but unknown. It was his final plea for a course of action befitting "friends."

Let us conclude our remarks on Lincoln's style by emphasizing that it reflected the same purposefulness that was characteristic of the arguments contained in the address. Through directness, clearness, dignity, and appropriately affective words, he sought to aid himself in achieving his ends.

One further means of persuasion may be noted, namely, that of his manner in oral presentation. Lincoln's delivery, of course, was significant chiefly to those who composed his immediate audience, and not to any great extent to the much larger audience throughout the country, except in so far as eyewitnesses and newspaper reports conveyed impressions pertaining to the character and personality of the speaker. It is undoubtedly true that Lincoln's manner contributed heavily to his effectiveness on this particular occasion. It may even be true that, had the whole country been immediately present, it would have found further grounds for trust. Ethical stature often shows itself not only in the selection of argument or the composition of words, but in those "echoes and values" that emanate from physical presence alone. "If I were to make the shortest list of the qualifications of the orator," Emerson once remarked, "I should begin with *manliness;* and perhaps it means here presence of mind."[193] It must be remembered that when Lincoln advanced to the platform to deliver his Inaugural, he did so in face of threats on his life. That he manifested little fear is apparent from practically all of the newspaper accounts of the day. The most usual observation indicated that "the great heart and kindly nature of the man were apparent in his opening sentence, in the tone of his voice, the expression of his face, in his whole manner and bearing."[194] In the judgment of many, he "gained the confidence of his hearers and secured their respect and affection."[195] Lincoln appears to have had a

---

[192] *Facsimile of the original suggestion of Seward as reprinted in* Abraham Lincoln: His Speeches and Writings, *edited by Roy P. Basler, pp. 589, 590.*

[193] "Eloquence," The Complete Works of Ralph Waldo Emerson *(New York: Sully and Kleinteich, 1875),* VIII, 123.

[194] *Chittenden,* loc. cit.

[195] Ibid., *p. 90.*

sense of communication, a complete awareness of what he was saying when he was saying it. His thought emerged clearly and appeared to be in no way obstructed by affectation or peculiarities of manner. With dignity and firmness coupled with mildness and humility he sought to enforce his plea by those powers that reside in personality. That they have stimulus value one can scarcely question.

Thirty-nine days after Lincoln delivered his Inaugural Address, Fort Sumter was fired upon. Civil war had begun. Lincoln had sought to save the Union by carefully reasoned argument, by regard for the feelings and rights of all the people, and by a solemn avowal of justice and integrity. That the Inaugural alone could not prevent the war is surely insufficient ground to condemn it for ineptness. "In speechmaking, as in life, not failure, but low aim, is crime."[196] There were many divisive forces, and these had gained great momentum by the time Lincoln addressed the American people. The South accepted the burden of his challenge, "In *your* hands, my dissatisfied fellow countrymen, and not in *mine*, is the momentous issue of civil war.

---

[196] *Parrish and Nichols,* op. cit., *p. 12.*

Lord Thomas Erskin: Modern Advocate

by Carrol C. Arnold

On January 10, 1750,[1] Thomas Erskine was born in Edinburgh, the youngest son of Henry David, tenth Earl of Buchan. He was fortunate in family, health, and natural intelligence, but unfortunate in being the third son of a "good family" whose patrimony had been wasted by previous generations. His parents had only meager funds for the education of their eldest and second sons and little but affection and guidance for the youngest.[2] Still, the accepted chronicle of Erskine's first fifty-six years is remarkably filled with fortunate coincidences and examples of determination and talent demanding and earning their proper rewards.

Erskine displayed apt scholarship and high spirits as a grammar school student, first in Edinburgh and then in St. Andrews. At the age of thirteen, he briefly attended lectures on science and mathematics at the University of St. Andrews, but could not afford to matriculate. For the same too-familiar reason he was unable to purchase the army commission he coveted; and so, assisted or perhaps pressed by friends and family, he enlisted as a sailor on the man-of-war, the *Tartar*, in the spring of 1764.

Thus entered upon service in His Majesty's forces, Erskine was probably expected to move through the ranks, carving for himself the standard naval career of an impecunious scion of good family. But fortune had better things in store. At eighteen, with a small inheritance from his father, he managed to purchase an ensign's commission in the First Royal Regiment of Foot. At twenty, and still without clear prospects, he foreclosed a common path to personal advancement by marrying for love a girl as poor as he. When his regiment was moved to Minorca for a period of two years, Erskine used his leisure to develop an extensive knowledge of English literary classics. Back in England, at twenty-three and with the rank of lieutenant, he is said to have visited, almost casually, a courtroom presided over by Lord Mansfield. On this day, so the story goes, he was invited to sit beside the distinguished jurist

---

Reprinted from *The Quarterly Journal of Speech* 44 (1958): 17-30 with permission of the Speech Communication Associaton.

[1] J. A. Lovat-Fraser in his *Erskine* (Cambridge, 1932) gives the date as January 10, 1749, Old Style, citing the Erskine family Bible as his source (p. 1). Almost all other sources give the birth year as 1750, though a few change the day to January 21 to accommodate it to the calendar change of 1752.

[2] The very brief biographical sketch here follows Lord James Campbell, *Lives of the Lord Chancellors* (New York, 1874-1881), VIII; Lloyd Paul Stryker, *For the Defense* (New York, 1947); and Lovat-Fraser, *Erskine*.

on the bench and later to dine with him, in consequence of which Erskine fixed his hopes upon a career at the bar. Whatever the genesis of Erskine's interest in the law, Lord Mansfield does appear to have encouraged it, and, receiving approval but virtually no aid from his family, Erskine enrolled as a student at Lincoln's Inn in April 1775. His chief source of support for himself, his wife, and his children was money realized from the sale of his lieutenancy.

A university degree reduced from five to three years the required period of enrollment at an Inn of Court; therefore, since university and law terms could be kept concurrently and since Erskine was entitled by rank to a degree without examination, he also matriculated at Trinity College, Cambridge. During the same period he regularly attended and engaged in debates and harangues at Coachmakers' Hall[3] and elsewhere in London. By thus telescoping his formal education, by living in what was at best embarrassing poverty, and by studying law, literature, and public life assiduously, Thomas Erskine secured an honorary A.M. from Cambridge in June 1778 and was called to the bar the following July. He was twenty-eight. He had been midshipman, army officer, university student, law student, and now he was a barrister without a brief.

Good fortune and evident intelligence brought Erskine from his ordinary station to the prospect of a great career in a single, giant stride. An invitation to dinner gave him the occasion to defend in conversation one Captain Baillie, formerly Lieutenant Governor of Greenwich Hospital but now under suit for libel against those responsible for the institution's support and administration. Captain Baillie, or it may have been the Captain's brother, was also at the dinner, heard Erskine's talk, and next day the young lawyer received his first fee and an invitation to serve as a junior counsellor in Baillie's trial. Erskine did the unexpected. He exercised his counsellor's privilege during the trial, despite his junior status, and delivered to Lord Mansfield and the other judges what Lord Campbell called, "all the circumstances considered, . . . the most wonderful forensic effort of which we have any account in our annals."[4] Baillie was acquitted, and Erskine's argument was credited with contributing greatly to the outcome. Thus the course of his career was settled; he would rise from success to success in pleading until, having once served as Lord Chancellor, he could no longer practice in the courts. Only then would his star slowly begin to set.

It is with the quality of Erskine's forensic pleas that this essay has to do.

---

[3] This hall, on Noble Street, was evidently used as a meeting place by a variety of groups. Just when Erskine participated in debates and harangues here, and on what subjects, I have not discovered. The Protestant Association, formed in 1779, met here and in this hall resolved on May 29, 1780 to accompany its President, Lord George Gordon, to the House of Commons to present the "Protestant Petition." The riots leading to Lord George's indictment for treason and Erskine's defense of him followed. See Walter Thornbury, *Old and New London: A Narrative of Its History, Its People, and Its Places* (London, 1873), I, 363.

[4] *Lives of the Lord Chancellors,* VIII, 29.

His courtroom arguments have been universally praised; but in this century, at least, we are in some danger of submerging his claim to greatness as a forensic *artist* beneath our enthusiasm for the political ideals into which his art breathed new life and vigor in an important but limited series of trials.

There is unquestionable nobility and significance in Erskine's iterated propositions that subversive *intent* must be shown before convictions for treason or libel can be just, and that *juries* must be allowed to judge *both* fact and intent where libel is charged. But others, before and after, spoke on these and equally noble themes without comparably influencing the course of law and without adding to our permanent literature. We shall err, therefore, if we suppose that Erskine's claim to continued attention springs primarily from the political position he took in a few momentous state trials. He was not, after all, a one-man Civil Liberties Union; neither was he a Clarence Darrow irrevocably committed to the cause of the underdog, though Stryker's biography and the foci of other recent studies might seem to imply that he was.[5]

Whether Erskine defended John Stockdale's publication of a pamphlet critical of the Government or prosecuted Thomas Williams for publishing Paine's *Age of Reason,* whether he prosecuted Benjamin Boddington for eloping with his cousin's wife or defended Richard Bingham who had eloped with the wife of Bernard Howard, Erskine's rhetorical artistry gave to each client his fullest, rightful claim to judicial attention and sympathy. It was by art more than by choice of briefs that he served the cause of justice, for in a wide variety of causes he gave full effect to the honorable tradition that if liberty and justice are to be wedded in the courts, each litigant must have the most persuasive representation the limits of fact and law allow. There is, I think, no other English-speaking pleader who, in the service of this tradition, achieved more completely the degree of creative excellence to which Cicero has Crassus allude in his question: "What is so admirable as, that, out of an infinite multitude of men, there should arise a single individual, who can alone, or with only a few others, exert effectually that power that nature has granted to all?"[6]

If we take Erskine's published forensic addresses as a whole, the leading and distinctive quality of his discourse is the congruity of the rhetorical forces

---

[5] Lovat-Fraser's view is expressed thus: "If he had been a great advocate only, he would soon have been forgotten. He is remembered because he was also a resolute champion of liberty, a valiant defender of freedom, and a noble and far-seeing patriot" (p. xi). Most academic investigations have also focused on the treason and libel pleas. See William E. Young, "The Rhetorical Methods of Thomas Erskine," unpublished M.A. thesis (State University of Iowa, 1928); Lloyd Watkins, "Argumentation of Thomas Erskine in the Trial of Thomas Hardy," unpublished M.A. thesis (University of Wisconsin, 1951); and Merrill T. Baker, "Rhetorical Analysis of Thomas Erskine's Courtroom Defenses in Cases Involving Seditious Libel" unpublished Ph.D. thesis (State University of Iowa, 1952). Lawrence R. Rumley's "The Pleas of Thomas Erskine in Selected Trials for Criminal Conversation, 1789-1805," unpublished M.A. thesis (Cornell University, 1951), is the only exploration of Erskine's nonpolitical pleading I know of.

[6] *De Oratore,* trans. J. S. Watson (London, 1881), I. viii.

he loosed in each persuasive effort. The most striking elements in this consonance of matter and manner seem to me to be three: his ability, within a single speech, to direct effective persuasion toward the predispositions of judges and jurors even when these two classes of auditors were differently inclined; the entire harmony of language, thought, and purpose which marks all his pleas; and, above all else, his ability to discover and make inescapable the *public* significance of each case for which he accepted a brief. These, I believe, are the features of pleading which set Erskine apart from the advocates who were his contemporaries and raise his addresses above those of the advocates who have followed. They are features the more striking because they appear in the speeches of one who spoke at a time when much English oratory was cluttered with vestiges of a rhetoric shorn of *inventio* and *dispositio* and burdened on the one hand by digression and ornament and on the other by dull detail.

Henry Roscoe asserted that the care and nicety with which Erskine joined fact, reason, and feeling to central principles of justice was "the most remarkable" of all the qualities that contributed to the success of his addresses. Roscoe continued:

> In every case he proposed a great leading principle to which all his efforts were referable and subsidiary, which ran through the whole of his address, arranging, governing, and elucidating every portion. As the principle thus proposed was founded in truth and justice, whatever might be its application to the particular case, it necessarily gave the whole of his speech an air of honesty and sincerity which a jury could with difficulty resist.[7]

Such centricity in composition has merit in almost any oral discourse but it contributes special force and effect to forensic argument, where facts of human actions and their relations to accepted systems of rules and policies are the bases of judgment. Harry Caplan has used the phrase, "the complete economy of the entire speech," to suggest this degree of centricity required in effective pleading.[8] This is precisely the degree of unity and systematic emphasis Erskine achieved. He created in each address a "complete economy" of thought and feeling in which a principle of truth or of justice became the adductive force and the decision called for became a necessary intermediate step in accepting the still more attractive central proposition.

The broad principles to which the rhetorical resources of Erskine's pleas had unbroken relationship were not usually rules of law. They were propositions about justice or the way to justice, about truth or the way to truth. They focused attention on the ends and methods of social organization.

---

[7] *Lives of Eminent British Lawyers* (London, 1830), p. 381.
[8] *Rhetorica Ad Herennium*, trans. Harry Caplan (London, 1954), 1.xvi.26. Caplan translates his author thus: "Once the Point to Adjudicate is found, the complete economy of the entire speech ought to be directed to it."

If they were also administrative rules or guides to legal interpretation, this was incidental. Characteristically, they suggested strongly but indirectly that judge and juror ought to *make* law, ought to refashion social patterns by *creating* precedents.

There were at least two strong reasons for the favor with which these subtly developed invitations to form or conserve social practices were received: 1) the "Point to Adjudicate," being relatively non-technical and therefore readily comprehensible, was inescapable, for it was central to everything in the entire plea; 2) jurors almost always, and judges very often, actively desire to influence the future, even though they know, intellectually, that they are expected to render decisions according to law and precedent alone. To put the matter another way, Erskine tempted his courtroom "deciders" to become policy makers too, a temptation few men even desire to resist.

Almost all of Erskine's defenses and prosecutions exemplify what has been said of the nature and function of pivotal propositions in his forensic addresses, but the defenses of Bingham[9] and Hadfield[10] furnish convenient illustrations unencumbered by the themes with which Erskine's name has been so exclusively associated in twentieth-century studies.

First to be noticed are the gradual, cautious, but always directly relevant stages by which Erskine advanced toward the principle of justice on which he would rest his plea. In Bingham's behalf the principle to be established was

---

[9] *Howard v Bingham,* Court of King's Bench, February 24, 1794; Lord Kenyon presiding. I have not seen the transcript of this famous trial, if one exists. Reports from *The Times,* February 25, 1794, and other sources such as C. A. Goodrich, *Select British Eloquence* (New York, 1880), pp. 708-713, are the bases for the following summary of facts.

Bernard Howard sought damages against Richard Bingham, charging criminal conversation with his wife, Elizabeth Howard. After four years of marriage to Howard and one child by him, Mrs. Howard eloped with Bingham. At the time of the trial Mrs. Howard was living with Bingham and was pregnant, admittedly by Bingham. The significant complication in the affair was that Mrs. Howard had been engaged to marry Bingham until her parents broke the engagement, determining she must make a better connection by marrying Howard, heir to the Duke of Norfolk. Under the law, Howard was clearly entitled to damages if Bingham had deprived him of "the society and comfort" of his wife. Erskine accepted Bingham's brief as an act of personal friendship.

Though Roscoe (p. 386) says there are "three or four instances" of Erskine's appearing for the defense in such cases, this is the only such plea appearing in any of the standard collections of his speeches or referred to by name in any of the standard biographical sources.

[10] *Rex v Hadfield,* Court of King's Bench, June 26, 1800; Lord Kenyon presiding. The record of the trial appears in *State Trials,* comp. T. B. and Thomas J. Howell (38-40 Geo. III) (London, 1820), XXVII, 1281-1356.

As to the facts, the case was simple, but Erskine's defense made the nature of insanity and the legal responsibilities of the insane the deciding issues. James Hadfield, a wounded veteran of the war with France, discharged a pistol loaded with two slugs at George III, as the king stepped forward in his box to receive the ovation of the audience at a command performance of Colley Cibber's *She Would and She Would Not,* in Drury Lane Theatre. The king was not harmed. Hadfield was dragged from his place in the pit to a room beneath the stage, where he was interrogated before being imprisoned. Trial evidence showed he had methodically procured the pistol, made the slugs, placed himself in a strategic spot in the theatre. Evidence also showed he was subject to fits of insanity.

As traditionally interpreted and as applied by the Crown, the law stipulated that to be unaccountable for crime one must be unable "to form a judgment of that which he proposed to do, of that which he did, and of that which he had designed."

that forced, loveless marriage is prostitution. Through the first two thirds of
the speech the coldness and degradation of the Howards' marriage are hinted
at, asserted, vivified, and finally traced to their source: "the legal prostitution
of parental choice in the teeth of affection." There follows the familiar social
application of the principle: the jury's decision must resoundingly condemn
marriages of arrangement and must teach the aristocracy to abandon practices
so morally reprehensible and so dangerous to established order. The jury was
only too willing to teach the lesson, and *The Times* did Erskine the honor of
copying out his homily.[11]

Erskine's plea for Hadfield was built around a basic principle of justice
too. He stated it in rather negative fashion at the close of the first third of his
address:

> He alone can be emancipated . . . [from criminal responsibility] whose
> reasoning and corresponding conduct, though governed by the
> ordinary dictates of reason, proceed upon something which has no
> foundation or existence.

Lord Kenyon endorsed this proposition and made it a principle of law by
interrupting the presentation of defense evidence to suggest a directed verdict
of acquittal by reason of insanity.[12] But Erskine had not taken the jurist's
mind by storm. His principle was a proposition of law as well as justice, and
he had woven the web of his discourse cautiously. By rhetorical necessity he
had to instruct the judges without seeming to invade the realm of their
privileged judgment, for he was not, as in the Bingham case, addressing
chiefly the less self-conscious jurors.[13]

The argument for Hadfield began conventionally enough. The advocate
praised the caution and generosity of English justice; he protested that the
case was not entirely as the prosecutor, Sir John Mitford, had represented it.

---

[11]Lord Campbell, Goodrich, James Ridgway, Lovat-Fraser, and others report that the jury tried to bring
in a verdict of damages against *Howard* but, being reminded by Lord Kenyon that the adultery was
admitted and Howard stood blameless before the law, granted Howard a trifling £500 where £10,000
would ordinarily be thought low. On the other hand, *The Times*, on the day after the trial, reported that
the plaintiff was awarded £1,000. In either case the award was extraordinarily small.

On February 26, 1794, *The Times* editorialized: "This trial ought to serve as a very serious warning
to parents, how they enforce matrimonial engagements on their children, without the parties having a
mutual inclination for each other."

[12]William C. J. Meredith says in his *Insanity as a Criminal Defense* (Montreal, 1931) that Erskine "upset
the doctrines which until then had generally been recognized as law" by removing from Lord Kenyon's
mind "the hitherto accepted doctrine of Coke and Hale" (pp. 118, 124). Twelve years after, Lord
Mansfield discarded Erskine's and Kenyon's "delusion theory" in favor of the thesis that ability to
distinguish right from wrong was a more precise test of sanity. Nonetheless, Erskine's argument for
his principle is generally credited with having opened the way for more realistic and more merciful
views of criminal insanity. See E. C. Mann, "Mental Responsibility and Diagnosis of Insanity in
Criminal Cases," in *Papers Read Before the Medico-Legal Society of New York*, 3rd Ser. (New York,
1886), p. 480; John C. Bucknill, *Unsoundness of Mind in Relation to Criminal Acts* (Philadelphia,
1856), pp. 21-23.

[13]Erskine's defense of Lord George Gordon offers a close parallel to the plea for Hadfield, both in the
rhetorical problem to be met and in the method of meeting it.

But even here he inserted the first hints of the psychological problem the court must resolve: the prisoner's obligation to British institutions, "if he had the consciousness and reason to reflect upon [them]," was deftly mentioned before the pleader passed on to explore the special difficulties of interpreting the legal responsibilities of the insane under British law. Having thus laid open the inadequacies of existing law, Erskine hastened to reassure his listeners that he had no revolutionary judicial interpretation in view; he would never, he insisted, apply in a criminal case such liberal definitions of insanity as Coke and Hale had applied in civil cases. Who could refuse fair and favorable attention to the case analysis that would follow from such conservative doctrine?[14]

Only after such cautious preparation did Erskine dare to assault directly Mitford's legal orthodoxy:

> If a total deprivation of memory was intended by these great lawyers to be taken in the literal sense of the words . . . [Mitford had so taken it] then no such madness ever existed in the world. It is idiocy alone which places a man in this helpless condition; where from an original mal-organization there is the human frame alone without the human capacity.

By now his argument clearly showed that Hadfield's ability to reason and plan could not be taken as proof of his *general* sanity, but Erskine did not rest content with this factual and theoretical invalidation of traditional views. He set about to justify his own theory of mental disease by illustrating from familiar cases at law the restricted character of insanity in some of its forms. It was thus that he cleared the way for his summary observations that "insane persons frequently appear in the utmost state of ability and composure" and that Hadfield's act was the "immediate, unqualified offspring of the disease." With the minds of the judges prepared by this chain of suggestion, direct refutation, and affirmative reasoning and evidence, Erskine felt secure enough to assert, in the most reserved language, the pivotal judicial principle I have already quoted. He did not neglect to add that the monarch's safety would be better served by justice to Hadfield than by an effort "to stretch the laws" to convict him.

When Erskine at last revealed the principle of justice for which he was arguing, one may suppose judges and jurors found it plausible and sanctified by reason and authority (though no authority had been adduced to support it directly). They received the new doctrine without shock, for the speaker had done nothing abruptly; from first to last his proofs were rendered acceptable by the method of *insinuatio* before being directly argued. Even Sir John Mitford appears to have been convinced by Erskine's argument, once

---

[14]The indirect suggestion that existing law was inadequate to render justice in this case may have had added force with the judges because the idea was familiar. Newspaper and magazine accounts of Hadfield's act and apprehension had represented Hadfield as a victim of mental disease.

evidence had established that Hadfield actually suffered from special and recurring delusions.[15]

Though one of the pleas just reviewed recommends a revolutionary interpretation of the marriage contract and the other extends the principles of civil law to a limited class of criminal cases, their general rhetorical design is the same. The arcs of discourse, as it were, rise gently and suggestively toward the proposition that sustains the plea, then inflect through an application of the principle, finally coming to rest on an aspect of Erskine's favorite topic of persuasion—the decision to be rendered must be that which best promotes the public good.[16]

When one remembers that judges in the late eighteenth century claimed authority to sit in judgment on fact as well as law and that juries were often restless under such judge-imposed restrictions on their powers, Erskine's subtle urgings that *both* classes of auditors assume deliberative authority seem especially well adapted to the sometimes conflicting inclinations of his two audiences. By so carefully clearing the way for his central propositions, he made it easy for even conservative judges to assume lawmaking functions, almost without realizing it. And since he asked that decisions be rendered on principles having considerable public significance, it became easier and seemingly justifiable for jurors to act upon the bases of their common sense and their impressions of society's needs.[17]

In selecting and structuring persuasive materials Erskine exhibited a fuller apprehension of the scope of forensic discourse and of the psychological process we call suggestion than did the rhetorical theorists of his own or

---

[15]When Lord Kenyon stopped the case to suggest acquittal and confinement of Hadfield as an insane person, Mitford observed: "With respect to his sanity immediately preceding and subsequent to the act, I have offered the evidence I had; unquestionably, the circumstances which have now been stated, were perfectly unknown to me." (*State Trials*, XXVII, 1354.) It was Garrow, assistant counsel for the Crown, who suggested that the jury be directed to "state in their verdict the grounds upon which they give it," and thus embodied Erskine's general principle in the verdict formally rendered (*ibid.*, 1356).

[16]Two of Erskine's published forensic addresses are exceptions: his plea for a new trial in the case of William Shipley, Dean of St. Asaph, and his defense of Stockdale. In both, the principle of judgment is asserted very early in the address. The former is an appellate plea and this may account for the difference in method, but why the proposition that the *whole intent* of a work must be the measure of its libelous character should have been announced at the outset of the plea for Stockdale eludes me. Erskine's method here may have allowed doubts to build up in the jurors' minds, for Lord Campbell observes that "it is a curious fact . . . that the jury deliberated two hours before they found a verdict of NOT GUILTY" (*Lives of the Lord Chancellors*, VIII, 80).

[17]Kenyon's almost casual promulgation of a new doctrine on criminal insanity, the jury's burst of sympathy for Elizabeth Howard and Richard Bingham, and Kenyon's frequently moralistic charges to juries in criminal conversation cases are all instances in point. Some writers imply that in the Hadfield case Kenyon was so far carried away by Erskine's supra-legal persuasions that he did not even realize he was radically changing the law by his disposition of the case. His colloquy with Mitford, the prosecutor, at the end of the trial, suggests this. Henry Weihofen, in *Insanity as a Defense of Criminal Law* (New York, 1933), says "the speech of the Counsel which practically put an end to the trial" led Kenyon to render a decision which could not stand for long because it failed to define the test it endorsed (pp. 21-23). Yet Kenyon, formerly a specialist in the law of conveyancing, was not given to looseness in definition and detail.

earlier times.[18] By unifying direct and indirect persuasion in the service of central purposes that reached beyond the confines of existing law and isolated cases, he almost imperceptibly raised his courtroom arguments to that level of thought which Aristotle considered "nobler and more statesmanlike than the branch that is concerned with the everyday relations between man and man."[19] His forensic addresses are, thus, subtle blends of forensic and deliberative elements in which, contrary to the advice of most rhetorical theorists, he extended to all parts of the discourse the method of *insinuatio*. These qualities were rare in eighteenth-century pleading and, I suggest, their presence in Erskine's pleas contributed greatly to the high proportion of unexpectedly favorable verdicts he obtained from juries and judges alike.

Not only did Erskine select and develop subtle arguments clustered closely but unobtrusively about principles of policy and justice, he exercised equal care and purposefulness in selecting the language that was to bear his thought. So far as I have been able to discover, only Sergeant William Draper Best and Sir Robert Dallas, among his contemporaries at law, even resembled him in these respects; and they resembled him but weakly. Certainly among his colleagues there was no other who succeeded in making history, law, and literature while pleading.[20] Best was thought "one of the principal ornaments" of the common law courts, but it was also said of him that, being superficial in both legal and general knowledge, he needed an able "junior" to handle the more formal aspects of difficult cases.[21] In his defense of E. M. Despard against charges of treason, Best had a splendid opportunity to emulate Erskine in thought development and style but fell far short of Erskine's artistry in both respects.[22] Sir Robert Dallas, who, like Erskine, had practiced

---

[18]Hugh Blair's Lecture XXVII sets out the general rule that English lawyers ought not follow too closely Ciceronian and Demosthenian arguments from topics of expediency and public welfare because at the English bar "the field of speaking is limited to precise law and statute" *(Lectures on Rhetoric and Belles Lettres)*. Only in discussing introductions and statements of facts does Blair touch on the value of preparing the minds of listeners by indirect means, and in this he follows the pattern of most classical treatments of "the subtle approach." George Campbell considered neither the uses of indirect argument nor the values of alternative methods of speech organization in his *Philosophy of Rhetoric*.

[19]*The Rhetoric of Aristotle*, trans. Lane Cooper (New York, 1932), I. 1. 1354ᵇ.

[20]Among those with whom and against whom Erskine served as counsel were: *Lloyd Kenyon*, later Lord Chief Justice of King's Bench; *John Scott*, later 1st Earl of Eldon, Chief Justice of Common Pleas, Lord High Chancellor, and dominant member of the Cabinet for most of the period, 1801-1827; *Edward Law*, later 1st Baron Ellenborough, Chief Counsel for Warren Hastings, Chief Justice of King's Bench, member of the All-the-Talents Administration; *Sir John Mitford*, afterwards Speaker of the House of Commons, Lord Chancellor of Ireland, writer on legal subjects; *Spencer Perceval*, Attorney General, Chancellor of the Exchequer and Prime Minister, 1809-1812. Others, who did not assume high public office, included *William Garrow, Edward Bearcroft, John Dunning, Sir Robert Dallas,* and *William Draper Best*, all greatly sought after as pleaders.

[21]"Amicus Curiae" [John Payne Collier], *Criticism on the Bar* (London, 1819), pp. 53, 59.

[22]See "Proceedings in the Trial of Edward Marcus Despard, Esq., for High Treason," in *State Trials*, XXVIII, 345-528. Best was chief counsel for Despard and, in the manner of Erskine, showed that treason should not be adjudged where *overt* acts of treason could not be proved. Having done this, he showed why some considered him a rather unsafe "leader" for he gave equal emphasis to the argument that Despard's intelligence and character were such as to make it impossible to believe he would choose to act as charged. The impossibility of demonstrating the second contention badly weakened the force of the first.

debate at Coachmakers' Hall, could isolate pivotal principles on which to rest a case and could bring circumstances within the vicarious experience of jurors; but beside Erskine's, his style is flat and wanting in vitality.[23] There is certainly little similarity between the bright efficiency of Erskine and Sir John Scott's "detail of facts, mixed up with protestations of his own honesty and good intentions," or Scott's carelessness "as to the structure of his sentences, or the order of his discourse."[24] Bearcroft's verbose circumlocutions clearly mark him as Erskine's inferior. It was with Edward Law that Erskine divided most of the business of the common law courts so long as Law remained in active practice, but Law's dry recitals of facts, his abruptness in argument, and his overly "cautious and calculating spirit"[25] deny him favorable comparison with Erskine.

The fact seems to be that in Erskine's day courtroom pleading was more often than not acute but dull; yet even those pleaders who were not dull usually exhibited a rhetoric less functional and hence less persuasive than Erskine's. James Macintosh's great address in the trial of Jean Peltier is justly famous; but in it Macintosh adopted a grand, discursive manner such as Erskine never used in court. In striking but diffuse fashion the plea for Peltier magnifies the domestic and European need for a free English press, it turns aside for extended condemnation of Bonaparte and the Jacobin spirit, it is threaded with literary allusion, analogy, and quotation, often more impressive than persuasive. The judges and jurors must be excused for finding much of the discourse irrelevant to the actions of Macintosh's client and the specific libel charged against him, so evocative and so generalized are the leading arguments for freedom of political expression.[26]

The Irish advocate John Philpot Curran was seldom if ever dull in pleading, yet Erskine's superiority in invention and style is at once apparent on comparison. Happily, very close comparison is possible, since Curran, with one Bartholomew Hoar, prosecuted a criminal conversation case almost exactly like the famous *Markham v Fawcett* cause in which Erskine appeared. In each instance a clergyman's wife had been seduced by one to whom her husband had extended his personal friendship. In 1802, Erskine sought damages for the Reverend George Markham, against John Fawcett, on such charges; and in 1804, Curran and Hoar represented the Reverend Charles Massy in a similar action against the Marquis of Headfort. Both cases were

---

[23]His plea in the trial of James O'Coigly and others for high treason, in 1798, is an excellent argument; but the style, though clear, seldom reinforces thought with feeling. See *State Trials*, XXVII, 53-90.

[24]Lord Campbell, *Lives of the Lord Chancellors*, "Lord Eldon," VIII, 434.

[25]Archer Polson, *Law and Lawyers* (Philadelphia, 1841), I, 188-192; "Amicus Curiae," p. 10.

[26]Attorney General Spencer Perceval neatly destroyed much of Macintosh's effect by his reply: "We are both agreed as to the illegality of printing and the illegality of publishing libels against those with whom we are at peace: the only question then for you to decide is this, whether or not these publications . . . were or were not published with the intention of vilifying the French Consul?" Lord Ellenborough [Edward Law] paraphrased Perceval in his charge, and the jury "immediately returned a verdict of—GUILTY." *State Trials*, XXVIII, 563-608, 615, 618-619.

tried in county courts, the former in Middlesex and the other in County Clare, Ireland. In each case it was imperative that the prosecutors magnify the offensiveness of the undeniable adultery by impressing upon their hearers that the wrong was the greater for being also a violation of friendship.

Hoar's treatment of this forensic commonplace is fairly represented by the following passage from his opening for Massy:

> The Cornish plunderer, intent on the spoil, callous to every touch of humanity, shrouded in darkness, holds out false lights to the tempest-tost vessel, and lures her and her pilot to that shore upon which she must be lost forever—the rock unseen, the ruffian invisible, and nothing apparent but the treacherous signal of security and repose. So, this prop of the throne, this pillar of the State, this stay of religion, the ornament of the Peerage, this common protector of the people's privileges and of the crown's prerogatives, descends from these high grounds of character to muffle himself in the gloom of his own base and dark designs; to play before the eyes of the deluded wife and the deceived husband the falsest lights of love to the one, and of friendly and hospitable regards to the other, until she is at length dashed upon that hard bosom where her honor and happiness are wrecked and lost forever. The agonized husband beholds the ruin with those sensations of horror which you can better feel than I can describe. Her upon whom he had embarked all his hopes and all his happiness in this life, . . . sunk before his eyes into an abyss of infamy, or if any fragment escape, escaping to solace, to gratify, and to enrich her vile destroyer.[27]

As Snyder says, "the striking parallel . . . with the treachery of the Cornish pirates . . . presents a graphic picture,"[28] but one must also add that the compensable anguish of the husband twice betrayed is enshrouded in words better calculated to sustain the orator's rhythmic flight than to mirror the poignancy of his client's suffering.

Curran's closing plea for the same plaintiff illustrates a similar sacrifice of sharp persuasiveness in favor of embellishment:

> There is another consideration, gentlemen, which, I think, most

---

[27]From the text as published by William L. Snyder, *Great Speeches by Great Lawyers* (New York, 1882), pp. 667-676. Bartholomew Hoar (or Hoare, or Hore) was born in the County of Cork, son of Benjamin Hoar, in 1754. He received the B. A. from the University of Dublin (Trinity College) in 1775, was called to the Irish Bar in 1778, and subsequently became a King's Counsel. For at least part of his active career he resided in Dublin. (I am indebted to Professor Lewis W. Morse, Librarian, Cornell Law School, and to Mr. Arthur Cox of Dublin for this information.) Exhaustive search of records might produce additional data on Hoar, but had he been a pleader of more than ordinary powers references to him would surely be more frequent in standard sources. Had he been an inferior pleader, he would hardly have opened in a case where Curran led the plaintiff's counsel and George Ponsonby led the defense. His address, neither better nor worse than many others of the period, doubtless entered the literature of forensic oratory because Curran and Ponsonby also spoke.
[28]*Ibid.*, p. 668.

imperiously demands even a vindictive award of exemplary damages, and that is the breach of hospitality. To us peculiarly does it belong to avenge the violation of its altar. The hospitality of other countries is a matter of necessity or convention; . . . but the hospitality of an *Irishman* is not the running account of posted and legered [*sic*] courtesies, as in other countries; it springs, like all his qualities, his faults, his virtues, directly from his heart. The heart of an Irishman is by nature bold, and he confides; it is tender, and he loves; it is generous, and he gives; it is social, and he is hospitable. This sacrilegious intruder has profaned the religion of that sacred altar so elevated in our worship, so precious to our devotion; and it is our privilege to avenge the crime. You must either pull down the altar and abolish the worship, or you must preserve its sanctity undebased. There is no alternative between the universal exclusion of all mankind from your threshold, and the most rigorous punishment of him who is admitted and betrays. The defendant has been so trusted, has so betrayed, and you ought to make him a most signal example.[29]

The profusion of religious symbols and the appeal to national pride make it easy for the listener to lose sight of the immediate issue before the court; the Reverend Mr. Massy ceases to be a husband-friend betrayed and becomes an abstraction, an artifact of Irish character and custom. The invocation of deliberative ends is so complete that "the everyday relations between man and man" are almost lost from view.

Erskine had the same argument to make in the Reverend Mr. Markham's behalf, but the manner of its making was profoundly different:

Invited into the house of a friend—received with the open arms of affection, as if the same parents had given them birth and bred them—in this situation this most monstrous and wicked defendant deliberately perpetrated his crime, and, shocking to relate, not only continued the appearances of friendship, after he had violated its most sacred obligations, but continued them as a cloak to the barbarous repetitions of his offence; writing letters of regard, whilst, perhaps, he was the father of the last child, whom his injured friend and companion was embracing and cherishing as his own. What protection can such conduct possibly receive . . . ? A passion for a woman is progressive; it does not, like anger, gain an uncontrolled ascendency in a moment, nor is a modest matron to be seduced in a day. Such a crime, can not, therefore, be committed under the resistless dominion of sudden infirmity; it must be wilfully, and wickedly committed. The defendant could not possibly have incurred the guilt of this adultery without often passing through his mind (for he had the education and principles of a gentleman) the very topics I

---

[29] *Ibid.*, pp. 691-707.

have been insisting upon before you for his condemnation. . . . He
was a year engaged in the pursuit; he resorted repeatedly to his
shameful purpose, and advanced to it at such intervals of time and
distance, as entitle me to say that he determined in cold blood to
enjoy a future and momentary gratification, at the expense of every
principle of honor which is held sacred amongst gentlemen, even
where no laws interpose their obligations or restraints.[30]

Curran and Hoar could not have claimed that their client must doubt the
parentage of a child he had thought his own, and it is true that Headfort
devoted but four months to his nefarious business. But Massy's advocates
might, like Erskine, have focused attention more clearly upon the
deliberateness of the deceit, the trust of the husband for his friend, and the
impossibility of excusing the Marquis on grounds of sudden weakness.[31]
Erskine's development of these standard topics of degree in wrongdoing is
stronger than the developments furnished by either of his Irish
contemporaries because, proceeding with economy and rigid relevancy, he
vividly "furthered the magnification of the crime against his client by creating
a hierarchy of loss: one item after another . . . added to the structure of the
argument until the crime became the worst of its kind and the loss suffered
by Erskine's client, the deepest."[32]

Other ways in which Erskine's art excelled that of his contemporaries are
also illustrated by the passages just quoted. In contrast to the practice of
Curran, Hoar, or Macintosh, Erskine admits to his discourse no allusion that
might draw the mind of a hearer from the quality of the human action he
examines. His language contains scarcely a hint of copy-book polish; yet he
is at great pains that the amplification of his topics shall recreate in the
vicarious experience of each auditor the most acute sensations of his client.
Figures of speech and thought, allusions, quotations—all the beautifying and
evocative resources of language—are cleanly functional; the presence of each
symbol is justified by its contribution to the sum of the advocate's *proof.*

But when Erskine stepped from the bar to the floor of the House of
Commons or, later, delivered his opinions in the House of Lords, it was as if
his wonted unity of thought, harmony of methods, and functionalism in style
had been left among his briefs and law books. In Parliament he cluttered his
speeches with *ad hominem* arguments, sprinkled them with lumbering
quotations from Dr. Johnson, with commentary to match, and only now and

---

[30]From the text as published in J. L. High, *Speeches of Lord Erskine* (Chicago, 1870), 4 vols., IV, 214
238.
[31]George Ponsonby did, in fact, use this topic in behalf of the Marquis, insisting that Mrs. Massy could
not have fallen so swiftly out of love with her husband unless he had, himself, been at fault (Snyder,
p. 690). Curran did not reply directly.
[32]Lawrence R. Rumley, p. 214. This characterization Rumley applies to "every trial which would support
such treatment."
[33]*Select British Eloquence,* p. 635.

then revealed his real powers in a telling proof of expediency or in-
expediency. He who, as Goodrich observed, never digressed in the courtroom
without bringing back from his excursion something important to his central
theme,[33] treated parliamentarians to so many autobiographical semi-
relevancies that he fairly justified the taunt in the suggestion that he be raised
to the title "Baron Ego, of Eye, in the county of Suffolk."[34] The texts of his
legislative addresses are at some points studded with parentheses, those
printers' accommodations to involved constructions and unmanaged
qualifications of thought.

Clearly Erskine was not a brilliant pleader because he possessed some
divine general gift of persuasive speech; had it been so, his deliberative
speaking must surely have been quickened. Though from the beginning he
was able to solve the rhetorical problems of courtroom discourse, he seems
never to have understood fully the ultimate ends and methods of advisory or
occasional speaking. Had he, then, only a special, limited knack? Or had he
studied and learned the art on which his profession depended? One may
speculate, but no clear answer is to be found.

Quite possibly poverty and ambition drove the highly intelligent Erskine
to induce the elements of the pleader's art from independent observation and
study.[35] Since he was already successful in his profession when he entered
Parliament, he was probably not similarly motivated to analyze the new
rhetorical problems that confronted him there, after 1783. Almost certainly,
too, legislation interested him less than advocacy.

If we were to judge from his deliberative oratory alone, we might
suppose him a child of the tradition that saw rhetoric as style or as delivery,
but his forensic principles could never have been derived from such sources.
The rhetorical works published in England during the period of his formal
and self-education offered little advice that would make for the qualities of
oratory he displayed in the courtroom.[36] It would be far easier to believe that
his achievements at the bar drew some guidance from that branch of
rhetorical theory which, during his earlier years, was beginning to move "out
of the intellectual vacuum in which Ward [and others] had kept it,
and . . . into line with contemporary developments in psychology,
epistemology, and literary criticism."[37]

[34]*Lives of the Lord Chancellors*, VIII, 307.
[35]One cannot assume that his legal study provided much experience in argumentation, for disputations
and moots were no longer generally practiced at the Inns of Court. See W. Herbert, *Antiquities of the
Inns of Court and Chancery* (London, 1804), pp. 180-181; and R. M. Jackson, *The Machinery of
Justice in England*, 2nd ed. (Cambridge, 1953), pp. 209-210. His participation in debates at
Coachmakers' Hall and elsewhere may, of course, have supplied enlightening experience.
[36]The list of leading English works on rhetoric published between his eleventh and twenty-fifth years
includes: Burgh's *Art of Speaking* (1761), Sheridan's *Lectures on Elocution* (1762), Leland's
Dissertation on the Principles of Human Eloquence (1764), Rice's *Introduction to the Art of Reading
with Energy and Propriety* (1765), Gibbons' *Rhetoric, or a View of its Principal Tropes and Figures*
(1767), Enfield's *The Speaker* (1774), Steele's *Prosodia Rationalis* (1775), Cockin's *The Art of
Delivering Written Language* (1775).
[37]Douglas Ehninger, "John Ward and His Rhetoric," *Speech Monographs*, XVIII (March 1951), 16.

Erskine's forensic practice might have derived from thoughtful application of the theoretical doctrines published by George Campbell in his *Philosophy of Rhetoric*, particularly those found in Book I, Chapters VII through IX.[38] There is no evidence that Erskine read this book by a fellow Scotsman, but Campbell stated the psychological premise that underlay all of Erskine's distinctive methods when he wrote, "It must be allowed there are certain principles in our nature, which, when properly addressed and managed, give no inconsiderable aid to reason in prompting belief."[39] Again, Campbell's concern with rhetorical adaptation to listeners, collectively and particularly, is an emphasis remarkably consistent with Erskine's principles of practice.

But to try to erect an hypothesis connecting Erskine's art with Campbell's body of theory would certainly strain the scattered bits of circumstantial evidence. Campbell's *Philosophy* was, after all, only one of a number of signs of rising interest in psychological principles, including those of communication. An alert and ambitious barrister-in-training, with even a general impression of the scientific and critical speculations emanating from his native Edinburgh, might well see for himself how completely the principles of persuasion derive from the natures of men in general and men in particular. The supposition that Erskine formulated his principles of pleading independently of contemporary theory and practice is strengthened by the fact that he extended the range of forensic thought and feeling considerably beyond the bounds Blair or Campbell prescribed.[40] At the same time, he was more rigid than they or his more systematically educated fellow barristers in measuring both substance and language by the test of *immediate* relevance.

Thus, the sources of Erskine's principles of advocacy remain obscure and uncertain; but whatever their derivation, his practice was distinctive. I have suggested as the essence of his forensic art the convergence of all the forces of discourse—as though this were their nature and not the orator's design—toward a clear and expedient rule for decision in a given case. In his forensic addresses there are no digressions inspired by models of another age or by a rhetoric confused with poetic. There are no vagrant thoughts; even vagrant words are few, considering the habits of the age. There is much that is striking and beautiful but it is as *proof*, not as formula, that style arrests or excites: consider the idyl on conjugal love in the plea for Bingham or the description of Hadfield's battle wounds.[41] Even when he rose to deliver his

---

[38] The work was published in 1776, while Erskine was studying law.

[39] *Philosophy of Rhetoric* (New York, 1841), p. 77.

[40] Blair's conception of the range of forensic speaking has been cited. Campbell devotes so little attention to this form of persuasion that it seems fair to assume he had no quarrel with restrictive definitions that confined the pleader to questions of fact and legal interpretation.

[41] It is worth noting that anthologists have singled out few passages from Erskine's forensic addresses as beautiful when considered apart from their context. The "Indian Chief" segment of his defense of Stockdale is such a passage, but it is the only one Goodrich was moved to call "beautiful in itself," though he published and annotated nine of Erskine's courtroom speeches.

first plea, for Captain Baillie, on November 24, 1778, Erskine gave notice that his was a fresh, broad-gauged theory of argument in which the structuring of listeners' predispositions, perceptions, and emotional energies was the end of all persuasive effort. His artistic command over the complex ideational and motivational resources of advocacy came to its full development in the last decade of the eighteenth century and reached its zenith, I believe, in the later treason and libel trials, in his defense of Bingham, and in his defense of Hadfield.

Almost without exception, Thomas Erskine's speeches at the bar illustrate that the best persuasion is unitary, that forensic rhetoric is neither reason on a work detail nor parade-ground polish on review. His rhetoric was an artistic integration of reason, suggestion, and functional symbols, organized to form a complete and dynamic economy. In this he was, and remains, a thoroughly modern practitioner of the art of rhetoric—though in one of its branches only. In the manner of the classical forensic orator, he perceived that, "There is indeed no cause in which the point that falls under dispute is considered with reference to the parties to the suit and not from arguments relating to questions in general."[42] In the modern manner he applied the method of *insinuatio*, "the subtle approach," in all the parts of his discourses. Again, exhibiting his modernity, he found the topics of forensic discourse not only in places having reference to particular and general questions of fact and justice, but in those reaches of popular thought where questions of expedient public policy are found and resolved. Finally, more than the ancients or his contemporaries, he devoted his rhetorical efforts to the end of evoking *and controlling* strongly motivated reason through rigorously organized and sharply relevant substance and symbols.

Immediate influence, not beauty or profundity, was Lord Erskine's goal in the courtroom; in consequence, he achieved all three. In the process he left his mark on Anglo-American law, advanced the general cause of political liberty, and, at so unlikely a place as the counsel's bench, he enlarged the store of imaginative literature in the English language. His life of influence through consummate art closed on February 7, 1806, when he accepted the seals of the Lord Chancellor's office and thereby closed his career as an advocate. He died on November 17, 1823. The intervening years were years of slow but steady decline, for the artist was denied the practice of his special, single art. His culture was denied the further contributions to law, politics, and literature that the challenge of courtroom advocacy might have inspired in Lord Thomas Erskine, Baron of Restormel Castle, whose motto was, "Trial by Jury."

---

[42]Cicero, *De Oratore*, II.xxxi.

"War Message," December 8, 1941: An Approach To Language

by Hermann G. Stelzner

I

Two recent books[1] are responses to an uneasiness with much rhetorical criticism which has appeared in print. In raising questions the authors hope to stimulate more meaningful and insightful analyses of rhetorical activities and processes. They goad critics to experiment, to describe and to evaluate in ways heretofore little practiced. Both authors ask that "beginnings" be made.

Reviewers have pointed to difficulties. Arnold's review of Nichols' work asks for a sample of the criticism "I am exhorted to produce. . . ." He feels that Nichols "does not illustrate in pointed ways how criticism may, in practice, resolve the . . . issues raised. . . ."[2] Responding to Black's work, Ehninger agrees with Black's assessment of much criticism but believes Black's alternatives "are not worked out in enough detail to be viable." The "ingredients are not developed into anything approaching a critical method" nor are "characteristics and possibilities . . . systematized into a program of attack and procedure which the critic . . . may apply."[3] Yet neither Black nor Nichols set out to develop systems. Black observes:

> We have not evolved any system of rhetorical criticism, but only, at best, an orientation to it. An orientation, together with taste and intelligence, is all that a critic needs. If his criticism is fruitful, he may end with a system, but he should not, in our present state of knowledge, begin with one. We simply do not know enough yet about rhetorical discourse to place our faith in systems, and it is only through imaginative criticism that we are likely to learn more.[4]

Concluding her remarks on I. A. Richards, Nichols states:

> One of the most useful things about I. A. Richards . . . is his demonstration of the possibility of finding an orderly

Reprinted from *Speech Monographs* 33 (1966), with permission of the Speech Communication Association.

[1] Marie Hochmuth Nichols, *Rhetoric and Criticism* (Baton Rouge, La., 1963); Edwin Black, *Rhetorical Criticism* (New York, 1965).
[2] Carroll C. Arnold, review of *Rhetoric and Criticism* in *Southern Speech Journal*, XXX (Fall 1964), 62.
[3] Douglas Ehninger, "Rhetoric and the Critic," *Western Speech*, XXIX (Fall 1965), 231.
[4] Black, p. 177.

methodology. . . . I do not mean that Richards' method should be adopted. . . . What I do mean is that we also should be looking for an orderly methodology.[5]

The thrust of Nichols' and Black's analyses is macrocosmic. Most criticism, Black states, is limited to "an estimate of the historically factual effects of the discourse on its relatively immediate audience."[6] He argues for enlargement, for an "interpretation of the discourse that realizes all that is in it and that aims 'to see the object as it really is'. . . ."[7]

A rhetorical act is both rich and complex. To probe it fully requires all the critical postures, approaches, and talents described by Stanley Hyman in his portrait of an "ideal" critic.[8] Full disclosure is the ideal.

The posture of this study is microcosmic. We center on the language of Franklin D. Roosevelt's "War Message" to Congress, December 8, 1941. The analysis is motivated by the treatment of language found in much traditional criticism. Often critics fragment discourse, investigate chosen samples of language as independent variables and draw conclusions. One analyst, after studying Stevenson's 1952 campaign addresses, reported that Stevenson had a "middle" style, "neither plain nor grand."[9] To the traditional procedures, Nichols has responded: "Hoary with age. . . ."[10] She believes that the usual approaches have failed to treat language adequately: "Year after year, language, if it is handled at all, gets a few words about rhetorical questions, antithesis, and metaphors. . . ."[11] Ehninger's description of existing criticism includes like comments:

> Instead of describing what is going on in a discourse as it works to achieve its ends, they [critics] focus on how the discourse came into being, on the circumstances under which it was delivered, and on the reactions or results it produced. Analysis of the speech itself not only is scanted, but to the extent that it is present it tends to consist of a classification of certain grosser properties, cast under the heads of the traditional modes and canons—to be a mechanical accounting or summing up of how well the speech fits an *a priori* mold.[12]

The present approach to Franklin D. Roosevelt's "War Message" is "topographical." The speech is the "particular place" and, to assess the configurations of its language, its "roads," "rivers," "cities," "lakes," and "relief" are examined. To shift the figure, fragments of language are not selected from the speech and regarded as the dominant lights, independent

[5] Nichols, pp. 106-107.
[6] Black, p. 48.
[7] *Ibid.*
[8] Stanley Edgar Hyman, *The Armed Vision* (New York, 1955), pp. 386-391.
[9] Nichols, p. 107.
[10] *Ibid.*
[11] *Ibid.*
[12] Ehninger, p. 230.

and autonomous. The concern is with the constellation, not the major stars alone. Interest centers on the order, movement, meanings, and interrelations of the language; the object is to discover not only what goes on, but how it goes on. The aim is full disclosure.

We explicate. We try, inductively, a kind of "statistical inspection"[13] to find out what goes on and how the "on-going" is generated. We note development *"from what through what to what,"*[14] shifting from grammar to syntax to diction to logic to rhythm to figure or whatever, when the speech itself demands a shift to account for the totality of tensions in the language. Speeches, including those of the expository genre, are more than collections of statements. Explicating is more than paraphrasing. It is "the e*xplicit*ation of the implicit."[15] We explore the lexical possibilities of words and word combinations. As a way of demonstrating what is going on in a speech, explication is analogous to Hyman's description of Burke's mode: "Use All There Is to Use," which means "the rather disorganized organizing principle of investigating every possible line of significance."[16]

The speech provides the clues. The available drafts of Roosevelt's address have been examined and, when variations in the drafts bear on the analysis, we cite them.[17] However, the primary purpose is not to trace the *development* of the "War Message" of December 8, 1941. How the speech *is*, not how it came to be, is the concern.

We do not suggest that Roosevelt himself consciously structured the relationships we explore and evaluate. It "cannot be said too often that a poet does not fully know what is the poem he is writing until he has written it"[18] applies to all composition. Burke argues it is not until *"after the completion of the work"*[19] that interrelationships in it can be analyzed; analysis of these involves both "quantitative and qualitative considerations":[20]

> Now, the work of every writer contains a set of implicit equations. ... And though he be perfectly conscious of the act of writing, ... he cannot possibly be conscious of the interrelationships among all these equations. ... The motivation out of which he writes is synonymous with the structural way in which he puts events and values together when he writes; and however consciously he may go about such

[13]Kenneth Burke, *The Philosophy of Literary Form* (New York, 1957), p. 59; on p. 75 Burke refers to the examination as an "inductive inspection."

[14]*Ibid.*, p. 60; italics his.

[15]W. K. Wimsatt, Jr., *The Verbal Icon* (Lexington, Ky., 1954), p. 249; italics his.

[16]Hyman, p. 390.

[17]The Franklin D. Roosevelt Library, Hyde Park, New York, has four drafts of this message. They were examined and are referred to by number. Changes from draft to draft are not extensive. Grace Tully, Roosevelt's secretary, indicates that the address was delivered in almost the identical form in which it was originally dictated to her by the President. See Grace Tully, *F. D. R., My Boss* (New York, 1949), p. 256.

[18]C. Day Lewis, *The Poetic Image* (London, 1947), p. 71.

[19]Burke, p. 18; italics his.

[20]*Ibid.*, p. 59.

work, there is a kind of generalization about these interrelations that he could not have been conscious of, since the generalization could be made by the kind of inspection that is possible only *after the completion* of the work.[21]

Because this analysis is limited to the language of a single speech, we cannot generalize from it to "style." The inability to generalize from a single example presents the reverse of a difficulty which reviewers saw in Nichols' and Black's macrocosmic postures: the difficulty of implementation. And microscopic analysis, no matter how successful, does not shed much light on discourse in general. Yet William E. Leuchtenburg's insightful essay, "The New Deal and the Analogue of War,"[22] offers possibilities for extending the analysis undertaken in these pages. He points out that much New Deal policy was accomplished through the figure of war. Roosevelt himself often applied the topic, "war," to social and economic problems. In a sense his December 8, 1941 "War Message" was but another treatment of that topic. Scrutiny of a number of his addresses might provide insights into his use of language, his "style," on the topic "war"; generalization would then be possible. Speaking to the point of generalization, Burke states that it is first necessary to trace down the "interrelationships as revealed by the objective structure of the book itself":

> The first step . . . requires us to get our equations inductively, by tracing down the interrelationships as revealed by the objective structure of the book itself. [Eventually one may] . . . offer 'generalizations atop generalizations' whereby different modes of concrete imagery may be classed together. That is, one book may give us 'into the night' imagery; another 'to the bottom of the sea' imagery; another the 'apoplectic' imagery . . . and we may propose some over-all category . . . that would justify us in classing all these works together on the basis of a common strategy despite differences in concrete imagery.[23]

The objective structure of a speech, as well as of a book, is a composite of subtly balanced meanings; all language is weighted toward something, hence away from something; for something, hence opposed to something. A "statistical inspection" of a speech reveals what the speaker talked about, and from that knowledge the balance of his meanings can be established. For example, in the "War Message" of December 8, 1941 "time" is central to Roosevelt's discussion. He uses the future and the past, even as he speaks in, about, and to the present. Future is balanced against Past; these are poles of a continuum along which "goods" and their opposites balance antithetically.

---

[21] *Ibid.*, p. 18; italics his.
[22] William E. Leuchtenburg, "The New Deal and the Analogue of War," in *Change and Continuity in Twentieth-Century America,* ed. John Braeman (Columbus, Ohio, 1964), pp. 81-143.
[23] Burke, p. 59.

The past is given negative valence in Roosevelt's address; and in like manner other concepts, entities, and conditions are antithetically balanced. The balanced meanings are listed below. Those on the left have "positive" quality; those on the right are "negative." *Successive* balances emerge as the speech advances and they, hence, constitute a structural pattern according to which analysis of the address may proceed.

Future time	Past time
God	"Devil"
United States	Japan
government	government
military	military
people	people
Absence of Danger	Presence of Danger
(presence of peace)	(absence of peace)
International involvement	Isolationistic non-involvement
"I" of address	Non-"I"[24]

An arrangement of the balanced meanings of an address, such as the arrangement just set forth, describes the relationships of the topics discussed by the speaker; the arrangement does not, however, explicate these relationships. There remains the task of revealing not only the weight of each pole in a particular balance of meaning but how the weighting, hence relationship, was rhetorically achieved.

We may turn now to the text of Roosevelt's address:

WAR MESSAGE[25]

1   Yesterday, December 7, 1941—a date which will live in infamy—the United
2 States of America was suddenly and deliberately attacked by naval and air forces of
3 the Empire of Japan.
4   The United States was at peace with that nation and, at the solicitation of
5 Japan, was still in conversation with its Government and its Emperor looking toward
6 the maintenance of peace in the Pacific.
7   Indeed, one hour after Japanese air squadrons had commenced bombing in the
8 American island of Oahu, the Japanese Ambassador to the United States and his colleague
9 delivered to our Secretary of State a formal reply to a recent American message. And
10 while this reply stated that it seemed useless to continue the existing diplomatic
11 negotiations, it contained no threat or hint of war or of armed attack.
12   It will be recorded that the distance of Hawaii from Japan makes it obvious that
13 the attack was deliberately planned many days or even weeks ago. During the inter-
14 vening time the Japanese Government has deliberately sought to deceive the United
15 States by false statements and expressions of hope for continued peace.

---

[24] In a speech situation, the speaker, the "I," is never wholly absent. Listeners may respond to his voice and/or his physical presence even when he handles materials largely denotative and expository in character. The continuum of "presence-absence" is one of convenience, establishing poles and making possible relative weighting.

[25] This text is the transcript of the message as delivered. Text from Franklin D. Roosevelt Library, Hyde Park, New York.

16   The attack yesterday on the Hawaiian Islands has caused severe damage to American
17 naval and military forces. I regret to tell you that very many American lives have
18 been lost. In addition American ships have been reported torpedoed on the high seas
19 between San Francisco and Honolulu.
20   Yesterday the Japanese Government also launched an attack against Malaya.
21   Last night Japanese forces attacked Hong Kong.
22   Last night Japanese forces attacked Guam.
23   Last night Japanese forces attacked the Philippine Islands.
24   Last night the Japanese attacked Wake Island.
25   And this morning the Japanese attacked Midway Island.
26   Japan has, therefore, undertaken a surprise offensive extending throughout the
27 Pacific area. The facts of yesterday and today speak for themselves. The people of
28 the United States have already formed their opinions and well understand the impli-
29 cations to the very life and safety of our nation.
30   As Commander-in-Chief of the Army and Navy I have directed that all measures
31 be taken for our defense. But always will our whole nation remember the character
32 of the onslaught against us.
33   No matter how long it may take us to overcome this premeditated invasion, the
34 American people in their righteous might will win through to absolute victory.
35   I believe that I interpret the will of the Congress and of the people when I
36 assert that we will not only defend ourselves to the uttermost but will make it
37 very certain that this form of treachery shall never again endanger us.
38   Hostilities exist. There is no blinking at the fact that our people, our
39 territory and our interests are in grave danger.
40   With confidence in our armed forces, with the unbounding determination of our
41 people, we will gain the inevitable triumph—so help us God.
42   I ask that the Congress declare that since the unprovoked and dastardly
43 attack by Japan on Sunday, December 7, 1941, a state of war has existed between the
44 United States and the Japanese Empire.

II

The man who writes or speaks of an anticipated war . . . must select his material out of the past and the present."[26] He is committed to speak in some fashion about history. On December 7, 1941, history was made suddenly and directly. The equally direct, initial, verbal response (1-3) parallels the historical facts which made statement necessary. Moreover, the mass media had described fully the international activities of December 7, 1941, and listeners could easily fit the speaker's initial statement into a larger and ordered background.

"Yesterday" quickly anchors the address to the immediate historical past, to the events of December seventh. It suggests that the speaker does not intend to go deeply into the past or to discuss it as part of the recommendations he will ultimately make.[27] The meaning of the immediate past was

[26]Burke, p. 203.
[27]Tully, p. 256, reports that when the message was being prepared Roosevelt called Secretary of State Cordell Hull to the White House to examine a draft. "The Secretary brought with him an alternative message drafted by Sumner Welles, longer and more comprehensive in its review of the circumstances leading to the state of war. It was rejected by the Boss. . . ."

clearly less important than the present and the future. This placement of yesterday contributes to the overall past-present-future structure of the address and to the connotative values of "time" in it. The direct announcement (1-3) ruptures "yesterday," a time of reasonable stability and peace. That mind which wished to wander even fleetingly back over time, is restrained and controlled by the appositive, December 7, 1941. The speaker acknowledges that his listeners understood (27-29) the "leisure," the peaceful "timelessness" of yesterday had gone; but he impresses the point upon them.

The appositive, December 7, 1941, not only defines the specific yesterday among the potentially many. It establishes the date, which for historical purposes is more important than the day, Sunday, here omitted. The personal value judgment—"a date which will live in infamy"—colors the appositive and introduces the future into the discussion. Introduced as an "aside," the future already acts, offering judgments about the present. The matter is carefully handled. The speaker did not say: the date will live in infamy. A shift from the indefinite to the definite article and the excision of the relative pronoun *which* makes the speaker's personal judgment categorical, forcing on the historical future a value judgment which only the historical future can rightfully make.

That a sense of and a sensitivity to history operates[28] can be seen by testing alternatives: *Yesterday, a day which will live in infamy.* . . . Here the appositive is omitted, a possibility because it was unlikely that any member of the immediate audience would have been unaware of the date. History, however, catalogues dates, not yesterdays or days; the date is supplied. Omitting the appositive also makes necessary the revision of "a date which" to "a day which"; the former is somewhat more precise and sustains better the historical overtones of the initial announcement (1-3). Thus, the first twelve words of Roosevelt's address join past and future; the present is represented by speaker and audience. And the immediate present—unsettled, disrupted, and anxiety-provoking—is somewhat stabilized by the past-future continuum which provides a sense of continuity. In the speaker's judgmental aside, the future renders a verdict on present activities which favors us; implicatively the future is on "our side."

The passive voice of the initial announcement makes possible some specific relationships between time, the actors in time, and the judgmental aside about the time. Though the statement's subject is the naval and air forces of the Empire of Japan, in the passive voice the subject becomes a marginal, omissible part of the sentence and its sense. The speaker could have said: . . . *the United States of America was suddenly and deliberately attacked.* But as delivered, the first statement treats the Japanese Empire as "marginal,"

---

[28]Roosevelt "regarded history as an imposing drama and himself as a conspicuous actor. Again and again he carefully staged a historic scene: as when, going before Congress on December 8, 1941 to call for a recognition of war with Japan, he took pains to see that Mrs. Woodrow Wilson accompanied Mrs. Roosevelt to the Capitol, thus linking the First and Second World Wars." Allan Nevins, "The Place of Franklin D. Roosevelt in History," *American Heritage*, XVII (June 1966), 12.

subordinate. The passive emphasizes the United States as receiver of the action on a specific date, a day of peace until the attack which was infamous in character. The interrelationship of the three allows the immediate audience and history to record these facts. The initial statement might have been active: *Yesterday, December 7, 1941, a date which will live in infamy, naval and air forces of the Empire of Japan suddenly and deliberately attacked the United States.* Not only would the Japanese Empire have become central and active, but the United States would have been removed from its relationship to time. Yet time is essential to the well-being of the country. Past time treated her badly; future time (33-34, 40-41) will heal her wounds.

Even as yesterday was ruptured, the formal, settled, and trusted diplomatic conventions (4-6) were in process. These, too, will be broken (9-15) as the speaker particularizes some of the specific details in the deliberations. The formal and elevated diplomatic language describes. "Nation" (4) is more formal and concrete than a possible alternative, *country*. "Solicitation" (4) is more formal than *request*, and "conversation" (5) is more formal than *discussion* or *conference*. Consistent with the formality of the language is its loose, alliterative quality, more pronounced here than in any section of the address. "Peace" (4, 6) opens and closes the section, its sound sense somewhat reinforced by a weak alliterative echo: "Pacific." Between these points, "nation," "solicitation," "conversation" occur in rapid order; "maintenance," modifies the pattern by introducing a different, though not wholly dissimilar, sound tension.

Time remains central to the development. "The United States was at peace"[29]—past, "still in conversation"—present, "looking toward the maintenance"—future. The actors in the drama are polarized. Responding to a Japanese "solicitation," we were still concerned with tomorrow, even as they were not. The formal, diplomatic language (4-6) symbolizes a mask behind which duplicity is hidden. The duplicity, one dimension of a key term, "infamous" (1), is woven into the texture of the address. For example, the close relationship of "yesterday" (1, 16, 20) to the repeated "deliberately" (2, 13, 14) intensifies and supports the duplicity or infamy. The formal language (4-6) foreshadows the recital of specific events (7-11).

"Indeed," injecting emphasis and force, begins the recitation and colors the neutrality of formal, diplomatic language. Not *yet, still, but*, nor *however* would have functioned as well to introduce the formal, but false, overtures of the Japanese. "Indeed" imprints a reaction of the individual "I" on the yet-to-be-stated particulars. Moreover, "indeed" gains force and support from the

---

[29] In drafts I, II, and III the line reads: "The United States was at the moment at peace. . . ." The "at the moment" phrase emphasizes time unnecessarily; it contributes little to clarity or sense, and its excision is merited. Further, its excision diminishes the possibility of the immediate listeners' setting up the balance: was at the moment—is at this moment. "At this moment" (i.e., the moment of the address) the United States was in practical terms at war. Yet the President was speaking formally to the Congress to whom the legal right formally to declare war belonged. "At this moment" we were "legally" still at peace. Excision of "at the moment" diminished the possibility of a mistaken response by either the Congressional or the general audience.

earlier "yesterday," "infamy," "deliberately," "at peace," "still in conversation," and "maintenance of peace." Following the expletive, the speaker says "one hour after" (7), not merely *after*. "One hour after" makes time concrete, supports the emotional dimensions of "indeed," and forecasts the brazen, formal action of the Japanese Ambassador and the duplicity behind his formality. Also supporting duplicity is a subdued temporal pattern (7-11): after Japanese air squadrons attacked—past, the Ambassador delivers his reply—present, concerning *future* relationships.

"Japanese air squadrons" (7) were the instruments of attack. The phrase might have been rendered: *after the Japanese air force* or *after Japanese air forces*. These alternatives parallel better the first reference to the Japanese military (2); but therein lies a weakness. The modified repetition provides some variety. More important is the matter of image. *Air force* and *air forces* denote and connote mass, a large quantity which blankets a sky. Such a mass moves, but in droning and lumbering fashion. "Air squadrons" is a sharper, definable form of the force, as an image in the mind's eye. The image is of small groups, of well-defined patterns in the total mass, of tightly knit units sweeping in and out over the target.

"Air squadrons" is quantitative, definitive, and repetitive. To the extent that squadrons are patterns, the image presents formal patterns inflicting damage. Formal patterns are the enemy: of the past—"one hour after" (7), as well as the near present—"the Japanese Ambassador . . . delivered" (8-9). The formality of pattern connoted by "Japanese air squadrons" is also explicitly denoted of the Ambassador's act; he delivers a "formal reply" (9), which is contrasted to a slightly less formal "American message" (9). Had the description been of an *American note,* it would have been overly informal. Slightly more formal and rigid than "our Secretary of State" (9) is "the Japanese Ambassador" (8). If there is in these lines a heightened sense of the "formal" and if formality marks the enemy, all formality becomes symbolic—a mask—for duplicity and infamy. The closed, distant, difficult-to-read "formal" opposes the somewhat easier-to-read, open "informality." Such suggestion is consistent with the Western, especially American, stereotype of the Orient and Oriental, *circa* 1941. Duplicity masked by formality is thus further intensified. On first glance the construction of line 11[30] appears anti-climactic. "War" (11) is more encompassing and potentially more dangerous than "armed attack." However, "war" connotes a formal, open declaration of conflict. The Japanese dispensed with that formality, favoring "armed attack," an action outside the conventions of diplomacy.

Thus far no objective evidence has been offered to support the charge of duplicity. The speaker has been reporting diplomatic relationships (4-6) which

---

[30]In draft II lines 10-11 read: "This reply contained a statement that it seemed useless to continue the diplomatic negotiations, but it contained no threat nor hint of war or of armed attack." Drafts III and IV are consistent with the final text (pp. 121-122). The draft II version is a compound sentence and fails to stress the "no threat nor hint of war. . . ." The revision, a dependent-independent arrangement, emphasizes the "no threat nor hint of war. . . ." It emphasizes duplicity.

the listeners themselves cannot verify; they are dependent upon him. But the shift is now to a geographical relationship (12) which supports the charge. "It will be recorded. ..." By whom? The immediate audience certainly, but the historical audience as well. The verb "record" alters the speaker's stance and the passive "will be recorded" his perspective. The speaker's verb refers to, points to, the intellectual activity of man. Together, in concert, the speaker and the listeners function as detached observers—they measure mileage—and as commentators. "Makes it obvious" (12) is a phrase which befits such activity—of seeing, of reasoning, of understanding. The passive allows the evidence to be offered in dependent clauses, which contain the signs upon which the conclusion depends; it provides the "distance" necessary to de-tached, intellectual analysis. All the signs, and especially the final, objective, mileage sign, which is positioned nearest the conclusion which all signs support, contribute to one judgement: infamous duplicity. Finally, "the distance of Hawaii from Japan" (12), a particular sign, is embedded in a sentence which itself spans syntactical distance.

The passive construction makes possible analysis of events which are outside the direct experience of the speaker. Events of the more immediate past (14-15) are handled differently; they are not in dependent clauses and the subject of detached, intellectual analysis. Of these events, the speaker has direct knowledge, and he shifts to the active voice. Japan acts. The language which responds is categorical and conclusive: "deliberately sought to deceive the United States by false statements and expressions of hope ..." (14-15). Was the deception successful? The ambiguous "sought" leaves the question open, even as the speaker's emphasis on Japan's deliberateness and falsity tend to forestall the asking of it.

As further details are enumerated, time shifts slightly in importance. In "the attack yesterday" (16), the act is more important than the time. The emphasis on time could have been maintained: *yesterday's attack*. The new arrangement is less emphatic. The shift in emphasis does not however alter the basic time-act or act-time relationship. A legitimate alternative would have considerably weakened, if not broken, it: *the attack on the Hawaiian Islands yesterday. ...*

From the description the personal "I" (17) emerges to link the speaker with the "blackest" event yet—the specific human tragedy. Both the "I" and the tragedy gain stature from the relationship. Had the "I" chosen a compound sentence, he could have avoided announcing the loss of life: *the attack ... caused ... damage to ... forces and very many American lives have been lost.* Or he might have said simply: *Very many American lives have been lost.* These choices diminish both the ethical posture of the "I" and the dignity of the men who lost their lives. The "I" reveals (17-18), explicitly and implicitly, something of his regard for life—he separates it from the materials of war—and of his concept of duty, as a human being and as President and Commander-in-Chief. He demonstrates his understanding of and his respect for the conventions of tragic announcement. Moreover, he emerges "to tell" (17) his listeners. The direct, common verb suggests closeness—he to them and they to him. A close relationship must exist between the bearer and the receivers of tragic tidings for the verb "tell" to operate. When there is distance the tendency is toward formality, neutrality, and elevation: to *inform*, to *report*, or to *announce*.

"In addition" (18) adds still another detail. Is it of equal, more, or less importance than others? That depends upon the reaction of the listener to the total configuration. But the speaker by his placement of it reveals his assessment of its importance. Japanese submarines have approached the United States; they act not at far-off Hawaii, but nearer home. For an already upset nation the news is serious and distressing. The distress is minimized somewhat by placing it following the announcement of the loss of life, which absorbed most, if not all, emotional energies. The statement which follows the news helps to minimize the danger from the submarines. Attention and concern are diverted by the quick, crisp movement to Malaya (20)—about as far as danger could be removed.

Additional forces further diminish the submarine threat; distance is achieved by having the ships torpedoed on the high seas between San Francisco and Honolulu. The language moves danger "away from" the shores of the United States. The proper nouns, San Francisco and Honolulu (19), are necessary to the overall effect. Let the speaker say: *In addition, American ships have been reported torpedoed on the high seas.* Responses become: Where? Everywhere? Close to the United States? How close? Distant? How distant? The proper nouns meet some of the questions. Where? On a direct path between San Francisco and Honolulu. One can almost see it on the wall map of the mind—the narrow, well-defined shipping route. Close? How close? Ambiguously the image suggests movement *away from*. One may speculate on the range of possible responses had the speaker said, *on the high seas between Honolulu and San Francisco,* or merely *on the high seas.*

The choice and arrangement of the proper nouns diminish danger; a vague term in the same sentence (18-19) functions similarly. "Have been reported torpedoed. . . ." said the speaker. "Reported" has truth-value, but relative to source and circumstance. Reports of that time were somewhat chaotic and unreliable. The speaker hints at doubt and uncertainty. The weight of the office of President and Commander-in-Chief does not support the reports. An alternative could diminish doubt: *American ships have been torpedoed.* The specific and the concrete joined in the same sentence to the vague and ambiguous moderate danger.

The announcement of the attack against Malaya (20), which partially relieved concern for the movement of Japanese submarines, has another function. It quietly extends the conflict, joining the United States as partner and ally of the British. The United States' involvement is not to be limited: it will become global. "Also" (20) signals this extension, though "Malaya" and "Hong Kong" must be heard to make the idea meaningful. The concluding generalization, "a surprise offensive extending throughout the Pacific area" (26-27), also quietly involves the country with allies and quietly prepares it for total involvement without the speaker's need to expend ethos to stress the necessity of all international commitment.[31]

The announcement of the attack against Malaya (20) also introduces a shift in the movement and tone of the address. The former will be quickened, the latter be made emphatic. The statement of the attack against Malaya parallels in substance lines 1-3; it begins "yesterday"; its subject is Japanese activity. However, its voice is active; it has neither qualifiers nor dependent clauses; its verb is simple, past tense. No other statement in the address thus far is as compressed or moves as quickly.

The "yesterday" which introduces the attack against Malaya concludes a compression among the yesterdays; note only the distance between them (1, 16, 20). This compression occurring over time and distance foreshadows, even as it is counterbalanced by, the tightly compressed "last night" series (21-24), including as well the modified restatement of time: "this morning" (25). These compressions of time herald the end of discussion about events in the immediate past. Attention will soon be directed (27-29) to what must be done today and tomorrow.

The tonalities of the "last night" series (21-25) are controlled by line 20 which begins formally: "the Japanese Government" The verb, "launched," quickly tarnishes the formal recognition. Rather than "launched," why not *began, commenced,* or the still simpler *attacked*? None of these verbs reinforces or sustains as well the connotations of "suddenly and deliberately attacked" (2) and "deliberately planned" (13), which emphasize that Japanese activities were outside the conventions of diplomacy. Had they been within those conventions, "launch" might have been an inappropriate description. A verb of strong thrust and impulse, "launch" has sufficient energy to encompass all remaining action (21-25).

Formal agents and agencies, "Japanese forces" (21-23), advance the action. Soon the less formal and somewhat ambiguous "the Japanese" (24-25) forward it. Is the referent only the Japanese Government and/or its agents? Or has there been a subtle expansion to include the citizens of Japan, as well? The choice of "Japan" (26) suggests the latter explanation. "Japan"—not the Empire of Japan, nor the Emperor, nor the Ambassador, nor the Government—merely Japan; the common term describes the nation. The Government and its agents are the explicit enemy; by implication the people are also numbered among the enemy. Nowhere before has the term, Japan, been used in this naked fashion. The "Japan" of line 5 occurs within the context of elevated, diplomatic language; in line 12 the reference is a straightforward, geographical one. The common term is later repeated (43) and tarnished completely by "unprovoked and dastardly" (42). The national name is finally too good to serve to describe the country. Reduction of Japan is effected by

---

[31]James Reston, *New York Times,* December 9, 1941, p. 5, wrote: "Two facts seemed to impress this gathering [Congress] more perhaps than the simple words of the speech. By not the slightest inflection did he suggest that the facts of the world situation had finally justified his policy, as even his opponents were admitting today he might very well have done."

carefully controlled and disciplined language. Men in the street could and did say "Japs." The speaker could not. To have done so would have diminished not only the stature of the office of President but also the occasion and the place, the formal chambers in which affairs of state were conducted. Equally important, to have said "Japs" would have reduced the leader to the level of the led; distance, however defined, is necessary to effective leadership.

The "last night" series (21-24) supports the pace and quality of the attacks. Logically, last night, a part of yesterday, is illogical. The compressed "last nights," figuratively ticking off the clock, bring yesterday to a climactic end. The three "yesterdays" (1, 16, 20) spanned time and space; the night and the events in the night move faster. Simple declarative sentences present facts—actor, action, acted upon. The lengthy iteration is necessary to establish the magnitude of the Japanese thrust. However, had it been extended by the addition of only a few details, it would have been compromised, having its force, pace, and energy enervated. Finally, the verb "launched" more than attacks; it launched a series of sentences which structurally (i.e., in form) harmonize with the acts embedded in them. The actions (i.e., their substance) and the manner of describing them (form) are one. The syntax is itself symbolic of the fast moving military operations.

The connotations from the cluster of "last nights" do more than support the emotional responses rising from "in the quiet of the night when all were abed and defenseless." The cluster is the turning point in a chain of emotive phrases. Prior to the "last night" series, descriptions are relatively mild and basically denotative: "suddenly and deliberately" (2), "deliberately planned" (13), "deliberately sought to deceive" (14), and "false statements" (15). Following the cluster and supported by it is a chain of increasingly stronger phrases: a mild "surprise offensive" (26), a slightly stronger "premeditated invasion" (33), the strong "this form of treachery" (37), and the vehement "unprovoked and dastardly" (42). As the descriptions of the Japanese actions become stronger, so also does the language which responds. Later shifts in verb and voice which describe the response of the United States will be noted.

Finally, the stress which the language contributes, sustains and intensifies the general emphasis of the "last night" passage (20-25). "Yesterday" has three syllables, the first being accented. The phrase "last night" has two accented syllables, relatively equal in stress. Each "last night" is encircled by "attack" or "attacked." The stress pattern of the language is a bombardment. The final line (25) begins with a conjunction which readies the listener for the final "to top it all off." Thus "and," too, is a term of some stress and strength. "And this morning," a phrase of four syllables, the first three accented, concludes the bombardment.

How well this discourse is managed is seen best by examining some alternatives. Compare "Last night Japanese forces attacked Hong Kong" (21) with: (a) *Japanese forces attacked Hong Kong last night,* or (b) *last night Hong Kong was attacked by Japanese forces.* Alternative (a) maintains the active voice, emphasizing Japanese forces. But the immediacy of "last night" is lost when the phrase concludes the thought. The arrangement also negates the effect produced by accent and stress. "Japanese" contains three syllables, relative stress being unaccented, unaccented, accented. Bombardment by stress is weaker. Further, alternative (a) significantly changes the range of the connotative values of "last night," which now modifies Hong Kong and which divides the emotional response. Sympathy goes out to the people of Hong Kong who experienced catastrophe during the night, yet this relieves somewhat the intensity of the negative emotional response centered on the Japanese, the central actors in the night. Alternative (b) is also unable to capitalize fully on the connotative values of "last night." The passive construction of (b) slows the pace; it also makes the subject, "Japanese forces," a marginal part of the sense. Yet the "last night" series (20-25) is the speaker's final statement about yesterday's activities. He soon directs his listeners (27-29) to respond positively. Their active responses are directed to and focused on something central, not marginal.

Finally, the passive construction of alternative (b) puts the places attacked prior to the act of attack and the attacking forces. Place names, Malaya, Hong Kong, Guam, are presented to the listener first, and though the places are scattered over geography, mentioning them first tends to fix them within a general geographical framework. Anchoring the place names makes the image somewhat static. In the active construction (20-25), the image has more movement. The attacks push on places which are in turn pushed over geographical distance enlarging the area of the conflict. The image thus better foreshadows the concluding, explicit reference to a surprise offensive "extending throughout the Pacific area" (26-27).

Roosevelt's conclusion is introduced by the formal, logical sign, "therefore" (26). His demonstration concluded, the speaker again shifts posture, removing himself altogether from the discussion. He chooses to let a transcendental power suggest action. He personifies: "The facts . . . speak for themselves" (27). The information could have been conveyed in other ways: *the facts . . . are clear; the facts . . . are obvious; the facts . . . are self-evident; the facts . . . are self-explanatory.* But, "facts . . . speak. . . ." To whom? Directly, which none of the alternatives above manages quite as well, to "the people of the United States," the subject of the following sentence. How do the people respond? What do they do? Verbs (28) indicate that they use their intellects and power to reason. They have "formed their opinions and well understand." So powerful were the facts that they spoke; so reasoned were the people that they needed no guidance to arrive at a conclusion. No intermediary stands between the facts and the people of intellect. What conclusion had the people "already" (28) reached? To support the action which the speaker announces he has "already" taken (30-32).

The people of the United States are presented as acting on the danger before their Government. Though the danger is not well defined, they understand the "implications" and react positively. When the speaker first mentions the danger he embeds it in his statement about the people (27-29). Their positive response envelops danger, thereby minimizing it.

The speaker's treatment of the situation and the course of action asserts a commonplace of democratic decision making: the people (27-29), the president (30), the troops (30-31) act jointly. Though they act jointly, the people are presented as having the power to effect decisions.[32] The point is demonstrated by rearranging the speaker's language so that it violates the commonplace:

> The facts of yesterday and today speak for themselves. As Commander-in-Chief of the Army and Navy, I have directed that all measures be taken for our defense. The people of the United States, understanding well the implications to the very life and safety of our nation, have already formed their opinions as to the necessity of this action.

To take the action which the logic of the people demanded, man must act. The speaker shifts stance to act in their behalf: "directed" (30) and "taken" (31) indicate reinvolvement with immediate circumstances. He has been reporting. Now he leads: "I direct" (31), "I believe" (35), "I interpret" (35), "I assert" (36), "I ask" (42). Henceforth energies are marshalled and thrust upon the circumstances which face the country. In the prepositional phrase of interrelation and interaction, "between the United States and the Japanese Empire" (43-44), the United States is mentioned first, giving an additional sense of thrust to our energies. After the speaker announces that the "facts of yesterday . . . speak for themselves," the United States becomes active and positive in its response to those facts. The shift in movement is marked when compared to earlier activity, lines 1-3 being but one example.

The turning point in this address having been reached, the events of yesterday now sustain and support the energy of the country. "That always will our whole nation remember the character of the onslaught against us"

---

[32]The power structure upon which the democracy rests compares favorably with that of the enemy: the Emperor, the troops, the people, the latter recognized by their omission. Two reasons partially explain the absence of any formal recognition of the Japanese people, thereby implicatively numbering them among the enemy. First, the conflict does not become one between people: the enemy scapegoat is clearly displayed and well-defined to allow reactions to center on it. Second, the people have to be handled as a totality, as an entity. Even were it possible to define some as "enemy" and others as "friend" the difficulties would have been great. Fine distinctions would have necessitated logical and legalistic development which would have slowed and weakened the movement of the address. The problem would have been only slightly less difficult had the speaker said categorically: The United States has no quarrel with the Japanese people. (Substitute the word German for Japanese in this sentence and it becomes Woodrow Wilson's position in his "War Message" on April 2, 1917. Roosevelt's treatment of the Japanese *people* is quite different from Wilson's treatment of the German *people*). Quite apart from the fact that the Japanese had made American citizens part of the conflict, the speaker, perhaps ahead of the mass of men, realized that such a statement, with its overtone of righteousness, had no place in the mid-twentieth century. War was total. To have said publicly that the people of Japan were not a part of the conflict would have involved the speaker in an untruth, at worst, or in "mere rhetoric," at best. These charges he had earlier levied against Japan.

(31-32)[33] is in a syntactically dependent position. Though the clause is somewhat awkward and forced, it does foreshadow the first comment about the ultimate outcome (33-34): "no matter how long it may take" (33) which tempers hopes of a quick conclusion. The introductory qualification needs its present emphasis so that listeners' hopes may not be falsely supported. Had the speaker said: *the American people ... will win through to absolute victory, no matter how long it may take,* listeners might have missed the qualification. Patience, determination, and fortitude are connoted to counterbalance the zeal with which the people, who had "already" (28) reached a judgment, meet the challenge. The zeal is not destroyed, but protected: zeal often becomes impatient when detours or setbacks delay progress. The "righteous might" (34) not only provides alliteration and balance for "premeditated invasion" (33), but also triggers a new chain of images: from "righteous might" (34) to "God" (41) to "Sunday" (43). "God" in medial position reflects backward and forward.

Though the specific "I" has emerged to act, his actions vary. What he is and what he does are partially revealed by the choice of verbs. Three verbs (35-37) point to intellectual activity: "I believe." "I interpret," "I assert." Having earlier "directed" and "taken" (30-31), he now becomes an observer of evidence and a commentator thereon. A slow reading of lines 35-37 reveals the tentative, cautious, distant quality of the prose. These lines contain three dependent clauses; no other lines in the address contain as many. Moving through the clauses, the speaker searches for and examines present signs as a basis for his "assertion" (36): "that this form of treachery shall never again endanger us."[34]

Following this intellectual-activity statement, long in the sense of distance and tone and by word count the longest in the address, Roosevelt shifts posture again, jolting listeners to a blunt recognition of present difficulty. "Hostilities exist" (38) is his shortest and most direct statement. Yet so mild, so objective, and so matter-of-fact is it that it functions as understatement. Responses spill out and over it; reactions are some variant of "that puts it mildly." Emotional responses to the events are stronger than this statement

---

[33]In drafts I, II, and III this line reads: "Long will we remember the character of the onslaught against us." In draft III "long" is struck and "always" substituted. "Always," positive and categorical, is stronger than "long," a relative term. "Always" also better suits the historical overtones in the address and the emphasis on future time. "Long" appears again in line 33, but the repetition serves no rhetorical purpose.

[34]In drafts I, II, and III line 35 begins: "I speak the will of the Congress and of the people. ..." This construction is much more emphatic and direct than what the speaker actually said, and he would not have been inaccurate had he said it. Yet his actual statement better suits the commonplace of democracy which holds that the President speaks as a result of what the people and their representatives will. He does not say: *I speak your will;* but rather, "as a result of your will, I speak." And he gives the appearance of "sounding out" the will and responding to it, even as he knows what that will is. Also in drafts I, II, and III lines 36-37, "but will make it very certain" read "but will see to it." The latter expresses the tone of determination but not the finality of the result. The actual statement is categorical in a way which "see to it" is not; moreover "see to it" is somewhat more colloquial than "make it very certain."

about the events. Thus, some response spills into lines 38-39 finding resolution in, and providing support for, the judgment, "grave danger" (39).

"Hostilities exist" has another function. Though the future is of concern, listeners could not long tolerate intellectual analysis of the present and future. They might allow the speaker to speculate, but their impulses were for direct action, having "already" (28) reached a judgment. Yet the distant quality of understated assessment dulls somewhat the listener's emotional edge, taking his mind momentarily off the present; it rests the mind before that mind has to accept the judgment of "grave danger" (39). When the speaker turns from intellectual analysis to the present, he indicates that he has not forgotten immediate concerns. He meets the present head-on.

Earlier the facts spoke to the people. They must now look directly at the facts: "There is no blinking at the fact that our people, our territory and our interests are in grave danger" (38-39). In the first three drafts, this line read: "There is no mincing the fact. . . ." The revision is clearer and stronger. To give "no mincing" meaning, an auditor might have to find a context which helped explain it; for example, I'll not mince words. "Blinking at" is clearer; its meaning is rooted in a common physiological process and in common usage. Moreover, a sound-sense equivalent to "blinking at" is "winking at"; and if sense were a problem the latter would easily furnish it. A sound-sense equivalent to "mincing" is "wincing"; the listener who sought meaning analogically would be mislead.

The degree of danger is finally stated explicitly. Though "grave" (39) is judgmental, it stands as "fact" (38). Heretofore "grave danger" has been suggested in various ways: "character of the onslaught against us," "premeditated invasion." The statement, "There is no blinking at the fact that our people, our territory and our interests are in grave danger," is a modified repetition and an extension of "The people of the United States have already formed their opinions and well understand the implications to the very life and safety of our nation." New meaning is given to "implications." They are "grave."

However, the gravity (38-39) is tempered by its position in the general pattern. It is preceded by the statement which indicates that we shall respond so that this "form of treachery shall never again endanger us" (35-37) and followed by a statement prophesying "inevitable triumph" (40-41). The tensions created by gravity are counterbalanced by terms of positive outlook and mounting force: "confidence," "unbounding determination," "inevitable triumph," "God." The danger, though grave, is relative and does not connote absolute destruction; "unbounding," "inevitable," and "God" are positive, categorical, and absolute. The swing of the pendulum of construction is longer, stronger, and more forceful than the swing of destruction. Contributing to the strength of the categorical language of lines 40-41 is the loose, but recognizable and felt, iambic meter, which moves firmly to the inevitable triumph, "so help us God."

"With confidence in our armed forces, with the unbounding determination of our people, we will gain the inevitable triumph, so help us God" is the leader-speaker's oath, publicly taken.[35] So commonplace is its structure, diction, and rhythm that once underway the line cannot be turned nor resisted. Its sweep catches all. The well-being of the country is set in the timeless future. Rearranging the structure, diction, and rhythm upsets the sweep of the statement and weakens it as an article of faith: *We have confidence in our armed forces; our people have unbounding determination; we will gain the inevitable triumph, so help us God.*

The oath taken, no further thematic development is necessary. Only the formal declaration of war (42-44) remains.[36] However, additional modified repetitions woven into the formal declaration enlarge and emphasize thoughts, values, and feelings in the address. "Unprovoked and dastardly" (42) not only balances but also intensifies and enlarges "suddenly and deliberately" (1). The common "Japan" (43) is elevated to the "Japanese Empire" (44) which parallels the formality of "Empire of Japan" (3). The final elevation is one of form only; "dastardly Japan" is the subject. The day, as well as the date, has value. "Sunday" (43) extends and reinforces the connotations of "last night"; its proximity to "dastardly" (43) intensifies the connotations of that term, even as "Sunday" itself gains value and support from its relationship to "God" (41).

The generic negation, the Devil term, is "dastardly" (42).[37] Its appearance is surprising; its choice, apt. Though not a term of the vernacular, it is clear, conveying a dimension of the speaker's moral indignation. As the Devil term, it stands in antithesis to "righteous might" (34), "Sunday" (43), and "God" (41). It has another function. It is as close as the President, speaking to the country in a public chamber, could come to profanity. The movement from "dastardly" to "bastardly" is slight and swift; the latter epitomizes one dimension of the public mood on December 8, 1941. Infamous duplicity has become bastardly duplicity. The leader-speaker controls his emotions before his public and again maintains his distance from his public. Yet the adroit and adept rhetorical choice effects a public catharsis.

The dependent clauses in the final statement (42-44) allow the speaker his judgment of "unprovoked and dastardly" and permit a return to the past: "a state of war has existed." Though the safe and settled formal language of diplomacy and the settled and safe historical past are upset and sundered by the declaration, its formality suggests that the United States respects the

---

[35]Lines 40-41 do not appear in drafts I, II, and III. Harry Hopkins suggested the addition, though his second phrase read: "with faith in our people." Roosevelt altered this to "with the unbounding determination of our people." Since Roosevelt's entire statement (40-41) is a confession of faith, the excision of "faith" in Hopkins' second phrase is appropriate. Too, "faith" has but one syllable, making Hopkins' second phrase shorter than his first and third and restricting somewhat the "swelling" movement of the entire confession. Roosevelt's "the unbounding determination of" is not only phonetically more expansive, but the additional syllables support better the rhythmical movement to the climactic "so help us God."

[36]In drafts I, II, and III line 42 begins: "I, therefore, ask that. ..." The formal, logical sign is unnecessary; Roosevelt's logical and rhetorical conclusion was lines 40-41; lines 42-44 are a formal, ceremonial statement dictated by the nature of the occasion and the place.

[37]For an interesting observation on the word "dastardly," which bears on the discussion here, see Barbara W. Tuchman, "History by the Ounce," *Harper's,* CCXXXI (July 1965), 74.

conventions of diplomacy even when confronted by dastardly actions outside the accepted conventions. Formality marks the conclusion as well as the beginning. The address has come full circle.

III

Elements of the "War Message," which sets forth Roosevelt's doctrine of demonology, need to be placed in the larger context of culture. We do not suggest that a direct, causal relationship exists between the speech and events in the culture. Cultural conditions have multiple causes; only rarely have they single causes. We do maintain that an address helps to create and sustain a "climate" which justifies activities, even though the speech itself is not *the* cause of any activity. The language of an address by the President of the United States in a time of crisis helps to create and sustain a "climate." It also begins to pattern the perceptions and the behaviors of those who hear it. Optimum language bears on perceptions and behaviors in a cohesive way.

The emphasis which Roosevelt gave to topics in his address provided his listeners an orientation to the Japanese and to the nature of the conflict: these had immediate and long-range consequences. He emphasized the infamous duplicity behind the Japanese attacks; they carefully and deliberately prepared their military onslaught, masking their preparations behind neutral and formal diplomatic negotiations. American political folklore and the folklore of the people generally hold such behavior in low esteem; the regard is revealed by popular maxims: the man who wears two hats; the man who works both sides of the street; the man who talks out of both sides of his mouth. Roosevelt's portrayal of the Japanese and their activities fits the sense of such widely known and well-understood commonplaces.

Too, the people of the United States generally knew little about the Orient, and stereotypes were associated with it and the Oriental long before December 7, 1941. Even in California, Washington, Oregon, and Arizona, where most of the Japanese in the United States lived, they were little known. The "War Message" enlarged and intensified the stereotypes. These long-standing cultural raw data were supported. On December 7-8, 1941, additional raw data came to the country from the news reports of the conflict. The latter data especially were confusing and anxiety-provoking. To them, Roosevelt gave meaning as he structured a climate of opinion and orientation.

The President's description of the Japanese Government as marginal, fraudulent, dangerous, and capable of dastardly-bastardly behavior has its parallels in the treatment of the Japanese people in the United States. For example, the Commanding General of the Western Defense Command, John L. DeWitt, agreed, as did others, that the Japanese on the West Coast had not engaged in any sabotage after Pearl Harbor. Yet on February 14, 1942, General DeWitt publicly cited the absence of sabotage as "a disturbing and confirming indication that such action will be taken."[38]

---

[38]Carey McWilliams, *Prejudice: Japanese-Americans, Symbol of Racial Intolerence* (Boston, 1945), p. 110; Dorothy S. Thomas and Richard S. Nishimoto, *The Spoilage* (Berkeley, Calif., 1946), p. 6.

On February 6, 1942 in Los Angeles, Mayor Fletcher Brown, "an able and honest public official,"[39] said in a radio broadcast: "If there is intrigue going on, and it is reasonably certain that there is, right here is the hot bed, the nerve center of the spy system, of planning for sabotage." The Mayor recommended "removal of the entire Japanese population—alien and native born—inland for several hundred miles."[40] Ultimately Japanese were removed to relocation centers, but those details lie outside the present concern.

United States military policy toward Nisei, American citizens of Japanese-American ancestry, reflected Roosevelt's portrayal of the Japanese in his "War Message." Nisei inducted into military service before Pearl Harbor were, shortly after December 7, 1941, given honorable discharges, with no specification of cause of dismissal. In March, 1942, potential Nisei inductees were arbitrarily assigned IV-F, ineligible for service because of physical defects; on September 1, 1942, this classification was changed to IV-C, the category ordinarily used for enemy aliens.[41]

Not until January 28, 1943 were Japanese-American citizens eligible for military service on the same basis as other citizens. President Roosevelt publicly approved, saying "no . . . citizen of the United States should be denied the democratic right to exercise the responsibilities of his citizenship, regardless of his ancestry."[42]

Of course the general anxiety of the civilian population immediately after December 7, 1941 contributed to development of hostility toward Japanese-Americans. It also made the civilian population susceptible to the rantings of professional patriots, witch hunters, alien haters, and others with private aims, who used the cover of wartime patriotism to achieve what they wanted to do in peace time—rid the West Coast of the Japanese.

Numerous private citizens and officials of Government sought to redress such attacks upon the Japanese-Americans. For example, the San Francisco *Chronicle*, December 9, 1941, said editorially: "The roundup of Japanese citizens in various parts of the country . . . is not a call for volunteer spy hunters to go into action. Neither is it a reason to lift an eyebrow at a Japanese, whether American-born or not. . . ."[43] On balance, the voices of tolerance and fair play were the weaker.

President Roosevelt's "War Message" prepared the United States for a long military operation against the Japanese Empire. The nature of the political and military enemy abroad was clear. Indirectly, he supported a civilian army, equally anxious to do its duty, in its march against the civilian "enemy" at home. The "War Message" offered no protection to Japanese-Americans. In the terms of the analysis here presented these people were given "no weight." Two phrases, "the people of the United States" (27-28)

[39]McWilliams, p. 252.
[40]Alexander H. Leighton, *The Governing of Men* (New York, 1961), p. 20.
[41]Thomas and Nishimoto, p. 56.
[42]*Ibid.*
[43]*Ibid.*, pp. 17-18. Also see, McWilliams, pp. 271-273.

and "the American people" (33-34), only implicitly recognize this group, and as a group they were a minority and a marginal part of the culture. Moreover, the two phrases do not contain positive terms; they contain dialectical terms, which reflect value judgments.[44] In this connection, note that Roosevelt's public statement in support of the induction of Nisei into the military service (p. 435) did contain the positive term, "citizen," which transcends even as it anchors such dialectical phrases as "the American people."

We do not suggest that had the "War Message" contained and emphasized the term, citizen, the address itself would have diminished attacks upon Japanese-Americans in the United States. We note only the absence of any protection, a matter of weighting, and thus conclude that the address contributed to the development of a climate for the attacks by strengthening the attitudes of those who, for whatever reasons, wished to attack. Equally important, those wishing to counter such attacks could find in the "War Message" of the President little to support them and the Japanese-Americans.

Though the primary concern of this analysis has been the language of the "War Message," we have in the paragraphs above extended the analysis and speculated upon possible cultural effects. We have done so because the major elements of any speech work on listeners' perceptions and when other factors, rhetorical and non-rhetorical, are present, perceptions become translated into behavior.

IV

We have centered on the language of an address because in much published criticism language has been neglected in favor of analysis of other factors in the rhetorical environment. What goes on in a speech? has been the question. To say that the "last night" series (20-25) is parallel and repetitive, thus contributing force and energy, is to say too little. We have tried to link the section with preceding and following configurations of language and to analyze closely the section itself. The "last night" series is not in the active voice merely because the active voice is clear, direct, and emphatic, among other things. Had the series been structured differently, the image would have become static and less able to sustain the speaker's conclusion about the magnitude of Japanese activity: "a surprise offensive extending throughout the Pacific area" (26-27). The "last night" series is the turning point in the address; following it the United States becomes active, reacting to the events of yesterday. Had the series been structured differently, the Japanese actors would have become less central and the reaction of the United States more difficult to direct and focus. Though it makes sense for the speaker to choose to handle the Japanese Empire as "marginal" in his first recognition of the enemy (1-3), it makes equal sense for him to place the Japanese in a central position in the "last night" series. To expose linguistic strategies of rhetoric

---

[44]Richard M. Weaver, *The Ethics of Rhetoric.* (Chicago, 1953), pp. 16; 187-188.

one needs thus to see language as "moving," as "linking," and as "ordering a hierarchy."

The critical posture here has been microcosmic; the analysis, microscopic. Such analysis does not reveal much about discourse in general. Yet it may be helpful to those who search for orderly methodologies for dealing with all rhetorical activities and processes. The interplay of the microcosmic and the macrocosmic may yield insights which will lead to more fruitful and productive rhetorical criticism.

A Rhetoric of Facts:
Arthur Larson's Stance as a Persuader
by Robert L. Scott

The notion that man can know a reality which, when known, will clearly dictate proper behavior is at least as old as Plato. To focus on reality, men began to shift their gaze in the sixteenth century from the empyrean to earth, from what was somehow mysteriously manifested in the nature of things to what was manifest to the senses observing nature. The result was a number of scientific revolutions; indeed, the result was science itself.

The chief maker of one of these revolutions, Charles Darwin, described his own perception of his procedure: "I worked on true Baconian principles, and without any theory collected facts on a wholesale scale. . . ."[1] The *activity* of facts in dictating conclusions was even more clearly highlighted in the work of Darwin's great defender, Thomas Huxley, who wrote, for example, "This conclusion is thrust upon us by analogous facts in every part of the sentient world. . . ."[2] Although the sense of *facts* in Darwin and Huxley goes beyond the notion that they have a certain hardness making them resist erroneous hypotheses and that they tend somehow to reach out to shape their own explanations, both were too wise not to sense how men tend to shape facts through their use of symbol systems. Darwin understood *genus* for what it is, a concept, an artifice imposed by man for his convenience in dealing with the hardness of the phenomenal world; and he began to suspect that *species* was likewise a linguistic convenience.[3] Huxley saw that it was necessary to restrict the sense of *nature* to those parts of the phenomenal world in which man does not play "the part of immediate cause. . . ."[4] But today, with knowledge of genetic code growing and with the possibility of manipulating the gene structure of individuals, that which Huxley wished to exclude from *nature*—man's art, society, and morals—has potential actually to direct the future of biological evolution. Huxley's distinction made good

Reprinted from *Communication Monographs* 35 (1968): 109-121 with permission of the Speech Communication Association.

[1] *The Autobiography of Charles Darwin*, "Residence at Down; My Several Publications," (London, 1958), p. 119.
[2] "The Struggle for Existence in Human Society," in *Evolution and Ethics* (New York, 1899), p. 197.
[3] *On the Origin of Species by Means of Natural Selection*, reprint of 1st ed. (London, 1950), Ch. XIV, passim; esp. pp. 401, 410-11.
[4] Huxley, p. 202.

sense in its time, but it was arbitrary in minimizing man's participation in framing the meanings of facts.

If Darwin and Huxley were scientists too good to miss the limitations of their own participation as observers, the same cannot be said of all who in the late nineteenth century were entranced with the idea of evolution. John D. Rockefeller, Andrew Carnegie, and James D. Hill were delighted with the justification for business competition seemingly supplied by applications of the "laws of nature."[5] They were further aided to see the meanings of facts by a growing number of social Darwinists, men like William Graham Sumner. "Sumner's speaking was an extension of his faith in facts," Fred Kauffeld concludes, "a faith he attempted to communicate to his audience so that their perceptions would be shaped by a consciousness of the antagonism between facts and notions."[6]

Advice to "get the facts" and appeals "well based on facts" are familiar to anyone who participates in argument today. The locutions so common in Sumner's work are common still. My purpose is not to trace the history of this tendency but to explore some implications that confidence in the prepotency of facts has for rhetoric. What does it mean to assume that facts exist in such a way as to justify arguments on social issues? When in the process of living together in communities ranging from families to international organizations we make recommendations and rules to govern our behaviors, how do we and how should we view "the facts of the matter" in so recommending and ruling?

Theorists, critics, and teachers of rhetoric are prone to see rhetoric as the handmaiden of truths somehow fixed outside of and prior to efforts to relate symbolically environment, others, and self at specific moments. Critics of rhetorical discourse remain quick to enlist "factual" as a term of positive evaluation. Teachers often assume that getting and presenting *facts* is a rudimentary concern doubly desirable because it is apt to be simultaneously effective and ethical. "Make an orderly statement of facts" is a familiar ideal in standard discussions of rhetorical theory and practice, yet as a philosophy of rhetoric the ideal has serious shortcomings.

In order to make the case implied by the last statement above, I shall take as illustrative the rhetoric of Arthur Larson. His is a rhetoric in two senses: he has a theory of communication and he practices his theory vigorously. To the degree that the ideal just mentioned permeates writing and teaching about public address in America, my criticism of Larson's assumptions about good discourse may be applied to much discourse about us. Moreover, if criticism of Larson's conception of the role of fact in social suasion proves well founded, the criticism is criticism of method rather than of rhetorical ends.

---

[5] See Richard Hofstadter, *Social Darwinism in American Thought*, rev. ed. (Boston, 1955), pp. 44-50.
[6] "A Burkean Analysis of Selected Speeches of William Graham Sumner," unpubl. M.A. thesis (University of Kansas, 1965), p. 53.

Arthur Larson's ends are laudable. He uses his means not only efficiently but scrupulously.

I shall first make a short survey of Larson's career and describe his speaking generally, then consider what appear to me the distinct difficulties in his "rhetoric of facts."

I.

"Americans first began to hear the name Arthur Larson during the Presidential campaign of 1956 when, as a ghost writer for President Eisenhower, he was dubbed the 'No. 1 Egghead' of the 'modern Republican' party."[7] It was a book, *A Republican Looks at His Party*,[8] which drew Eisenhower's attention to his Undersecretary of Labor. After the election the President named Larson Director of the United States Information Agency, a job in which the man who had been a Rhodes Scholar and Dean of the University of Pittsburgh School of Law did not long remain.

Mr. Larson resigned as head of the USIA in October, 1957, after Congress had cut his proposed budget by about one-third. He had become during that summer one of the foci of a struggle within his party. As Wilfred Parsons concluded in *America* magazine, "Make no mistake about it: the furor is not about money; it is a fight over Republican leadership in 1960 and about liberal policies at home and abroad."[9]

Larson became a special White House adviser. In less than a year he left the government to found the World Rule of Law Center at Duke University. As Director of this Center he has addressed the public through a series of pamphlets, magazine articles, and speeches reiterating the thesis that "in the presence of appalling danger, we too can and must do the impossible and bring about that rule of law between nations which is the last, best hope of earth."[10]

Larson might be accurately described as an apostle. His commitment is clear: "As a blueprint for an ultimate optimum system, to be accomplished by an intelligent revision of the United Nations Charter, the judicial, arbitral, and conciliation structure set forth in Clark and Sohn's *World Peace through World Law* would be difficult to improve upon."[11] His statement upon resigning as a White House adviser suggests that he saw his role at Duke as, to use Donald C. Bryant's phrase, one "of adjusting ideas to people and of people to ideas."[12] "The Law is a common concept of civilized peoples, a

[7] "Candled Egghead," *Newsweek*, L (October 28, 1957), 29-30.
[8] (New York, 1956).
[9] Wilfred Parsons, "On Again Looking into Larson's Odyssey," *America*, XCVII, (June 1, 1957), 277.
[10] "Address by Arthur Larson, Director Duke University World Rule of Law Center and Special Consultant to the President [of the United States], on the Occasion of the Second Annual Law Day Observances of Harvard Law School, May 1, 1959," mimeographed by the Duke World Rule of Law Center, p. 26.
[11] "Arms Control Through World Law," *Daedalus*, LXXXIX (Fall 1960), 1047. Larson's reference is to Grenville Clark and Louis B. Sohn, *World Peace through World Law* (Cambridge, Mass., 1958).
[12] "Rhetoric: Its Function and Its Scope," *Quarterly Journal of Speech*, XXXIX (December 1953), 413.

largely untapped reservoir of possible common understanding," Larson is quoted as having said. "Our big problem is getting it down out of the stratosphere to the level of something reasonably practical."[13]

From the beginning Larson looked at his task and that of the World Rule of Law Center as one entailing research as well as propagation of a doctrine. His *Design for Research in International Rule of Law*[14] sets forth briefly 113 projects in nine categories. A pamphlet from the Center describes this booklet as one published in the hope of arousing interest in and attracting support for basic research.[15] The word "design" in the title of Larson's booklet is well used. The research discussed is scarcely disinterested; it is part of an overall plan; it is purposive. The desired end of inquiry is the "international rule of law" which "refers to a world in which resort to law in the settlement of disputes and the conduct of international affairs is as habitual as it is on the domestic scene."[16] Nonetheless, Larson sees himself as a scientist for, as he has said several times, one may apply "the genuine scientific approach by first studying the facts, and then conceiving a definite design and building toward it."[17]

Larson's concept of research is two-pronged: it follows a design consistent with the facts and it provides facts consistent with the design. For him *facts* is a key word. "My research generates facts; I supply facts to others," would be a fair statement of his point of view.[18]

Larson's discourse reflects these two closely related purposes. First, one observes the purpose of providing facts to intelligent opinion leaders in the hope of convincing them and helping them to convince others that world peace through world law is a practical goal. Second, there is the more technical purpose of carrying out and reporting basic research which will demonstrate that there are principles of international law which can be used because they have been used. Here, the concern is to demonstrate that there are fundamental consistencies within the major legal systems of the world which form a basis for international, legal order; the belief is that knowledge of these facts will enable political leaders to reach more realistic international agreements. In the following analysis of Larson's persuasive discourse I shall deal primarily with speeches, articles, and pamphlets aimed at his first purpose.

By the criteria of rhetorical discourse emphasized in typical college

---

[13]Quoted in *Time*, LXXII (August 18, 1958), 12.
[14]World Rule of Law Center, Duke University, Durham, N. C., February, 1961. Hereafter this source will be referred to as *Design*.
[15]A pamphlet entitled "World Rule of Law Center," dated March, 1963. See also *Design*, p. 13.
[16]Earl D. Osborn, President, Institute for International Order, in the Preface to *Design*, p. 3.
[17]Arthur Larson, "Can Science Prevent War?" *Saturday Review*, XLVIII (February 20, 1965), 15. For a similar statement see "A Road Map for the U.N.," *Saturday Review*, XLV (April 28, 1962), 39.
[18]This point of view is readily discernible in a "Basic Guidance Paper" Larson wrote for his staff when he was Director of the USIA. Interestingly, he included excerpts from it in a book which represents a major World Rule of Law Center research project. See Larson and John B. Whitton, *Propaganda, Toward Disarmament in the War of Words* (Dobbs Ferry, N. Y., 1964), pp. 268-273.

public speaking classes and textbooks, Arthur Larson's public address is exemplary. If any discourse deserves to be described as clear, orderly, rational, and concrete, his does. In structure and form his articles and speeches are admirably suited to his purpose.

His introductions are short and pointed. Usually, he opens with a direct statement of his thesis. Consider one example: "There is only one rational and honorable way out of our present complicated position in Southeast Asia: we must proceed immediately to make maximum use of the instruments and organizations that we ourselves created for the express purpose of dealing with this kind of problem."[19] Ordinarily he divides his subject. His *Daedalus* article, which is longer and more complex than most of his essays, opens simply: "There are two main elements in world law relevant to arms control: settling disputes and ensuring compliance."[20] Occasionally he undertakes to clarify a key term or to offer a formal definition. In any case, his openings focus immediately upon his thesis or a statement that closely approximates the single proposition to which his essay or speech might be reduced. His discussion scrupulously adheres to the divisions he announces. In general his openings are calculated to arouse the expectation of a careful, factual discussion. Few so disposed by his introductions should be disappointed by what follows.

"Let us marshal the key facts bearing on each of these problems."[21] Remarks like this sprinkle Larson's rhetorical discourse. An example will also illustrate his characteristic method of developing a point. "It has also been charged that the General Assembly is completely irresponsible whenever the subject of colonialism comes up. This is not borne out by the record."[22] This assertion is followed by a series of cases which Larson presents as evidence of responsible action by the General Assembly on issues of colonialism. Elsewhere the same procedure recurs; claim is followed by enumeration of supporting facts.

Overwhelmingly, Larson's supportive material is what would be classified in most public speaking textbooks as factual examples. He selects examples carefully for their clarity and impact and limits their detail in ways that allow him to pack his discourse with the greatest number of instances possible. His disposition to repeat especially pointed examples is soon apparent to anyone reading the bulk of his work. Occasionally he uses hypothetical examples and analogies, which allow concise explanation of complex points. His argument seldom depends on testimony. When he does cite a person whose reputation might add weight to the argument, he is more apt to indicate an action the person took than to use his words. Even direct quotations function more as

---

[19] Co-author with Don R. Larson, "Plan for Peace in Viet Nam," *Saturday Review*, XLVIII (April 24, 1965), 24.
[20] "Arms Control through World Law." p. 1039.
[21] "Commonsense and the United Nations," *Saturday Review*, XLV (February 24, 1962), 18.
[22] "Road Map for the U.N.," p. 12.

examples than as testimony.

Larson's conclusions often indicate clearly the values to which he relates his arguments. Usually these are values that have been made explicit early in the speech or essay. Sometimes the values appealed to are both explicit and implicit. He opens one essay, "My argument for the repeal of the 'self-judging' clause in the American acceptance of the World Court's jurisdiction will be addressed solely to cold-blooded American self-interest."[23] By this he means economic interest but, as his conclusion indicates, there is another value involved, one that undergirds his discourse generally. During his short term as Director of the USIA, he made a speech in which he said:

> You know, one of the most curious and inexplicable phenomena of our times is the fact that, although we live literally under the shadow of the possibility that one day the whole human race might be extinguished in a nuclear holocost [sic], we still don't seem to absorb that idea and let it affect the everyday making of plans, the formulation of strategy.[24]

Clearly Larson believes that human survival is involved in major public decisions and that humans can be made to respond to what they ought hold in the highest regard. Survival, as a value, is frequently appealed to implicitly in discourse otherwise directed explicitly.

In addition to survival and material self-interest, Larson believes that Americans have a strong sense of the individual integrity and self-determination coupled with high agreement on means of implementing these ideals. He often argues, in effect, "Be consistent with your ideals." Although he does not ordinarily spell out these ideals in his discourses on world law, he set them forth in describing the "Authentic American Center" in *A Republican Looks at His Party* and even more specifically in his *What We Are For.*[25]

The most striking impression that arises from my study of Larson's persuasive efforts is of the stability of his practice. Form and content differ little whether he is writing a pamphlet to be distributed by the World Rule of Law Center, an article for the *Saturday Review,* or a speech. His propositions, values, and procedures remain substantially the same.

Even his books take the shape which I have described. One can predict that a chapter will be formed by Larson's making an assertion or raising a

---

[23]"The Self-Judging Clause and Self-Interest," mimeographed by the World Rule of Law Center, n.d., p. 7. The same essay was published by the *American Bar Association Journal,* XLVI (July 1960), 721-30.
[24]"While the Reds Are on the Run, This Is the Time to Pour It On," *U. S. News and World Report,* XLII (May 10, 1957), 91. Speech to the National Press Club, Washington, D. C., April 30, 1957.
[25](New York, 1956 and New York, 1959.) In the latter book he argues that the "key lies in one word: 'identification' " (p. 5). Our effort overseas ought not be to tell others what they should do but to try to make clear that our interests and the interests of the developing nations coincide. These nations find freedom as precious as we do and are learning that "Enterprise Democracy" is the means of gaining material well being while maintaining human dignity (see esp. p. 15).

key question, dividing the subject, and developing each part in turn, mainly by examples. The book he co-authored with John B. Whitton, *Propaganda, towards Disarmament in the War of Worlds,* follows substantially the same pattern even though it is the result of a major research project carried out by the Center.[26]

Larson's adaptations to various audiences are slight. Only in referring to immediate circumstances that have brought about his speaking or writing or in taking advantage of the time or space a particular medium allows him, does he adapt. Larson seems to assume an interested, intelligent audience. He approaches his readers and listeners rationally, treating them as persons who will respect and use the facts he provides and who will be motivated by a few fundamental values which are ordinarily quite clear in his discourse.

With these descriptive observations I conclude my direct consideration of Larson's persuasive campaign on behalf of World Law and turn to the larger problem of this inquiry: the potentialities and limitations of the "rhetoric of facts" which Larson's discourse so conveniently illustrates.

In rhetorical intention, outlook, and method Arthur Larson and the World Rule of Law Center are not unique. They represent institutionalized rhetoric dominated by a sense of commitment to propositions allegedly grounded in fact, by the view that more supportive fact must be generated by research, and by methods deriving from a belief that providing facts to others will be ultimately socially decisive. Like most who will read this essay, I am inclined to admire Arthur Larson and the World Rule of Law Center and to disparage Billy Joe Hargis and his battery of researchers at the Christian Anti-Communist Crusade University in Tulsa.[27] Yet the two enterprises have characteristics and assumptions in common. If one wishes to attack a rhetorical ideal, he may be well advised to observe a practitioner with whom he can sympathize rather than one he cannot. But it will be useful to remember that a hallmark of many important American persuaders in the second half of the twentieth century is a rhetoric using a variety of written and spoken means of addressing the public through discourse which is remarkably stable in form and seeks to persuade through "making an orderly statement of facts." One's preference for goals does not alter the potentialities of rhetorical methods shared by widely differing publicists.

II.

The practice of Arthur Larson and Billy Joe Hargis indicates that "a rhetoric of facts" may be the method of quite different sorts of persons. Obviously the word *fact* can be used in a multitude of ways. For Larson, and most others, *fact* has a special status. Facts make up reality. As reality, facts

---

[26](Dobbs Ferry, N. Y., 1964). This book is apparently part of the results of research carried out at the Center and described as "Project 27. *Illegal Propaganda*" in *Design*, pp. 36-37.

[27]See Dale G. Leathers, "A Descriptive Study of the Revolutionary Reaction of the 1960's: The Rhetoric of Salvation," unpubl. diss. (University of Minnesota, 1965), pp. 107-130.

dictate relationships. The relationships of facts will operate in spite of our wishes or desires. I had better know the facts about certain liquids before I undertake to quench my thirst. Not to know is hazardous, to myself and to others.

Clearly implied in this point of view is a value. That this value operates with prime importance in Larson's rhetoric is indicated by the constant occurence of the words *facts* and *factual.* But what the *facts* are and how they may serve decision making on social matters are themselves serious problems for Larson or anyone using like methods. If one fails to carry his analysis beyond general endorsement of appeals to data, important implications will be missed.

I shall take, as bases for considering further the functioning of *facts* in rhetoric, two consecutive paragraphs and part of a third from Larson's remarkable essay, "Can Science Prevent War?" The first paragraph:

> Before the Age of Science, if you wanted to find out what the inside of the human body was like, you did not open a human body; you opened Aristotle. When Galileo, to test whether the speed of falling objects increased with their weight, dropped two balls of differing weights from the Leaning Tower of Pisa instead of accepting the answer contained in the books, it was considered a piece of impertinence. Today this fact seems almost unbelievable—yet for the most part our conduct of political and international affairs is still dominated by pre-Galileo methods.[28]

These statements beg for dozens of remarks, but two errors are most interesting. Galileo did not drop two balls (or any number as far as careful research has been able to determine) from the Tower of Pisa; if he had, the experiment would have been ineffective as scientific demonstration.[29]

My point is not to catch Larson in a factual error. This would be insignificant. What is significant is the ease with which one may argue, before I am finished, that to criticize is to quibble. One may say that for Larson's argument it makes no difference whether or not Galileo dropped the balls. This comes down to saying that a fiction does as nicely as a fact for his persuasive purposes. Ironically, the fiction serves where the fact would not. For Larson to explain Galileo's experiments would be distracting to his audience; to explain them in detail would even be to weaken his conclusion, which is based on a questionable picture of human behavior before the "Age of Science."

That Larson said that Galileo dropped two balls is a fact. That most people believe that Galileo dropped two balls is also a fact. And to make these statements is to uncover the conclusion that *fact* operates on different

---

[28] *Saturday Review,* XLVIII (February 20, 1965), 15.
[29] See J. Bronowski and Bruce Mazlish, *The Western Intellectual Tradition* (New York, 1962), pp. 118-119. See also Lane Cooper, *Aristotle, Galileo, and the Tower of Pisa* (Ithaca, N. Y., 1935), p. 14.

levels of interpretation and is a highly relative sort of evidence.

Consider a second, less precise feature of *fact* as used here. Larson's picture of the behavior of the thinkers of the Middle Ages in regard to Aristotle's work may be the reflection of a contemporary myth. It may be a shortcut we take through several centuries in order to thump our own tubs of superiority without recognizing our multitude of debts. Stephen Toulmin, for one, believes that medieval thinkers did much more than simply rehash Aristotle and that what they did was important in the evolution of conditions that made contemporary science possible.[30] It may be argued that the common criticism of them is an example of what Michael Polanyi calls the "rationalist fallacy," criticizing someone for failing to consider something he could not possibly consider at a given time in a given place.[31] To put the matter another way, this error is to assume that man can know all that it is necessary to know to make decisions and that he can calculate the effects of those decisions as precisely before deciding as afterward.

With this possibility in mind, take a second paragraph from "Can Science Prevent War?"

> World Wars have been started with what seems to have been less real investigation of the facts bearing on the probable outcome than a scientist would put into the dietary habits of an obscure insect. How much research did the Kaiser conduct to support his conviction that the British would never enter World War I, not to mention the United States? With this lesson of history behind him, Hitler nevertheless, made precisely the same error of fact with similar results [32]

Does Larson assume that the Kaiser was (1) in a position to do whatever research might seem necessary from the point of view of our hindsight, (2) in a position to act on such research, and (3) prepared to use both advantages to avert World War I? Or, to proceed further, assuming that the Kaiser started World War I in a rather singlehanded fashion having, but shunning, advantages similar to those of the entomologist, should we go on to say that Hitler's was "precisely the same error"?

Hitler had evidence from his experience with British behavior. Although he may have made some decisive errors, should his procedure be called less *factual* than the argument Larson apparently recommends: that Britain and the United States entered World War I, therefore these nations will enter a second general war in Europe? To do so is to take drastic advantage of a superior point of view provided by passing time. Certainly from Hitler's point of view, the appeasement of the thirties provided *facts* as relevant as those of World

---

[30]*Foresight and Understanding, An Enquiry into the Aims of Science* (New York, 1963), pp. 106-109. Thomas S. Kuhn writes, "Galileo's contributions to the study of motion depended closely upon difficulties discovered in Aristotle's theory by scholastic critics." See his *The Structure of Scientific Revolutions* (Chicago, 1962), p. 67.
[31]*The Study of Man* (Chicago, 1963), pp. 86-88.
[32]*Saturday Review*, XLVIII (February 20, 1965), 15.

War I.

A few lines of a third paragraph:

> Similarly, millions of Soviet citizens have repeatedly been
> brought to the verge of starvation because of a slavish adherence to
> doctrinaire ideology rather than reliance on observable facts on how
> to get crops and livestock produced. [33]

To broaden our consideration of Larson's rhetoric I shall here make the
assumption that Larson did not observe personally the facts to which he
refers—the starvation, the decisions, the carrying out of decisions, and the
causal connections. To make such an assumption implies that criteria may be
set for deciding what to judge fact and what not. It implies that the claim a
"fact" may have upon our acceptance may vary according to standards set
against the "fact" as stated and against the conditions of its statement.

We are dealing here with rhetoric, hence with *statements* of or about
"facts." When one calls some object, event, or relationship a *fact,* he makes a
statement about it, describes it at least to the extent of assigning it the
property of *fact* as contrasted to whatever he would call *non-fact.* It follows
that discussion of "a rhetoric of facts" will be facilitated by asking what
standards may be used to evaluate close use or loose use of *facts* in discourse.
Let me, then, suggest three criteria by which we might designate *facts* in a
close sense. The first two are common to discussions of fact; the third is not.

1. What we call *facts* should be verifiable; we should be able to
   agree on the reports.
2. What we call *facts* should be reports of sense data.
3. What we call *facts* should be present while we report them.

The first criterion needs little illustration. It recognizes the public nature
of what we call *facts.* We expect competent persons with similar opportunities
to observe to make reports which agree in important details. Often, however,
one can also find agreement on reports which one would hesitate to call
factual. Agreement, then, is not the sole measure of factualness. An evaluative
statement such as, "Riots are bad," may be verifiable in the sense that most
competent persons would agree to it, but the statement, "There were riots in
Newark, Detroit, and Minneapolis in the summer of 1967" is a verifiable
statement of a different order. Which brings us to the second suggested
criterion stipulating what is *fact* and what is *non-fact.*

The reports we are most prone to call factual are reports of sense data. I
may observe certain behaviors that I call *riots,* but I do not observe the
badness attributed by that label.[34] I do not observe *riots* unless I somehow

---

[33]*Ibid.*
[34]That the word *riots* tends to have the value built in is demonstrated by the preference strongly
expressed by many Negroes for the word *rebellions.* "And don't you ever call those things riots
because they are rebellions, that's what they are." Stokely Carmichael in a speech given in Cobo
Arena, Detroit, July 30, 1966, transcribed from a tape-recorded re-broadcast by WKNR, Detroit.

connect what I see to my system of values, which is what I am quite likely to do if I observe destruction of property, personal injury, and loss of life. Thus in much that we report as *facts,* we report both direct descriptions of sense data and conclusions based on these and on application of some clear value. But to say the applied value is *clear* tends to beg the question of what is *fact,* so it is not at all easy to determine fact-ness by saying *facts* in rhetoric are those statements that report sense data. And application of this criterion is especially difficult if we modify it to admit statements a step removed from reports of sense data—as we are often impelled to do.

The third criterion offered above may seem corrective of the difficulties encountered in applying the second. If observers report to one another in the presence of the phenomena in question, they can probably guard against slipping onto an evaluative plane or can at least stipulate more objectively the values they attribute to the phenomena being observed. But rhetoricians will seldom find themselves in such fortunate circumstances. An advantage of several branches of the physical sciences is the ability of the observers to produce in a given instance phenomena of the sort about which they wish to make verifications; hence the timelessness of some science.[35] In any case, however, statements of *facts* that satisfy our third criterion will be in reference to a point in time; the report can be called *fact* only for an instant, whether or not it is probable that like reports would have equal factualness in subsequent instants.

This is not the place to discuss how or whether sense data can really be factually reported through discourse or what sorting processes and categories contribute to the highest degree of shared verification. I am seeking to emphasize by reference to the criteria just discussed that statements of *fact* will always be relative in some way to human purposing. No matter how consistent we are, we humanize our facts to some degree and our reports about facts are always colored accordingly.

If even when dealing with physical phenomena we must admit at least slight disclaimers toward our ability to be purely factual, we must recognize that selecting and interpreting those events relevant to our economic, social, and political affairs—precisely the tasks of rhetoricians—make perfect

---

[35]The natural sciences, being evolutionary, are historical; they are in time. But not all philosophers of science would agree to label the physical sciences as timeless. Stephen Toulmin, for example, argues that even physics and chemistry are bodies of knowledge that have evolved and are evolving and are then very much in time. See his *Foresight and Understanding,* especially Chapter 6, "The Evolution of Scientific Ideas." See also Thomas S. Kuhn, *The Structure of Scientific Revolutions,* especially Chapter 10, "Revolutions as Changes of World View".

fulfillment of the criteria for fact an unattainable ideal.[36] In short, *the appeal to facts in these realms must always be insufficient and ought to be recognized as such by any who would influence the behavior of others.*

Another example from Arthur Larson's "Can Science Prevent War?" will help illustrate the sorts of difficulties that tend to be compounded by a rhetoric of facts.

> A rational approach to any problem begins with getting the facts—facts which are accurate and current. International relations today are being conducted on the basis of facts that are from eighteen to 300 years out of date.
>
> A partial check-list of current misconcepts of fact bearing on the ultimate issue of war and peace may serve to support this statement.
>
> The first misconcept is that diplomacy is the only valid method of settling international disputes. The fact is that old-fashioned power-politics diplomacy is virtually obsolete as a method of settling major disputes.[37]

Would these purported facts satisfy the criteria I have suggested? Could anyone even begin such an examination? The statement is disabled by the word *only*. Undoubtedly Larson could find some who would claim that "diplomacy is the only valid method," but how many, how recently, and how similar would their meanings of *diplomacy* be? But of course Larson modifies his statement immediately by referring to "old-fashioned power-politics diplomacy," which would have to hark back at least eighteen years. If a reader were to take these paragraphs in an utterly straightforward way, in what sort of light would anyone be put who undertook to defend diplomacy?

From the standpoint of the demands that ought to be made on a "rhetoric of facts" Larson's argument directed toward diplomacy is disreputable. If anyone objects that this judgment is too harsh, he may be saying in effect, "Come now, let's not hold Larson too strictly to narrow criteria. True, he continually gives his statement the ringing appeal of the word *fact,* but this is merely a way of being emphatic." This hypothetical retort cuts to the heart of the matter. Would the typical reader of *Saturday Review* take the statements cited in an utterly straightforward way? Probably not. Taken as common rhetorical heightening, one can see Larson arguing that there are tendencies that he finds alarming; one can then readily share his point of view and his

---

[36]If anyone espousing a "rhetoric of facts" argues that striving for an unattainable ideal is good, he should recognize that the purported basis of his rhetoric has shifted drastically. First, "the orderly presentation of facts" becomes a complex affair which can scarely be recommended as rudimentary, i.e., the least that can be expected of a speaker or writer. Second, one relinquishes the pose of objectivity, which in effect says, "What I am saying anyone could, and even should, say if he is interested in the facts." This attitude is highly questionable for two reasons: (1) it tends to be non-responsible, if not irresponsible, and (2) it tends to attribute poor procedure, if not bad faith, to those who speak otherwise.

[37]"Can Science Prevent War?" p. 16.

temper at least for a few moments. This sort of sharing is important to human communication; but attitudes, not sense data, are its basis.

Rhetorical heightening can be so extreme as to deserve condemnation. Drawing that line is admittedly difficult, but my argument is that "make an orderly statement of facts" is not a satisfactory solution to the difficult problem. It is not a satisfactory solution because it pledges a rhetor to a simple standard which he cannot meet but which, paradoxically, charges his statements with goodness for those who value science as method.

Larson is again a case in point. He repeatedly suggests an idea of science that will seem strange to one who takes the ordinary conceptions of physical science as a model. One reads, for example, "The true fact is that at certain key points in our history Americans have applied the genuine scientific approach by first studying facts, then conceiving a definite design and building toward it."[38] A prime example? The American Constitution!

The human purposing, risking, and working that have place in this conception of science do not partake of a passive, disinterested ideal. Larson's campaign for World Rule of Law is based on a view of science which Michael Polanyi aptly expressed: "I am merely referring to the important fact that you cannot discover or invent anything unless you are convinced that it is there, ready to be found."[39] And yet it is not clear that Larson and others like him, who claim to persuade by orderly presentations of *facts*, fully recognize the subjective qualities of their facts and presentations thereof.

The man with convictions who undertakes to impress others with those convictions ought to recognize that he evaluates as he symbolizes. Striking the stance of simply presenting facts is apt to put him in awkward positions, as Arthur Larson's failure as Director of the USIA strikingly demonstrates. The Hearings in which Larson appeared before the Subcommittee of the Senate Appropriations Committee in the spring of 1957 merit study by any student of persuasion for their indications of how limited a "rhetoric of facts" must be as a basis for achieving communication.[40]

One magazine writer said, "The Senate subcommittee . . . did more than cut the United States Information Agency appropriation from the requested $140 million to $90.2 million—it cut USIA director Arthur Larson into pieces."[41] The *New Republic* was principally interested in the political alignments involved, but the conclusion of its report applies also to Larson's defense of his agency's persuasive mission. The senators revealed a basic mistrust of persuasion. Their questioning exhibited at least a surface commitment to a "rhetoric of facts" which might be summarized thus: If one is right, will not self-evident facts bring the truth to the fore? Further, will not

---

[38] *Ibid.*, p. 15.
[39] *The Study of Man*, p. 35.
[40] *Hearings before the Subcommittee of the Committee on Appropriations, United States Senate, Eighty-fifth Congress, First Session on H. R. 6871 . . .* , pp. 488ff. (Referred to below as *Hearings*.)
[41] "Arthur Larson Testifies," *New Republic*, CXXVI (May 27, 1957), 5.

natural processes (e.g., ordinary news coverage by the press services) bring the facts to view? If so, does the USIA have a defensible function?

Larson's exchange with Senator Fulbright along these lines is most significant. Fulbright finally said concerning Larson's explanations of the agency's function: "Well, this is a very interesting subject. I would not want to minimize the difficulty, either by simply saying that you have not made it clear. Certainly all Members of Congress have struggled with it. ... It is a very difficult thing to sit here in peacetime and feel that it is constructive."[42] My own evaluation of the interchange is that Larson had difficulty making clear the necessity for an agency like the USIA because basically he agreed with Senator Fulbright. His own relatively uncritical commitment to a doctrine of facts made it difficult for him to respond to the senator's line of questioning.

Fulbright's remark about peacetime indicates that those who espouse a rhetoric of facts are likely to believe that persuasion is sufferable only in unusual circumstances, e.g., wartime. Another move tempting to those who assume that facts can speak for themselves is indicated in Fulbright's response to Larson's insistence that the United States must counter the propaganda of Russia: "That makes sense to me in what I call an underdeveloped, backward country. In France they are quite as capable as you or I in distinguishing propaganda from Russia. ... Even the USIA cannot tell the French the facts of life."[43] The statement implies that there are two ways of speaking—one appropriate between equals and another between superiors and inferiors. Such a position is attractive, smacking as it does of Plato's recommendation of dialectic for the Guardians and noble lies for everyone else, but it is antithetical to the democratic values to which both Senator Fulbright and Arthur Larson had often committed themselves.

In writing about the war in Vietnam, Larson has made a statement with which Senator Fulbright would probably sympathize:

> The sad thing about all this is that it has not been brought about by a conscious act of national judgment, policy, or will. It has come about by a process of creeping involvement, of almost imperceptible increases in American participation from week to week, which have drastically altered our basic position and purpose from one of technical assistance and military advice to one of apparently open-ended involvement in all out war against both internal and external enemies of the South Vietnam regime, using our own planes and men.[44]

The recognition that events are made by human purposing or lack of purposing and are meaningful as humans make them meaningful is here, but

---

[42] *Hearings*, p. 530.
[43] *Ibid.*
[44] "A Plan for Peace in Viet Nam," p. 24.

the recognition is inconsistent with Larson's (and Fulbright's) constant stance relative to communication and persuasion: that *facts* speak for themselves in an ideal rhetoric. Larson's difficulties in explicating the functions of an "information" agency and Fulbright's difficulties in coming to a clear understanding of how "informing" processes do and ought to occur illustrate the consequences of an unexamined commitment to a rhetoric of facts.

III.

"An orderly presentation of facts" is an unsatisfactory ideal for a rhetoric. It is inconsistent with the facts of human involvement. It can even lead toward intolerance.

Consider one final quotation from Larson.

> Crucial decisions reflecting public information and attitudes on the U. N. are being made frequently. Since every time one more person learns one more true fact about the United Nations it is a significant contribution to world peace, there is no finer or more urgent use to which persons engaged in research, communication and education can apply their resources than this task of creating a sound base of understanding and confidence on which to build a future for the United Nations.[45]

"True fact" needs comment. What Larson wants is not facts located indiscriminately by anyone. He wants facts selected and in part created by those committed to a design for the future. I say *created* because being committed to the design Larson designates must be a part of the fact if the fact is to work in the evolution of the design. A "true fact" is thus a design-bound fact. Just here the rhetoric of the World Rule of Law Center and of the Christian Anti-Communist Crusade share a philosophical premise potentially intolerant.

Lying outside human perception and beyond human use—if we may so conceive them—"facts are facts and flinch not" as Browning said. Seen, interpreted, integrated, and socially used by men, "facts" become humanized. The consequence may be social good or social ill. Uncritical assumptions that "facts" retain the disinterested nature of matter, even in human discourse, debar rhetoricians and critics from understanding their own failures in communication and criticism, and promulgation of a "rhetoric of facts" as ideally dispassionate hides the role of human choice and design in all discourse, thereby covering over the seat of tolerance and intolerance.

---

[45]"A Road Map for the U. N.," p. 40.

Darwin and *The Origin of Species:*
The Rhetorical Ancestry of an Idea

by John Angus Campbell

One of the most important persuasive events to occur in the last hundred and ten years was the publication in 1859 of Charles Darwin's *On The Origin of Species.* Though mid-century philosophy and metaphysical theology had advanced far beyond the Platonic conception of a great static chain of being in the organic world, in both Europe and America the idea of natural organic development remained unpopular and commonly regarded as thoroughly discredited.[1] *The Origin* was important not only for the new fields of research which it opened in the natural sciences, but for the marked influence which it had on such diverse fields as sociology, economics, philosophy, anthropology, and theology.[2] The advent of Darwin's book has justly been compared in its epoch-making significance with the French Revolution and the American Civil War.[3] Even as these two events brought to an end centuries-old social systems and marked the birth of quite different societies, so, in the world of ideas, *On the Origin of Species* brought to an end an entire Anglo-American tradition in the relationship between science and religion and saw the birth of radically altered views of the proper relationship between man, the physical universe, and God.

The Origin is of scientific importance not because of its absolute originality, for, as historians of science have noted, there was little in it that was genuinely new, but because in it the significance of natural selection was first fully grasped and systematically applied as an adequate explanation of the principal mechanism of organic change.[4] All of the elements for a

---

Reprinted from *Speech Monographs* 37 (1970): 1-14 with permission of the Speech Communication Association.

[1]For the classic account of the great chain of being see Arthur O. Lovejoy, *The Great Chain of Being* (New York, 1965). For the predominant attitude of scientists toward organic development see Charles C. Gillispie, *Genesis and Geology* (New York, 1959).

[2]For an extensive bibliography on the range of the Darwinian influence see Gail Kennedy (ed.), *Evolution and Religion* (Boston, 1957), pp. 110-114.

[3]Harry K. Girvetz, "Philosophical Implications of Darwinism," *The Antioch Review,* XIX (1959), 19.

[4]For the fullest treatment of Darwin's predecessors see Bentley Glass, Owsei Temkin, and William L. Straus, Jr. (eds.), *Forerunners of Darwin, 1745-1859* (Baltimore, 1959). The reader who examines Glass, however, should also take into consideration the critique of this volume in Donald Fleming, "The Centenary of The Origin of Species," *Journal of The History of Ideas,* XX (1959), 437-446. Particularly helpful concerning the anticipators of the mechanism of natural selection is Loren C. Eiseley, *Darwin's Century* (Garden City, New York, 1961), pp. 100-140.

successful developmental theory were implicit in the advances of science in the first half of the nineteenth century, but before Darwin no one possessed both the scientific competence and the imaginative vision to bring these parts into a coherent, persuasive, whole. In addition to being a landmark in the history of science, *On The Origin of Species* was a rhetorical masterwork as well. It is with *The Origin* as a persuasive document that the present study is concerned. Specifically, I will attempt to demonstrate that an important but insufficiently noted source of *The Origin's* success lay in Darwin's singular ability to harmonize conflicting though common conventions of discourse to gain acceptance for a familiar but unpopular idea.

Because history has passed a basically favorable judgment upon Darwin's theory, it is tempting to assume that Darwin's success was inevitable. Far from being inevitable, given the context of nineteenth-century science, Darwin's success was unexpected and remarkable. Darwin's success was unexpected because the established doctrine of creation was thought to be not only firmly established upon empirical grounds, but established beyond hope of successful challenge by any possible theory of organic development. Darwin's success was remarkable because belief in natural development was just beginning to take hold of the public imagination at the very time Darwin's particular theory was receiving what amounted to a substantial refutation.[5] Modern historians of science recognize that Darwin's theory could not have been true on the basis of the mistaken assumptions of genetics and physics on which Darwin had to operate. Indeed, based upon these assumptions, objections logically fatal to the theory were voiced by scientists within seven years after the appearance of *The Origin*. Nevertheless, public acceptance of natural evolution proceeded apace.[6] The argument for natural organic development was not so strong by 1867—the year the last major objection to it became known—as to compel belief in it, yet man's belief in it was beginning. Why this change of opinion? The answers seem to lie not so much in the evidence as in the willingness of men to believe.

It is with the issue of men's willingness to believe that the rhetorical dimensions of Darwin's accomplishment become fully visible. A decade after the appearance of *The Origin* the evidence for natural development was not different in kind from what it had been before *The Origin*. The difference was that the traditionally accepted doctrine was no longer regarded as credible, and while Darwin's theory was badly flawed, men in increasing numbers were coming to believe that something like it *had* to be true. Darwin's victory, although clearly advancing science and won through the medium of a scientific treatise, is comparable to the victory of a major poet or novelist

---

[5]Probably the best account of the speed with which developmentalism became the new orthodoxy is contained in Gertrude Himmelfarb, *Darwin and The Darwinian Revolution* (Garden City, New York, 1959), pp. 307-309.

[6]The major objection to Darwin from physics was voiced by Lord Kelvin in the early 1860's. See Eiseley, pp. 237-241. The major objection to Darwin's physics was raised by Fleming Jenkyn. See Eiseley, p. 209.

who succeeds in changing the sensibility of his age. Darwin's victory was very much a victory over the imagination of his time, and indeed victories over men's imaginations may finally be the most important ones of all. As E. A. Burtt has observed, "In the last analysis it is the ultimate picture which an age forms of the nature of its world that is its most fundamental possession. It is the final controlling factor in all thinking whatever."[7] To understand the means by which Darwin's victory was won we must examine Darwin's rhetorical inheritance, that tangled legacy of incompatible assumptions—of scientific assumptions based partially on religion and of religious assumptions bolstered partially by science—that both invited the conception of developmental theories and then so often disowned and stifled them at birth.

The Legacy of Natural Science

Whatever reasons may be advanced to account for the failure of men prior to Darwin to accept the idea of natural organic development, their failure to do so cannot be explained by any supposed widespread unfamiliarity with science or lack of interest in scientific data. Quite to the contrary, the first half of the nineteenth century was a period which witnessed extraordinary popular interest in virtually every aspect of natural science. C. F. A. Pantin has commented upon the importance of the popularity of science in preparing the public for *The Origin:*

> Innumerable books on the phenomena of the natural world were published in the first half of the nineteenth century. Many of their beautiful plates of flowers and butterflies are now to be seen in art shops where they may be bought at an exorbitant price. The books dealt with the systematics and classification of plants and animals. Their authors were by no means confined to academic scientists, though *The Conchologists First Book, or a System of Testaceous Malacology arranged expressly for the use of schools . . .* by Edgar A. Poe, Philadelphia 1839 is perhaps unexpected. Interest in such books was widespread. Young ladies grew ferns in "Wardian cases" and wrangled over new species. Charles Kingsley comments upon the prevailing "'Pteridomania" and paterfamilias preferred that his daughters should entertain themselves in this way rather than reading novels which only put ideas into their heads. But such things did put one important idea into people's heads. The educated mid-Victorian had a much better idea of what a species was than does the educated man of today. And the problem of the origin of species was one the significance of which he could fully grasp.[8]

Geology was studied with an especial interest. Herbert Spencer has recorded

[7] E. A. Burtt, *The Metaphysical Foundations of Modern Science* (Garden City, New York, 1954), p. 17.
[8] C. F. A. Pantin, "Darwin's Theory and The Causes of Its Acceptance," *School Science Review.* XXXII (1951), 318.

the excitement which railroad construction crews took in the discovery of
fossil remains. Visitors to England during this period have commented upon
the major role which geological hikes and minor expeditions played in the
recreation of a country weekend.[9]

Most important from the perspective of the present investigation, for at
least sixty days prior to the publication of *The Origin,* the preponderant
majority of scientists and laymen had already begun to view the natural world
from a perspective which may be broadly termed "evolutionary," though their
evolutionism expressly denied the competency of natural causes to produce
new species. Indeed, it might well be claimed that the form of evolution
which was accepted prior to Darwin led to a scientific dead end, since instead
of focusing men's attention upon potential natural explanations it tended to
lead men to despair of natural explanations almost altogether, especially on
the question of the origin of species.[10] From a rhetorical perspective, however,
this earlier form of evolutionism was to be of considerable importance in
preparing the public for Darwin. The older view of evolution provided a basic
motif which Darwin radically temporalized and then represented as something
which the public had accepted all along.

Evolutionary belief prior to Darwin took the form of geological
catastrophism. In the first two decades of the nineteenth century the evidence
that certain animate forms had become extinct and that other previously
unknown forms had appeared forced the final abandonment of the idea of the
great chain of being, an idea which had informed metaphysical theologies
since the time of Plato.[11] In place of the venerable, static conception that no
form of life had been created or destroyed since the beginning, the dynamic
theory that creation was a temporal ongoing process which proceeded by
successive destructions and higher recreations became widely accepted by the
second decade of the nineteenth century. In an early refutation of Darwin, the
pioneer American geologist, Edward Hitchcock, quoted the French geologist,
D'Orbigny, for an authoritative statement of what long before mid-century
had come to be the predominant view of the pattern of creation:

> A first creation took place in the Silurian stage. After that was
> annihilated by some geological cause, and after a considerable time,
> a second creation took place in the Devonian stage, and successively,
> twenty-seven times, have distinct creations repeopled all the earth
> with plants and animals; following, each time, some geological
> disturbance, which had totally destroyed living nature. Such is the
> certain but incomprehensible fact, which we are bound to state,

[9]Himmelfarb, p. 232. See also Gillispie, p. 187.
[10]On this point see especially, William Whewell, *History of The Inductive Sciences* (New York, 1858),
   II, 573-577. See also Louis Agassiz, *Essay On Classification* ed. Edward Lurie (Cambridge, Mass.,
   1962), pp. 12-18.
[11]For an excellent discussion of the impact of the discovery that certain fossils no longer had living
   counterparts see John C. Greene, *The Death of Adam* (New York, 1961), pp. 96-130.

without trying to pierce the superhuman mystery that envelopes it.[12]

One could scarcely ask for a better statement of the dominant view of creation which it was the task of Darwin's theory to supplant. Yet, considered from the perspective of the rhetorical legacy bequeathed to later controversy, this view of creation did much to prepare the public for the very theory whose truth it expressly denied. On the one hand, as A. O. Lovejoy has observed, the progress of geology had increased "the resort to supernatural agency in the accounts of the genesis of organisms" and had substituted "for one great obscure miracle at the origination of the universe . . . a long succession of relatively petty and definite miracles."[13] Nevertheless, at the same time as it erected barriers in the path of organic development, geological catastrophism popularized the notion that creation was a process which unfolded over time and followed an overall pattern of development from the simpler to the more complex levels of animate being. Thus, though catastrophism saw each creation as distinct and genetically unconnected with either preceding or following creations, the catastrophists did not lose sight of the evolutionary character of the creative process. Yet despite the warming assurances of the genial arch-catastrophist, Louis Agassiz, that species were connected with one another only by thought in the mind of God and not by genetic descent, the catastrophist interest in tracing out "the plan of creation" inevitably turned up what on occasion could be embarrassing similarities between the lower and higher forms of life.[14] Indeed less than three months before publication of *The Origin's* first English edition, a revealing article in the American periodical *Christian Examiner* probed the most embarrassing similarity of all. The author, who clearly revealed his adherence to catastrophism, uncomfortably pondered the narrowness of the chasm separating man from his nearest relations. Notwithstanding the excessive theism of geological catastrophism, the evolutionary character of the philosophy had unmistakably led this writer to the very brink of a conclusion that popularization of Darwinism was soon to render commonplace:

When he [man] examines . . . step by step, the progressive development of lower life, and finds nowhere any break; when he examines the structure of the highest forms of brute life, and finds a caricature of himself; when he sees the skeleton of the orangoutang hanging by the side of the human skeleton, and seeming to cast towards it a grin of recognition and relationship; when he studies the more internal faculties of the higher animal, and finds there in germ the types of all or nearly all his own;—he is for the moment startled. The gulf which was infinite appears narrow, as if a leap might pass

---

[12]Edward Hitchcock, "The Law of Nature's Constancy Subordinate To The Higher Law of Change," *Bibliotheca Sacra,* XX (July, 1863), 515.
[13]Arthur O. Lovejoy, "The Argument For Organic Evolution Before The Origin of Species, 1830-1858," in Glass, pp. 364-365.
[14]Agassiz, pp. 10-12.

it. He feels at first somewhat like a man who, having been raised from some low estate to the midst of wealth and fashion, trembles whenever he sees one of his old neighbors and kinsfolk, fearing lest he should recognize and betray him, and the world of fashion should cast him out, and he should topple back again into the depths which he would fain forget. So man, with one hand warm in the grasp of the angels, shudders to feel upon the other the clammy fingers of the chimpanzee.[15]

The evolutionism of the catastrophists did not pass unquestioned. The challenge to catastrophism was launched in Charles Lyell's mighty "summa geologica," the *Principles of Geology,* which appeared from 1830-1833.[16] It is indeed ironic that the source to which Darwin owed his greatest rhetorical debt should have expounded a position which was radically anti-evolutionary. Lyell championed the geological uniformitarianism which Hutton had enunciated in the first really scientific book of geology, his 1795 *Theory of The Earth.* In contrast to the gigantic and tumultuous forces of catastrophism, Lyell's uniformitarianism was a rather dull affair. According to Lyell, continents, mountain ranges and great valleys did not make their appearances suddenly or as a result of unprecedented outbursts of force, but owed their original appearance and present condition to the operation of the same natural forces which daily may be seen functioning around us.

Although Lyell is credited with having helped prepare the way for Darwin, Lyell himself—much to Darwin's displeasure—vacillated back and forth between qualified acceptance and outright rejection of Darwin's theory. Lyell's failure to immediately embrace Darwin's theory has puzzled historians of science and until recently was regarded as "a sort of logical peccadillo or an inconsistent attempt to avoid making concessions to opposition."[17] W. F. Cannon has advanced the simplest explanation for Lyell's behavior; progressivism or evolutionism of any kind went directly contrary to a root assumption of Lyell's uniformitarianism.

> By uniformity of "causes" Lyell meant not merely that the same geological agents . . . have been at work in the past as in the present, but also that the quantity and intensity of the actions of these agents have never varied. His view of the past was one of "endless variation" leading nowhere in particular, an apparent ceaseless repetition of continent-raising and continent-eroding processes. Moreover in keeping with his belief that geology can never penetrate back beyond these repetitive cycles to an original or primitive state of

---

[15]"The Future of Man and Brute," *Christian Examiner,* LXVII (Sept., 1859), 158. *The Origin* appeared sometime between November 23 and November 26. See Morse Peckham (ed.), *Charles Robert Darwin, The Origin of Species: A Variorum Text* (Philadelphia, 1959), p. 18.

[16]The expression "summa geologica" is Charles C. Gillispie's.

[17]Walter F. Cannon, "The Uniformitarian-Catastrophist Debate," *Isis,* LI (1960), 39. Cannon specifically cites as guilty of this error Gillispie, p. 131 and Eiseley, p. 109.

the earth, he flatly denied that geology could show any over-all development of the surface of the earth in any particular direction from any knowable original state. He coupled to this assertion, a full-length refutation of the theories of Humphry Davy and of Lamarck as to "the successive development of animal and vegetable life, and their progressive advancement to a more perfect state." ....
"If, as is customary, we use the term "evolutionary" to refer to any process of significant directional cumulative change over time, it is evident that, as compared to Catastrophism, Lyell's Uniformitarianism was an anti-evolutionary creed postulating repetition rather than cumulative development as the net result of eons of geological time.[18]

Opposed as the scientific positions of Darwin and Lyell clearly were, this opposition should not lead us to conclude that there was no important similarity between them. That competent historians of science have been so impressed by the similarities between Darwin and Lyell as to have overlooked the important differences between them invites closer inquiry into the nature of these similarities. I hold that the contribution of Lyell to Darwin was real and important, but that it was rhetorical and strategic rather than primarily scientific.[19]

The essential similarity between *The Origin* and the *Principles* is that both works employ similar overall rhetorical strategies. Both works attempt to create and to satisfy certain expectations, but the *Principles,* unlike *The Origin*, created expectations which it could not and did not satisfy because the scientific foundations of the *Principles* prevented their satisfaction. To clarify and substantiate this claim we must examine the rhetorical structure of Lyell's work in closer detail.[20]

The *Principles* begins with an exhaustive review of geological thought from its very beginnings up to and including then comtemporary theories. One of the prime points that Lyell repeatedly brings to the reader's attention throughout this survey is that whenever investigators have placed their trust in known present causes, and by analogy have assumed the action of these causes in the past, advances in geological knowledge have been made. He follows this with a demonstration employing apt and telling examples of the absurd conclusions which will be forced upon the investigator who proceeds on any other supposition. In the body of the work itself the reader is constantly reminded of one principal idea: the ability of present forces acting in times past as they now act to produce the geological characteristics of the earth. In example after example from points all over the globe, Lyell illustrates this single, simple idea. Only the cast of characters varies, never

[18]Cannon, pp. 38-39.
[19]Though commenting from a somewhat different perspective C. F. A. Pantin has made suggestive observations on the similarities in style between Lyell and Darwin. See Pantin, p. 313.
[20]The following discussion is based upon the ninth American edition of the *Principles.* Charles Lyell, *Principles of Geology* (Boston, 1853).

the main theme, as Lyell discusses the ability of various forces or combinations of forces acting uniformly in times past to accomplish immense results over time. Lyell literally wears the reader down by small degrees in the manner of the very forces he discusses. With the length of the book serving as time, Lyell's seemingly endless, thorough and well-written rehearsal of the same story forces even the skeptical reader to share with the author the uniformitarian experience.

Lyell's scientific legacy to Darwin was the vast amounts of time his geology provided for the operation of the principle of natural selection, and his implicit suggestion (which his own principles prevented him from developing) that the large changes that had resulted in the sphere of geology from the sum of small ones would have a biological counterpart. Lyell's rhetorical legacy to Darwin was his manner of making this miniscule and prolonged accumulation convincing

The essence of this technique lay in going far beyond what was merely logically or even psychologically necessary for creating a bare presumption in favor of the point to be established. As we have seen, Lyell created a presumption in favor of his general case, introduced means conceivably sufficient for attaining those ends, and then illustrated the operation of those means. Establishing the presumption and introducing the means requires scarcely one quarter of his book. The bulk of the treatise is an illustration of the operation of those means. Lyell makes his case convincing by accumulating example after example rather than by resting his case with a single demonstration or with a limited group of demonstrations. The effect of this strategy is cumulative. At first the reader is led to understand Lyell's principles conceptually, next he finds himself able to anticipate his explanations almost in detail. Finally the effect of continued exposure to seemingly endless illustrations surely suffices for all but the most skeptical of readers to produce the illusion of having witnessed mountains worn down and continents submerged beneath the sea.

This strategy was to be of particular importance to Darwin, for the evidence available to him to establish the efficacy of natural selection was much more fragmentary than the evidence available to Lyell to demonstrate the sufficiency of present natural causes to have produced geologic change. Scientifically, Darwin could only demonstrate variation within specific limits. Rhetorically, Darwin had so forcefully to impress the reader with the ability of natural selection to preserve variations cumulatively that the reader would be able and willing to follow him over important gaps in the evidence without losing the thread or sacrificing the force of the argument.

In short, Lyell's rhetoric—his manner of making his case convincing—was so effective and seemed so strongly to cry out for a biological counterpart that only recently have historians of science become aware of the fairly evident reasons why it was impossible for Lyell to supply that counterpart and even more difficult for him to accept it. *The Origin of Species* certainly is the counterpart of the *Principles of Geology,* but the complement is more rhetorical and stylistic than scientific.

Lyell's rejection of evolutionism and his inability to find a natural explanation for the introduction of the animate world left the whole question of the origin of species in the province of natural theology. For all his opposition to the catastrophists, Lyell remained very much a special creationist. As far as I can understand Lyell's view, Lyell believed species to have been divinely but randomly created, their appearance revealing no sort of progression. However much Lyell may have helped pave the way for Darwin in the long run, in the short run his firm rejection of developmental theories served to strengthen special creationism. Until Lyell publicly sided with Darwin, clerics could use the *Principles* as a refutation of *The Origin.*[21]

The Legacy of Natural Theology

The express theism which we have seen articulated in the theories of the catastrophists and the uniformitarians was complemented by the emphasis on science reflected in theological thought. Indeed so close was the relationship between natural science and natural theology in the first half of the nineteenth century that no hard and fast line can be drawn between them. Scientific writers were often as keen about exclaiming over the goodness of God as manifested in the creation as were the natural theologians themselves. This enthusiasm was only to be expected since the natural scientists and the natural theologians were often the same men. Even such relatively non-theological naturalists as Lyell were not immune from the prevailing enthusiasm of their time. In the *Principles* Lyell had exclaimed, "In whatever direction we pursue our researches, whether in time or in space, we discover everywhere the clear proofs of a Creative Intelligence and of His foresight, wisdom, and power."[22] So widespread was natural theologizing that one German visitor commenting on the British scene observed: "The English have a peculiar love of regarding nature from a theological point of view."[23] The rhetorical legacy of this "peculiar love" is clearly stamped not only on the fly-leaf of *The Origin,* but also in the questions which Darwin asked himself and in the very language of his answers. To appreciate the more than vestigial character of natural theology in *The Origin,* we must first take a closer look at the Anglo-American tradition of natural theology.

The work of natural theology whose tone and delightful style set the model par excellence for all of the others was William Paley's *Natural Theology: or, Evidences of the Existence and Attributes of The Deity Collected from The Appearances of Nature,* published in 1802. For over half a century Paley's *Natural Theology* was a standard text in Protestant theological seminaries. As a divinity student at Cambridge Darwin read Paley

[21]Samuel Wilberforce, "Darwin's Origin of Species," *Quarterly Review,* CVIII (July, 1860), 264.
[22]Lyell, p. 799.
[23]Gillispie, p. 200.

and recalled years later in his autobiography that Paley had been one of the few authors who made the slightest impression upon him.

> The logic of this book [*Evidences of Christianity*] and I may add of his *Natural Theology* gave me as much delight as did Euclid. The careful study of these works, without tempting to learn any part by rote, was the only part of the Academical Course, as I then felt and as I still believe, was of the least use to me in the education of my mind. I did not at that time trouble myself about Paley's premises, and taking these on trust I was charmed and convinced by the long line of argumentation.[24]

Paley's basic argument was exceedingly simple and easily understood. The hallmark of Paley's argument and of the numerous variations and developments of it by others was "contrivance." God might have made man and most other forms of life much simpler than he did, Paley argues, but had he done this the proofs of his existence would have been correspondingly decreased. If men and animals had been quite simply constructed then it would be quite natural to suppose that they had been the products of blind chance. Since, to the contrary, men were a combination of pipes, ducts, tubes, and articulated structure, all neatly packaged so as to avoid damage or dislocation by sudden movement, only a fool could believe that men and animals were not the end-products of specific and deliberate design. In a characteristic piece of argument, having discoursed upon the structure of the windpipe and the gullet, Paley continued:

> Reflect how frequently we swallow, how constantly we breathe. In a city feast, for example, what deglutition, what anhelation! yet does this little cartilege the epiglottis so effectually interpose its office, so securely guard the entrance of the windpipe, that whilst morsel after morsel, draught after draught are coursing one another over it, an accident of a crumb or a drop slipping into this passage (which nevertheless must be open for breath every second of time), excites in the whole company, not only alarm by its danger, but surprise by its novelty. Not two guests are choken in a century.[25]

The Paleyan enterprise of combining solid science with sound religion probably reached its most extended treatment in the Bridgewater treatises of the mid-1830's. The Eighth Earl of Bridgewater had charged the executors of his estate to commission each of eight scientific authors to write a dissertation from his particular specialty demonstrating "The Power, Wisdom, and Goodness of God, as manifested in the Creation." The usual topics—the moral nature of man, the adaptation of external nature to the physical nature

[24]Nora Barlow (ed.), *The Autobiography of Charles Darwin* (New York, 1959).
[25]William Paley, *Natural Theology, or, Evidence of The Existence and Attributes of The Deity, Collected From The Appearances of Nature* (Boston, 1863), pp. 105-106.

of man, the human hand, etc.—were all covered in great depth and at interminable length. The permanent impact of these treatises can be seen in the first wave of anti-Darwinian literature which was often peppered by citations from these works.

The rhetorical legacy of natural theology to Darwin was perhaps the most vital legacy of all because it firmly established and legitimized certain theological expectations of science in the larger public. Indeed, natural theologizing was such an accepted convention that it would have been remarkable had *The Origin* been free of it. The polemics surrounding Darwin's book and the decidedly anti-religious turn which the controversy took have obscured a very important rhetorical debt which Darwin owed to Paley and the natural theologians.

Beginning with the first edition of *The Origin* and continuing with some variation through the sixth and final edition three separate citations favorable to natural theology appeared on the fly-leaf of Darwin's book. One of these citations was from the Bridgewater treatises, one was from Bishop Butler's *Analogy,* and one was from Bacon's *Advancement of Learning.* The *Analogy* citation which appeared in all but the first and fourth editions, especially invited readers to understand *The Origin* from a theistic point of view. The quotation read: "The only distinct meaning of the word 'natural' is *stated, fixed,* or *settled;* since what is natural as much requires and presupposes an intelligent agent to render it so, i.e., to effect it continually or at stated times, as what is super-natural or miraculous does to effect it for once."[26] Even in the process of posing to himself the questions which he proposed to answer, Darwin betrayed his debt to Paley and the Bridgewater treatises.[27] In one particularly eloquent passage Darwin exclaimed:

> How have all those exquisite adaptations of one part of the organization to another part, and to the conditions of life, and of one distinct organic being to another being, been perfected? We see these beautiful co-adaptations most plainly in the woodpecker and the mistletoe; and only a little less plainly in the humblest parasite which clings to the hairs of a quadruped or feathers of a bird; in the structure of a beetle which dives through the water; in the plumed seed which is wafted by the gentlest breeze; in short, we see beautiful adaptations everywhere and in every part of the organic world.[28]

Here Darwin speaks the very language of natural theology; he does so right down to the level of noting the testimony of the parasites, those real, but nonetheless embarrassing, little witnesses to the providential design. So firmly established was the convention of viewing the adaptations of nature as

---

[26]Peckham, p. ii.
[27]All citations are from the first edition of *The Origin. Charles Robert Darwin. On The Origin of Species: A Facsimilie of The First Edition,* with an introduction by Ernst Mayr (Cambridge, Mass., 1964).
[28]Darwin, 1964, pp. 60-61.

the result of foresight, intelligent planning, and craftsmanly skill that Darwin did not even escape it in his description of the very mechanism which Huxley claimed had administered the "death blow" to teleology. In the following passage Darwin fully personifies nature giving it the attributes of a purposive and ruthless deity.

It may be said that natural selection is daily and hourly scrutinising, throughout the whole world, every variation, even the slightest; rejecting that which is bad, preserving and adding up all that is good; silently and insensibly working, whenever and wherever opportunity offers, at the improvement of each organic being in relation to its organic and inorganic conditions of life.[29]

While the internal evidence of *The Origin*, which here we have but touched upon, provides clearest evidence of natural theology's place in Darwin's persuasive strategy, Darwin's behavior in the early years of the controversy manifested his intent that the public should see his theory and natural theology as fully compatible. In 1860 the American botanist, Asa Gray, wrote a series of articles for the *Atlantic Monthly*, proposing a reconciliation between natural selection and natural theology. Though Darwin could not accept Gray's argument, at his own expense Darwin republished Gray's articles in booklet form, personally entitled the collection *Natural Selection Not Incompatible With Natural Theology*, and ordered copies of the booklet sent to a long list of scientists and laymen throughout England including such eminent divines as Samuel Wilberforce and Charles Kingsley.[30]

The Legacy of Science vs. Religion Controversy

Contradictory as were the rhetorical legacies examined thus far, these legacies were none the less "positive" for they familiarized the public with the very elements out of which Darwin was to weave his synthesis. Not all schools of science-religion discussion, however, even unwittingly helped prepare the way for Darwin. Though both scientists and natural theologians had reached a generally satisfactory agreement before mid-century, two small but vocal groups—the popular scientific-religious left and the religious right—were not party to this agreement. An understanding of the place and role of these groups in the broader controversy will reveal the rhetorical pitfalls which Darwin avoided and will shed light upon a common source of misunderstanding concerning the identity of Darwin's real enemies.

Despite Herbert Spencer's phenomenal success as the most voluminous advocate of evolution after Darwin, Spencer's thought was not of primary importance in shaping public attitudes toward evolution before Darwin. The

[29]*Ibid.,* p. 84.
[30]A. Hunter Dupree, *Asa Gray,* 1810-1888 (Cambridge, Mass., 1959), pp. 298-301. The third and fourth editions of *The Origin* contained a special postscript in the opening pages which specifically recommended Gray's *Atlantic Monthly* articles and the booklet *Natural Selection Not Incompatible With Natural Theology* to the readers. See Peckham, pp. 788-789.

principal source which shaped public attitudes toward evolution before Darwin was a small volume anonymously written by Robert Chambers, a Scottish publisher and minor literary figure. In 1844, fourteen years after publication of Lyell's *Principles* and fifteen years before publication of *The Origin, Vestiges of the Natural History of Creation* made its appearance. *Vestiges* was a remarkable book.[31] In the space of 280 pages Chambers derived the universe from the expansion and contraction of a primordial "Fire Mist," explained the formation of the various earth strata, described the major characteristics of the fossil remains to be discovered in each, accounted for the appearance of all living creatures and man out of "globules forming within globules," explained the emergence of civilization out of savagery, examined the philological evidences for unity of the human race, demonstrated the necessary but incidental character of evil, and reconciled the whole with the goodness of God who dearly loved and cared for each individual though he operated only through uniform and fixed laws which he impressed upon matter from the beginning.

Vestiges may fairly be characterized as "sense impregnated with nonsense." Particularly in the later portions of the book, scarcely a chapter did not contain some profound insight illustrated by the most absurd or improbable examples. Though the central idea which Chambers was urging— that the organic sphere is governed by a natural law of development—was sound, his manner of explanation poorly served his argument. Though in the earlier portions of the book Chambers, as an amateur geologist, could argue with some force for the operation of natural laws in the formation of the features of the earth, his suggestion in the later portions that under certain circumstances geese might give birth to rats and fish to reptiles seemed to make a mockery of the very notion of a biological analogue to the laws in the inorganic sphere. Though *Vestiges* succeeded in making a few converts, the legacy which it bequeathed to Darwin was overwhelmingly negative. Virtually every scientist of importance in the English speaking world came out in print against *Vestiges* and against the idea of natural organic development. At the same time as *Vestiges* was familiarizing the public with the idea of organic development, it was informing them that the idea was

---

[31]This discussion is based upon the second edition of the work, see: Robert Chambers, *Vestiges of the Natural History of Creation* (New York, 1845). Later editions, as Darwin was to observe, were "much improved." The essential impact of the work, and the public's general conception of it were created by the earlier editions. For a complete discussion of *Vestiges* see Milton Millhauser, *Just Before Darwin* (Middletown, Conn., 1959), pp. 86-115.

[32]Considerable evidence could be cited in *Vestiges'* favor. Certainly its impact, both direct and indirect, upon the educated classes was great. Milton Millhauser has shown the influence of *Vestiges* on, among other sources, Tennyson's *The Princess* and *In Memoriam* and Schopenhauer's *Parerga und Paralipomena* and *The Will In Nature.* See Millhauser, pp. 156-158. One early convert to the Vestiges was Abraham Lincoln. William H. Herndon and Jessie William Weik, *Herndon's Lincoln* (Chicago, 1889), III, 436-438. It should be kept in mind, however, that *Vestiges* made powerful enemies, not the least of whom were Darwin's later defenders, Thomas Henry Huxley and Asa Gray. My judgment against a positive rhetorical legacy for *Vestiges* is based upon an examination of the type of clerical objections raised against Darwin and will be dealt with in the course of a later article on the response of American Christianity to Darwin.

without scientific merit.[32]

Though no less an historian than Arthur O. Lovejoy has urged that the case for organic evolution was complete with the appearance of Chambers' book and ought to have been recognized as such, his judgment has not been sustained by other historians of science. In answering Lovejoy's case for a more prominent place for Chambers in the history of science, Donald Fleming put his finger on a very important source of Darwin's persuasive success which lay at the very root of Chamber's failure.

> A book of science will inevitably be judged not only by the wisdom the author conveys but the unwisdom he abstains from. Where a revolutionary new hypothesis is in question, a sense of rigor and discipline at work and sure instincts in command may deservedly tip the balance in its favor; and the other way around. ....
>
> The *Origin of Species* was commended by what it did not treat of. Unlike Chambers, Darwin did not attempt to supply a cosmogony. Unlike Chambers, he did not attempt to account for the origin of life. Suppose, he says, 'some few beings' to have lived 'before the first bed of the Silurian system was deposited,' this is what ensued. Unlike Chambers he did not discuss the notoriously tricky subject of the origin of the races of mankind.[33]

If with Whitehead we can view style as "the fashioning of power, the restraining of power," and the ability to attain one's end directly "without side issues, without raising undesirable inflamations," then it is not too much to claim that a major source of Darwin's persuasive success may be attributed to his sense of style.[34] When we consider the inviting but not directly relevant issues which the theory of evolution suggested and when we consider the range of evolutionary subjects covered by Darwin's later writings, then the sheer quantity of the "undesirable inflammations" which Darwin avoided raising in *The Origin,* becomes in itself as eloquent testimony to Darwin's rhetorical mastery as the positive skill manifested in his reconciliation of conflicting legacies. In short, the rhetorical legacy of what for convenience I have called the popular scientific-religious left, was negative. Rather than preparing the way for Darwin, the rhetoric of the early popularizers of evolution functioned to erect formidable barriers of popular prejudice in his path.

The religious right, the second major dissenting party from the prevailing religion-science synthesis, played no major role either in preparing the broader Victorian public to oppose evolution or in leading the attack on Darwin's book. Darwin's most excited opponents were not those who refused all compromise with science, but those who had compromised most. The

---

[33]Fleming, p. 442-443.
[34]Alfred North Whitehead, *The Aims of Education & Other Essays* (New York, 1964), p. 24.

pious citations on the flyleaf of *The Origin* and the theological citations within the work were not directed at the literalists who regarded the reigning religion-science synthesis as far too heavily weighted in favor of science, but at the religious moderates whose very position depended upon agreement with science. Not until the late 1870's and early 1880's, when moderate clerics began finding their way to belief in some form of developmentalism, did the fundamentalists become, as they have remained into our own time, the major opponents of evolutionary science. At mid-century, however, the persuasive efforts of the fundamentalists to discredit virtually all science were held in check by the religious moderates who needed science because of the support it offered to natural theology. Thus, though the religious right was not even included in the audience to which *The Origin* was primarily addressed, the persistence and tenacity of fundamentalist opposition has left to our own time a legacy of misunderstanding about the beliefs of Darwin's original foes which must be dispelled if we are to achieve historical perspective on the evolutionary dispute.

At mid-century the main enemy of natural evolutionism was not fundamentalism—enemy though fundamentalism surely was—but special creationism. However much special creationism may suggest Biblical literalism to modern readers, it should be remembered that special creationism, as that term came to be understood in the first two decades of the nineteenth century, was a teaching of science before it was a doctrine of religion.[35] Indeed, during this period, reconciling "Genesis with Geology" largely meant reconciling the once-and-for-all creation of the six days of Genesis with the "27" distinct creations, destructions, and recreations of geological catastrophism. While religious moderates were able to understand the special creations of catastrophist geology in a manner that harmonized them with the Biblical record, men of heterodox religious convictions or even men who violently hated any form of Biblically-based religion could be found in the ranks of those who stoutly upheld the special creationist position.

In America, for example, the great "prince of science," Louis Agassiz, affirmed that even as the various animal species were products of separate and distinct creations so also were the separate races of men.[36] In short, in affirming his particular brand of special creationism Agassiz was denying the historical character of the Biblical record. Despite his vigorous advocacy of arguments from design, despite his ultra-creationism and his complete lack of hostility toward religion, refutations of Agassiz' version of creation were

---

[35]For an excellent account of how science rather than simple Biblical literalism had the upper hand even in most religious quarters, see John Dillenberger, *Protestant Thought and Natural Science* (Garden City, New York, 1960), esp. pp. 137-138.

[36]Louis Agassiz, "Geographical Distribution of Animals," *Christian Examiner*, XLVIII (March, 1850), 181-204. Louis Agassiz, "The Diversity of Origin of The Human Races," *Christian Examiner*, XLIX (July, 1850), 110-145.

carried forward into the early years of the Darwinian controversy by orthodox clerics and scientists.[37]

Further evidence of the ideological ubiquity of special creationism may be found in the weighty volumes of those notorious apologists for slavery, Messrs. Gliddon and Nott. Agassiz' denial of the genetic unity of the human race served the purposes of these authors well. Though Agassiz did not share Gliddon and Nott's blunt and vehement opposition to any attempt at reconciliation with Genesis, he, for reasons known only to himself, contributed prefatory articles to the two books which these gentlemen authored. Thus, strange as it may sound to contemporary ears, Gliddon and Nott upheld special creationism *against* the Bible and did so in the name of science.[38]

Darwin's biggest challenge then came not from religious fundamentalism nor even from theistic pressures outside of science, but from established theistic traditions within science. Indeed, as we have seen, the very doctrine of special creation which Darwin had to overthrow was based more upon science than upon any strict reading of Genesis.[39]

Darwin's Rhetorical Synthesis

Viewed from the context of the universe of discourse to which *The Origin* belonged, Darwin's persuasive victory was indeed ironic. From a series of parts—of rhetorical legacies—none of which added up to natural organic development, Darwin was able to derive a developmental synthesis. Truly, Darwin's ability to appropriate many of the very argumentative elements of his opponents to his own use made *The Origin* equally elegant whether viewed from a rhetorical or a scientific point of view. In the rhetoric of the geological catastrophists and the geological uniformitarians, Darwin had inherited two mutually-opposed legacies. The catastrophists believed in evolution, but vehemently denied the ability of natural causes to bring about evolution. The uniformitarians denied that there had been cumulative progress in any particular direction, but affirmed the ability of natural forces to bring about random change. In his exposition of the mechanism of natural selection Darwin employed the uniformitarians' manner of explanation to establish on naturalistic grounds the evolutionary conclusions of the catastrophists. To a public steeped in a theological tradition which taught men to view the adaptations of the organic world as the artifacts of a conscious designer, Darwin presented natural selection under the metaphor of a conscious, choice-making intelligence. Finally, on issues where the premature and often

---

[37]Joseph P. Thomson, "Quatrefages and Godron In Reply To Agassiz on The Origin and Distribution of Mankind," *Bibliotheca Sacra,* XIX (July, 1862), 607-632.

[38]J. C. Nott and George R. Gliddon, *Types of Mankind* (Philadelphia, 1854), pp. 49-61.

[39]In the end design was more important to American clerics than orthodoxy, for when it became clear that the battle with Darwin was to be fought in earnest, Agassiz' deviations were conveniently forgotten and his works were judiciously quoted to support the beleaguered battlements of orthodoxy.

fantastic explanations of others had made the very idea of natural evolution a laughing-stock, Darwin was either silent or conventional. In *The Origin* Darwin said nothing about the beginning of the universe, nothing about the ancestry of man; for the beginning of the first forms of life from which all of the rest were derived, he spoke of a special divine interposition and continued to do so throughout all six editions of his book.

A principal result of Darwin's synthesis was to render the traditional weapons of the opposition of little effect. The really interesting aspect of the mid-Victorian response to Darwin was not the shrillness of the initial opposition, but the speed of its evaporation. It is tempting to speculate that Darwin's opponents had difficulty attacking Darwin without firing on their own lines as well. In any event, restatements of special creationism seemed increasingly doomed to failure. The most effective means of combating Darwin, as the more perceptive clerics and their scientific apologists soon discovered, was to accept evolution and to deny Darwin's version of it. Thus, in many instances, even when Darwin appeared to be losing he was, in fact, winning. Much seeming outright opposition to Darwin was actually only a polemical smokescreen to cover the reluctant abandonment of no longer tenable positions.

The Second Persona

by Edwin Black

The moral evaluation of rhetorical discourse is a subject that receives and merits attention. It is not necessary to dwell on why rhetorical critics tend to evade moral judgments in their criticism, or on why the whole subject has the forbiddingly suspicious quality of a half-hidden scandal. Suffice it to note that the motives for doubting the enterprise are not frivolous ones. Most of us understand that the moral judgment of a text is a portentous act in the process of criticism, and that the terminal character of such a judgment works to close critical discussion rather than open or encourage it.

Moral judgments, however balanced, however elaborately qualified, are nonetheless categorical. Once rendered, they shape decisively one's relationship to the object judged. They compel, as forcefully as the mind can be compelled, a manner of apprehending an object. Moral judgments coerce one's perceptions of things. It is perhaps for these reasons that critics are on the whole diffident about pronouncing moral appraisals of the discourses they criticize. They prefer keeping their options open; they prefer allowing free play to their own perceptual instruments; they prefer investigating to issuing dicta. These are preferences that strongly commend themselves, for they are no less than the scruples of liberal scholarship.

Nevertheless there is something acutely unsatisfying about criticism that stops short of appraisal. It is not so much that we crave magistracy as that we require order, and the judicial phase of criticism is a way of bringing order to our history.

History is a long, long time. Its raw material is an awesome garbage heap of facts, and even the man who aspires to be nothing more than a simple chronicler still must make decisions about perspective. It is through moral judgments that we sort out our past, that we coax the networks and the continuities out of what has come before, that we disclose the precursive patterns that may in turn present themselves to us as potentialities, and thus extend our very freedom. Even so limited a quest as conceiving a history of public address requires the sort of ordering and apportioning that must inevitably be infected with moral values. The hand that would shape a "usable past" can grasp only fragments of the world, and the principles by which it makes its selections are bound to have moral significance.

Reprinted from *The Quarterly Journal of Speech* 56 (1970), with permission of the Speech Communication Association.

The technical difficulty of making moral judgments of rhetorical discourses is that we are accustomed to thinking of discourses as objects, and we
are not equipped to render moral judgments of objects. Ever since
Prometheus taught us hubris, we in the West have regarded objects as our
own instruments, latent or actual, and we have insisted that an instrument is a
perfectly neutral thing, that it is solely the use to which the instrument is put
that can enlist our moral interest. And it was, of course, the ubiquitous
Aristotle who firmly placed rhetoric into the instrumental category.[1] Thanks in
part to that influence, we are to this day disposed to regard discourses as
objects, and to evaluate them, if at all, according to what is done with them.
If the demagogue inflames his audience to rancor, or the prophet exalts their
consciousness, in either case we allow ourselves a judgment, but the judgment is of consequences, real or supposed. We do not appraise the discourse
in itself except in a technical or prudential way. Our moral judgments are
reserved for men and their deeds, and appropriately the literature of moral
philosophy is bent toward those subjects. My purpose here is by no means to
challenge this arrangement. Instead, I propose exploring the hypothesis that if
students of communication could more proficiently explicate the saliently
human dimensions of a discourse—if we could, in a sense, discover for a
complex linguistic formulation a corresponding form of character—we should
then be able to subsume that discourse under a moral order and thus satisfy
our obligation to history.

This aspiration may seem excessively grand until we remember that we
have been at least playing about its fringes for a long time in criticism. The
persistent and recurrently fashionable interest among rhetorical and literary
critics in the relationship between a text and its author is a specific expression
of the sort of general interest embodied in the hypothesis. Despite our
disputes over whether the Intentional Fallacy is really a fallacy, despite our
perplexities over the uses of psychoanalysis in criticism and the evidentiary
problems they present, despite even the difficulties posed the critic by the
phenomenon of ghost writing, where the very identity of the author may be
elusive, we still are inclined to recognize, as our predecessors have for many
centuries, that language has a symptomatic function. Discourses contain
tokens of their authors. Discourses are, directly or in a transmuted form, the
external signs of internal states. In short, we accept it as true that a discourse
implies an author, and we mean by that more than the tautology that an act
entails an agent. We mean, more specifically, that certain features of a
linguistic act entail certain characteristics of the language user.

The classic formulation of this position is, of course, in the *Rhetoric* and
the *Poetics*. There we find the claim developed that a speech or set of
speeches, constituting either the literal discourse of a public man or the lines
associated with a role in a play, reveal two dimensions of character: the moral
and the intellectual. It is common knowledge that the discussion of moral

---

[1] Aristotle, *Rhetoric*, 1355a-b.

character—ethos—in the *Rhetoric* is for many reasons an intriguing account, that the discussion of intellectual character—dianoia—which appears mainly in the *Poetics* is cryptic and evidently incomplete in the form in which we have it, and that there are ample textual hints that we are to take ethos and dianoia as distinguishable but complementary constituents of the same thing. They are aspects of the psyche. In a play their tokens suggest to the audience the psyche of a character. In a speech they suggest the speaker.

It is also common knowledge that today we are not inclined to talk about the discursive symptoms of character in quite the way men did in Aristotle's time. We are more skeptical about the veracity of the representation; we are more conscious that there may be a disparity between the man and his image; we have, in a sense, less trust. Wayne Booth, among others, has illuminated the distinction between the real author of a work and the author implied by the work, noting that there may be few similarities between the two, and this distinction better comports than does the classical account with our modern sense of how discourses work.[2] We have learned to keep continuously before us the possibility, and in some cases the probability, that the author implied by the discourse is an artificial creation: a persona, but not necessarily a person. A fine illustration of this kind of sensibility appears in a report on the 1968 Republican convention by Gore Vidal:

> Ronald Reagan is a well-preserved not young man. Close-to, the painted face is webbed with delicate lines while the dyed hair, eyebrows, and the eyelashes contrast oddly with the sagging muscle beneath the as yet unlifted chin, soft earnest of wattle soon-to-be. The effect, in repose, suggests the work of a skillful embalmer. Animated, the face is quite attractive and at a distance youthful, particularly engaging is the crooked smile full of large porcelain-capped teeth. The eyes are the only interesting feature: small, narrow, apparently dark, they glitter in the hot light. . . .[3]

Note that last twist of the knife: the eyes are *"apparently* dark." Not even the windows of the soul can quite be trusted, thanks to optometry.

The Vidal description is more nearly a kind of journalism than a kind of criticism, but its thrust is clearly illustrative of the distinction we have become accustomed to making—the distinction between the man and the image, between reality and illusion. And we have to acknowledge that in an age when seventy percent of the population of this country lives in a preprocessed environment, when our main connection with a larger world consists of shadows on a pane of glass, when our politics seems at times a public nightmare privately dreamed, we have, to say the least, some adjustments to make in the ancient doctrine of ethical proof. But however revised,

[2] Wayne C. Booth, *The Rhetoric of Fiction* (Chicago, 1961), esp. Part II, "The Author's Voice in Fiction."
[3] "The Late Show," *The New York Review of Books,* XI (September 12, 1968), 5.

we know that the concept amounts to something, that the implied author of a discourse is a persona that figures importantly in rhetorical transactions.

What equally well solicits our attention is that there is a second persona also implied by a discourse, and that persona is its implied auditor. This notion is not a novel one, but its uses to criticism deserve more attention.

In the classical theories of rhetoric the implied auditor—this second persona—is but cursorily treated. We are told that he is sometimes sitting in judgment of the past, sometimes of the present, and sometimes of the future, depending on whether the discourse is forensic, epideictic, or deliberative.[4] We are informed too that a discourse may imply an elderly auditor or a youthful one.[5] More recently we have learned that the second persona may be favorably or unfavorably disposed toward the thesis of the discourse, or he may have a neutral attitude toward it.[6]

These typologies have been presented as a way of classifying real audiences. They are what has been yielded when theorists focused on the relationship between a discourse and some specific group responding to it. And we, of course, convert these typologies to another use when we think of them as applying to implied auditors. That application does not focus on a relationship between a discourse and an actual auditor. It focuses instead on the discourse alone, and extracts from it the audience it implies. The commonest manifestation of this orientation is that we adopt when we examine a discourse and say of it, for example, "This is designed for a hostile audience." We would be claiming nothing about those who attended the discourse. Indeed, perhaps our statement concerns a closet speech, known to no one except ourselves as critics and its author. But we are able nonetheless to observe the sort of audience that would be appropriate to it. We would have derived from the discourse a hypothetical construct that is the implied auditor.

One more observation must be made about these traditional audience typologies before we leave them. It is that one must be struck by their poverty. No doubt they are leads into sometimes useful observations, but even after one has noted of a discourse that it implies an auditor who is old, uncommitted, and sitting in judgment of the past, one has left to say—well, everything.

Especially must we note what is important in characterizing personae. It is not age or temperament or even discrete attitude. It is ideology—ideology in the sense that Marx used the term: the network of interconnected convictions that functions in a man epistemically and that shapes his identity by determining how he views the world.

Quite clearly we have had raging in the West at least since the Reformation a febrile combat of ideologies, each tending to generate its own

---

[4] Aristotle, Book I, Ch. 3.
[5] Aristotle, Book II, Chs. 12-13.
[6] See for example Irving L. Janis, Carl I. Hovland, *et al.*, *Personality and Persuasibility* (New Haven, 1959), esp. pp. 29-54.

idiom of discourse, each tending to have decisive effects on the psychological character of its adherents. While in ages past men living in the tribal warmth of the *polis* had the essential nature of the world determined for them in their communal heritage of mythopoesis, and they were able then to assess the probity of utterance by reference to its mimetic relationship to the stable reality that undergirded their consciousness, there is now but the rending of change and the clamor of competing fictions. The elegant trope of Heraclitus has become the delirium of politics. Thus is philosophy democratized.

It is this perspective on ideology that may inform our attention to the auditor implied by the discourse. It seems a useful methodological assumption to hold that rhetorical discourses, either singly or cumulatively in a persuasive movement, will imply an auditor, and that in most cases the implication will be sufficiently suggestive as to enable the critic to link this implied auditor to an ideology. The best evidence in the discourse for this implication will be the substantive claims that are made, but the most likely evidence available will be in the form of stylistic tokens. For example, if the thesis of a discourse is that the communists have infiltrated the Supreme Court and the universities, its ideological bent would be obvious. However even if a discourse made neutral and innocuous claims, but contained the term "bleeding hearts" to refer to proponents of welfare legislation, one would be justified in suspecting that a general attitude—more, a whole set of general attitudes were being summoned, for the term is only used tendentiously and it can no more blend with a noncommittal context than a spirochete can be domesticated.

The expectation that a verbal token of ideology can be taken as implying an auditor who shares that ideology is something more than a hypothesis about a relationship. It rather should be viewed as expressing a vector of influence. These sometimes modest tokens indeed tend to fulfill themselves in that way. Actual auditors look to the discourse they are attending for cues that tell them how they are to view the world, even beyond the expressed concerns, the overt propositional sense, of the discourse. Let the rhetor, for example, who is talking about school integration use a pejorative term to refer to black people, and the auditor is confronted with more than a decision about school integration. He is confronted with a plexus of attitudes that may not at all be discussed in the discourse or even implied in any way other than the use of the single term. The discourse will exert on him the pull of an ideology. It will move, unless he rejects it, to structure his experience on many subjects besides school integration. And more, if the auditor himself begins using the pejorative term, it will be a fallible sign that he has adopted not just a position on school integration, but an ideology.

Each one of us, after all, defines himself by what he believes and does. Few of us are born to grow into an identity that was incipiently structured before our births. That was, centuries ago, the way with men, but it certainly is not with us. The quest for identity is the modern pilgrimage. And we look to one another for hints as to whom we should become. Perhaps these reflections do not apply to everyone, but they do apply to the persuasible, and that makes them germane to rhetoric.

The critic can see in the auditor implied by a discourse a model of what the rhetor would have his real auditor become. What the critic can find projected by the discourse is the image of a man, and though that man may never find actual embodiment, it is still a man that the image is of. This condition makes moral judgment possible, and it is at this point in the process of criticism that it can illuminatingly be rendered. We know how to make appraisals of men. We know how to evaluate potentialities of character. We are compelled to do so for ourselves constantly. And this sort of judgment, when fully ramified, constitutes a definitive act of judicial criticism.

A Paradigm

Since a scruple of rationality mandates that claims be warranted, and since the most convincing sanction of a critical position is its efficacy, we turn now to a test. That test will be an essay in the original sense of the word: a trial, an attempt, an exploration. The subject of the essay is a small but recurrent characteristic of discourses associated with the Radical Right in contemporary American politics. That characteristic is the metaphor, "the cancer of communism."

The phrase, "the cancer of communism," is a familiar one. Indeed, it may be so familiar as to approach the condition of a dead metaphor, a cliché. What is less familiar is that this metaphor seems to have become the exclusive property of spokesmen for the Radical Right. Although speakers and writers who clearly are unsympathetic to the Right do sometimes use "cancer" as the vehicle of metaphors, the whole communism-as-cancer metaphor simply is not present in "liberal" or Leftist discourses.[7] Yet it seems to crop up constantly among Rightists—Rightists who sometimes have little else in common besides a political position and the metaphor itself. Perhaps the best source of illustration of the metaphor is the Holy Writ of the John Birch Society, *The Blue Book* by Robert Welch. More than most of his compatriots, Welch really relishes the metaphor. He does not simply sprinkle his pages with it, as for example does Billy James Hargis. Welch amplifies the figure; he expands it; he returns to it again and again. For example:

". . . every thinking and informed man senses that, even as cunning, as ruthless, and as determined as are the activists whom we call Communists with a capital 'C', the conspiracy could never have reached its present extensiveness, and the gangsters at the head of it could never have reached

---

[7] Norman Mailer, for example, has lately been making "cancer" and "malignancy" the vehicles of frequent metaphors, but the tenor of these metaphors, usually implied, seems to be something like "the dehumanization that results from technological society." It clearly is not "communism," although Soviet society is not exempt from Mailer's condemnations. One can also find occasional references to the "cancer of racism" among left-of-center spokesmen, but these references seem to be no more than occasional. Where, as in Mailer, cancer is a frequently recurring metaphorical vehicle, the analysis that follows may, with appropriate substitution of tenors, be applied. In Mailer's case, at least, it works.

their present power, unless there were tremendous weaknesses to make the advance of such a disease so rapid and its ravages so disastrous."[8] And again: "An individual human being may die of any number of causes. But if he escapes the fortuitous diseases, does not meet with any fatal accident, does not starve to death, does not have his heart give out, but lives in normal health to his three score years and ten and then keeps on living—if he escapes or survives everything else and keeps on doing so, he will eventually succumb to the degenerative disease of cancer. For death must come, and cancer is merely death coming by stages, instead of all at once. And exactly the same thing seems to be true of those organic aggregations of human beings, which we called cultures or civilizations."[9] And again: ". . . collectivism destroys the value to the organism of the individual cells—that is, the individual human beings—without replacing them with new ones with new strength. The Roman Empire of the West, for instance, started dying from the cancer of collectivism from the time Diocletian imposed on it his New Deal."[10] And again: "Until now, there is a tremendous question whether, even if we did not have the Communist conspirators deliberately helping to spread the virus for their own purposes, we could recover from just the natural demagogue-fed spread of that virus when it is already so far advanced."[11] And again: "We have got to stop the Communists, for many reasons. One reason is to keep them from agitating our cancerous tissues, reimplanting the virus, and working to spread it, so that we never have a chance of recovery."[12] And finally: "Push the Communists back, get out of the bed of a Europe that is dying with this cancer of collectivism, and breathe our own healthy air of opportunity, enterprise, and freedom; then the cancer we already have, even though it is of considerable growth can be cut out."[13]

There are other examples to be taken from Welch's book, but we have a sample sufficient for our biopsy. Welch, of course, is an extreme case even for the Radical Right. He cultivates the metaphor with the fixity of a true connoisseur. But though the metaphor is not present in the discourses of all Rightists, it seems almost never to appear in the discourses of non-Rightists. It is the idiomatic token of an ideology, the fallible sign of a frame of reference, and it is what we essay to explore.

This metaphor is not the only idiomatic token of American rightwing ideology. There is, to name another, the inventory of perished civilizations that crops up in discourses that are right of center. It is a topos that goes a long way back into our history, and that has evidently been associated with a Rightist orientation for more than a century. Perry Miller, writing of the political conservatism of nineteenth-century revivalism, notes of a sermon

[8] Robert Welch, *The Blue Book of the John Birch Society* (Belmont, Mass., 1961), p. 41.
[9] *Ibid.,* p. 45.
[10] *Ibid.,* p. 46.
[11] *Ibid.,* pp. 53-54.
[12] *Ibid.,* p. 55.
[13] *Ibid.*

delivered in 1841 that it "called the roll . . . of the great kingdoms which had perished—Chaldea, Egypt, Greece, Rome—but gave America the chance, unique in history, of escaping the treadmill to oblivion if it would only adhere to the conserving Christianity. In the same year, George Cheever, yielding himself to what had in literature and painting become . . . a strangely popular theme in the midst of American progress, told how he had stood beneath the walls of the Colosseum, of the Parthenon, of Karnak, and 'read the proofs of God's veracity in the vestiges at once of such stupendous glory and such a stupendous overthrow.' "[14] Miller goes on to observe, "William Williams delivered in 1843 a discourse entitled 'The Conservative Principle,' and Charles White one in 1852 more specifically named 'The Conservative Element in Christianity.' These are merely examples of hundreds in the same vein, all calling attention to how previous empires had perished because they had relied entirely upon the intellect, upon 'Political Economy,' and upon 'false liberalism.' "[15]

That topos is with us yet, and it is almost as much a recurrent feature of Rightist discourse as the communism-as-cancer figure. Both the topos and the metaphor are examples of an idiomatic token of ideology.

Regarding the communism-as-cancer metaphor, it could make considerable difference to critical analysis whether a preoccupation with or morbid fear of cancer had any psychopathological significance, whether such a fear had been identified by psychiatrists as a symptom of sufficient frequency as to have been systematically investigated and associated with any particular psychological condition. If that were the case—if psychiatry had a "line" of any kind on this symptom—such clinical information could be applicable in some way to those people who are affected by the communism-as-cancer metaphor. Moreover, if an obsessive fear of cancer were the symptom of an acknowledged and recognizable psychological condition, the tendency of Rightist discourse to cultivate this fear may work to induce in its auditors some form of that psychological condition. Such would be the enticing prospects of a marriage between science and criticism, but unfortunately both psychiatry and clinical psychology are frigid inamoratas, for the literature of neither recognizes such a symptom. It remains, then, for the critic alone to make what sense he can of the metaphor:

1) Cancer is a kind of horrible pregnancy. It is not an invasion of the body by alien organisms, which is itself a metaphor of war, and therefore suitable to the purposes of the Radical Right. Nor is it the malfunction of one of the body's organs—a mechanical metaphor. The actual affliction may, of course, be related to either or both of these; that is, some kinds of cancer may in fact be produced by a virus (invasion), or they may be the result of the body's failure to produce cancer-rejecting chemicals (malfunction), but these are only the hypotheses of some medical researchers, and not associated with

[14]*The Life of the Mind in America* (New York, 1965), pp. 70-71.
[15]*Ibid.*, p. 71.

the popular conception of cancer. Cancer is conceived as a growth of some group of the body's own cells. The cancer is a part of oneself, a sinister and homicidal extension of one's own body. And one's attitude toward one's body is bound up with one's attitude toward cancer; more so than in the case of invasions or malfunctions, for neither of these is an extension of oneself. It is a living and unconscious malignancy that the body itself has created, in indifference to, even defiance of, the conscious will. And because one's attitude toward one's body is bound up with one's attitude toward cancer, we may suspect that a metaphor that employed cancer as its vehicle would have a particular resonance for an auditor who was ambivalent about his own body. We may suspect, in fact, that the metaphor would strike a special fire with a congeries of more generally puritanical attitudes.

2) In the popular imagination, cancer is thought to be incurable. Now this is a curious aspect of the metaphor. If the metaphor serves to convey the gravity, agony, and malignancy of communism, why would it not convey also its inexorability, and thus promote in the auditor a terror that robs him of the will to resist? That consequence would seem to be contrary to the Rightist's objectives. Why, then, is the metaphor not excessive?

Some auditors possibly are affected by the metaphor or understand it in this way—that is, as a metaphor conveying not just the horror of communism but also the inevitability of its triumph. Hence, Rightists seem less inhibited by the fear of nuclear war than others. Perhaps there is associated with this metaphor not a different estimate of the probable effects of nuclear war, but rather a conviction that the body-politic is already doomed, so that its preservation—the preservation of an organism already ravaged and fast expiring—is not really important.

We must understand the *Weltansicht* with which the metaphor is associated. The world is not a place where one lives in an enclave of political well-being with a relatively remote enemy approaching. No, the enemy is here and his conquests surround one. To the Rightist, communism is not just in Russia or China or North Vietnam. It is also in the local newspaper; it is in the magazines on the newsstand; it is in television and the movies; it has permeated the government at all levels; it may even be in the house next door. We understand well enough that when the Rightist speaks of communism he refers to virtually all social welfare and civil rights legislation. What we understand less well is that when he refers to America, he refers to a polity already in the advanced stages of an inexorable disease whose suppurating sores are everywhere manifest and whose voice is a death rattle.

And what organs of this afflicted body need be spared amputation? The country is deathly ill. Its policies are cowardly; its spokesmen are treasonous; its cities are anarchical; its discipline is flaccid; its poor are arrogant; its rich are greedy; its courts are unjust; its universities are mendacious. True there is a chance of salvation—of cure, but the chance is a slight one, and every moment diminishes it. The patient is *in extremis*. It is in this light that risks must be calculated, and in this light the prospect of nuclear war becomes thinkable. Why not chance it, after all? What alternative is there? The patient is dying; is it not time for the ultimate surgery? What is there to lose? In such a context, an unalarmed attitude toward the use of atomic weapons is not just reasonable; it is obvious.

3) The metaphor seems related to an organismic view of the state. The polity is a living creature, susceptible to disease; a creature with a will, with a consciousness of itself, with a metabolism and a personality, with a life. The polity is a great beast: a beast that first must be cured, and then must be tamed. The question arises, what is the nature of other organisms if the state itself is one? What is the individual if he is a cell in the body-politic? Contrary to what one might expect, we know that the Rightist places great emphasis on individualism, at least verbally. Recall, for example, Goldwater's often used phrase, "the whole man," from the 1964 campaign.[16] It is true, the Rightist is suspicious of beards, of unconventional dress, of colorful styles of living. He has antipathy for deviance from a fairly narrow norm of art, politics, sex, or religion, so that his endorsement of individualism has about it the aura of a self-indulgent hypocrisy. Nonetheless, there is something of great value to him that he calls individualism, and if we would understand him, we must understand what he means by individualism. He probably acts consistent with his own use of the term.

It appears that when the Rightist refers to individualism, he is referring to the acquisition and possession of property. Individualism is the right to get and to spend without interference, and this is an important right because a man asserts himself in his possessions. What he owns is what he has to say. So conceived, individualism is perfectly compatible with an organismic conception of the polity. And moreover, the polity's own hideous possession—its tumor—is an expression of its corruption.

4) At first glance the metaphor seems to place communism in the category of natural phenomena. If one does not create a cancer, then one cannot be responsible for it, and if communism is a kind of cancer, then it would seem that one cannot develop a moral attitude toward its agents. This would constitute a difficulty with the metaphor only if people behaved rationally. Fortunately for the metaphor—and unfortunately for us—there is a demonstrable pervasive and utterly irrational attitude toward cancer that saves the metaphor from difficulty. Morton Bard, a psychologist who investigated the psychological reactions of a hundred patients at Memorial Sloan-Kettering Cancer Center, found that forty-eight of them spontaneously expressed beliefs about the cause of their illness that assigned culpability either to themselves or to others or to some supernatural agent.[17] His study suggests, in other words, that an extraordinarily high proportion of people who have cancer— or for our purposes it may be better to say *who become convinced* that they have cancer—are disposed to blame the cancer on a morally responsible

---

[16]For example, roughly the last third of Goldwater's speech accepting the Republican nomination in 1964 was a panegyric to individuality and nonconformity.

[17]"The Price of Survival for Cancer Victims," *Trans-action*, III (March/April 1966), 11.

agent. Surely it is no great leap from this study to the suspicion that an auditor who is responsive to the metaphor would likely be just the sort of person who would seek culpability. The link between responsiveness to the metaphor and the disposition to seek culpability lies, perhaps, in religious fundamentalism. Various studies indicate that the members of Radical Right organizations tend also to be affiliated with fundamentalist religious sects.[18] Surely it is possible that a life-time of reverent attention to sermons that seek a purpose behind the universe can end by developing a telic cast of mind, can end by inducing some people to seek purpose and plan behind everything, so that they must explain political misfortunes and illness alike by hypothesizing conspiracies.

5) Cancer is probably the most terrifying affliction that is popularly known. So terrible is it, in fact, that medical authorities have reported difficulty in inducing people to submit to physical examinations designed to detect cancer. For many, it seems, cancer has become unthinkable—so horrifying to contemplate that one cannot even admit the possibility of having it. The concept of cancer is intimately connected with the concept of death itself. Thus, to equate communism with cancer is to take an ultimately implacable position. One would not quit the struggle against death except in two circumstances: either one acknowledged its futility and surrendered in despair, or one transmuted the death-concept into a life-concept through an act of religious faith.

Given the equation, communism = cancer = death, we may expect that those enamored of the metaphor would, in the face of really proximate "communism," tend either to despairing acts of suicide or to the fervent embrace of communism as an avenue to grace. The former, suicidal tendency is already discernible in some Rightist political programs, for example, the casual attitude toward nuclear warfare that has already been remarked in another connection. If it were possible for a communist agency to increase its pressure on the United States, we could expect to see the latter tendency increasing, with some of our most impassioned Rightists moving with equal passion to the Left. John Burnham, Elizabeth Bentley, Whitaker Chambers, and others famous from the decade of the fifties for having abandoned the Communist Party have already traveled that road in the opposite direction. The path clearly is there to be trod.

6) Finally, we may note the impressive measure of guilt that seems to be associated with the metaphor. The organism of which one is a cell is afflicted with a culpable illness. Can the whole be infected and the part entirely well?

As the Archbishop in the second part of *Henry IV* says in the midst of political upheaval:

---

[18]See, for example *The Radical Right*, ed. Daniel Bell (Garden City, N.Y., 1964), esp. Seymour Martin Lipset, "Three Decades of the Radical Right: Coughlinites, McCarthyites, and Birchers (1962)," pp. 373-446.

> *. . . we are all diseas'd;*
> *And with our surfeiting and wanton hours*
> *Have brought ourselves into a burning fever,*
> *And we must bleed for it . . .*

The guilt is there. Coherence demands it, and the discourse confirms it. It finds expression in all the classic patterns: the zealous righteousness, the suspiciousness, the morbidity, the feverish expiations. The condition suits the metaphor; the metaphor, the condition.[19]

What moral judgment may we make of this metaphor and of discourse that importantly contains it? The judgment seems superfluous, not because it is elusive, but because it is so clearly implied. The form of consciousness to which the metaphor is attached is not one that commends itself. It is not one that a reasonable man would freely choose, and he would not choose it because it does not compensate him with either prudential efficacy or spiritual solace for the anguished exactions it demands.

In discourse of the Radical Right, as in all rhetorical discourse, we can find enticements not simply to believe something, but to *be* something. We are solicited by the discourse to fulfill its blandishments with our very selves. And it is this dimension of rhetorical discourse that leads us finally to moral judgment, and in this specific case, to adverse judgment.

If our exploration has revealed anything, it is how exceedingly well the metaphor of communism-as-cancer fits the Rightist ideology. The two are not merely compatible; they are complementary at every curve and angle. They serve one another at a variety of levels; they meet in a seamless jointure. This relationship, if it holds for all or even many such stylistic tokens, suggests that the association between an idiom and an ideology is much more than a matter of arbitrary convention or inexplicable accident. It suggests that there are strong and multifarious links between a style and an outlook, and that the critic may, with legitimate confidence, move from the manifest evidence of style to the human personality that this evidence projects as a beckoning archetype.

---

[19] Some illuminating comments on the component of guilt in Rightist style and ideology can be found in Richard Hofstadter, "The Paranoid Style in American Politics," *The Paranoid Style in American Politics and Other Essays* (New York, 1967), esp. pp. 30-32.

Lincoln at Cooper Union:
A Rhetorical Analysis of the Text
by Michael C. Leff and Gerald P. Mohrmann

When Abraham Lincoln spoke at the Cooper Union on the evening of February 27, 1860, his audience responded enthusiastically, and the speech has continued to elicit praise throughout the intervening years. Biographers, historians, and literary scholars agree that it was "one of his most significant speeches,"[1] one that illustrated "his abilities as a reasoner,"[2] and one to which posterity has ascribed his "subsequent nomination and election to the president."[3] Ironically, however, this model of "logical analysis and construction"[4] has failed to generate a critical response in kind. Most of what has been written treats of the background, and, too often, the man as myth has intruded; caught up in the drama of the performance, writers find no bit of information too trivial to report, whether it be the price of tickets or the fit of Lincoln's new shoes.[5] Such details can deepen our appreciation of the event, but they do not illuminate the speech as a speech.

Unhappily, little light is shed by those who do comment on the speech text. Nicolay and Hay assert, for example, that Lincoln's conclusions "were irresistibly convincing,"[6] but their sole piece of supporting evidence is a four-hundred word excerpt. And if they happen to be "firmly in the hero-worshipping tradition,"[7] those of sterner stuff fare no better. Basler makes the curious claim that the rhetorical "high-water mark" occurs toward the end of the first section;[8] Nevins mistakenly argues that the speech "fell into two halves";[9] reputable scholars equate summary and quotation with explication;[10]

Reprinted from *The Quarterly Journal of Speech* 60 (1974): 346-358 with permission of the Speech Communication Association.

[1] J. G. Randall, *Lincoln the President* (New York: Dodd, Mead, 1945), I, 135.

[2] Howard Mumford Jones and Ernest E. Leisy, eds., *Major American Writers* (New York: Harcourt, Brace, 1945), p. 681.

[3] Benjamin Barondess, *Three Lincoln Masterpieces* (Charleston: Education Foundation of West Virginia, 1954), p. 3.

[4] R. Franklin Smith, "A Night at Cooper Union," *Central States Speech Journal* 13 (Autumn 1962), 272.

[5] The most influential account of this sort is Carl Sandburg, *The Prairie Years* (New York: Harcourt, Brace, 1927), II, 200-216, but the most complete is Andrew A. Freeman, *Abraham Lincoln Goes to New York* (New York: Coward-McCann, 1960).

[6] John G. Nicolay and John Hay, *Abraham Lincoln: A History* (New York: Century, 1917), II, 219-220.

[7] Richard Hofstadter, *The American Political Tradition* (New York: Alfred A. Knopf, 1948), p. 364.

[8] *Abraham Lincoln: His Speeches and Writings*, ed. Roy P. Basler (Cleveland: World, 1946), p. 32.

[9] Allan Nevins, *The Emergence of Lincoln* (New York: Charles Scribner's Sons, 1950), II, 186.

[10] Randall, pp. 136-137; Basler, pp. 32-33; Nevins, pp. 186-187; Reinhard H. Luthin, *The Real Abraham Lincoln* (Englewood Cliffs, New Jersey: Prentice-Hall, 1960), p. 210.

and it is generally accepted that Lincoln demonstrated a conciliatory attitude toward the South.[11]

Certainly all is not dross in previous studies, but wherever one turns in the literature, no satisfying account of the speech is to be found.[12] We are convinced that a systematic rhetorical analysis can help rectify the situation, and what follows is our attempt to accomplish such an analysis. In that attempt, we center on the text of the speech, but our purpose demands some preliminary remarks about the rhetorical context.

Although it was not until after the speech that Lincoln frankly admitted his presidential aspirations, saying, "The taste *is* in my mouth a little,"[13] he had been savoring the possibility for months. The preceding November, he had written that the next canvas would find him laboring "faithfully in the ranks" unless "the judgment of the party shall assign me a different position,"[14] but even as he wrote, Lincoln was grasping for a different assignment, "busy using the knife on his rivals . . . and doing all he could to enhance his reputation as an outstanding Republican leader."[15] Small wonder that he decided early to "make a political speech of it" in New York.[16] Here was the opportunity to make himself more available to Republicans in the East. The appearance alone would make for greater recognition, but political availability required more; Lincoln had to be an acceptable Republican, and he had to be an attractive alternative to the Democratic candidate.

William A. Seward and Stephen A. Douglas were the presumptive nominees, and they, patently, were Lincoln's antagonists. Moreover, their views on slavery created an intertwining threat that menaced his conception of the party and his personal ambitions. When Seward spoke about a "higher law" and an "irrepressible conflict," he strained Lincoln's sense of moral and political conservatism; these pronouncements smacked too much of radicalism.[17] Douglas, meanwhile, exacerbated the situation with his doctrine of popular sovereignty. Lincoln feared that this siren song would cause wholesale apostasy in Republican ranks, an eventuality all the more likely if the party nominee was tinctured with radicalism. He knew, however, that a

---

[11]Randall, p. 136; Barondess, p. 18; Nicholay and Hay, p. 220, Nevins, p. 186; Luthin, pp. 243-244.

[12]Freeman treats of the text briefly, pp. 84-88, and although Barondess ranges from preparation to audience reaction, pp. 3-30, Hofstadter's observation applies, n. 7 above. Earl W. Wiley discusses the address in *Four Speeches by Lincoln* (Columbus: Ohio State Univ. Press, 1927), pp. 15-27, but he limits analysis to the first section of the speech, a limitation also applied in his "Abraham Lincoln: His Emergence as the Voice of the People," in *A History and Criticism of American Public Address*, ed. William N. Brigance (New York: McGraw-Hill, 1943), II, 859-877. In the same volume, the speech is the basis for comments on delivery in Mildred Freburg Berry, "Abraham Lincoln: His Development in the Skills of the Platform," pp. 828-858.

[13]Letter to Lyman Trumbull, April 29, 1860, *The Collected Works of Abraham Lincoln*, ed. Roy P. Basler (New Brunswick, New Jersey: Rutgers Univ. Press, 1955), IV, 45.

[14]Letter to William E. Frazer, November 1, 1859, *Collected Works*, III, 491.

[15]Richard N. Current, *The Lincoln Nobody Knows* (New York: McGraw-Hill, 1958), p. 199. For an indication of Lincoln's activities see *Collected Works*, III, 384-521.

[16]Letter to James A. Briggs, *Collected Works*, III, 494.

[17]See Letter to Salmon P. Chase, June 9, 1859, *Collected Works*, III, 384; Letter to Nathan Sargent, June 23, 1859, *Collected Works*, III, 387-388; Letter to Richard M. Corwine, April 6, 1860, *Collected Works*, IV, 36.

middle ground existed, and he long had occupied it with his insistence that slavery should be protected but not extended. Consequently, when Lincoln addressed the Eastern Republicans, both principle and expediency permitted, even dictated, that he speak for party and for self and that he maintain party and self in a position between those taken by Seward and Douglas.

That he took such a course is revealed by an examination of the speech text, but all the external evidence shows a man running hard, if humbly, for political office, and while Lincoln spoke for his party, he spoke first for his own nomination. In fact, the Cooper Union Address is best characterized as a campaign oration, a speech designed to win nomination for the speaker. This identification of genre is basic to our analysis, and the nature of the genre is suggested by Rosenthal's distinction between nonpersonal and personal persuasion;[18] in the former, the speaker attempts to influence audience attitudes about a particular issue, and ethos is important insofar as it lends credence to the substance of the argument. In the latter the process is reversed. The focal point is the speaker, and the message becomes a vehicle for enhancing ethos. Campaign orations, on this basis, tend to be examples of personal persuasion, for while "the ostensible purpose of a given speech may be to gain acceptance of a particular policy, . . . the actual purpose is to gain votes for the candidate."[19] In other words, the ultimate goal of the campaign orator is to promote himself as a candidate. Both policies and character are in question, but the treatment of issues is subsidiary to the purpose of creating a general identification between the speaker and the audience. The objective, then, in a campaign oration is ingratiation.

With genre and purpose in mind, we can approach the speech through familiar topics. Addressing himself first to the people of New York, then to the South and finally to the Republican Party, Lincoln divides his speech into three sections, and this pattern of organization invites seriatim analysis of the major dispositional units. Furthermore, argument and style immediately loom as important elements, since they disclose essential characteristics in and significant interrelationships among the main units of the discourse. Consequently, our critique will follow Lincoln's pattern of organization and will have special reference to matters of argument and style. This approach, however, is not without its hazards. The convenience of tracing the natural sequence of the argument may foster fragmentary analysis and obscure the dominant rhetorical motive. Yet to be mindful of the genre is to find a corrective. The central concern is ingratiation, and recognition of this purpose unifies the elements of analysis by giving them a more precise focus; awareness of the ultimate goal becomes shuttle to the threads of structure, argument, and style.

In the address, Lincoln deals exclusively with slavery, and although this

---

[18]Paul I. Rosenthal, "The Concept of Ethos and the Structure of Persuasion," *Speech Monographs* 33 (June 1966), 114-126.
[19]Rosenthal, p. 120.

inflammatory issue might seem a shaky bridge to ingratiation, the choice is a fitting response to the rhetorical problem. What better point of departure than the paramount issue of the day, the issue with which he was most closely identified, and the issue that had spawned the Republican Party?[20] And Lincoln starts with the very motivation that had driven men to Ripon only a few years before, the question of slavery in the territories. Capitalizing on these initial associations, he counters the emotionalism inherent in the topic by assuming a severely rational posture and enunciating a moderate but firm set of principles. The approach distinguishes him from his chief rivals and solicits an intensified association from Eastern Republicans. These objectives govern the matter and manner of the opening argument, and this argument lays a foundation for subsequent developments in the speech. In the opening section and throughout, Lincoln associates himself and Republicans with the founding fathers and Constitutional principle, and he dissociates rival candidates and factions from those fathers and that principle.

Acknowledging his "fellow citizens of New York," Lincoln begins by adopting a "text for this discourse."[21] The text is a statement in which Stephen A. Douglas had asserted, "Our fathers, when they framed the government under which we live, understood this question just as well and even better than we do now." Defining terms in catechistic sequence, Lincoln maintains that "the frame of government under which we live" consists of the Constitution and the "twelve subsequently framed amendments" and that "our fathers" are "the 'thirty-nine' who signed the original instrument." He then asks, what is the question "those fathers understood 'just as well and even better, than we do now'?" The answer "is this: Does the proper division of local from Federal authority, or anything else in the Constitution, forbid our Federal Government to control as to slavery in our Federal Territories?" The question joins the issue because it is a matter upon which "Senator Douglas holds the affirmative, and the Republicans the negative."

That Douglas should play the foil is most fitting. National newspaper coverage of the 1858 senatorial campaign had linked the two men together,

---

[20]In 1854, "northern whigs persuaded that their old party was moribund, Democrats weary of planting dominance, and free-soilers eager to exclude slavery from the territories began to draw together to resist the advance of the planting power"; Charles A. Beard and Mary R. Beard, *The Rise of American Civilization* (New York: Macmillan, 1937), II, 22. Cf. Don E. Fehrenbacher, "Lincoln and the Formation of the Republican Party," in *Prelude to Greatness* (Stanford: Stanford Univ. Press, 1962), pp. 19-47.

[21]We follow the text in *Complete Works*, ed. John G. Nicolay and John Hay (New York: Francis D. Tandy, 1905), V, 293-328; we include no footnotes because aside from unimportant exceptions, citations are sequential. This text is more conservative in typography than that edited and published as a campaign document by Charles C. Nott and Cephas Brainerd. The latter appears in *Collected Works*, III, 522-550; 1860, p. 1. Substantive variations in extant see also the *New York Times*, February 28, texts are minuscule, and this consistency deserves comment. Lincoln ignored suggested alterations in the original (Sandburg, II, 210 and 215-216); he proofread the newspaper copy (Freeman, pp. 92-93); pamphlet copies were available by the first of April (*Collected Works*, IV, 38-39); and Lincoln adamantly resisted editorial changes by Nott (*Collected Works*, IV, 58-59). This evidence emphasizes the care with which he constructed the speech, but it also suggests that he anticipated a wider audience from the outset. Publication practices and his own experience told Lincoln that he would reach many who would not hear him speak.

and the debates were to be published in March.[22] Moreover, Lincoln had continued the argument during 1859, worrying whether the Republican Party would "maintain it's [sic] identity, or be broken up to form the tail of Douglas' new kite."[23] Nevertheless, Lincoln knew that Douglas was vulnerable. The Freeport Doctrine had convinced many in the North that the man was only too "willing to subordinate moral considerations to political expediency."[24] Douglas, then, was an established rival, one whom Lincoln perceived as a threat to party unity, and one whose strategic position was open to attack from principle.

On a tactical level, the "text" quoted from Douglas affords Lincoln an ideal starting point. The allusion to the fathers is a symbolic reference with the potential for universal respect, and Douglas' implicit attack upon the principles that had generated the Republican Party creates an antithesis binding speaker and audience together in opposition to a common enemy. This antithesis is a channel for ingratiation; Lincoln makes Republicanism the voice of rational analysis, and the precise terms of Douglas' assertion form the premises of logical inquiry. Moving into the inquiry, Lincoln pursues a vigorous *ad hominem* attack.[25] He accepts Douglas' logic and then turns it against him.

The argument of the first section develops out of a single hypothetical proposition: if the better understanding evinced by our fathers shows that they believed nothing forbade control of slavery in the territories, then such regulatory power is inherent in the governmental frame. Lincoln affirms the antecedent with an elaborate chain of inductive evidence. Instances in the induction consist of actions by the fathers before and after they signed the Constitution because the question "seems not to have been directly before the convention."[26] From the Northwest Ordinance of 1784 to the Missouri Compromise of 1820, Lincoln enumerates seven statutes regulating slavery in

---

[22]General interest in the debates is underlined by the favorable editorial notice appearing in the Brooklyn *Daily Times*, August 26, 1858, an editorial written by one Walt Whitman; Walt Whitman, *I Sit and Look Out*, ed. Emory Holloway and Vernolian Schwartz (New York: Columbia Univ. Press, 1932), p. 96. For letters referring to publication of the debates, see *Collected Works*, III, 341, 343, 372-374, 515, and 516.

[23]Letter to Lyman Trumbull, Dec. 11, 1858, *Collected Works*, III, 345.

[24]Harry J. Carman and Harold C. Syrett, *A History of the American People* (New York: Alfred A. Knopf, 1952), I, 588, Cf. Fehrenbacher, "The Famous 'Freeport Question,' " in *Prelude to Greatness*, pp. 121-142.

[25]Logicians often define *ad hominem* as a fallacy resulting from an attack upon the character of a man rather than the quality of argument. In this essay, however, we use the term as Schopenhauer does in distinguishing between *ad hominem* and *ad rem* as the two basic modes of refutation. He differentiates in this manner: "We may show either that the proposition is not in accordance with the nature of things, *i.e.*, with absolute, objective truth [*ad rem*]; or that it is inconsistent with other statements or admissions of our opponent, *i.e.*, with truth as it appears to him [*ad hominem*]"; Arthur Schopenhauer, "The Art of Controversy," in *The Will to Live: Selected Writings of Arthur Schopenhauer*, ed. Richard Taylor (New York: Anchor Books, 1962), p. 341. See Henry W. Johnstone, Jr., "Philosophy and *Argumentum ad Hominem*," *Journal of Philosophy* 49 (July 1952), 489-498.

[26]Lincoln undoubtedly knew that James Wilson, Patrick Henry and Edmund Randolph had discussed the topic (See *Collected Works*, III, 526-527, n. 9.), but he is accurate in asserting that the subject did not come "directly" before the convention.

the territories, and he accounts for votes by twenty-three of the fathers.[27] Twenty-one voted in favor of such regulation. Since these men were bound by "official responsibility and their corporal oaths" to uphold the Constitution, the implication of their affirmative votes is beyond question. To conclude that the twenty-one would have condoned federal regulation if they thought it unconstitutional would be to accuse these fathers of "gross political impropriety and willful perjury," and "as actions speak louder than words, so actions under such responsibility speak still louder."

Emphasizing deeds and "adhering rigidly to the text," Lincoln cannot offer evidence "whatever understanding may have been manifested by any person" other than the thirty-nine, nor can he cite the sixteen who left no voting records. But the latter include the likes of Franklin, Hamilton, and Morris, and he believes that this group "would probably have acted just as the twenty-three did." In any event, "a clear majority of the whole" understood that nothing "forbade the Federal Government to control slavery in the Federal Territories," and with the remaining fathers probably agreeing, there can be little doubt about "the understanding of our fathers who framed the original Constitution; and the text affirms that they understood the question 'better than we.' "

Lincoln now uses this understanding to discredit arguments based on the fifth and tenth amendments; he says it is "a little presumptuous" to suggest that the fathers embraced one principle when writing the Constitution and another when writing the amendments. And does not this suggestion "become impudently absurd when coupled with the other affirmation, from the same mouth, that those who did the two things alleged to be inconsistent, understood whether they really were inconsistent better than we—better than he who affirms that they are inconsistent?" The touch of sarcasm reveals a more aggressive attitude, but it is justified by the inductive process; Douglas' own criterion forces the conclusion that he does not comprehend the understanding of the fathers. Lincoln will become even more combative before he brings the first section to a close, but some comments on style are merited, and they will lead us into his conclusion.

The style of this section is entirely consistent with Lincoln's severely rational approach. The audience probably did not expect the "rhetorical fireworks of a Western stump-speaker,"[28] but Lincoln is most circumspect. There are none of the "many excuses" that made him a Uriah Heep to some of his opponents,[29] and he avoids all display, indulging neither in anecdotes nor figurative language. The syntax is complex at times, but the complexity is that of legal rather than literary prose, as is evidenced in the following sentence: "It, therefore, would be unsafe to set down even the two who voted

[27]Washington's vote was his signature, as President, on the Act of 1789 which enforced the Ordinance of 1787.
[28]Nicolay and Hay, *Abraham Lincoln*, II, 220.
[29]See Hofstadter, p. 94; *Collected Works*, III, 396.

against the prohibition as having done so because, in their understanding, any proper division of local from Federal authority, or anything in the Constitution, forbade the Federal Government to control as to slavery in Federal territory."

The preceding quotation, with its echo of the text, points to a noteworthy stylistic element: repetition. Lincoln includes fifteen extended citations of the issue and an equal number from the "text," repetitions that accentuate the single line of argument. He adds to the emphasis by stressing certain key words and phrases. For example, there are over thirty uses of the root "understand," usually in the participial "understanding," and Lincoln alludes to the "fathers" more than thirty-five times. None of these repetitions is blatant or forced because he weaves them into the fabric of the inductive process. Furthermore, the repetitions concomitantly reinforce and control the emotional association with the fathers and their understanding of the Constitution. This point is crucial to an appreciation of Lincoln's rhetorical method. Both the direction of the argument and the symbols expressing it are fiercely emotional; yet, all is enmeshed in an incisive logical and linguistic structure, and while the tone remains rationalistic and legalistic, it also creates a subtle emotive nexus between the Republican audience and the founding fathers.

As noted above, style and argument shift in the concluding paragraphs, after Lincoln already has established his logical credentials. The argument becomes bolder, and the style alters appropriately. When developing the induction, Lincoln refers to the framers of the Constitution as the "thirty-nine," but they become "our fathers" again in the conclusion of the long first section of the speech. And there periods become more polished and sophisticated:

> If any man at this day sincerely believes that a proper division of local from Federal authority, or any part of the Constitution, forbids the Federal Government to control as to slavery in the Federal Territories, he is right to say so, and to enforce his position by all truthful evidence and fair argument which he can. But he has no right to mislead others, who have less access to history, and less leisure to study it, into the false belief that 'our fathers who framed the government under which we live' were of the same opinion—thus substituting falsehood and deception for truthful evidence and fair argument.

This passage completes the negative phase of Lincoln's argumentation. Both matter and manner drive a rational wedge between the speaker and his rivals. Clearly, Lincoln suggests that Douglas may be guilty of deliberate "falsehood and deception," and just as clearly, his own position represents "truthful evidence and fair argument." Lincoln, one of those with "access to history" and some "leisure to study it," attempts to set the record straight. Another direct slash at Douglas, the very source of the text and issue. At the same time, Lincoln indirectly differentiates himself from Seward and his radical posture. Lincoln's position is more to the right, closer to the demands of objective inquiry, closer also to the demands of political availability, and it is important to remark that he achieves this dissociation without recourse to divisive rhetoric. The foray against the man and his position is patent, but it is completely inferential.

Although less obtrusive than the refutation, an equally important constructive movement exists within this part of the oration. Not only does Lincoln distinguish himself from his opponents, he nurtures Republican unity because he makes himself and party the vessels for transmitting the faith of the fathers. Avoiding self-references, he presents himself as the voice of Republicanism, and he caps this appeal with words both to and from the party:

> But enough! Let all who believe that 'our fathers who framed the government under which we live understood this question just as well, and even better, than we do now,' speak as they spoke, and act as they acted upon it. This is all Republicans ask—all Republicans desire—in relation to slavery. As those fathers marked it, so let it be again marked, as an evil not to be extended, but to be tolerated and protected only because of and so far as its actual presence among us makes that toleration and protection a necessity. Let all the guarantees those fathers gave it be not grudgingly, but fully and fairly, maintained. For this Republicans contend, and with this, so far as I know or believe, they will be content.

At this point in the speech, Lincoln has associated himself and his audience with the spirit, the principles and the actions of the founding fathers, and in doing so, he has taken the first steps toward ingratiation.

Comprising nearly half the speech, this initial section is so clearly logical that it regularly is cited as a demonstration of Lincoln's powers as a reasoner, but to say no more is to grossly underestimate his achievement. The next section, too, is remarkable for its logical development, and all that follows in the speech is anticipated and controlled by the attack upon Douglas. Failure to appreciate this unity has confounded commentators, and their confusion is strikingly illustrated in the generally accepted conclusion that Lincoln follows his attack with remarks "conciliatory toward the South."[30]

The second section does begin with an ostensible change in audience: "And now, if they would listen,—as I suppose they will not,—I would address a few words to the Southern people." But we learn more about the beholders than the object when we are told that the next twenty-six paragraphs are filled with "words of kindly admonition and protest,"[31] words of "sweet reasonableness to allay Southern fears."[32] Presuming that he will not be heard, Lincoln notes that "our party gets no votes" in the South, and

---

[30]Randall, I, 136.
[31]Nicolay and Hay, *Abraham Lincoln*, I, 220.
[32]Nevins, II, 186.

he flatly asserts later that "the Southern people will not so much as listen to us." These are not idle reservations. They represent the realistic assessment of an astute politician who knows that the coming election will be won or lost in the North; it is hardly plausible that this man would detract from his ultimate purpose by directing nearly forty per cent of his speech to an unavailable audience.

In truth, the audience does not change. Lincoln merely casts the second section of the speech in the form of a *prosopopoeia*, a figure he had rehearsed five months earlier in Cincinnati.[33] The device suits his purposes admirably. It enables him to create a mock debate between Republicans and the South, a debate in which he becomes spokesman for the party. In this role, Lincoln can strengthen the identification between himself and the available Republican audience. He is careful to extend the refutation of Douglas into the second section and thus carry over the lines of association and disassociation begun earlier in the discourse. If Lincoln leaves Douglas with little ground on which to stand, he performs the same argumentative service for the South, and the debate he manufactures is far from being conciliatory.

The *prosopopoeia* develops into another *ad hominem* argument. This time, however, the presentation is complicated by the need to deal with the collective contentions of a collective opposition. To provide control, Lincoln again begins by stressing reason, saying to the South, "I consider that in the general qualities of reason and justice you are not inferior to any other people." Yet, in the specific case, rational discourse is stymied because the Southerners never refer to Republicans except "to denounce us as reptiles, or, at the best, as no better than outlaws." Such responses are unjust to both sides. The proper course would be to "bring forward your charges and specifications, and then be patient long enough to hear us deny or justify." Obviously, the South is unwilling and unable to follow this procedure, and becoming persona for both Republicanism and reason, Lincoln reconstructs the charges and specifications; these include sectionalism, radicalism, agitation of the slavery question, and slave insurrections.

The putative debate begins: "You say we are sectional. We deny it. That makes an issue; and the burden of proof is upon you." The crux of the matter is whether Republicans repel the South with "some wrong principle." Republican principle, however, is based in the beliefs and actions of the fathers, and Lincoln challenges the South to respond to this fact. "Do you accept the challenge? No! Then you really believe that the principle which 'our fathers who framed the government under which we live' thought so clearly right as to adopt it, and indorse it again and again, upon their official oaths, is in fact so clearly wrong as to demand your condemnation without a moment's consideration." Closing and reinforcing this line of reasoning

---

[33]*Collected Works*, III, 438-454. Speaking at Cincinnati, September 17, 1859, Lincoln directs so much of his speech across the river "to the Kentuckians" (p. 440.) that one listener complained aloud, "Speak to Ohio men, and not to Kentuckians!" (p. 445.) Interestingly, Nevins appreciates the *prosopopoeia* in this speech, noting that Lincoln was "ostensibly speaking to Kentuckians," II, 56.

Lincoln refers to the pre-eminent father: "Some of you delight to flaunt in our faces the warning . . . given by Washington in his Farewell Address," but if he were to speak for himself "would he cast the blame of that sectionalism upon us, who sustain his policy, or upon you, who repudiate it? We respect that warning of Washington, and we commend it to you, together with his example pointing to the right application of it."[34] Thus, the South claims to be the injured party, but analysis of the charge proves that the wounds are self-inflicted.

Lincoln uses the same refutational method for each of the other issues; first defining the charge with a series of rhetorical questions, he then turns the argument against the adversary. The South proclaims itself the bastion of conservatism and denounces Republican radicalism, but "what is conservatism? Is it not adherence to the old and tried, against the new and untried? We stick to, contend for, the identical old policy . . . which was adopted by 'our fathers who framed the government under which we live'; while you with one accord reject, and scout, and spit upon that old policy, and insist upon substituting something new." The South alleges that Republicans have made the slavery issue more prominent. True, the issue is more prominent, but this situation arose because the South "discarded the old policy of the fathers." Finally, Southerners complain that Republicans foment insurrection among the slaves, but they can adduce no evidence to support this allegation, cannot "implicate a single Republican" and ignore that "Republican doctrines and declarations are accompanied with a continual protest against any interference whatever" with the institution in the slave states. Indeed, were it not for the loud and misleading protestations of Southern politicians, the slaves would hardly know that the Republican Party existed. Worse yet, the South refuses to acknowledge a simple truth contained in Republican doctrine, a truth articulated "many years ago" when Jefferson indicated that the cause of slave insurrections was slavery itself. Like Jefferson, Republicans would not interfere with slavery where it exists, but Republicans do insist, as the fathers did, that the federal government "has the power of restraining the extension of the institution—the power to insure that a slave insurrection shall never occur on any American soil which is now free."

Finishing his treatment of specific charges, Lincoln builds to a more forceful and aggressive tone, just as he did at the end of the first section. His arrangement of responses to Southern allegations is itself climactic, the issue of insurrections being both last and most critical. Always volatile, this issue had become extremely explosive in the wake of the Harper's Ferry raid and the trial of John Brown, and Lincoln understandably chooses this matter as the instrument for his most extensive defense of party and principle. He is not

---

[34]The varied interpretations of Washington's warning and their longevity are illustrated in debates, early in 1850, over the purchase of the Farewell Address manuscript for the Library of Congress. Much of the debate is reproduced in William Dawson Johnston, *History of the Library of Congress* (Washington: Government Printing Office, 1904), I, 326-340.

content, however, to assume a merely defensive posture; the entire pattern of his argumentation reveals a movement from reply to attack that gathers momentum as the discourse proceeds. Thus, having disposed of the insurrection controversy, Lincoln assails the very character of the Southern position, and he concludes this section with an examination of threats emanating from the South.

The South hopes to "break up the Republican organization." That failing, "you will break up the Union rather than submit to a denial of your constitutional rights." This is a course of "rule or ruin"; the union will be destroyed unless people are permitted to take slaves into the federal territories. But no such right exists in the Constitution, and Southern threats are fruitless. Neither the Constitution nor the Republican Party are so malleable as to bend at the touch of Southern fancy. Not even the Dred Scott decision offers a refuge. That verdict was made "in a divided court, by a bare majority of the judges, and they not quite agreeing with one another in the reasons for making it." The decision rests upon "the opinion that 'the right of property in a slave is distinctly and expressly affirmed in the Constitution,' " but careful analysis shows that this right is not even implied. Surely it is reasonable to expect the Court to retract "the mistaken statement" when apprised of its error. Furthermore, the verdict runs contrary to the judgment of the fathers, those who decided the same question long ago "without division among themselves when making the decision," without division "about the meaning of it after it was made," and without "basing it upon any mistaken statement of facts." Having thus contrasted the babel of the Court with the unity of the fathers and their lineal descendants, Lincoln builds to a striking analogy:

> Under these circumstances, do you really feel yourselves justified to break up this government unless such a court decision as yours is shall be at once submitted to as a conclusive and final rule of political action? But you will not abide the election of a Republican president! In that supposed event, you say, you will destroy the Union; and then, you say, the crime of having destroyed it will be upon us! That is cool. A highwayman holds a pistol to my ear, and mutters through his teeth, 'Stand and deliver, or I shall kill you, and then you will be a murderer!'

Adding that the highwayman's threat can "scarcely be distinguished in principle" from "the threat of destruction to the Union," Lincoln completes his *ad hominem* assault against the Southern position, and the *prosopopoeia* ends.

The parallels and interrelationships between the first and the second sections of the speech are evident. Some shifts in invention and style between the two sections are occasioned by the change of antagonist, but it is more significant that Lincoln elects to argue against adversaries in both and that he uses the same fundamental argument to dispatch them all. In both sections, he strives to become spokesman for the party by demonstrating that he is a man of reason and that this characteristic melds himself and party with the principles of the founding fathers. In addition, the same characteristic distinguishes him from other candidates. Finally, each section is based on a severely rational framework and builds to a terminal climax that unifies and heightens logical and emotional dimensions.

Merging style and argument within and between parts of the discourse, Lincoln unquestionably remains in touch with his immediate audience, and he unquestionably has his eye on ingratiation. In the first movement, he separates himself and party from Douglas and Seward; in the second, he favorably contrasts the position of the party with that of its most vociferous opponent.[35] But one further step remains. To this juncture, the identification of speaker, party, and principle has been closely tied to a series of negative definitions. A positive gesture seems necessary, and in the final section of the speech, Lincoln fuses his audience together through more directly constructive appeals.

He begins by saying he will address "a few words now to Republicans," and though he puts aside both text and issue, his remarks evolve naturally from what has proceeded. Once more reason is the point of departure. Having, in the highwayman metaphor, implied a contrast between cool reason and hot passion, Lincoln urges Republicans to "do nothing through passion and ill-temper" that might cause discord within the nation, and, as he draws out the ultimate implications of the Southern position, antithesis becomes the dominant mode of argument and style. The section centers on a contrast between the Republicans and the South (between "we" and "they"); it extends and amplifies the distinction between word and deed that is present throughout the speech; and the argument is couched in and reinforced by antithetical syntax.

Recognizing Southern intransigence, Lincoln still wants his party to "calmly consider their demands" and reach conclusions based on all "they say and do." Pursuing the inquiry, he asks, "Will they be satisfied if the Territories be unconditionally surrendered to them? We know they will not." And "will it satisfy them if, in the future, we have nothing to do with invasions and insurrections? We know it will not." It will not because past abstention has not exempted "us from the charge and the denunciation." To satisfy them, "we must not only leave them alone, but we must somehow convince them that we do let them alone." Experience shows that this is no easy task because Republican policy and actions have been misconstrued consistently. The only recourse seems to be "this and only this: cease to call

---

[35]The second movement continues the implicit attack upon Seward, and all texts indicate a mimicking of Douglas' "gur-reat pur-rinciple" Buchanan also is a victim here, for he had championed popular sovereignty in his "Third Annual Message," December 19, 1859; *The Works of James Buchanan*, ed. John Bassett More (1908-1911; rpt. New York: Antiquarian Press Ltd., 1960), X, 342. Lincoln's efforts were not lost on a New York *Evening Post* reporter who wrote that "the speaker places the Republican party on the very ground occupied by the framers of our constitution and the fathers of our Republic" and that "in this great controversy the Republicans are the real conservative party." His report is reprinted in the *Chicago Tribune*, 1 Mar. 1860, p. 1.

slavery wrong, and join them in calling it right. And this must be done thoroughly—done in acts as well as words. Silence will not be tolerated—we must place ourselves avowedly with them." Republicans must suppress all "declarations that slavery is wrong," must return "fugitive slaves with greedy pleasure," and must pull down all free state constitutions "before they will cease to believe that all their troubles proceed from us."

Most Southerners, Lincoln admits, would not put the argument in this extreme form. Most would simply claim that they want to be left alone, but "we do let them alone." Consequently, it is apparent that "they will continue to accuse us of doing, until we cease saying." Given the nature of their arguments and the character of their actions, the Southerners cannot stop short of the demand that all Republicans desist from speaking and acting out of conviction. Those who hold that "slavery is morally right and socially elevating" must necessarily call for its recognition "as a legal right and a social blessing." Stripped of its veneer and examined in the cold light of reason, the Southern position reveals the disagreement governing the entire conflict; it also underscores the principle from which Republicans cannot retreat. Lincoln expresses both points in a final antithesis that reduces the issue of slavery to a matter of right and wrong, to a matter of moral conviction:

> Their thinking it right and our thinking it wrong is the precise fact upon which depends the whole controversy. Thinking it right, as they do, they are not to blame for desiring its full recognition as being right; but thinking it wrong, as we do, can we yield to them? Can we cast our votes with their view, and against our own? In view of our moral, social, and political responsibilities, can we do this?

Providing no answers because they are only too obvious, Lincoln moves on to merge self and party with the fathers, and Washington is the exemplar.

Style changes appropriately as Lincoln makes his final call for unity. Antithetical elements appear in the penultimate paragraph, but the opposed clauses are subordinated within the long, periodic flow of the final sentence, a flow that builds emotionally to a union with Washington's words and deeds. Lincoln repeats that slavery can be left alone where it exists, but he insists that there can be no temporizing when it comes to the extension of slavery:

> If our sense of duty forbids this, then let us stand by our duty fearlessly and effectively. Let us be diverted by none of those sophistical contrivances wherewith we are so industriously plied, and belabored—contrivances such as groping for some middle ground between the right and the wrong: vain as the search for a man who should be neither a living man nor a dead man; such as a policy of 'don't care' on a question about which all true men do care; such as Union appeals beseeching true Union men to yield to Disunionists, reversing the divine rule, and calling, not the sinners, but the righteous to repentance: such as invocations to Washington, imploring men to unsay what Washington said and undo what Washington did.

Neither let us be slandered from our duty by false accusations against us, nor frightened from it by menaces of destruction to the government, nor of dungeons to ourselves. Let us have faith that right makes might, and in that faith let us to the end dare to do our duty as we understand it.

This short third section, constituting less than fifteen per cent of the text, is a fitting climax to Lincoln's efforts. Rational principle develops into moral conviction, and the resulting emotional intensity emerges from and synthesizes all that has gone before. Yet the intensity is controlled. Speaker and audience are resolute and principled, but at the same time, they are poised and logical. Others may indulge in "false accusations" and "menaces of destruction," but Lincoln and Republicans will have faith in right and in their understanding.

With this closing suggestion of antithetical behavior, Lincoln harks back to all he has said, and with it, he completes his exercise in ingratiation. Douglas is a pitiful example of one who argues misguided principle in maladroit fashion, and Seward's notion of an irrepressible conflict is at odds with the true spirit of the Republican Party, a party whose words and deeds follow from what the framers of the government said and did. Neither opponent measures up to the new and higher self-conception that the speaker has created for his audience. Furthermore, Lincoln has, by this very performance, demonstrated that he is the one who will best represent party and principle. Starting with reason and principle, he has shunted aside opposition, differentiated between Republicans and the South, and pushed on to unite the party in the faith that will "let us to the end dare to do our duty as we understand it."

The very wording of the concluding paragraphs reflects the organic quality of Lincoln's quest for unity. "Understand" echoes the "text"; Washington is a synecdochic reminder of the fathers; and the antithetical language recalls dissociations that are fundamental. In examining the discourse, we have attempted to explicate this internal coherence by tracing the sequence of arguments and images as they appear in the text, by dealing with the speech on its own terms. We are satisfied that the analysis has produced a reading that is more accurate than those previously available, a reading that goes farther toward explaining why the Cooper Union Address was one of Lincoln's most significant speeches.

Our interpretation is at odds, of course, with the conventional wisdom concerning his attitude toward the South. Where others have found him conciliatory, we argue that his position on slavery was calculated to win the nomination, not to propitiate an unavailable audience. That he had made "many similar declarations, and had never recanted any of them"[36] unquestionably contributed to the triumph of availability that was to be his,

---

[36]Abraham Lincoln, "First Inaugural Address," in *Collected Works,* IV, 263.

but his position ultimately pointed to an ideological conflict between North and South. Some Southerners took solace from Lincoln's assurances that slavery would be left alone where it existed, but extremists perceived him as the personification of Black Republicanism, even as the source of the irrepressible conflict doctrine.[37] The latter perceptions were distorted. So are ours, if we blink the realities of political rhetoric, and whatever else the speech might have been, it was certainly an oration designed to meet the immediate problems of a political campaign.

This perspective emphasizes that alternatives sometimes really do exclude and that rhetoric may nurture exclusion. Such a perspective may be uncomfortable for those who want to cast Lincoln as the Great Conciliator, but we are convinced that an accurate reading of the Cooper Union Address demands a frank recognition of the immediate rhetorical motives. Despite the mythology, the man was human, perhaps gloriously so, and it does him no disservice to accept this speech as evidence of his political skill, as evidence that "he was an astute and dextrous operator of the political machine."[38] Nor does this acceptance detract from the speech as literature and as logical exposition. The political artistry and the rhetorical artistry are functions of each other, and an appreciation of this coalescence can only enhance our understanding of the Cooper Union Address. And viewing the speech as a whole, we are quite content to close with a slightly altered evaluation from another context: "The speech is—to put it as crudely as possible—an immortal masterpiece."[39]

---

[37]Michael Davis, *The Image of Lincoln in the South* (Knoxville: Univ. of Tennessee, 1971), pp. 7-40; traces Southern views from nomination through inauguration. See *Southern Editorials on Secession*, ed. Dwight L. Dumond (1931; rpt. Gloucester, Mass.: Peter-Smith, 1964), pp. 103-105, 112-115, 159-162, *et passim*.

[38]David Donald, *Lincoln Reconsidered* (New York: Alfred A. Knopf, 1956), p. 65.

[39]The original is Randall Jarrell's comment on a poem, Robert Frost's "Provide Provide," in *Poetry and the Age* (New York: Vintage-Knopf, 1953), p. 41.

Stanton's "The Solitude of Self": A Rationale for Feminism

by Karlyn Kohrs Campbell

In 1892, near the end of her long career as a leader in the woman's rights movement,[1] Elizabeth Cady Stanton made her farewell address to the National American Woman Suffrage Association. The speech, "The Solitude of Self," is unlike the usual rhetoric of social activists of any period, and it is a startling departure from the typical speeches and arguments of nineteenth century feminists. The address is extraordinary because it is a philosophical statement of the principles and values underlying the struggle for woman's rights in the United States. It is also extraordinary because it is a social reformer's defense of humanistic individualism and because it is a rhetorical statement of the limits of those things which can be altered by words. In analyzing Stanton's address, I have two purposes: first, to use the speech as a means to discover and detail the ideology of nineteenth century feminism and, second, to examine its unusual features, particularly its lyric tone and its tragic perspective, to discover how and why it still has the power to speak to and move today's audience.

"The Solitude of Self" was delivered three times near the end of the long public career of Elizabeth Cady Stanton. It was first presented to the House Committee on the Judiciary on the morning of 18 January 1892. That afternoon Stanton delivered it to the twenty-fourth national convention of the National American Woman Suffrage Association as its retiring president. Two days later she repeated the speech at a hearing before the Senate Committee

Reprinted from *The Quarterly Journal of Speech* 66 (1980): 304-312 with permission of the Speech Communication Association.

[1]The best history of the woman's rights movements in the United States is Eleanor Flexner, *Century of Struggle*, rev. ed. (Cambridge: Harvard Univ. Press, 1975). See, also, Andrew Sinclair, *The Better Half: The Emancipation of the American Woman* (New York: Harper, 1965). Stanton's leadership is demonstrated in many ways: She was one of the five women who organized the Seneca Falls, N.Y., Convention in 1848; she edited *The Revolution* (1868-1870); and she was president of the National Woman Suffrage Association (1869-1890) and of the combined National American Woman Suffrage Association (1890-1892).

on Woman Suffrage.[2] The text of the speech was published subsequently in *The Woman's Journal.*[3] As presented to the congressional committees, the speech was part of the yearly lobbying effort of the association, made in conjunction, with its national convention in Washington, D.C., to persuade Congress to pass a federal suffrage amendment.

Elizabeth Cady Stanton was a skilled rhetor who had spoken and testified frequently before legislative groups since her address to the New York State Legislature in 1854. Her earlier speeches demonstrate an ability to marshal evidence and to make cogent arguments and moving appeals. In 1892 she was seventy-six years old, and the wary contemporary critic may wonder whether the qualities of the speech reflect her rhetorical skills or her recognition of approaching death. Stanton lived for ten more years, however, and, in the period between the speech and her death, she published, with others, the two volumes of *The Woman's Bible,*[4] a work that is strong evidence of her energy, mental acuity, and continued dedication to social change. In sum, "The Solitude of Self" was addressed to policy makers and fellow activists by a highly skilled rhetor who, despite advanced age, was fully alert and actively engaged in efforts for reform.

Stanton was a prolific writer and speaker, but "The Solitude of Self" is unlike her other efforts. Although unusual, it was highly praised by her contemporaries. Susan Anthony, Stanton's close friend and co-worker, thought it "the speech of Mrs [sic] Stanton['s] life";[5] Anna Howard Shaw, an outstanding speaker in the early movement, called it "an English classic";[6] "it . . . is considered by many to be her masterpiece."[7] Rhetorically, the address violates nearly all traditional canons. It makes no arguments; it provides no evidence. The thesis, if it can be called that, is

> The strongest reason for giving woman all the opportunities for higher education, for the full development of her faculties, forces of mind and body; for giving her the most enlarged freedom of thought and action; a complete emancipation from all forms of bondage, of

[2]The speech was read for Stanton before the House Committee on the Judiciary, but she delivered it herself before the convention and before the Senate Committee on Woman Suffrage. See Aileen S. Kraditor, *The Ideas of the Woman Suffrage Movement, 1890-1920* (New York: Columbia Univ. Press, 1965), p. 46. The speech was favorably received by the congressional committees: "The Senate Committee made a favorable majority report. The House Committee were so impressed by her speech that they had 10,000 copies reprinted from the Congressional Record and sent throughout the country." See Alma Lutz, *Created Equal: A Biography of Elizabeth Cady Stanton, 1815-1902* (New York: John Day, 1940), p. 290.

[3]*The Woman's Journal,* 23 January 1892, pp. 1 and 32. All citations from the speech are from this source, and all subsequent references will be in the text.

[4]Elizabeth Cady Stanton and others, *The Woman's Bible,* Two parts (New York: European Publishing Co., 1895, 1898). In addition to Stanton, seven persons wrote commentaries for volume one, eight persons for volume two. Altogether twenty women collaborated on what was called "The Revising Committee" that produced these works. The volumes were reprinted in 1972 by Arno Press, New York.

[5]Susan B. Anthony to Elizabeth Boynton Harbert, 12 August 1901, Harbert Papers, Radcliffe Women's Archives, cited by Kraditor, p. 46, n. 4.

[6]Lutz, p. 290.

[7]Susan B. Anthony and Ida Husted Harper, eds., *History of Woman Suffrage,* IV, 1883-1900 (Rochester, N.Y.: Charles Mann, 1902), 186.

custom, dependence, superstition; from all the crippling influences of fear—is the solitude and personal responsibility of her own individual life. (p. 1)

It has no logical structure. It refers briefly at the outset to some shared values, but it makes no appeal to them. It has no proper introduction, and it ends abruptly with a pointed but poignant question. Yet, it retains still its power to speak, and, like John Chapman's address at Coatesville, it is "strange and moving."[8]

The Lyric Mode

The speech is unusual, first, because it is a rhetorical act in the lyric mode. As a literary form, the lyric is defined as "a category of poetic literature that is distinguished from the narrative and dramatic . . . and is . . . characterized by subjectivity and sensuality of expression."[9] Lyric structure, in contrast to the narrative form of a novel or the climactic form of drama, is associative and develops through enumeration. Typically, the lyric poem attempts to explore and express all facets of a feeling or attitude in a series of statements related by the fact that they are all about a single subject; the parts are related to each other as the spokes of a wheel are related to the axle. A paradigmatic case is Elizabeth Barrett Browning's "How do I love thee? Let me count the ways." In addition, the lyric is intimate in tone, relies on personal experience, and uses sensual or aesthetic materials, including metaphor, to induce participation by the audience. The tone of the lyric is so subjective that it seems rhetorically inappropriate, as if one were washing emotional linen in public. For this reason, the lyric is described as a kind of indirect address that is "overheard" by the audience.

Stanton's speech exhibits these lyric qualities. It explores a single concept—the solitude of the human self, the idea that each person is unique, responsible, and alone. It begins with a string of associations: "The point I wish plainly to bring before you on this occasion is the individuality of each human soul; our Protestant idea, the right of individual conscience and judgment, our republican idea, individual citizenship" (p. 1). It develops by presenting a hierarchy in terms of which to discuss the rights of woman. Most fundamental is what belongs to her as an individual; next are her rights as a citizen; third are her rights which arise from the "incidental relations of life such as mother, wife, sister, daughter" (p. 1). The speech concerns itself exclusively with the most basic of these, her rights as an individual. Structurally, the speech is an exhaustive enumeration of human solitude in all its dimensions—through the stages of one's life from childhood to old age; in the varied roles of wife, mother, and widow; and in the extremities of

---

[8]Edmund Wilson's assessment of Chapman's speech is cited by Edwin Black, *Rhetorical Criticism: A Study in Method* (New York: Macmillan, 1965), p. 83.
[9]*The American Heritage Dictionary of the English Language* (Boston: Houghton Mifflin, 1969).

poverty, childbirth, old age, catastrophe, and death. To encounter the speech
is to experience the magnitude of human solitude.

Consistent with its lyric structure, the tone of the speech is intimate, and
its language is sensual and figurative. As a member of the audience one
confronts the existential reality of one's lonely life through imagery: Life is
a solitary voyage that each makes alone; each person is a soldier who
requires provisions from society but bears the burdens of fighting alone. The
human condition is like the terrible solitude of Jesus—fasting and tempted
on the mountain top, praying alone in Gethsemane, betrayed by a trusted
intimate, and, in the agonies of death, abandoned even by God. In a
concluding series of figurative comparisons, Stanton says,

> And yet, there is a solitude which each and every one of us has
> always carried with him, more inaccessible than the ice-cold
> mountains, more profound than the midnight sea; the solitude of
> self. Our inner being which we call ourself, no eye nor touch of
> man or angel has ever pierced. It is more hidden than the caves of
> the gnome; the sacred adytum of the oracle; the hidden chamber of
> Eleusinian mystery, for to it only Omniscience is permitted to enter.
> (p. 32)

Another paragraph illustrates the lyric tone and style, the appeal to
personal experience and to the emotions engendered by extreme situations:

> Alike amid the greatest triumphs and darkest tragedies of life,
> we walk alone. On the divine heights of human attainment,
> eulogized and worshipped as a hero or saint, we stand alone. In
> ignorance, poverty and vice, as a pauper or criminal, alone we
> starve or steal; alone we suffer the sneers and rebuffs of our
> fellows; alone we are hunted and hounded through dark courts and
> alleys, in by-ways and highways; alone we stand in the judgment
> seat; alone in the prison cell we lament our crimes and misfortunes;
> alone we expiate them on the gallows. In hours like these we realize
> the awful solitude of individual life, its pains, its penalties, its
> responsibilities. (p.32)

Repetition and parallelism are much used; the structure is associative;
the evidence is the evocation of personal experiences. Consistent with other
lyrical elements, Stanton's relationship to the audience is a kind of indirect
address. Only the opening and closing sentences betray an unambiguous
awareness of an immediate audience. The implied audience of the address
is not composed of the delegates at the convention or the members of the
congressional committees; it includes all persons. Stanton appears to be
"musing aloud" about what it means to be a human being, and the audience
is permitted to eavesdrop.

How does the lyric become rhetoric? How do these materials become
instrumental to achieving woman's rights? The experience of the "solitude
of self" breathes new life into the ideas of religious and political

individualism. That individuals are unique, responsible, and alone is the philosophical basis for the Protestant concept of the priesthood of believers and the republican notion that rights are not granted by governments but inhere in persons. Members of the audience affirm these values more intensely because of the evocation of the experience of human solitude which underlies them.

Despite the universal appeals of such ideas, Stanton creates a sharp contrast between the condition of all humans and the special nature of woman's place. At one point the discrepancy is expressed in a vivid allusion:

> Shakespeare's play of "Titus Andronicus" contains a terrible satire on woman's position in the 19th century. Rude men (the play tells us) seized the king's daughter, cut out her tongue, cut off her hands, and then bade her to go call for water and wash her hands. What a picture of woman's position! Robbed of her natural rights, handicapped by law and custom at every turn, yet compelled to fight her own battles, and in the emergencies of life to fall back on herself for protection. (p. 32)

Stanton's speech tells one that woman, in all stages and conditions of life, is handicapped and yet responsible for her life. Woman's solitude of self becomes a dramatic refutation of the argument that woman is dependent on man or that she can be protected by man:

> Whatever the theories may be of woman's dependence on man, in the supreme moments of her life, he cannot bear her burdens. Alone she goes to the gates of death to give life to every man that is born into the world; no one can share her fears, no one can mitigate her pangs; and if her sorrow is greater than she can bear, alone she passes beyond the gates into the vast unknown. (p. 32)

Similarly, the unique quality of each individual is a refutation of the inferiority of woman, and individual solitude and responsibility entail the right to education and to other opportunities for development and the exercise of choice. Stanton comments, "The talk of sheltering woman from the fierce storms of life is the sheerest mockery, for they beat on her from every point of the compass, just as they do on man, and with more fatal results, for he has been trained to protect himself, to resist, and to conquer" (p. 32). The concept of self-sovereignty refutes the view that man can act for woman at the ballot box, in legislatures, on juries. Stanton's conclusion is a pointed question: "Who, I ask you, can take, dare take on himself, the rights, the duties, the responsibilities of another human soul?" (p. 32). That each person is unique, responsible, and alone refutes the view of woman as property; it implies her right to her wages, to own property, to sue and contract, to have a role in the custody of her children. Despite its associative structure, subjective tone, figurative language, and rather indirect address, the speech is a forceful rationale for the specific rights claimed by nineteenth century feminists.

The Tragic Perspective

The form of the speech and its modes of expression are lyric, but its perspective is tragic, a philosophical stance common in literature but rare in rhetoric. Many analysts of literature see distinctions between comedy and tragedy as fundamental and significant. Langer describes them as the basis for two great artistic rhythms, and Frye treats them as two fundamental literary modes (*mythoi*).

As literary forms, comedy and tragedy have certain distinctive characteristics. The focus of tragedy is destiny or fate. Ordinarily, the protagonist is a hero or leader whose end is the inevitable outcome of a situation. Tragedy typically isolates the individual from the community whereas comedy incorporates the protagonist into society, and its happy, unifying ending is often related to the cleverness of the protagonist. Langer summarizes these differences:

> Destiny . . . as a future shaped essentially in advance and only incidentally by chance happenings, is Fate; and Fate is the "virtual future" created in tragedy. The "tragic rhythm of action" . . . is the rhythm of man's life at its highest powers in the limits of his unique, death-bound career. Tragedy is the image of Fate, as comedy is of Fortune. . . . [T]ragedy is a fulfillment, and its form therefore is closed, final and passional. Tragedy is a mature art form . . . Its conception requires a sense of individuality which some religions and some cultures—even high cultures—do not generate.[10]

Briefly, then, tragedy emphasizes the isolation of the individual; comedy emphasizes integration into the community. Tragedy focuses on beginnings and endings, comedy on continuity. Tragedy reflects self-actualization—the individual at moments of greatest testing and achievement—whereas comedy affirms the cyclical survival of the species. Tragedy develops through inexorable fate; comedy involves fortune, which persons may influence through their wits. Langer, Frye, and Burke all recognize the relationship between these modes and philosophical perspectives. Langer notes the relationship between tragedy and individualism; Frye speaks of a tragic philosophy of fate and a comic philosophy of providence;[11] Burke identifies the "tragic frame of acceptance" as the perspective which sets in motion what he calls the iron law of history.[12]

The tragic perspective in Stanton's speech is evident. Like tragedy, the speech focuses on the life of the individual. It emphasizes beginnings and endings; in fact, it reminds one vividly that suffering and death are the inevitable lot of humans. It isolates the individual from the community,

---

[10]Susanne K. Langer, *Feeling and Form* (New York: Scribner's, 1953), pp. 333-34.
[11]Northrop Frye, *Anatomy of Criticism* (Princeton: Princeton Univ. Press, 1957), p. 64.
[12]Kenneth Burke, *The Rhetoric of Religion: Studies in Logology* (Boston: Beacon, 1961), pp. 4-5.

focuses on fate as an element in human affairs, and emphasizes the crises in human experience. The tragic perspective limits rhetorical acts severely. Rhetoric usually is comic because, given its commitment to the efficacy of deliberation and social action, it must opt to emphasize rationality, the community, cyclical survival, and progress. In Stanton's tragic view, feminism cannot change the human condition. If all the laws are passed and all the changes made, humans, both male and female, will remain unique, responsible, and solitary individuals, forced to confront their inevitable trials in the solitude of their selves:

> But when all artificial trammels are removed, and women are recognized as individuals, responsible for their own environments, thoroughly educated for all positions in life they may be called to fill; with all the resources in themselves that liberal thought and broad culture can give; guided by their own conscience and judgment, trained to self-protection, by a healthy development of the muscular system, and skill in the use of weapons of defense; and stimulated to self-support by a knowledge of the business world and the pleasure that pecuniary independence must ever give: when women are trained in this way, they will in a measure be fitted for those hours of solitude *that come alike to all, whether prepared or otherwise.* (p. 32; emphasis added)

Stanton's tragic perspective limits her appeal although it offers some rhetorical advantages. For supporters, her tragic view of life dampens enthusiasm and lessens motivation for social reform as it reminds women of the limits of what can be achieved through the movement for women's rights. As depicted here, human life is a pain-filled struggle, a condition no reform can alter. Philosophically, Stanton denies the traditional American view of "progress," but her perspective has an important advantage. If one accepts the human ontology articulated in this speech, woman's rights are not a matter for justification or argument; they are entailed by the human condition.

For legislators and the public, her point of view has similar advantages and disadvantages. Her perspective has some force because it is fresh and unusual. Similarly, the speech indicates that women do not expect legislators to enact laws to usher in the golden age; as redefined by Stanton, legislation extending woman's rights simply provides an opportunity for individual effort. However, Stanton's perspective has the potential to intensify conflict. To deny Stanton's claims is to reject the concept of humankind affirmed by the dominant political philosophy and system of religious beliefs. One who disagrees is compelled to argue that women are not persons who may rightfully claim their rights as citizens or as children of God. Arguments based on such fundamental values polarize the audience and heighten disagreement.

However, it is not sufficient to describe Stanton's viewpoint as tragic, for her perspective is also existential, an emphasis which serves to qualify and modify the attitudes expressed in the speech.

Humanism:
The Lyric Modification of Tragedy

The interrelationship between form and substance in rhetoric is illustrated in this speech by the ways in which the qualities of lyric form, particularly its emphasis on the subjective and sensual, come to modify Stanton's tragic perspective.

Stanton's apparent choice of individualism as a philosophical posture could be rhetorically as well as axiologically problematic. Individualism can take the form of a malign social Darwinism used to blame individuals, including women, for their own oppression,[13] a point of view which rejects all reform efforts. Political individualism can become an anarchism that precludes social movements; and religious individualism, at its extreme, produces what Kierkegaard described as the "tragic hero," who acts on the dictates of his conscience to transcend the ethical rules of the community and whose reasons for actions are incommunicable to others.[14]

Stanton avoids these extremes because she opts, not for the philosophy or doctrine of individualism, but for a humanistic concern for the existential individual—the experience of the living person in the here and now. The changes Stanton seeks will alter the individual lives of real persons in the present, but there is in the speech no dream of progress toward a utopian state. In fact, as Stanton describes it, there is an element of absurdity in all reform efforts. No matter what is done to alter the circumstances of women and of men, they will continue to be unique, responsible, and alone; reforms may ease the struggles of individuals, but they cannot change the givens of every human life.[15] As she expresses it, "Rich and poor, intelligent and ignorant, wise and foolish, virtuous and vicious, man and woman; it is ever the same, each soul must depend wholly on itself" (p. 32). Stanton's tragic perspective is modified by an existential emphasis on the individual and an absurdist recognition of the limits of social change. These modifications produce a perspective that is philosophically humanistic.

---

[13]See particularly the speech of the Reverend Antoinette Brown Blackwell in the debate on resolutions concerning marriage and divorce at the National Woman's Rights Convention, New York, 1860, in Elizabeth Cady Stanton, Susan B. Anthony, and Mathilda Joslyn Gage, eds., *The History of Woman Suffrage,* I, 1848-1861 (Rochester, N.Y.: Charles Mann, 1887), 724-29.

[14]Soren Kierkegaard, *Fear and Trembling: Dialectical Lyric,* trans. Walter Lowrie (1941; rpt. New York: Anchor, 1954), pp. 64-77, 91-129.

[15]The philosophy of individualism is one which places the interests of the individual above those of the society or social group, and it is illustrated in the political philosophy of Thomas Hobbes or the views currently expressed by Ayn Rand. In contrast, humanism is a philosophy or attitude concerned with the achievement, interests, and welfare of human beings rather than with abstract beings or theoretical concepts. Stanton's humanism is quite similar to the existential and absurdist humanism articulated by Jean-Paul Sartre in "Existentialism is a Humanism," in *Existentialism from Dostoevsky to Sartre,* ed. Walter Kaufmann (Cleveland: Meridian, 1956), pp. 287-311, and in "Introduction to *Les Temps Modernes,*" trans. Françoise Ehrmann, in *Paths to the Present: Aspects of European Thought from Romanticism to Existentialism,* ed. Eugen Weber (New York: Dodd, Mead, 1962), 432-41. Sartre there wrote that human life is limited by certain givens, "the necessity of being born and dying, of being *finite,* and existing in a world among other men" (p. 438).

As many of the citations have indicated, the speech concerns the conditions of humans, not just the concerns of females. The inclusion of and the appeals to males are both strategically desirable and philosophically consistent. Strategically, the agents of change in her immediate audience were males who held virtually all political and economic power. In this circumstance, there appears to be little conflict between pragmatic requirements and Stanton's principles. Early in the speech, as Stanton dismisses the significance of "social roles" as a basis for woman's rights, she uses the male as the standard from which the conclusion is drawn:

> In discussing the sphere of man, we do not decide his rights as an individual, as a citizen, as a man, by his duties as a father, a husband, a brother or a son, relations he may never fill. Moreover, he would be better fitted for these very relations, and whatever special work he might choose to do to earn his bread, by the complete development of all his faculties as an individual.
> Just so with woman. (p. 1)

Similarly, when she refers to the uniqueness of the individual, she says, "There can never again be just such . . . environments as make up the infancy, youth and manhood of this one," and she illustrated the need to rely on one's own resources with the example of Prince Piotr Alekseyevich Kropotkin's experiences in a Russian prison. Although nearly all of the examples in the speech are applicable to females in particular, one passage is noteworthy for its understanding of the constraints created by the male role:

> When suddenly roused at midnight, with the startling cry of "Fire! Fire!" to find the house over their heads in flames, do women wait for men to point the way to safety? And are the men, equally bewildered, and half suffocated with smoke, in a position to do more than try to save themselves? (p. 32)

In other words, not only are men incapable of protecting women from the vicissitudes of life, but it is unjust to demand that they should attempt to do so. Clearly, the philosophical bases of feminism are, for Stanton, humanistic, and the goals of the movement are goals for persons, for human beings. In Stanton's words, "We see reason sufficient in the outer conditions of human beings for individual liberty and development, but when we consider the self-dependence of every human soul we see the need of courage, judgment and the exercise of every faculty of mind and body, strengthened and developed by use, *in woman as well as man*" (p. 32; emphasis added).

As Stanton addressed male legislators and her brothers and sisters in the National American Woman Suffrage Association, she reminded them of the common philosophical precepts which are alike the foundations of Protestantism, republicanism, and feminism—the principles of humanism. She also reminded them of the wider meaning of feminism; it is a movement not solely aimed at the vote for women, but at equality and opportunity in all areas of life and for all persons. This is a speech for woman's rights broadly conceived; more properly, it is a speech for human rights.

In her first public speech at the convention in 1848 at Seneca Falls, New York, Stanton said:

> Woman herself must do this work; for woman alone can understand the height, the depth, the length, and the breadth of her own degradation. Man cannot speak for her, because he has been educated to believe that she differs from him so materially, that he cannot judge of her thoughts, feelings, and opinions by his own. Moral beings can only judge of others by themselves.[16]

Now, at the end of her speaking career, Stanton demonstrates her moral pre-eminence as one who can see and feel the conditions of others through herself. As a result, she speaks for all women, of all ages, in all roles, and in all conditions of life; indeed, she speaks for all persons, rich and poor, male and female, educated and uneducated. What she expresses and evokes is the nature of the human condition, and what her audience experiences is the lonely and troubled solitude of the individual for which each person requires all of the opportunities that can be provided by society.

Reformers, especially those who seek significant social change, are more than a little threatening. One fears the changes they seek and their energetic, sure-minded persistence. Rarely, if ever, do they show that they know the limits of the benefits that can be wrought through political, social, and economic reform. Although Stanton's depiction of the human condition is a terrifying one, it is reassuring to discover that a determined activist understood the inevitable and immutable elements of human life. As presented by Stanton, feminism is a humanistic movement for individual opportunity and choice, but it will not solve the problems of human life.

Conclusion

"The Solitude of Self" is a statement about the meaning of feminism. Philosophically, it reminds us of the conditions of every human life: that each of us is unique, responsible, and alone. These conditions entail the republican principle of natural rights and the religious principle of individual conscience. If women are persons, they merit access to every opportunity that will assist them in the human struggle. Stanton's speech enables us to understand why, by its nature and from its inception, feminism is grounded in humanism.

The address is also a rhetorical act that achieves its ends through poetic means. In contrast to more familiar forms of logical argumentation, the speech is nondiscursive and nonpropositional. However, as we encounter the solitude of human life as evoked through imagery, description, and example, we recall and reaffirm the bases for our most fundamental beliefs.

---

[16]*Proceedings of the Woman's Rights Conventions, Held at Seneca Falls & Rochester, N.Y., July & August, 1848* (New York: Johnston, 1870), p. 3.

Stanton's speech is a rare moment in the protest rhetoric of a social movement. The address hardly mentions, and quickly abandons, the specific justifications for woman suffrage. There is mention made of, but only the slightest emphasis placed upon, the need to grant women the vote, educational and economic opportunity, and legal equality. It might seem that the speech would fail because it had lost sight of its purpose, but, in fact, the speech succeeds because it has set forth a new and deeper purpose. No matter what else is true of the oppression of women, whenever the right to vote and to legal, educational, and economic equality are denied them, men are presuming, out of motives malign or benign, to take responsibility for those women. And it is just here that Stanton's argument, lyric and tragic though it is, attains its full power. Men cannot take responsibility for women, as Stanton's examples so simply demonstrate. Men can take responsibility only for themselves, and, of course, women are the only ones who can be responsible for themselves. As presented in the speech, the rights of women are not achieved at the cost of the rights of others; woman's rights are a natural and necessary part of the human birthright.

Although the laws that interfere with this individual responsibility must be changed, Stanton was entirely aware that such changes will mean only that men and women will face the crucial moments of their lives in equal solitude. The reforms Stanton desired would result in precious little change, but how precious that little.

Genre Criticism and Historical Context: The Case of George Washington's First Inaugural Address

by Stephen E. Lucas

There can be no doubt that the explosion of interest in genre studies during the past decade has invigorated the practice of rhetorical criticism and the development of rhetorical theory. If the promise of genre studies is to be fully realized, however, one major obstacle must be overcome—the tendency to treat the identification of genres as an end in itself. Rather than moving centrifugally from the classification of discourse to the illumination of broader critical and theoretical issues, the study of rhetorical genres appears to be moving centripetally toward increasingly narrow studies that seek to tuck "each of the world's little speeches into its own little generic bed."[1]

The problem is that this approach leaves unanswered the most crucial questions about the nature and role of generic constraints in rhetorical transactions. It invites attention to what rhetorical genres look like, rather than to how they function. What we need are not more studies describing the formal properties of rhetorical genres, but studies that investigate the functional attributes of generic discourse.

One way to do this is by studying the creation, evolution, and operation of rhetorical genres in their historical contexts. We know next to nothing about how rhetorical genres come into being, even less about how they pass out of existence, and astonishingly little about what happens to them in between. Nor are we likely to enhance our understanding appreciably until we look beyond the formal traits of rhetorical genres to the interconnections between generic discourse and the situational constraints that shape both its form and its function.

To take but a single example, let us look briefly at George Washington's first inaugural address. Washington's speech, presented to Congress on April 30, 1789, invites attention if for no other reason than that it was the initial instance of a major genre of American political discourse. As such, it invites speculation about its origins. Where did the first inaugural come from?

Reprinted from *Southern Speech Communication Journal* 51 (1986), with permission of the publisher.
[1] Roderick P. Hart, "Public Address: Should It Be Disinterred?", paper presented at the Speech Communication Association annual meeting, Denver, Colorado, November 1985, 15.

I

Kathleen Jamieson suggests one answer. Washington's address, she holds, reveals the "chromosomal imprint of ancestral genres" that is customarily evident at the conception of a new genre. Noting the pronounced religious tone of Washington's speech, she contends that it was shaped by "the American tradition of theocratic address." "One does not have to vivisect the inaugural," she says, "to see the imprint of the sermonic form." To be sure, she avers, at least twice in the speech Washington states that it has grown from the situation. But, she argues, "although Washington indicates that the speech is responding to the dictates of the occasion, his perception of the rhetoric demanded by that occasion and his perception of the occasion itself is colored by the rhetoric and role of the theocratic leader. Consequently, major portions of the address could have been comfortably delivered by a New England preacher to his parishioners."[2]

Jamieson does not purport to provide a complete account of Washington's speech, and her position is best seen as a speculative hypothesis rather than a fully developed historical argument. But the impact of antecedent rhetorical genres on the first inaugural—or on any other speech—cannot be confirmed in the absence of historical inquiry. It is important to distinguish between placing a text in a general rhetorical tradition and claiming that a text was modeled on a specific antecedent genre. The former can be substantiated simply on the basis of situational, structural, thematic, or stylistic consonance between the text in question and other texts within the tradition. The latter, however, is a more complex claim about the creation of a particular text. Its corroboration depends not merely on the generic features of the text, but also on the immediate rhetorical situation and the motives, knowledge, and perceptions of the rhetor.[3]

In the case at hand, we can confidently say that the religious portions of Washington's inaugural instantiate a tradition of theocratic discourse that runs deep into the history of Western civilization. But broad similarities in topic and tone are not enough to establish that either the content or the form of Washington's speech can be traced to the customs of sermonic address in New England. Even if the religious portions of Washington's address *could have been* comfortably delivered by a New England preacher—which is open to question—it does not necessarily follow that they *were* modeled on the

---

[2] Kathleen M. Hall Jamieson, "Generic Constraints and the Rhetorical Situation," *Philosophy and Rhetoric*, 6 (1973): 163-165.

[3] On rare occasions corroboration can be provided by direct evidence. We know, for example that John F. Kennedy had his speechwriters study the inaugural speeches of previous Presidents for guidance in creating his inaugural address. In most cases, however, including that of Washington's first inaugural, the case for generic influence must be built upon indirect evidence and informed inference. For the drafting of Kennedy's inaugural consult Theodore C. Sorensen, *Kennedy* (New York: Harper and Row, 1965) 240-243. What we know about the composition of Washington's first inaugural is summarized in note 24 below.

rhetoric of New England preachers.[4] If we are to find the chromosomal imprint of the New England sermon in Washington's inaugural, we shall need evidence that whatever similarities may have existed between the two are not simply coincidental.

Such evidence is hard to come by. Washington was a Virginian. Like most Americans before the Revolution, he had little knowledge of customs and traditions in the other colonies. So great was the heterogeneity of Americans before the Revolution that John Adams never ceased to marvel at the union they achieved in 1776. "The colonies," he said, "had grown up under constitutions of government so different, there was so great a variety of religions, they were composed of so many different nations, their customs, manners, and habits had so little resemblance, and their intercourse had been so rare, and their knowledge of each other so imperfect, that to unite them in the same principles in theory and the same system of action, was certainly a very difficult enterprise.[5] Washington had almost no exposure during his formative years to the kind of sermonic discourse typically heard in New England. Like most Virginia gentry, he was steeped in the moderate, rationalistic, enlightened religion of the Church of England, which was a far cry from New England Puritanism. Nor was there a tradition in Virginia of sermonic discourse in which religious and political themes were commonly intertwined. The feeling of most Anglican ministers during the colonial period was that "Political Subjects do not belong to the Pulpit."[6]

Notwithstanding a brief visit to Boston earlier in 1756, Washington was almost completely ignorant about New England before the beginning of the Revolution. His first sustained contact with New Englanders came in 1774, when he was a delegate to the First Continental Congress. His first—and only—lengthy stay in the region began in the summer of 1775, when he assumed command of the Continental Army outside Boston. After reoccupying the city from the British ten months later, he left New England and did not return for thirteen years, when he toured the region after his inauguration as President. Although he attended religious services during his

---

[4] Washington's sentiments are couched in the vocabulary of eighteenth-century deism. At no time does he use the language of pietistic Christianity so evident in New England sermons. He does not speak of "God," "Christ," "the Lord," or "our Saviour." Instead he refers to the Deity as "that Almighty Being who rules over the Universe," as "the Great Author of every public and private good," as "the invisible hand which conducts the Affairs of men," and as "the benign parent of the human race." Nor does Washington mention the divinity of Christ or doctrinal Christianity, both of which were standard features of sermonic discourse in New England. George Washington, "First Inaugural Address," in *The Writings of George Washington*, ed. John C. Fitzpatrick, XXX (Washington, D.C.: Government Printing Office, 1939) 291-296. In all quotations from this and other eighteenth-century sources I have modernized punctuation and spelling but have retained the original capitalization.

[5] John Adams to Hezekiah Niles, February 13, 1818, in *The Works of John Adams*, ed. Charles Francis Adams, X (Boston: Little, Brown, 1856) 283.

[6] William Tennent, *An Address Occasioned by the Late Invasion of the Liberties of the American Colonies by the British Parliament* (Philadelphia: William and Thomas Bradford, 1774) 6. For Washington's religious views and the course of Anglicanism in eighteenth-century Virginia, see Paul F. Boller, Jr., *George Washington and Religion* (Dallas: Southern Methodist University Press, 1963); George M. Brydon, *Virginia's Mother Church*, II (Richmond: Virginia Historical Society, 1952).

stay in Massachusetts as commander-in-chief, he does not appear to have been taken with the sermons he heard. Indeed, his correspondence shows that he was little impressed with either the place or its people. He described New England militia officers, for example, as "the most indifferent kind of People I ever saw." The enlisted men, he thought, "would fight very well (if properly Officered) although they are an exceedingly dirty and nasty people."[7] In short, there is nothing to indicate that Washington, who at the time he became President had spent less than one of his fifty-seven years in New England, was sufficiently familiar with or captivated by its tradition of sermonic discourse to have incorporated significant features of it into his inaugural address.

The most notable parallel between the first inaugural and New England sermons is Washington's affirmation of the role of divine providence in human affairs in general and in American history in particular. But one need never have set foot in or have read a piece of discourse from New England to express such ideas. They had been cardinal tenets of the rhetoric of the Revolution and were widely accepted in all parts of America during the 1780s. Washington himself had often stated such ideas, and they constituted a particularly conspicuous theme in his private letters during and after the debate over ratification of the Constitution. Their appearance in the inaugural address may be seen as a natural outgrowth of his deep personal belief that "the kind interposition of Providence, which has been so often manifested in the affairs of this country, must naturally lead us to look up to that divine source for light and direction in this new and untried Scene."[8]

They may also be seen as performing a crucial strategic function in the speech. The recently completed battle over ratification of the Constitution had provoked deep and bitter divisions among Americans. At the time of Washington's inaugural, two states—Rhode Island and North Carolina—had yet to adopt the new frame of government. Moreover, many Antifederalists in the other eleven states were far from reconciled to it—especially since it lacked a bill of rights—and some were still hopeful of calling a second constitutional

---

[7] George Washington to Lund Washington, August 20, 1775, in *The Writings of George Washington*, ed. John C. Fitzpatrick, III (Washington, D.C.: Government Printing Office, 1931) 433. On other occasions Washington complained of "an unaccountable kind of stupidity" shown by Massachusetts military men, of the "dirty, mercenary spirit" of Connecticut troops, and of the lack of "that patriotic Spirit which I was taught to believe was characteristic of this people." As late as February 1776, after seven months among New Englanders, he remained convinced that they were "not to be depended upon" in battle. See his letters to Richard Henry Lee, August 29, 1775, in Fitzpatrick, *Writings*, III, 450; to Joseph Reed, November 28, 1775, to Philip Schuyler, November 28, 1775, and to Joseph Reed, February 10, 1776, in *The Writings of George Washington*, ed. John C. Fitzpatrick, IV (Washington, D.C.: Government Printing Office, 1931) 124-125, 127, 320.

[8] George Washington to William Heath, May 9, 1789, in Fitzpatrick, *Writings*, XXX, 315. Similarly, see Washington to Charles Cotesworth Pinckney, June 28, 1788, to Benjamin Lincoln, June 29, 1788, to James McHenry, July 31, 1788, to Annis Boudinot Stockton, August 31, 1788, and to Philip Schuyler, May 9, 1789, in Fitzpatrick, *Writings*, XXX, 10, 11, 30, 76, 317. For the general currency of such ideas in American political discourse during the 1770's and 1780's see Catherine L. Albanese, *Sons of the Fathers: The Civil Religion of the American Revolution* (Philadelphia: Temple University Press, 1976).

convention to rectify the handiwork of the first. Nor did Federalists know whether the new government would work well enough to secure the support and affection of the people. They realized that many Americans shared at least a portion of the Antifederalists' fear that the Constitution was calculated to work against the interests of ordinary citizens and endangered the liberties secured only a few years before in the war for independence. Cloaking the government with the mantle of divine consecration was one way to allay those fears and to create trust in the new government.[9]

That Washington may have been thinking along these lines is suggested by the speech itself. For the most part, its religious references are oriented toward the future and move from supplicating for divine blessing to predicting that such blessing will be forthcoming and will ensure the success of the government created by the Constitution. This pattern is clearly evident in paragraph two, which contains the bulk of Washington's statements about religion. There he begins by hoping that the "Almighty Being who rules over the Universe" will "consecrate" the government and enable everyone "employed in its administration to execute with success the functions allotted to his charge." That the Almighty Being is likely to do so is suggested by the fact that "every step" in the quest for independence from Great Britain "seems to have been distinguished by some token of providential agency." The "tranquil deliberations" that produced the Constitution are further cause for "pious gratitude." And these past blessings, Washington says, justifiably lead to "an humble anticipation of . . . future blessings." He then concludes the paragraph by saying, "These reflections, arising out of the present crisis, have forced themselves too strongly on my mind to be suppressed. You will join with me I trust in thinking that there are none under the influence of which the proceedings of a new and free Government can more auspiciously commence."[10] It is this conclusion that constitutes the essential message of the paragraph. The lengthy invocation of divine support that precedes it provides the evidence and warrant upon which it is based and is best seen, not as the impress of antecedent rhetorical genres, but as a statement of Washington's personal convictions and as a strategic response to the problem of developing confidence in the new government.

When one looks beyond Washington's religious remarks, one finds even

---

[9] Although opposition to the Constitution would dissolve quickly in the months after Washington's inauguration, neither Washington nor his closest colleagues were taking anything for granted in April of 1789. They were cautiously optimistic that the new government would succeed, but they remained concerned about Antifederalist intrigues, about the lack of a quorum in Congress, and about how smoothly the untried system of government could be put into operation. See, for example, Samuel Powel to George Washington, January 6, 1789, in The Papers of George Washington, Library of Congress; George Washington to Henry Knox, March 25, 1789, privately owned, from a copy in The Papers of George Washington, Alderman Library, University of Virginia; George Washington to James McHenry, April 10, 1789, in Fitzpatrick, *Writings*, XXX, 280; Benjamin Lincoln to George Washington, April 18, 1789, in Papers of George Washington, Library of Congress; Edmund Pendleton to Harry Innes, August 11, 1790, in *Letters and Papers of Edmund Pendleton, 1734-1803*, ed. David John Mays, II (Charlottesville: University Press of Virginia, 1967) 571.
[10]Fitzpatrick, *Writings*, XXX, 292-293.

less to indicate that "the sermon is the rhetorical ancestor of the presidential inaugural."[11] The rest of the speech advances four major sets of ideas. First, Washington explains that he is leaving retirement to become President out of "veneration and love" for America, but not without anxiety about "the weighty and untried cares" awaiting him. Second, under the guise of praising Congress, Washington admonishes it to make sure that "no local prejudices or attachments, no separate views nor party animosities, will misdirect the comprehensive and equal eye" that ought to guide its proceedings. Third, Washington offers a carefully worded endorsement of amending the Constitution so as to settle "the degree of inquietude" aroused by the absence of a bill of rights. Fourth, he declines to receive a salary as President and requests that his remuneration "be limited to such actual expenditures" as he may confront in office. This was the same request he had made when becoming commander-in-chief during the Revolution. By repeating it upon his inauguration as President, he hoped to underscore the rectitude of his intentions in coming out of what he had characterized in 1783 as a permanent retirement from public life.[12]

The first three sets of ideas had been extensively rehearsed in Washington's correspondence during the months preceding his inauguration, while the fourth treated one of his major concerns about accepting the presidency. Their appearance in the inaugural address can be accounted for by Washington's personal apprehensions and by what he judged to be the most pressing rhetorical exigencies facing America as it set out on a new course designed to preserve the fragile experiment in republicanism begun in 1776.[13]

The extent to which Washington's first inaugural address was shaped by the immediate circumstances of April 1789 is further underscored when we compare it with his second inaugural, presented in the Senate chamber on March 4, 1793. In that speech of 135 words, by far the briefest of all presidential inaugurals, Washington perfunctorily acknowledged his re-election and signified his commitment to the oath of office he was about to take. He also indicated that the situation did not call for a more extended address. "When the occasion proper for it shall arrive," he said, "I shall endeavor to express the high sense I entertain of this distinguished honor, and of the confidence which has been reposed in me by the people of united America."[14] Not until December 3, 1793, in his fifth annual message to Congress, did Washington express the kinds of sentiments we usually expect to find in a presidential

[11]Jamieson, "Generic Constraints," 168.
[12]Fitzpatrick, *Writings*, XXX, 290-296. Washington's farewell address of 1783 is in *The Writings of George Washington*, ed. John C. Fitzpatrick, XXVI (Washington, D.C.: Government Printing Office, 1938) 483-496.
[13]For Washington's thinking about the presidency in late 1788 and early 1789 see Douglas Southall Freeman, *George Washington: A Biography*, VI (New York: Scribner's, 1954) 141-166; James Thomas Flexner, *George Washington and the New Nation, 1783-1793* (Boston: Little, Brown, 1969) 153-168.
[14]*The Writings of George Washington*, ed. John C. Fitzpatrick, XXXII (Washington, D.C.: Government Printing Office, 1939) 374-375.

inaugural.[15] Although the unusual nature of his second inaugural has perplexed many scholars, it is explained when we understand that he wanted a simple ceremony without the great pomp and extravagance of his first inauguration.[16] In Washington's view, the rhetorical situation of March 1793 did not require more than a few brief comments before being sworn into office for a second term, while that of April 1789 had demanded a major speech designed to get the new government off to a smooth start.[17]

II

This is not to say that antecedent rhetorical forms had no influence whatever on Washington's speech. Washington was doubtless constrained by the rhetorical customs of his age—as is any writer or speaker. There were at least two, and perhaps three, antecedent rhetorical genres with which Washington was familiar that could well have influenced both the form and content of the first inaugural. One was the rhetoric of office-taking, whether in politics, religion, or the military. In the eighteenth century such rhetoric was a highly ritualized form of discourse designed, in large measure, to safeguard the reputation of the new office-holder should he fail to discharge his duties successfully. When accepting his position, the new office-holder typically acknowledged the person or persons responsible for granting the office, noted the magnitude and/or importance of the duties attached to that office, expressed humility about his capacity to carry out those duties, and pledged his utmost effort to meet his responsibilities ably and honorably. In some cases the new office-holder also expressed a need for assistance from those who would be working with him and/or from the interdiction of divine providence.

There was, moreover, a characteristic style associated with the rhetoric of office-taking. The style bespoke gratitude and humility in such a way as to reinforce the thematic commonplaces of the genre. As a typical example, we might take Patrick Henry's speech of July 1776 accepting his election as first governor of the state of Virginia. Henry expresses his thanks "in the strongest

---

[15]*The Writings of George Washington*, ed. John C. Fitzpatrick, XXXIII (Washington, D.C.: Government Printing Office, 1940) 163-169.

[16]See *The Papers of Thomas Jefferson*, ed. Paul Leicester Ford, I (New York: Putnam's, 1892) 221-222; *The Papers of Alexander Hamilton*, ed. Harold C. Syrett and Jacob E. Cooke, XIV (New York: Columbia University Press, 1969) 169-170, 176; James Thomas Flexner, *George Washington: Anguish and Farewell, 1793-1799* (Boston: Little, Brown, 1969) 16.

[17]While Washington's first inaugural established a prototype followed by all subsequent Presidents, his second inaugural did not. The prototype for second inaugurals is the 2,159-word speech delivered by Thomas Jefferson on March 4, 1805, in *The Chief Executive: Inaugural Addresses of the Presidents of the United States from George Washington to Lyndon B. Johnson*, ed. Arthur Schlesinger, Jr., and Fred L. Israel (New York: Crown, 1965) 18-23. For the characteristics of presidential inaugural addresses as a genre of political discourse see Donald L. Wolfarth, "John F. Kennedy in the Tradition of Inaugural Speeches," *Quarterly Journal of Speech*, 47 (1961): 124-132; Karlyn Kohrs Campbell and Kathleen Hall Jamieson, "Inaugurating the Presidency," *Presidential Studies Quarterly*, 15 (1985): 394-411.

terms of acknowledgment" to the Convention for "the high and unmerited honor" it has conferred upon him. After explaining that the many perils facing Virginia "at this truly critical conjuncture" require that the state be "managed by great abilities," Henry says: "I lament my want of talents, I feel my mind filled with anxiety and uneasiness, to find myself so unequal to the duties of that important station to which I am called by the favor of my fellow citizens." In such a situation, he can only promise his "unwearied endeavors to secure the freedom and happiness of our common country," and he will rely upon "the known wisdom and virtue" of the Convention to make up for his own "defects."[18]

The same style and commonplaces are clearly evident in the opening paragraphs of Washington's first inaugural. He begins by acknowledging Congress' notification of his election and states that he has been "summoned" to the presidency by his country. But, he says, "no event could have filled me with greater anxieties," for "the magnitude and difficulty of the trust to which the voice of my Country called me, being sufficient to awaken in the wisest and most experienced of her citizens a distrustful scrutiny into his qualifications, could not but overwhelm with despondence one who, inheriting inferior endowments from nature and unpracticed in the duties of civil administration, ought to be peculiarly conscious of his own deficiencies." Shortly after this statement Washington again mentions his "incapacity as well as disinclination for the weighty and untried cares" before him and hopes that his errors will be palliated by the high motives that led him to accept the office of President. This is followed by the second paragraph, in which Washington offers his lengthy "fervent supplications" to divine providence that "every instrument" of the new government will discharge its responsibilities skillfully and successfully.[19]

In making these remarks, Washington was not just conforming to rhetorical tradition. Such ideas had been evident in his correspondence for several months and reflected his deep concern about the uncharted course facing him and his country in 1789. But some variation of these ideas—even if only a perfunctory expression of them—would likely have appeared in his first inaugural address regardless of the political situation, just as similar ideas appeared in other of his speeches and letters accepting political or military posts.[20]

---

[18] *Official Letters of the Governors of the State of Virginia,* ed. H. R. McIlwaine, I (Richmond: Virginia State Library, 1926) 3-4. Also see Peter Beverley, speech to the Virginia House of Burgesses, December 7, 1700, in *Journals of the House of Burgesses, 1695-1702,* ed. H. R. McIlwaine (Richmond: Virginia State Library, 1913) 206; Lewis Burwell, Address to the Virginia Council, November 21, 1750, in *Executive Journals of the Council of Colonial Virginia,* ed. Wilmer L. Hall, V (Richmond: Virginia State Library, 1945) 345; Thomas Jefferson, First Inaugural Address, March 4, 1801, in Schlesinger and Israel, *Chief Executive,* 13-18; and the speeches cited in notes 20, 22, and 25 below.

[19] Fitzpatrick, *Writings,* XXX, 291-293.

[20] In his speech to the Continental Congress accepting appointment as commander-in-chief of the American army, June 16, 1775, Washington said: "Tho' I am truly sensible of the high Honor done me in this Appointment, yet I feel great distress from a consciousness that my abilities and Military

Another potential model for Washington's address was the initial speech to Parliament by British monarchs after their accession to the throne. In 1603 James I began the practice of delivering this speech personally, rather than having it read by the Lord Chancellor, but the unsettled state of the monarchy throughout the seventeenth century inhibited the development of a well-established genre of accession speeches. By the eighteenth century, however, the monarchy was again a stable institution. Moreover, following a practice begun during the Glorious Revolution and codified during the reign of Queen Anne, Parliament could now remain in session for up to six months following a change of rulers. In this situation, it became customary in the eighteenth century for British monarchs to go to the House of Lords shortly after ascending the throne to address both houses of Parliament.[21]

These accession speeches follow a fairly regular pattern. They begin by lamenting the death of the previous ruler and noting the great weight of responsibility placed on his or her successor. They then express confidence that the support of Parliament, the affection of the people, and/or the blessings of God will assure a successful reign. This is followed by a brief enunciation of the new monarch's determination to uphold the constitution and to maintain the Protestant succession. After reflecting briefly on the immediate state of the kingdom, the speeches end by reminding the House of Commons of its duty to provide sufficient revenue for the Civil List and by directing a few general comments to the House of Lords. Unlike the speech from the throne opening each new session of Parliament during a monarch's reign, the accession speeches typically do not contain extensive policy recommendations.[22]

---

experience may not be equal to the extensive and important Trust. However, as the Congress desires I will enter upon the momentous duty, and exert every power I Possess In their Service for the Support of the glorious Cause. I beg they will accept my most cordial thanks for this distinguished testimony of their Approbation. But lest some unlucky event should happen unfavorable to my reputation, I beg it may be remembered by every Gentleman in the room, that I this day declare with the utmost sincerity, I do not think myself equal to the Command I am honored with" (in Fitzpatrick, *Writings*, III, 292-293). Also see Washington's address to Charles Thomson upon being officially notified of his election as President, April 14, 1789, in Fitzpatrick, *Writings*, XXX, 285, and his letter to John Adams stating his willingness to head the armies of the United States in the event of war with France, July 13, 1798, in *The Writings of George Washington*, ed. John C. Fitzpatrick, XXXVI (Washington, D.C.: Government Printing Office, 1941) 327-329.

[21]The accession speech should not be confused with the monarch's speech from the throne at the beginning of each new session of Parliament. The typical speech from the throne contains none of the rhetoric typically associated with office-taking and is devoted to outlining an agenda for parliamentary legislation. This speech—along with its American analogue, the royal governor's speech to the colonial Assembly at the start of a new legislative session—provided the model for Washington's annual messages to Congress. See Michael MacDonagh, *The Pageant of Parliament*, I (London: Unwin, 1921) 201-217; Charles Warren, *Odd Byways in American History* (Cambridge, Mass.: Harvard University Press, 1942) 136-158; Kathleen M. Jamieson, "Antecedent Genre as Rhetorical Constraint," *Quarterly Journal of Speech*, 61 (1975): 406-415.

[22]See Queen Anne, speech to both houses of Parliament, March 11, 1702, in *Cobbett's Parliamentary History of England from the Earliest Period to the Year 1803*, VI (London: R. Bagshaw, 1810) 5-6; George II, speech to both houses of Parliament, June 27, 1727, in *Cobbett's Parliamentary History of England from the Earliest Period to the Year 1803*, VIII (London: Longman, Hurst, Rees, Orme, and Co., 1811) 595-596; George III, speech to both houses of Parliament, November 18, 1760, in *Cobbett's*

The situation for Washington's first inaugural was analogous in a number of ways to that for the eighteenth-century British accession speeches. In both cases a new national ruler addressed both houses of the legislature to punctuate his ascendancy, to ease the transition from the old regime, to establish his image as a good ruler, and to set a positive tone for his relationship with the legislature. It should not be surprising, then, that Washington's inaugural address shares several thematic and structural affinities with the accession speeches.

We must be exceedingly careful, though, in appraising those affinities. On the one hand, many of them are rooted in the rhetoric of office-taking and cannot with confidence be traced to the genre of accession speeches. There were only four accession speeches by British monarchs in the eighteenth century, and the last—George III's—was delivered in 1760, twenty-nine years before Washington's inauguration. Moreover, given the claims of Antifederalists that the Constitution granted the President dangerously king-like power, Washington certainly did not want his inaugural to convey any tincture of monarchy.

On the other hand, we know the American Revolutionaries modeled some of their most crucial rhetorical documents—including the Declaration of Independence—on English precedents from the seventeenth century and earlier. We also know that the Constitution was based in part on the British system of government and that the Federalists often looked to English practices for guidance in putting the new government into operation.[23] In light of this, it is not inconceivable that Washington—or James Madison, the brilliant young scholar-politician who helped draft the first inaugural—might have turned to the eighteenth-century British accession speeches as potential

---

Parliamentary History of England from the Earliest Period to the Year 1803, XV (London: Longman, Hurst, Rees, Orme, and Co., 1813) 981-985. George I, Elector of Hanover, did not arrive in England until six weeks after the death of Queen Anne and was the only eighteenth-century British ruler not to deliver an accession speech. Many of the functions of that speech were fulfilled, however, by the Lord Chancellor's address to both houses on August 5, 1714, in *Cobbett's Parliamentary History of England from the Earliest Period to the Year 1803,* XII (London: Longman, Hurst, Rees, Orme, and Browne, 1812) 3-4. The tradition of the accession speech was well enough established by the nineteenth century that George IV's failure to present such a speech after the death of George III touched off considerable debate in the House of Commons. See especially the comments of Mr. Tierney, in *Parliamentary Debates from the Year 1803 to the Present Time,* XLI (London: Baldwin, Cradock, and Joy, 1820) 1606-1608.

[23]Stephen E. Lucas, "The Rhetorical Ancestry of the Declaration of Independence," presented at the biennial meeting of the International Society for the History of Rhetoric, Oxford, England, August 1985; C. Ellis Stevens, *Sources of the Constitution of the United States Considered in Relation to Colonial and English History* (New York: Macmillan, 1894); Burleigh C. Rodick, *American Constitutional Custom: A Forgotten Factor in the Founding* (New York: Philosophical Library, 1953); Andrew C. McLaughlin, *The Foundations of American Constitutionalism* (New York: New York University Press, 1932).

models for the first presidential inaugural address.[24]

But it was not necessary to look across the Atlantic for precedents. Another potential model for Washington's inaugural could be found much closer to home. That model was the speech delivered to the Virginia Council and House of Burgesses by a new royal governor at the opening of the first legislative session after his arrival in the colony. Although this speech was delivered several months after the governor had taken his oath of office, by Washington's lifetime it had become, in essence, an inaugural address in which the governor typically reconfirmed his appointment by the crown, noted the important trust and great weight of responsibility assigned to him, announced the general principles that would guide his administration, mentioned one or two specific issues of pressing importance, praised the legislature for its knowledge, virtue, and loyalty, and urged that it avoid faction and promote the public weal in every respect.[25]

Washington was unquestionably familiar with these speeches and his first inaugural manifests a strikingly similar pattern.[26] In addition, the ceremonies surrounding Washington's inauguration reenacted—albeit on a much grander scale—those surrounding the inauguration of royal governors in colonial America. The delegations of local dignitaries that greeted him in town after town as he traveled from Mount Vernon to New York, the formal procession and cheering crowds that accompanied him to Federal Hall for his inauguration, the cry of "Long live George Washington, President of the United States!" after he took the oath of office, the receptions and entertainment that followed the inauguration—all were heartfelt expressions of hope for America

---

[24]Much of the process by which the first inaugural was composed remains shrouded in mystery. We know with confidence only that Washington rejected a 73-page draft by David Humphreys and turned to Madison for assistance in preparing a briefer, more suitable address. There are no surviving drafts by either Washington or Madison. Nor do either man's private papers reveal how the final version was written. If Madison was responsible for much of the prose—as seems likely—the speech as a whole unquestionably reflected Washington's thinking and, as we have seen, expressed ideas that had appeared time and again in his correspondence. For what remains of Humphreys' draft, see Fitzpatrick, *Writings*, XXX, 296-308; Nathaniel E. Stein, "The Discarded Inaugural Address of George Washington," *Manuscripts*, X (1958) 2-17. Madison's role is summarized in *The Papers of James Madison*, ed. Charles F. Hobson and Robert A. Rutland, XII (Charlottesville: University Press of Virginia, 1979) 120-121.

[25]This pattern is most evident in the speeches of William Gooch, February 1, 1728, in *Journals of the House of Burgesses of Virginia, 1727-1740*, ed. H. R. McIlwaine (Richmond: Virginia State Library, 1910) 4-5, where it is incorrectly dated February 1, 1727; Robert Dinwiddie, February 27, 1752, in *Journals of the House of Burgesses of Virginia, 1752-1758*, ed. H. R. McIlwaine (Richmond: Virginia State Library, 1909) 4-5; Francis Fauquier, September 15, 1758, in *Journals of the House of Burgesses of Virginia, 1758-1761*, ed. H. R. McIlwaine (Richmond: Virginia State Library, 1908) 4-5; Baron Norborne Berkeley de Botetourt, May 8, 1769, in McIlwaine, *Journals, 1758-1761*, 188-189; John Murray, Earl of Dunmore, February 10, 1772, in *Journals of the House of Burgesses of Virginia, 1770-1772*, ed. John P. Kennedy (Richmond: Virginia State Library, 1906) 154-155.

[26]The governors' inaugural addresses attracted considerable attention in colonial Virginia and were regularly printed in the *Virginia Gazette* after its founding in 1736. As a member of the House of Burgesses from 1759 to the Revolution, Washington was in the audience for Botetourt's speech of May 8, 1769, though he arrived in Williamsburg too late to hear Dunmore's address of February 10, 1772. See Douglas Southall Freeman, *George Washington: A Biography*, III (New York: Scribner's, 1951) 216-217, 289.

and respect for Washington, but all had roots in the political ceremonies of colonial America and, of course, in the ancient rituals of British politics. It is also noteworthy in this regard that Washington's inaugural, like the inaugural speeches of Virginia's colonial governors (and the accession speeches of British monarchs), was delivered to the legislature behind closed doors and was followed by an exchange of formulaic replies between the legislature and the executive.[27]

There was, of course, no exact template for the first presidential inaugural. The speech Washington delivered on April 30, 1789, was shaped above all by his personal beliefs and by his view of the rhetorical situation as he assumed the presidency. His response to that situation, however, appears to have been modulated by a set of generic constraints derived from the rhetoric of office-taking, from the inaugural speeches of Virginia's colonial governors, and, perhaps, from the accession speeches of eighteenth-century British monarchs. Seen in this way, the first presidential inaugural emerges as a blend of the old and the new, as a product of personal considerations, situational constraints, and rhetorical customs.

If this inquiry has illuminated the origins of Washington's first inaugural, it should also remind us that assessing the impact of antecedent rhetorical forms upon any given rhetorical transaction requires rigorous investigation. Rhetorical critics would seem well advised to give more intensive consideration to the interplay of generic constraints and the particular historical situations out of which rhetorical genres evolve and in which they operate. This is one step to producing a more powerful body of scholarship that moves beyond describing what rhetorical genres look like to explaining why they look that way and how they function.

---

[27]See Leonard Woods Labaree, *Royal Government in America: A Study of the British Colonial System before 1783* (New Haven: Yale University Press, 1930) 84-91, for the inauguration of colonial governors. The ceremonies of Washington's inauguration are detailed in Frank Monaghan, *Notes on the Inaugural Journey and the Inaugural Ceremonies of George Washington as First President of the United States* (New York: privately printed, 1939), while the messages exchanged between Congress and Washington in the days after the inaugural are printed in *A Compilation of the Messages and Papers of the Presidents*, ed. James D. Richardson, I (New York: Bureau of National Literature, 1897) 46-49.

Constitutive Rhetoric:
The Case of the *Peuple Québécois*

by Maurice Charland

In the *Rhetoric of Motives,* Kenneth Burke proposes "identification" as an alternative to "persuasion" as the key term of the rhetorical process. Burke's project is a rewriting of rhetorical theory that considers rhetoric and motives in formal terms, as consequences of the nature of language and its enactment. Burke's stress on identification permits a rethinking of judgment and the working of the rhetorical effect, for he does not posit a transcendent subject as audience member, who would exist prior to and apart from the speech to be judged, but considers audience members to participate in the very discourse by which they would be "persuaded." Audiences would embody a discourse. A consequence of this theoretical move is that it permits an understanding within rhetorical theory of ideological discourse, of the discourse that presents itself as always only pointing to the given, the natural, the already agreed upon.[1] In particular, it permits us to examine how rhetoric effects what Louis Althusser identifies as the key process in the production of ideology: the constitution of the subject, where the subject is precisely he or she who simultaneously speaks and initiates action in discourse (a subject to a verb) and in the world (a speaker and social agent).[2]

As Burke recognizes, "persuasion," as rhetoric's key term, implies the existence of an agent who is free to be persuaded.[3] However, rhetorical theory's privileging of an audience's freedom to judge is problematic, for it assumes that audiences, with their prejudices, interests, and motives, are *given* and so extra-rhetorical. Rhetorical criticism, as Grossberg points out, posits the existence of transcendental subjects whom discourse would mediate.[4] In

Reprinted from *The Quarterly Journal of Speech* 73 (1987): 133-150 with permission of the Speech Communication Association.

[1]By ideology I mean a symbolic system, the discourse of which (1) is "false" in the sense that it is based on the presuppositions of some "terministic screen," (2) denies its historicity and linguisticality—pretending to but present a naturally or self-evidently meaningful world, (3) denies or transforms contradictions and (4) legitimates and structures power relations. As such, my usage is much like the one suggested in, Anthony Giddens, *Central Problems in Social Theory: Action, Structure and Contradiction in Social Analysis* (Berkeley: University of California Press, 1979), 165-197.

[2]For a discussion of discourse-based theories of the subject, see, Kaja Silverman, *The Subject of Semiotics* (New York: Oxford University Press, 1983), 43-53, 126-131.

[3]Kenneth Burke, *A Rhetoric of Motives* (1950; rpt. Berkeley: University of California Press, 1969), 50.

[4]Lawrence Grossberg, "Marxist Dialectics and Rhetorical Criticism," *Quarterly Journal of Speech* 65 (1979): 249.

other words, rhetorical theory usually refuses to consider the possibility that the very existence of social subjects (who would become audience members) is already a rhetorical effect. Nevertheless, much of what we as rhetorical critics consider to be a product or consequence of discourse, including social identity, religious faith, sexuality, and ideology is beyond the realm of rational or even free choice, beyond the realm of persuasion. As Burke notes, the identifications of social identity can occur "spontaneously, intuitively, even unconsciously."[5] Such identifications are rhetorical, for they are discursive effects that induce human cooperation. They are also, however, logically prior to persuasion. Indeed, humans are constituted in these characteristics; they are essential to the "nature" of a subject and form the basis for persuasive appeals. Consequently, attempts to elucidate ideological or identity-forming discourses as persuasive are trapped in a contradiction: persuasive discourse requires a subject-as-audience who is already constituted with an identity and within an ideology.

Ultimately then, theories of rhetoric as persuasion cannot account for the audiences that rhetoric addresses. However, such an account is critical to the development of a theoretical understanding of the power of discourse. If it is easier to praise Athens before Athenians than before Laecedemonians, we should ask how those in Athens come to experience themselves as Athenians. Indeed, a rhetoric to Athenians in praise of Athens would be relatively insignificant compared to a rhetoric that constitutes Athenians as such. What I propose to develop in this essay is a theory of constitutive rhetoric that would account for this process. I will elaborate this theory of constitutive rhetoric through an examination of a case where the identity of the audience is clearly problematic: the independence movement in Quebec, Canada's French-speaking province. There, supporters of Quebec's political sovereignty addressed and so attempted to call into being a *peuple québécois* that would legitimate the constitution of a sovereign Quebec state.

Central to my analysis of the constitutive rhetoric of Quebec sovereignty will be Althusser's category of the subject. Examining what Michael McGee would term Quebec's rhetoric of a "people," I will show how claims for Quebec sovereignty base themselves upon the asserted existence of a particular type of subject, the "Québécois." That subject and the collectivized "peuple québécois" are, in Althusser's language, "interpellated" as political subjects through a process of identification in rhetorical narratives that "always already" presume the constitution of subjects. From this perspective, a subject is not "persuaded" to support sovereignty. Support for sovereignty is inherent to the subject position addressed by *souverainiste* (pro-sovereignty) rhetoric because of what we will see to be a series of narrative *ideological effects.*

[5]Kenneth Burke, *Language as Symbolic Action: Essays on Life, Literature, and Method* (Berkeley: University of California Press, 1966), 301.

The Quest for Quebec Sovereignty

In 1967, the year of Canada's centennial, a new political association was formed in Quebec. This organization, the *Mouvement Souveraineté-Association (MSA),* dedicated itself to Quebec's political sovereignty as it proclaimed the existence of an essence uniting social actors in the province. In French, Quebec's majority language, the *MSA* declared: "Nous sommes des Québécois" ("We are *Québécois")* and called for Quebec's independence from Canada.[6] This declaration marked the entry of the term "Québécois" into the mainstream of Quebec political discourse. Until that time, members of the French-speaking society of Quebec were usually termed "Canadiens français" ("French-Canadians"). With the *MSA,* a national identity for a new type of political subject was born, a subject whose existence would be presented as justification for the constitution of a new state. Thus, the *MSA's* declaration is an instance of constitutive rhetoric, for it calls its audience into being. Furthermore, as an instance of constitutive rhetoric, it was particularly effective, for within a decade of the creation of that *mouvement,* the term "Québécois" had gained currency even among certain supporters of the Canadian federal system, and Quebec voters had brought the *MSA's* successor, the *Parti Québécois (PQ),* to power.

Quebec voters gave the *Parti Québécois* control of the Quebec government on November 15, 1976. The party obtained 41.4% of the popular vote and won 71 of 110 seats in the *Assemblé nationale,* Quebec's legislature.[7] This election marked a major transformation in Canada's political life, for the *PQ* asserted that those in Quebec constituted a distinct *peuple* with the right and duty to political sovereignty, and was committed to leading Quebec, Canada's largest and second most populous province, out of Canada.

The *PQ's* major campaign promise was to hold a referendum on Quebec's political sovereignty during its first term of office. In preparation of this plebiscite, the Quebec government issued, on November 1, 1979, a formal policy statement, a "white paper," that outlined a proposed new political order in which Quebec would be a sovereign state associated economically with Canada.[8] While the Quebec-Canada economic association would include free trade, a customs union, a shared currency and central bank as negotiated, and the free movement of persons across the Quebec-Canada border, each

---

[6]Mouvement Souveraineté-Association, founding political manifesto, 1968, in *Le manuel de la parole: Manifestes québécois,* ed. Daniel Latouche and Diane Poliquin-Bourassa (Sillery, Quebec: Editions du boréal express, 1977) vol. 3, 97.

[7]André Bernard and Bernard Descrôteaux, *Québec: élections 1981* (Ville LaSalle, Québec: Editions Hurtibise HMH, Limitée, 1981), 15, 23.

[8]Quebec (Prov.), Conseil exécutif, *La nouvelle entente Québec-Canada: Proposition du Gouvernement du Québec pour une entente d'égal à égal: La souveraineté-association.* Quebec: 1979. This document, a soft cover book sold in bookstores, consists of a foreword, six chapters which explain the Quebec government's reasons for seeking sovereignty, and a concluding direct address by Quebec's premier, René Levesque, calling for a OUI vote in the forthcoming referendum. The significance of the document arises from its clear articulation of Quebec's rhetoric of sovereignty as it had developed for over a decade in Quebec public address, and from its institutional status, offering the official rhetoric of the government's pro-sovereignty position.

government would have the full sovereignty of a nation-state.[9] The White Paper asserted that those in Quebec constituted a *peuple* and called upon them to support this project by voting OUI in a forthcoming referendum. Such a positive vote by the Quebec electorate would mandate their provincial government to negotiate for the envisioned new constitutional status with the federal government in Ottawa.[10]

The White Paper, as it articulated the reasons for Quebec's political independence, was a rhetorical document. It offered a variety of arguments demonstrating that *Québécois* were an oppressed *peuple* within the confines of Canada's constitution who would be better off with their own country. These arguments were presented in the context of the constitutive rhetoric of the "peuple québécois." This constitutive rhetoric took the form of a narrative account of Quebec history in which *Québécois* were identified with their forebears who explored New France, who suffered under the British conquest, and who struggled to erect the Quebec provincial state apparatus.

The Referendum on sovereignty-association was held May 20, 1980. Although a majority of the populace voted against the measure, over 45% of the French-speaking population assented to their provincial government's interpretation of Quebec society.[11] Those voting OUI granted the legitimacy of the constitutional claims the White Paper asserted. Clearly, even if a majority of *Québécois* were not ready to seek sovereignty, a *malaise* powerful enough to dominate political debate and government priorities existed in the province. There was a strong sense in which "Québécois" was a term antithetical to "Canadien."

The election of the *Parti Québécois* and the strength of its *souverainiste*

---

[9]Quebec, *La nouvelle entente,* 62-64.

[10]As adopted by the Quebec *Assemblé nationale,* 20 March 1980, the following question appeared on the ballot:

"Le Gouvernement du Québec a fait connaitre sa proposition d'en arriver, avec le reste du Canada, à une nouvelle entente fondée sur le principe de l'égalité des peuples; cette entente permettrait au Québec d'acquérir le pouvoir exclusif de faire ses lois, de percevoir ses impôts et d'établir ses relations extérieurs, ce qui est la souveraineté—et, en même temps, de maintenir avec le Canada une association économique comportant l'utilisation de la même monnaie; aucun changement de statut politique résultant de ces négociations ne sera réalisé sans l'accord de la population lors d'un autre référendum; en conséquence accordez-vous au Gouvernement du Québec le mandat de négocier l'entente proposée entre le Québec et le Canada?
                                       OUI   NON

The Government of Québec has made public its proposal to negotiate a new agreement with the rest of Canada, based on the equality of nations; this agreement would enable Québec to acquire the exclusive power to make its laws, levy its taxes and establish relations abroad—in other words, sovereignty— and at the same time, to maintain with Canada an economic association including a common currency; no change in political status resulting from these negotiations will be effected without approval by the people through another referendum; on these terms, do you give the Government of Québec the mandate to negotiate the proposed agreement between Quebec and Canada?
                                       YES   NO."

Quebec (Prov.), Directeur Général des élections, *Rapport des résultats officiels du scrutin, référendum du 20 mai 1980,* 9.

[11]In the May 1980 referendum on "sovereignty-association," 85.6% of eligible voters cast valid ballots. Of these, 40.4% voted OUI. See, *Rapport des résultats,* 19. Among francophones, the vote was slightly higher and is estimated at 46%. See, Jean-Claude Picard, "Le gouvernement et le Parti Québécois analysent l'échec référendaire de mardi," *Le Devoir,* Thursday, 22 May 1980.

option in the Referendum reveals the significance of the constitutive rhetoric of a "peuple québécois." While some might consider the White Paper to be a rhetorical failure because less than half of Quebec's French-speaking population opted for independence, the outcome of the Referendum reveals that its constitutive rhetoric was particularly powerful. This rhetoric, which presents those in Quebec as *Québécois* requiring and deserving their own state, constituted at least close to half of Quebec voters such that they, as an audience, were not *really* Canadians.

What the debate in Quebec reveals is that the very character of a collective identity, and the nature of its boundary, of who is a member of the collectivity, were problematic. In other words, in Quebec there existed a struggle over the constitution of political subjects. In Quebec, the possibility of an alternative *peuple* and history was entertained. Thus, the movement for sovereignty permits us to see how peoples are rhetorically constituted.

"Peuple" as Legitimating Principle

As Michael McGee has noted, the term "people" can rhetorically legitimate constitutions.[12] Not surprisingly then, the independence debate in Quebec, as it developed since the formation of the *MSA,* centered upon whether *a peuple québécois* exists, and more importantly, on whether that *peuple* is the kind of "people" that legitimates a sovereign state. In Quebec, competing claims were made as to the nature of the *peuple.* Consider, for example, Claude Morin's polemical history of Quebec-Ottawa constitutional disputes from 1960 to 1972, where he distinguishes the emergent Quebec collectivity from its predecessor, French-Canada, as he identifies the perspective of the Quebec government: "Like many other peoples, Quebeckers have experienced an awakening of self-consciousness. They want to assert themselves, not as French-speaking Canadians, but as Québécois, citizens who, for the moment, suffer the want of a country that is their own."[13] In Morin's view, not only are those in Quebec *Québécois,* but they constitute the kind of *peuple* that warrants a sovereign state. Morin's observation confirms that populations can at different historical moments gain different identities that warrant different forms of collective life. Furthermore, if we consider that Morin's observation is contentious and partisan,[14] and that many in Quebec would contest his assessment of their collective identity, we find confirmation of McGee's further assertion that the identity of a "people," as a rhetorical construct, is not even agreed upon by those who would address it.[15] Rather, supporters and opponents of Quebec sovereignty both seek to

---

[12]Michael C. McGee, "In Search of 'The People': A Rhetorical Alternative," *Quarterly Journal of Speech* 61 (October 1975): 239.

[13]Claude Morin, *Quebec versus Ottawa: The Struggle for Self-Government, 1960-1972,* trans. Richard Howard (Toronto: University of Toronto Press, 1976), 5.

[14]Claude Morin's text was written as a reflection on his experience of federal-provincial relations as a high-ranking civil servant. He was also an early and active proponent of sovereignty and member of the *PQ* who became a cabinet minister in the *PQ* government.

[15]McGee, 246.

justify their position on the basis of what they assert is a will intrinsic to their version of the *peuple's* very being. Their rhetoric is grounded in the constitution of *Québécois* as political subjects.

The debate over sovereignty in Quebec clearly reveals the degree to which peoples are constituted in discourse. Those in Quebec could be "Québécois"; they could also be "Canadiens français." The distinction is crucial, for only the former type of "peuple" can claim the right to a sovereign state. Indeed, the debate in Quebec permits us to see the radical implication of McGee's argument, for not only is the character or identity of the "peuple" open to rhetorical revision, but the very *boundary* of whom the term "peuple" includes and excludes is rhetorically constructed: as the "peuple" is variously characterized, the persons who make up the "peuple" can change. Thus, consider the rather extreme counter-argument to Morin's claim that a *peuple québécois* exists and is gaining self-awareness, as articulated by William Shaw and Lionel Albert, two Quebec opponents of sovereignty, who conversely assert that no Quebec *peuple* exists, that the term "Québécois" properly only applies to residents of the City of Quebec, and that the term as used by Quebec nationalists constitutes a "semantic fraud":

> Separatists measure the degree of their penetration of the public consciousness by the extent to which the people are willing to call themselves *Québécois*. The more they can persuade the French Canadians in Quebec to call themselves *Québécois,* the easier the task of insinuating the idea that those French Canadians who happen to live in eastern or northern Ontario or in northern New Brunswick are somehow "different" from those living in Quebec. Once that idea has been established, then the idea that Quebec's borders, which are criss-crossed daily by tens of thousands of French Canadians, could somehow be thought of, not as casual signposts along the highway, but as a full-fledged international boundary, can also be established.[16]

Shaw and Albert display a keen sensitivity to the workings of the *péquiste* rhetoric of collective identity, even if as advocates, these opponents of Quebec independence assert that a French-Canadian *peuple* "really" exists outside of rhetorical construction. What Shaw and Albert ignore, of course, is that the French-speaking *peuple* or nation that they assert exists also becomes real only through rhetoric. Indeed, the possibility of political action requires that political actors be within a "fictive" discourse. More precisely, as Althusser asserts: "there is no practice except by and in an ideology."[17] Political identity must be an ideological fiction, even though, as McGee

---

[16]William F. Shaw and Lionel Albert, *Partition* (Montreal: Thornhill Publishing, 1980), 143-144.
[17]Louis Althusser, *Lenin and Philosophy and other Essays,* trans. Ben Brewster (New York: Monthly Review Press, 1971), 170.

correctly notes, this fiction becomes historically material and of consequence as persons live it.

The Rhetoric of Interpellation

As we have seen, rhetorical claims for a sovereign Quebec are predicated upon the existence of an ideological subject, the "Québécois," so constituted that sovereignty is a natural and necessary way of life. Furthermore, and hardly surprisingly, the ultimate justification for these claims is the subject's character, nature, or essence. This is so because this identity defines inherent motives and interests that a rhetoric can appeal to. The ideological "trick" of such a rhetoric is that it presents that which is most rhetorical, the existence of a *peuple,* or of a subject, as extrarhetorical. These members of the *peuple* whose supposed essence demands action do not exist in nature, but only within a discursively constituted history. Thus, this rhetoric paradoxically must constitute the identity "Québécois" as it simultaneously presumes it to be pregiven and natural, existing outside of rhetoric and forming the basis for a rhetorical address.

We find a treatment of this constitutive phenomenon in Edwin Black's discussion of the "second persona."[18] As Michael McGuire observes, Black's process of transforming an audience occurs through *identification,* in Burke's sense.[19] However, to simply accept such an account of this process would be inadequate. It would not fully explain the significance of becoming one with a persona, of entering into and embodying it. In particular, to simply state that audiences identify with a persona explains neither (1) the ontological status of those in the audience before their identification, nor (2) the ontological status of the persona, and the nature of identifying with it. In order to clarify these ontological issues, we must consider carefully the radical edge of Burke's identificatory principle. Burke asserts that, as "symbol using" animals, our being is significantly constituted in our symbolicity. As Burke puts it, "so much of the 'we' that is separated from the nonverbal by the verbal would not even exist were it not for the verbal (or for our symbolicity in general[)]."[20] In this, Burke moves towards collapsing the distinction between the realm of the symbolic and that of human conceptual consciousness. From such a perspective, we cannot accept the 'givenness' of "audience," "person," or "subject," but must consider their very textuality, their very constitution in rhetoric as a structured articulation of signs. We must, in other words, consider the textual nature of social being.

The symbolically based critique of humanist ontology implicit in Burke has been developed in a tradition sharing much with him, that of

---

[18]Edwin Black, "The Second Persona," *Quarterly Journal of Speech* 56 (April 1970): 109-119.
[19]Michael D. McGuire, "Rhetoric, Philosophy and the *Volk*: Johann Gottlieb Fichte's *Addresses to the German Nation,*" *Quarterly Journal of Speech* 62 (April 1976): 135-136.
[20]Burke, *Symbolic Action,* 5.

structuralism.[21] Structuralist semiotics and narrative theory have deconstructed the concept of the unitary and transcendent subject. And, with rhetorical theory, they share an appreciation of the power of discourse, of its effects. Thus, in order to develop the radical implications of Burke's lead, it is to this tradition that I will turn.

Althusser describes the process of inscribing subjects into ideology as "interpellation";[22]

> I shall then suggest that ideology "acts" or "functions" in such a way that it "recruits" subjects among the individuals (it recruits them all), or "transforms" the individuals into subjects (it transforms them all) by that very precise operation which I have called *interpellation* or hailing, and which can be imagined along the lines of the most commonplace everyday police (or other) hailing: "Hey, you there!"[23]

Interpellation occurs at the very moment one enters into a rhetorical situation, that is, as soon as an individual recognizes and acknowledges being addressed. An interpellated subject participates in the discourse that addresses him. Thus, to be interpellated is to become one of Black's personae and be a position in a discourse. In consequence, interpellation has a significance to rhetoric, for the acknowledgment of an address entails an acceptance of an imputed self-understanding which can form the basis for an appeal. Furthermore, interpellation occurs rhetorically, through the effect of the addressed discourse. Note, however, that interpellation does not occur through persuasion in the usual sense, for the very act of *addressing* is rhetorical. It is logically prior to the rhetorical *narratio*. In addition, this rhetoric of identification is ongoing, not restricted to one hailing, but usually part of a rhetoric of socialization. Thus, one must already be an interpellated subject and exist as a discursive position in order to be part of the audience of a rhetorical situation in which persuasion could occur.

The "Peuple" as Narrative Ideological Effect

Events in Quebec demonstrate that the "peuple" is a persona, existing in rhetoric, and not in some neutral history devoid of human interpretation. But

---

[21]Burke reveals a structuralist tendency in his discussions of the formal interplay between the elements of his "pentad," which are constitutive of motives. While Burke differs with the French structuralist tradition, particularly in holding on to the concept of "act," his denial of a foundational character for any of his pentadic terms and his sensitivity to unresolvable ambiguities do lead him, just like the French structuralists, to consider the agent's constitution in symbolic structures. See Frank Lentricchia, *Criticism and Social Change* (Chicago: University of Chicago Press, 1983), 66-83.

[22]"Interpeller" is a rather commonly used French verb which designates the act of calling upon someone by name and demanding an answer. It is not surprising that Althusser, in the quote that follows, uses the example of a policeman's hailing, since a person who is *interpellé* is usually under some constraint to respond. Thus, the term is used to refer to the questioning of ministers by members of parliament and to the formal address of a judge or bailiff as part of a legal act. *Petit Larousse illustré*, 1979, s. v. "interpeller," "interpellation."

[23]Althusser, 174.

note, personae are not persons; they remain in the realm of words. As McGee observes, a "people" is a fiction which comes to be when individuals accept living within a political myth.[24] This myth would be ontological, constitutive of those "seduced" by it. In Quebec, what McGee terms the myth of the "people" is articulated in the Quebec government's White Paper. This document, speaking in the name of the independence movement, as institutionalized in a party and a government, offers a narrative of Quebec history that renders demands for sovereignty intelligible and reasonable.

The White Paper's narrative of the *peuple* since the founding of New France, through the British Conquest, the development of Canada into a federated state, and the setting up of the Referendum on Quebec sovereignty is, in McGee's sense, a myth. It paradoxically both reveals the *peuple* and makes it real. This making real is part of the ontological function of narratives. Indeed, as Jameson points out, "history . . . is inaccessible to us except in textual form, and . . . our approach to it and the Real itself necessarily passes through its prior textualization, its narrativization in the political unconscious."[25] Because the *peuple* exists as a subject in history, it is only intelligible within a narrative representation of history. In other words, this *peuple,* and the individual subject, the *Québécois,* exist as positions in a text.

Narratives "make real" coherent subjects. They constitute subjects as they present a particular textual position, such as the noun-term "peuple québécois" as the locus for action and experience. Roland Barthes well expresses this ultimate textuality of narratives when he asserts that: "Narrative does not show, does not imitate; the passion which may excite us . . . is not that of a 'vision' (in actual fact, we do not 'see' anything)."[26] In other words, narratives work through a representational *effect.* Texts are but surfaces; characters are, in a sense, but "paper beings," to use Barthes' phrase. These paper beings *seem* real through textual operations. The distinct acts and events in a narrative become linked through identification arising from the narrative form. Narratives lead us to construct and fill in coherent unified subjects out of temporally and spatially separate events. This renders the site of action and experience stable. The locus of yesterday's acts becomes that of today's. Consequently, narratives offer a world in which human agency is possible and acts can be meaningful.

All narratives, as they create the illusion of merely revealing a unified and unproblematic subjectivity, are ideological, because they occult the importance of discourse, culture, and history in giving rise to subjectivity, and because, as G. H. Mead and Freud have made clear, subjectivity is always social, constituted in language, and exists in a delicate balance of

[24]McGee, 244.
[25]Fredric Jameson, *The Political Unconscious: Narrative as a Socially Symbolic Act* (Ithaca: Cornell University Press, 1981), 35.
[26]Roland Barthes, *Image, Music, Text,* trans. by Stephen Heath (New York: Hill & Wang, 1977), 124.

contradictory drives and impulses. Narratives suppress the fact that, in a very real sense, no person is the same as he or she was a decade ago, or last year, or indeed yesterday. In raising the ultimate "falsity" of narratives, my intention is not, however, to decry them and hold out for some unmediated consciousness. Nor am I here concerned with a philosophical critique of the subject in Western civilization. My intention is to show the degree to which collective identities forming the basis of rhetorical appeals themselves depend upon rhetoric; the "peuple québécois," and "peoples" in general, exist only through an ideological discourse that constitutes them. Furthermore, if the subject in all narratives is ideological, a "peuple" is triply so, for it does not even have a unitary body corresponding to its imputed unitary agency and consciousness. The persona or subject "peuple québécois" exists only as a series of narrative ideological effects.

In the rhetoric of Quebec sovereignty, the "Québécois" is a collective subject. It offers, in Burke's language, an "ultimate" identification permitting an overcoming or going beyond of divisive individual or class interests and concerns.[27] This identity transcends the limitations of the individual body and will. This process of constituting a collective subject is the *first ideological effect* of constitutive rhetoric. If a *peuple* exists, it is only in ideology, as McGee makes clear. That ideology arises in the very nature of narrative history. To tell the story of the *Québécois* is implicitly to assert the existence of a collective subject, the protagonist of the historical drama, who experiences, suffers, and acts. Such a narrative renders the world of events understandable with respect to a transcendental collective interest that negates individual interest. Consider the following passage from the White Paper's account of early French North America:

> Our ancestors put down their roots in American soil at the beginning of the 17th century, at the time the first English settlers were landing on the East coast of the United States. As they were clearing the land of the St. Lawrence valley, they explored the vast continent in all directions, from the Atlantic to the Rocky Mountains, and from Hudson Bay to the Gulf of Mexico. Through discovering, claiming, and occupying the land, *Québécois* came to consider themselves North-Americans.
>
> In 1760, our community was already an established society along the St. Lawrence. North American by geography, French by language, culture, and politics, this society had a soul, a way of life, traditions, that were its very own. Its struggles, its successes, and its ordeals had given it an awareness of its collective destiny, and it was with some

---

[27]Burke, *Rhetoric of Motives,* 194.

impatience that it tolerated the colonial tie.[28]

In a radically empiricist mood, I could assert that a society *qua* society has no soul, no struggles, no successes. Clearly, history proceeds by the acts of individuals. But, of course, individuals can act in concert or as a mass, they can respond to apersonal historical forces, and we can interpret the sum total of their individual actions with respect to a collective agent. Historical narratives offer such interpretations. In the telling of the story of a *peuple,* a *peuple* comes to be. It is within the formal structure of a narrative history that it is possible to conceive of a set of individuals as if they were but one. Thus, the "struggles" and "ordeals" of settlers, as a set of individual acts and experiences, become identified with "community," a term that here masks or negates tensions and differences between members of any society. The community of *Québécois* is the master agent of a narratized history.

In the above passage, note also how the past is presented as an extension of the present through the use of the pronoun "our" and the term "Québécois" as signifiers of both eighteenth century settlers who termed themselves "Canadiens" and those living in Quebec today. The White Paper, and histories of peoples in general, offer a "consubstantiality," to use Burke's expression, between the dead and the living. This positing of a transhistorical subject is the *second ideological effect* of constitutive rhetoric. Here, ancestry is offered as the concrete link between the French settlers of North America, those in Quebec today, and a collectivity. Time is collapsed as narrative identification occurs: today's Quebec residents constitute a *peuple* and have a right to their own state because members of their community have discovered, claimed, and occupied the land. This interpretive stance is perfectly reasonable. It is also perfectly tautological, for it is a making sense that depends upon the a priori acceptance of that which it attempts to prove the existence of, a collective agent, the *peuple québécois,* that transcends the limitations of individuality at any historical moment and transcends the death of individuals across history.

Form renders the "Québécois" a real subject within the historical narrative. The "Québécois" does not, however, become a free subject. Subjects within narratives are not free, they are *positioned* and so constrained. All narratives have power over the subjects they present. The endings of narratives are fixed before the telling. The freedom of the character in a

---

[28]Québec, *La nouvelle entente,* 3. The primary language of Quebec public discourse is French. As such, political life proceeds through a French "terministic screen." To be true to the political consciousness of that society, this essay is based on the analysis of the French primary texts. It is for this reason that I continue to use the terms "peuple" and "Québécois" throughout this essay. Note specifically that "peuple," the French term for "people" is a singular noun; in French, one would write "the people is." Note also that there is no adequate translation of "Québécois." The closest equivalent, "Quebecker," lacks all of the French term's nationalist connotations. While analyzed in French, cited passages are presented in English translation for the reader's convenience. My translation is in large measure based on the simultaneously published official English version of the White Paper: *Québec-Canada a New Deal: The Québec Government Proposal for a New Partnership between Equals: Sovereignty-Association* (Quebec: 1979).

narrative is an illusion, for narratives move inexorably toward their *telos.* The characters in a story are obviously not free. Only in Woody Allen's *The Purple Rose of Cairo* can characters abandon their script and walk off the screen. What Allen's film and Barthes' analysis of narratives so clearly illustrate is that narratives are but texts that offer the illusion of agency. The subject is constituted at the nodes of a narrative's surface. What Walter Fisher terms "narrative probability" is a formal and ideological constraint upon the subject's possibilities of being.[29] To be constituted as a subject in a narrative is to be constituted with a history, motives, and a *telos.* Thus, in the rhetoric of Quebec sovereignty, "Québécois" is not merely a descriptive term, but identifies and positions the Quebec voter with respect to his or her future.

The White Paper presents *Québécois* as agents, capable of acting freely in the world. However, the narrative's existence as a text is predicated upon *Québécois* asserting their existence as a collective subject through a politics of independence. In the White Paper on sovereignty, *Québécois* are constituted in the choice of national solidarity. As Burke observes is the case in ideological narratives, the White Paper effects an identification of the temporal sequence of its plot with the logical development of an ultimate principle.[30] In the resultant hierarchy, *Québécois* are free to choose only one course of action:

> The Will to Survive
>
> Sooner or later, this society would have shaken off the colonial yoke and acquired its independence, as was the case, in 1776, for the United States of America. But in 1763 the hazards of war placed it under British control. . . . Faced with this defeat, francophones spontaneously chose to be faithful. There could be no question of passing over to the winner's camp to reap the benefits that awaited them. They would adapt to the new situation, come to terms with the new masters, but above all preserve the essential of that which characterized our *peuple:* its language, its customs, its religion. At all costs, they would survive.[31]

The freedom of the protagonist of this narrative is but an illusion. This illusion of freedom is the *third ideological effect* of constitutive rhetoric. Freedom is illusory because the narrative is already spoken or written. Furthermore, because the narrative is a structure of understanding that produces totalizing interpretations,[32] the subject is constrained *to follow through,* to act so as to maintain the narrative's consistency. A narrative, once written, offers a logic of meaningful totality. *Québécois,* precisely because

---

[29]Walter Fisher, "Narration as a Human Communication Paradigm: The Case of Public Moral Argument," *Communication Monographs* 51 (March 1984): 8.

[30]Burke, *Rhetoric of Motives,* 197.

[31]Quebec, *La nouvelle entente,* 3-4.

[32]Paul Ricoeur, *Hermeneutics and the Human Sciences,* ed. and trans. John B. Thompson (New York: Cambridge University Press, 1981), 278-279.

they are the subjects within a text, within a narrative rhetoric, must follow the logic of the narrative. They must be true to the motives through which the narrative constitutes them, and thus which presents characters as freely acting towards a predetermined and fixed ending.

The Effective Power of Constitutive Rhetoric

The ideological effects of constitutive rhetoric that I have outlined are not merely formal effects inscribed within the bracketed experience of interpreting a text. In other words, these do not only permit a disinterested understanding of a fictive world. What is significant in constitutive rhetoric is that it positions the reader towards political, social, and economic action in the material world and it is in this positioning that its ideological character becomes significant. For the purpose of analysis, this positioning of subjects as historical actors can be understood as a two-step process. First, audience members must be successfully interpellated; not all constitutive rhetorics succeed. Second, the tautological logic of constitutive rhetoric must necessitate action in the material world; constitutive rhetoric must require that its embodied subjects act freely in the social world to affirm their subject position.

Audiences are, to use Althusser's famous phrase, "always already" subjects. This is to say that if we disregard the point at which a child enters language, but restrict ourselves to "competent" speakers within a culture, we can observe that one cannot exist but as a subject within a narrative. The necessity is ontological: one must already be a subject in order to be addressed or to speak. We therefore cannot say that one is persuaded to be a subject; one is "always already" a subject. This does not imply, however, that one's subject position is fixed at the moment one enters language. Indeed, the development of new subject positions, of new constitutive rhetorics, is possible at particular historical moments. The subject is a position within a text. To be an embodied subject is to experience and act in a textualized world. However, this world is not seamless and a subject position's world view can be laced with contradictions. We can, as Burke puts it, encounter "recalcitrance."[33] In addition, as Stuart Hall observes, various contradictory subject positions can simultaneously exist within a culture:[34] we can live within many texts. These contradictions place a strain upon identification with a given subject position and render possible a subject's rearticulation. Successful new constitutive rhetorics offer new subject positions that resolve, or at least contain, experienced contradictions. They serve to overcome or define away the recalcitrance the world presents by providing the subject with new perspectives and motives.

---

[33]Kenneth Burke, *Permanence and Change: An Anatomy of Purpose*, 2nd rev. ed. (Indianapolis: The Bobbs-Merrill Company, Inc., 1954), 255.
[34]Stuart Hall, "Signification, Representation, Ideology: Althusser and the Post-Structuralist Debates," *Critical Studies in Mass Communication* 2 (June 1985): 107-113.

Thus, for example, the subject position "Québécois" arises from a rearticulation of two positions, that of "Canadien français," and that of the Quebec resident and voter with a collective will ostensibly represented by the Quebec government. Because some French-Canadians live outside of Quebec and not all those in Quebec are French-speaking, the identity "Canadien français" cannot permit the articulation of a French-speaking nation-state in North America. As the White Paper never fails to remind its audience, to be "Canadien français" is to be a member of an impotent minority without a proper homeland. The White Paper, penned by the Quebec government, invokes the contradiction of being a member of a French-speaking collectivity, or *nation*, that does not have a sovereign state apparatus, for the Quebec government remains subject to Canada's Federal government in Ottawa, and French-Canadians are subjects of the Federal state, a state that can be represented as ultimately foreign.

French-Canadians in Quebec had to live the contradiction of not being exclusively subjects of the state they collectively controlled. "Québécois" resolves this contradiction at the discursive level, by identifying the populace with a territory and a francophone state, rather than with an ethnic group. Constitutive rhetorics of new subject positions can be understood, therefore, as working upon previous discourses, upon previous constitutive rhetorics. They capture alienated subjects by rearticulating existing subject positions so as to contain or resolve experienced dialectical contradictions between the world and its discourses. The process by which an audience member enters into a new subject position is therefore not one of persuasion. It is akin more to one of conversion that ultimately results in an act of recognition of the 'rightness' of a discourse and of one's identity with its reconfigured subject position.

The White Paper's constitutive rhetoric, as it articulates the meaning of being "Québécois," is not a mere fiction. It inscribes real social actors within its textualized structure of motives, and then inserts them into the world of practice. The White Paper offers a collectivized subject position that constitutes those in Quebec as members of a *peuple* which is transcendent of the limits of their biological individuality. This position thus opens the possibility for them to participate in a collective political project. The White Paper's narrative is characterized by a set of formal ideological effects that permit it to be intelligible as one accepts and enters into the collective consciousness it articulates. The White Paper offers, therefore, a particular instance of narrative rhetoric that, in Fisher's language, "give[s] order to human experience and . . . induce[s] others to *dwell in [it]* to establish ways of living in common, in communion in which there is sanction for the story that constitutes one's life" (italics added).[35] This dwelling place is, of course, prerequisite to the power of the rhetoric of Quebec sovereignty. To be

---

[35]Fisher, 6.

Québécois as configured by the White Paper is to embody in the world the narrative and the motives it ascribes to members of the *peuple*.

To enter into the White Paper's rhetorical narrative is to identify with Black's second persona. It is the process of recognizing oneself as the subject in a text. It is to exist at the nodal point of a series of identifications and to be captured in its structure and in its production of meaning. It is to be a subject which exists beyond one's body and life span. It is to have and experience the dangerous memories of British conquest and rule. It is to live towards national independence. Then, the power of the text is the power of an embodied ideology. The form of an ideological rhetoric is effective because it is within the bodies of those it constitutes as subjects. These subjects owe their existence to the discourse that articulates them. As Burke puts it: "An 'ideology' is like a god coming down to earth, where it will inhabit a place pervaded by its presence. An 'ideology' is like a spirit taking up its abode in a body: it makes that body hop around in certain ways; and that same body would have hopped around in different ways had a different ideology happened to inhabit it."[36] Thus, from the subjectivity or point of view of the embodied *souverainiste* discourse, not only would there exist "good reasons" for supporting sovereignty, but good *motives* as well, motives arising from the very essence of the *Québécois'* being. Within the White Paper's account is embedded a "logic," a way of understanding the world, that offers those in Quebec a position from which to understand and act.

Identification with a Constitutive Rhetoric

If the White Paper and historical narratives were but dead history, mere stories, their significance to ideology could easily be dismissed. However, constitutive rhetorics, as they identify, have power because they are oriented towards action. As Althusser and McGee both stress, ideology is material, existing not in the realm of ideas, but in that of *material practices.* Ideology is material because subjects enact their ideology and reconstitute their material world in its image.[37] Constitutive rhetorics are ideological not merely because they provide individuals with narratives to inhabit as subjects and motives to experience, but because they insert "narratized" subjects-as-agents into the world.

The insertion of subjects into the world is a product of both the identificatory and referential functions of the White Paper's historical narrative and its ideological effects. In particular, it is the third ideological

---

[36]Burke, *Symbolic Action,* 6.

[37]McGee and Althusser adopt a similar strategy in order to assert the materiality of meaning. Althusser argues that, "Ideology . . . prescrib[es] material practices governed by a material ritual, which practices exist in the material actions of a subject in all consciousness according to his belief" (Althusser, 170). Similarly, McGee, after tracing out the relationship of myth to ideology, asserts: "Though [myths] technically represent 'false consciousness,' they nonetheless function as a means of providing social unity and collective unity. Indeed, 'the people' *are* the social and political myths they accept" (McGee, 247).

effect, the constitution in action of a motivated subject, that orients those
addressed towards particular future acts. Since narratives offer totalizing
interpretations that ascribe transcendent meanings to individual acts, the
maintenance of narrative consistency demands that a certain set of acts be
chosen. This is amplified in the White Paper because it offers a narrative
without closure. The White Paper offers an unfinished history: the *peuple
québécois* has yet to obtain its independence. Thus, the *Québécois* addressed
by the White Paper must bring to a close the saga begun by the subjects of
the White Paper's history. In other words, while classical narratives have an
ending, constitutive rhetorics leave the task of narrative closure to their
constituted subjects. It is up to the *Québécois* of 1980 to conclude the story
to which they are identified. The story the White Paper offers is of a besieged
peuple that has always continued to struggle in order to survive and to assert
its right to self-determination. Nevertheless, in this account, each advance is
blocked by the colonial power. The story proceeds through the recounting of
a series of episodes, each exhibiting the same pattern.

As we have already seen, the White Paper asserts that the new *peuple's*
aspirations were blocked by British conquest. This act of conquest recurs in
other guises at other moments in the *peuple's* saga. Thus, in the rhetoric of
Quebec sovereignty, for example, the victims of the conquest of 1760 become
the protagonists in the parliamentary wrangles of 1837. Individual subjects,
the *Québécois,* and their collective subject, the *peuple,* are somehow the
same, even though the actual personages, institutions, material conditions, and
struggles have changed. *Québécois* as explorers become political subjects.
Thus, the White Paper asserts:

> The Parliament of Lower Canada, where the language was
> French, proposed laws and a budget that were submitted for approval
> to the Governor, who exercised executive power on behalf of
> London. The *peuple's* will was often blocked by the veto of the
> Governor, particularly sensitive to the interests of the English
> minority of Lower Canada and those of the imperial power. The
> consequent tension was leading, by 1830, to exasperation. The
> representatives drew up a set of resolutions in which they expressed
> their demands: control by the Assembly of taxes and spending, and
> the adoption of urgent social and economic measures. The Governor
> refused and dissolved the House. In the elections that followed, the
> *Patriotes,* headed by Papineau, won 77 out of 88 seats with 90% of
> the vote. To the same demands, the Governor responded by dissolving
> the House once again.[38]

The rhetorical significance of this passage is twofold. First, it typifies the
text's constitution of a subject subjugated by Britain. Note how it confronts
victory with power. In doing so, it highlights what can be presented as an

---

[38]Quebec, *La nouvelle entente,* 5.

inherent contradiction of "French-Canadian" as a subject position that interpellates French-Canadians both as French ethnic subjects and Canadian political subjects. Second, this passage, again typically, rearticulates this subject position: it articulates "Québécois" as a *political* subject battling on the terrain of parliament. In doing so, it dissolves any possible contradiction between loyalty to an (ethnic) nation and the federal state and it articulates both a site for and an object of struggle: the Quebec state apparatus and its legitimated institutions.

The White Paper offers a narrative characterized by a teleological movement towards emancipation. If the root cause of the struggle of the *peuple* is the natural impossibility of the *peuple* to exist without self-determination, control of the state machinery becomes the point of resolution of a drama that began while *Québécois* were still under the rule of the French king. The narrative offers sovereignty as the ultimate point that must be reached in order to attain narrative closure and liberate its subjects. The White Paper offers no alternative but for *Québécois* to struggle against annihilation. To offer but one example among many, the recounting of the 1837 uprising by a nationalist party known as the *Patriotes* and their speedy defeat makes clear that *Québécois* are constituted in a struggle for life itself, a struggle, furthermore, that cannot be won militarily:

> After their lone victory at Saint-Denis, the *Patriotes* were crushed at Saint-Charles and Saint-Eustache. The repression was cruel: hundreds of *Patriotes* were imprisoned and twelve were hanged; here and there, farms were ablaze.[39]

Within the context of contemporary attempts to secure Quebec's independence, the White Paper offers a condensed historical narrative of the *peuple québécois* as teleologically moving towards emancipation. The historical account of the White Paper is decidedly presentist and rhetorical, for a society of the seventeenth century is identified with a society today: the seventeenth century colonists who termed themselves "Canadiens" are termed "Québécois"; past struggles are presented as warranting action in the present. The particular issues over which nineteenth century parliamentarians battled are rendered in ideological terms that are then applied to current battles between Quebec and Canada's Federal government. Each episode in the history moves the *peuple* as subject towards the Quebec Referendum on sovereignty-association. The narrative form provides a continuity across time in which the practices of the past are increasingly identified with the present day order. Thus, the British Conquest, parliamentary wrangles, and the rebellions of 1837, find their counterpart in the "imposition" of a Canadian constitution:

> At the constitutional conferences of 1864 and 1866, the Quebec delegates and those of the other provinces were pursuing very

---

[39]Quebec, *La nouvelle entente*, 6.

different goals. Upper Canada in particular wanted a supraprovincial parliament, endowed with as many and as important powers as possible, that would have presided over the fates of the new country; Quebec, on the other hand, wanted to grant itself a responsible government, enjoying a large degree of autonomy, that would guarantee once and for all the existence and progress of the Quebec *peuple*—and that would have been its *real* government. The opposition between a centralized federalism and a decentralized confederation was already making itself felt. The first idea finally won out. Granted, *Québécois* acquired an autonomous responsible government, but with its autonomy limited to jurisdictions seen then as being primarily of local interest.[40]

The *peuple québécois* is presented as preceding the Canadian state. Confederation, like the Conquest, the defeat of the *Patriotes,* and the unification in 1849 of the predominantly English-speaking colony of Upper Canada with the predominantly French-speaking colony of Lower Canada disrupted the movement of the *peuple* towards the "natural" ideal of its own constitution, responsible government, and a state. The implicit presumption that political structures should provide a means for the articulation and execution of a *peuple's* aspirations, as connoted by the term "peuple" itself, is set in opposition to this account of Canada's formation. The government in Ottawa is not a *real* government. Ottawa's power is represented as illegitimate. The Quebec *peuple* is frustrated, denied progress and its very existence. This narrative's movement towards closure is frustrated by the English presence. The emancipation of the *peuple* is blocked by the pattern of conquest and resistance (*narratio interrupta*). The conquerors stand against narrative teleology as well as history's grand laws.

In the rhetoric of Quebec sovereignty then, the Government of Canada does not arise from the Quebec *peuple* and hence disrupts the teleological flow of history that the narrative form provides. Canada is an antagonist in this life-drama of a *peuple*. As such, Canada must be overcome so that the tensions in the mythic narrative and in history can be resolved. The "natural" principle that *peuples* attain control of their future is denied because Ottawa will preside over destiny. Within the context of the repression of the *Patriotes*, this new order does not arise from the *peuple québécois* but from external constraints. Confederation is but another manifestation of the Conquest to which, in this account, the *peuple* never assented: *Québécois* never acquiesce, but always struggle within the constraints of the possible. The change heralded by Confederation was but a small gain within the British system. Confederation is not the end of the struggle, only a new battleground. On this terrain, the *peuple* is threatened by a political reality that denies its

---

[40]Quebec, *La nouvelle entente,* 7-8.

very being.

The White Paper, having constituted *Québécois* in a struggle for survival, moves them and the narrative into the present. The current constitution that the independence movement opposes is represented as forming the basis for the continued subjugation of the *peuple:*

> The institution of the Canadian federal regime thus sanctioned, and favored as well, the hegemony of a Canada become English. It is quite natural that in such a regime the interests and aspirations of *Québécois* and Francophones in other provinces should take second place. In 1885, for example, all Quebec took the side of Louis Riel, who was fighting for the survival of francophone communities in the West. On the other hand, the federal government fought him and Louis Riel died on the scaffold.[41]

Any possibility that Confederation was advantageous for Quebec is denied. The will of the *peuple*, as instantiated in historical practice, is shown to be undermined in the federal regime. The White Paper describes various defeats of the will of the *peuple* in Confederation: Louis Riel fought for "survival" and climbed the scaffold; rights to French language education outside Quebec were denied; *Québécois* were forced to participate in British wars.[42] The accounts form a tragic tale; the francophones in Canada including the *peuple québécois* are without control of their circumstances.

The narrative concludes by identifying a threat to its very existence as a narrative. Canadian Confederation would deny that Québécois exist and so would deny the very possibility of this constitutive rhetoric and so of an audience inhabiting it. As the White Paper puts it: "The very balance of the system, as the Canadian majority wants it, requires that Quebec remain a province—or perhaps a territory—among ten others, and forbids the formal and concrete recognition of a Quebec nation."[43] This version of Quebec would require a revision of the meaning of "Québécois" such that it no longer positioned its subjects as members of both a nation and state. The "Québécois" would be but the Quebec resident, who might also be a French-Canadian defined in ethnic terms. Thus, in its concluding summary exhorting *Québécois* to vote OUI in the Referendum on sovereignty-association, the White Paper characterizes a NON vote as constituting:

> Only a brutal ending to the healthiest form of progress, one that leads an entire *peuple,* as naturally as an individual, to its maturity. We would simply fall back into line, remain in the state of oblivion kindly granted us by those outsiders who have been keeping a close eye on our progress. ...
> On the contrary, we believe that we are mature enough, and big

---

[41]Quebec, *La nouvelle entente,* 11.
[42]Quebec, *La nouvelle entente,* 11-12.
[43]Quebec, *La nouvelle entente,* 44-45.

enough, and strong enough, to come to terms with our destiny. Because that is what is true.[44]

To be constituted as a *Québécois* in the terms of this narrative is to be constituted such that sovereignty is not only possible, but necessary. Without sovereignty, this constitutive rhetoric would ultimately die and those it has constituted would cease to be subjects, or at least would remain, like children, partial and stunted subjects, lacking maturity, responsibility, and autonomy. In consequence, true *Québécois* could not vote NON. Only a OUI vote would be in harmony with their being and their collective destiny: "Indeed, the choice should be easy, for the heart as well as the mind. We need only give a little thought to how faithful we have been in the past and how strong we are at present; we must think also of those who will follow us, whose futures depend so utterly on that moment."[45]

In sum, the White Paper calls on those it has addressed to follow narrative consistency and the motives through which they are constituted as audience members. Its rhetorical effect derives from their interpellation as subjects and on their identification with a transhistorical and transindividual subject position. It is in this sense of textualizing audiences, therefore, that we can understand the process Black treats in his discussion of the second persona and McGee discusses in his study of the "people." From this perspective, we can see that audiences do not exist outside rhetoric, merely addressed by it, but live inside rhetoric. Indeed, from the moment they enter into the world of language, they are subjects; the very moment of recognition of an address constitutes an entry into a subject position to which inheres a set of motives that render a rhetorical discourse intelligible. These subject positions are bequeathed by the past, by yesterday's discourses. Furthermore, the contradictions between discourses as well as the dialectic between discourse and a changing concrete world open a space for new subject positions. Tensions in the realm of the symbolic render possible the rhetorical repositioning or rearticulation of subjects.

Conclusion

Early in this essay, I identified two problems deserving examination: the first regarding the ontological status of those addressed by discourse before their successful interpellation; the second regarding the ontological status of the persona and the process by which one is identified with it. I have treated the latter problem by introducing the concept of the subject and by showing that audiences are constituted as subjects through a process of identification with a textual position. This identification occurs through a series of ideological effects arising from the narrative structure of constitutive rhetoric. As for the first problem I posed, I have in a sense circumvented it through

---

[44]Quebec, *La nouvelle entente,* 109-110.
[45]Quebec, *La nouvelle entente,* 118.

my analysis. Persons are subjects from the moment they acquire language and the capacity to speak and to be spoken to. As such, constitutive rhetoric is part of the discursive background of social life. It is always there, usually implicitly, and sometimes explicitly articulated. It is more than a set of commonplaces, but is the con-text, the pre-rhetoric that is necessary to any successful interpellation.

Our first subject positions are modest, linked to our name, our family, and our sex. As we enter the adult world, they become more complex, as different constitutive rhetorics reposition us with respect to such formal and informal institutions as the state, the economy, the church, and the school. Thus, though we are subjects through language, and indeed can only speak as subjects, our subjectivity and ideological commitments are not fixed at our first utterance. As Quebec public address illustrates, particular subject positions can undergo transformation: "Canadien français" can become "Québécois," an identity permitting claims for a new political order. At particular historical moments, political rhetorics can reposition or rearticulate subjects by performing ideological work upon the texts in which social actors are inscribed.

In this essay, I have suggested that Burke's privileging of the term "identification" and an understanding of rhetoric's constitutive and ontological effect, as suggested by structuralist discourse theory, have certain consequences for the theory and practice of rhetoric. A theory of constitutive rhetoric leads us to call into question the concept, usually implicit to rhetoric's humanist tradition, of an audience composed of unified and transcendent subjects. If we are left with a subject, that subject is partial and decentered. History, and indeed discourse itself, form the ground for subjectivity. Consequently, even what Fisher terms "narrative fidelity" has an ideological character, for the experiential ground to which narratives would be faithful are always already ideologically framed within the very being of the experiencing subject.[46]

Because ideology forms the ground for any rhetorical situation, a theory of ideological rhetoric must be mindful not only of arguments and ideographs, but of the very nature of the subjects that rhetoric both addresses and leads to come to be. Indeed, because the constitutive nature of rhetoric establishes the boundary of a subject's motives and experience, a truly ideological rhetoric must rework or transform subjects. A transformed ideology would require a transformed subject (not a dissolving of subjectivity). Such a transformation requires ideological and rhetorical work. This can proceed at two levels: (1) it can proceed at the level of the constitutive narrative itself, providing stories that through the identificatory principle shift and rework the subject and its motives; (2) it can also proceed at the aesthetic level of what Williams terms the "structure of feeling" and

---

[46]Fisher, 8.

Grossberg describes as the "affective apparatus."[47] Since, as Fisher observes, the truth of a narrative resides in its "fidelity," which is an aesthetic quality, new true narratives become possible as new modes of aesthetic experience emerge and gain social meaning. Ideological rhetorical practice is not restricted to explicitly political public address, but can include a range of aesthetic practices, including music, drama, architecture, and fashion, that elicit new modes of experience and being.

The significance of the rhetorical tradition is that it has long realized that discourse has eminently political and practical effects. In recognizing the contingency of the social, it offers the possibility of social critique and the development of *praxis*. However, in order to overcome the constraints of ideology, rhetorical theory must see through the 'givenness' of what appears to be the delimitable rhetorical situation, where the ontological status of speaker, speech, audience, topic, and occasion offer themselves as unproblematic. It must recognize that ultimately, the position one embodies as a subject is a rhetorical effect.

[47]Raymond Williams, *Marxism and Literature* (New York: Oxford University Press, 1977), 128-135; Lawrence Grossberg, "Is There Rock after Punk," *Critical Studies in Mass Communications* 3 (March 1986): 69-70.

Bibliography

Abrams, M. H. *The Mirror and the Lamp: Romantic Theory and the Critical Tradition*. New York: Oxford University Press, 1953.

Andrews, James R. "The Passionate Negation: The Chartist Movement in Rhetorical Perspective." *Quarterly Journal of Speech* 59 (1973): 196-208.

____. *The Practice of Rhetorical Criticism*. 2d ed. New York: Longman, 1990.

____. "Rhetoric in the Creation of Social Reality: Radical Consciousness and Whig Strategy in Parliamentary Reform." *Quarterly Journal of Speech* 69 (1983): 401-412.

Arnold, Carroll C. *Criticism of Oral Rhetoric*. Columbus, OH: Merrill, 1974.

Atkins, J. W. H. *Literary Criticism in Antiquity: A Sketch of Its Development*. 2 vols. Cambridge: Cambridge University Press, 1934.

Baskerville, Barnett. "Joe McCarthy: Briefcase Demagogue." *Today's Speech* 2 (September 1954): 8-15.

Bakhtin, M. M. *The Dialogic Imagination*. Trans. Caryl Emerson, and Michael Holquist. Austin: University of Texas Press, 1981.

Barthes, Roland. *Image-Music-Text*. Trans. Stephen Heath. New York: Noonday, 1977.

____. *Mythologies*. Trans. Annette Lavers. New York: Hill and Wang, 1972.

Bass, Jeff D. "The Appeal to Efficiency as Narrative Closure: Lyndon Johnson and the Dominican Crisis, 1965." *Southern Speech Communication Journal* 51 (1984): 103-120.

Bazerman, Charles. *Shaping Written Knowledge: The Genre and Activity of the Experimental Article in Science*. Madison: University of Wisconsin Press, 1988.

Bazerman, Charles, and James Paradis, eds. *Textual Dynamics of the Professions: Historical and Contemporary Studies of Writing in Professional Communities*. Madison: University of Wisconsin Press, 1991.

Bender, John, and David E. Wellbery, eds. *The Ends of Rhetoric: History, Theory, Practice*. Stanford, CA: Stanford University Press, 1990.

Benson, Thomas W., ed. *American Rhetoric: Context and Criticism*. Carbondale, IL: Southern Illinois University Press, 1989.

Benson, Thomas W., and Carolyn Anderson. *Reality Fictions: The Films of Frederick Wiseman*. Carbondale: Southern Illinois University Press, 1989.

Birdsell, David. "Ronald Reagan on Lebanon and Grenada: Flexibility and Interpretation in the Application of Kenneth Burke's Pentad." *Quarterly Journal of Speech* 73 (1987): 267-279.

Bitzer, Lloyd. "The Rhetorical Situation." *Philosophy and Rhetoric* 1 (1968): 1-14.

Bitzer, Lloyd F., and Edwin Black, eds. *The Prospect of Rhetoric*. Englewood Cliffs, NJ: Prentice-Hall, 1971.

Black, Edwin. *Rhetorical Criticism: A Study in Method*. Madison, WI: University of Wisconsin Press, 1978.

____. *Rhetorical Questions*. Chicago: University of Chicago Press, 1992.

Blair, Carole. "From 'All the President's Men' to Every Man for Himself: The Strategies of Post-Watergate Apologia." *Central States Speech Journal* 35 (1984): 250-260.

Booth, Wayne C. *The Company We Keep: An Ethics of Fiction*. Berkeley: University of California Press, 1988.

____. *Critical Understanding: The Powers and Limits of Pluralism*. Chicago: University of Chicago Press, 1979.

____. *The Rhetoric of Fiction*. 2d ed. Chicago: University of Chicago Press, 1983.

Bordwell, David. *Making Meaning: Inference and Rhetoric in the Interpretation of Cinema*. Cambridge, MA: Harvard University Press, 1989.

Bormann, Ernest G. "Fantasy and Rhetorical Vision: The Rhetorical Criticism of Social Reality." *Quarterly Journal of Speech* 58 (1972): 396-407.

____. *The Force of Fantasy: Restoring the American Dream*. Carbondale, IL: Southern Illinois University Press, 1985.

Branham, Robert, and W. Barnett Pearce. "A Contract for Civility: Edward Kennedy's Lynchburg Address." *Quarterly Journal of Speech* 73 (1987): 424-443.

Brigance, William Norwood, ed. *History and Criticism of American Public Address*. 2 vols. New York: McGraw-Hill, 1943.

Brock, Bernard L., Robert L. Scott, and James W. Chesebro, eds. *Methods of Rhetorical Criticism: A Twentieth-Century Perspective*. 3d ed. Detroit, MI: Wayne State University Press, 1989.

Brockriede, Wayne. "Rhetorical Criticism as Argument." *Quarterly Journal of Speech* 60 (1974): 165-174.

Browne, Nick. "The Spectator-in-the-Text: The Rhetoric of *Stagecoach*." *Film Quarterly* 29 (Dec. 1975): 26-38.

Browne, Stephen H. *Edmund Burke and the Discourse of Virtue*. Tuscaloosa: University of Alabama Press, 1993.

Brummet, Barry. *Rhetorical Dimensions of Popular Culture*. Tuscaloosa: University of Alabama Press, 1991.

Bryant, Donald C. *Rhetorical Dimensions in Criticism*. Baton Rouge, LA: Louisiana State University Press, 1973.

Burke, Kenneth. *The Philosophy of Literary Form*. 3d ed. Berkeley: University of California Press, 1973.

____. *A Rhetoric of Motives*. Berkeley: University of California Press, 1969.

Campbell, John Angus. "The Polemical Mr. Darwin." *Quarterly Journal of Speech* 61 (1975): 375-390.

Campbell, Karlyn Kohrs. *Critiques of Contemporary Rhetoric*. Belmont, CA: Wadsworth, 1972.

____. "The Rhetoric of Women's Liberation: An Oxymoron." *Quarterly Journal of Speech* 59 (1973): 74-86.

Campbell, Karlyn Kohrs, and Kathleen Hall Jamieson. *Deeds Done in Words: Presidential Rhetoric and the Genres of Governance.* Chicago: University of Chicago Press, 1990.

Cavell, Stanley. *Pursuits of Happiness: The Hollywood Comedy of Remarriage.* Cambridge, MA: Harvard University Press, 1981.

Chatman, Seymour. *Coming to Terms: The Rhetoric of Narrative in Fiction and Film.* Ithaca, NY: Cornell University Press, 1990.

Chesebro, James. "Paradoxical Views of Homosexuality in the Rhetoric of Social Scientists: A Fantasy Theme Analysis." *Quarterly Journal of Speech* 66 (1980): 127-139.

Clifford, James, and George E. Marcus, eds. *Writing Culture: The Poetics and Politics of Ethnography.* Berkeley: University of California Press, 1986.

Corbett, Edward P. J., ed. *Rhetorical Analyses of Literary Works.* New York: Oxford University Press, 1969.

Cox, Robert. "The Die Is Cast: Topical and Ontological Dimensions of the *Locus* of the Irreperable." *Quarterly Journal of Speech* 68 (1982): 227-239.

DeMan, Paul. *Blindness and Insight: Essays in the Rhetoric of Contemporary Criticism.* New York: Oxford University Press, 1983.

Dolan, Frederick M., and Thomas L. Dumm, eds. *Rhetorical Republic: Governing Representations in American Politics.* Amherst, MA: University of Massachusetts Press, 1993.

Dorfman, Ariel, and Armand Mattelart. *How to Read Donald Duck: Imperialist Ideology in the Disney Comic.* New York: International General, 1975.

Edelman, Murray. *Constructing the Political Spectacle.* Chicago: University of Chicago Press, 1988.

Farrell, Thomas, and Thomas Goodnight. "Accidental Rhetoric: The Root Metaphors of Three Mile Island." *Communication Monographs* 49 (1981): 271-300.

Fisher, Walter R. *Human Communication as Narration: Toward a Philosophy of Reason, Value, and Action.* Columbia, SC: University of South Carolina Press, 1987.

Foss, Sonja K., ed. *Rhetorical Criticism: Exploration and Practice.* Prospect Heights, IL: Waveland, 1989.

Greenblatt, Stephen. *Renaissance Self-Fashioning: From More to Shakespeare.* Chicago: University of Chicago Press, 1980.

Gregg, Richard B. "The Criticism of Symbolic Inducement: A Critical-Theoretical Connection." *Speech Communication in the 20th Century.* Thomas W. Benson (ed.). Carbondale: Southern Illinois University Press, 1985. 41-62.

____. "The Ego-Function of the Rhetoric of Protest." *Philosophy and Rhetoric* 4 (1971): 71-91.

Gross, Alan G. *The Rhetoric of Science.* Cambridge: Harvard University Press, 1990.

Hart, Roderick P. *Modern Rhetorical Criticism*. Glenview, IL: Scott, Foresman/Little, Brown, 1990.

_____. *The Political Pulpit*. Lafayette, IN: Purdue University Press, 1977.

_____. *The Sound of Leadership: Presidential Communication in the Modern Age*. Chicago: University of Chicago Press, 1987.

_____. "Theory-Building and Rhetorical Criticism: An Informal Statement of Opinion." *Central States Speech Journal* 27 (1976): 70-77.

Hatzenbuehler, R., and Robert Ivie. *Congress Declares War: Rhetorical Leadership and Partisanship in the Early Republic*. Kent, OH: Kent State University Press, 1983.

Hikins, James W. "The Rhetoric of 'Unconditional Surrender' and the Decision to Drop the Atomic Bomb." *Quarterly Journal of Speech* 69 (1983): 379-400.

Hillbruner, Anthony. *Critical Dimensions: The Art of Public Address Criticism*. New York: Random House, 1966.

Hirsch, E. D. *Validity in Interpretation*. New Haven: Yale University Press, 1967.

Hogan, J. Michael. *The Panama Canal in American Politics: Domestic Advocacy and the Evolution of Policy*. Carbondale, IL: Southern Illinois University Press, 1986.

Iser, Wolfgang. *The Implied Reader: Patterns of Communication in Prose Fiction from Bunyan to Beckett*. Baltimore, MD: Johns Hopkins University Press, 1974.

Ivie, Robert L. "Images of Savagery in American Justifications for War." *Communication Monographs* 47 (1980): 279-294.

Jameson, Frederic. *The Political Unconscious: Narrative as a Socially Symbolic Act*. Ithaca, NY: Cornell University Press, 1981.

Jamieson, Kathleen Hall. *Dirty Politics*. New York: Oxford University Press, 1992.

_____. *Eloquence in an Electronic Age*. New York: Oxford University Press, 1988.

Japp, Phyllis. "Esther or Isaiah: The Abolitionist-Feminist Rhetoric of Angelina Grimke." *Quarterly Journal of Speech* 71 (1985): 335-348.

Kerr, Harry P. "Politics and Religion in Colonial Fast and Thanksgiving Sermons, 1763-1783." *Quarterly Journal of Speech* 46 (1960): 372-382.

Lake, Randall A. "Enacting Red Power: The Consummatory Function in Native American Protest Rhetoric." *Quarterly Journal of Speech* 69 (1983): 127-142.

Leff, Michael C., and Fred J. Kauffeld, eds. *Texts in Context: Critical Dialogues on Significant Episodes in American Political Rhetoric*. Davis, CA: Hermagoras Press, 1989.

Lentricchia, Frank. *Criticism and Social Change*. Chicago: University of Chicago Press, 1983.

Longinus. *"Longinus" on Sublimity*. Trans. D. A. Russell. Oxford: Clarendon Press, 1965.

Lucaites, John Louis, and Celeste Condit. "Reconstructing <Equality>: Culturetypal and Counter-Cultural Rhetoric in the Martyred Black Vision." *Communication Monographs* 56 (1990): 5-24.

Lucas, Stephen E. *Portents of Rebellion: Rhetoric and Revolution in Philadelphia, 1765-1776.* Philadelphia: Temple University Press, 1976.

Mailloux, Steven. *Rhetorical Power.* Ithaca, NY: Cornell University Press, 1989.

McCloskey, Donald N. *The Rhetoric of Economics.* Madison, WI: University of Wisconsin Press, 1985.

McGuire, Michael D. "Mythic Rhetoric in *Mein Kampf*: A Structuralist Critique." *Quarterly Journal of Speech* 63 (1977): 1-13.

Medhurst, Martin J. "*Hiroshima, Mon Amour*: From Iconography to Rhetoric." *Quarterly Journal of Speech* 68 (1982): 345-370.

Medhurst, Martin J., and Thomas W. Benson, eds. *Rhetorical Dimensions in Media: A Critical Casebook.* 2d ed. Dubuque, IA: Kendall/Hunt, 1991.

Mohrmann, G. P., and Michael C. Leff. "Lincoln at Cooper Union: A Rationale for Neo-Classical Criticism." Quarterly Journal of Speech 60 (1974): 459-467.

Nelson, John S., Allan Megill, and Donald N. McCloskey, eds. *The Rhetoric of the Human Sciences: Language and Argument in Scholarship and Public Affairs.* Madison, WI: University of Wisconsin Press, 1987.

Newton, K. M. *Interpreting the Text: A Critical Introduction to the Theory and Practice of Literary Interpretation.* New York: St. Martin's Press, 1990.

Nichols, Marie Hochmuth. *History and Criticism of American Public Address.* Vol. 3. London: Longmans, Green, 1955.

Olson, Lester C. *Emblems of American Community in the Revolutionary Era.* Washington, DC: Smithsonian Institution Press, 1991.

Philipsen, Gerry. "Speaking 'Like a Man' in Teamsterville: Cultural Patterns of Role Enactment in an Urban Neighborhood." *Quarterly Journal of Speech* 61 (1975): 13-22.

Radway, Janice. *Reading the Romance: Women, Patriarchy, and Popular Literature.* Chapel Hill, NC: University of North Carolina Press, 1984.

Roberts, R. H., and J. M. M. Good, eds. *The Recovery of Rhetoric: Persuasive Discourse and Disciplinarity in the Human Sciences.* Charlottesville, VA: University Press of Virginia, 1993.

Rosenfield, Lawrence W. "The Anatomy of Critical Discourse." *Speech Monographs* 35 (1968): 50-69.

____. "The Experience of Criticism." *Quarterly Journal of Speech* 60 (1974): 489-496.

Rothman, William. *Hitchcock: The Murderous Gaze.* Cambridge, MA: Harvard University Press, 1982.

Rushing, Janice Hocker. "The Rhetoric of the American Western Myth." *Communication Monographs* 50 (1983): 14-32.

Russell, D. A. *Criticism in Antiquity.* London: Duckworth, 1981.

Simons, Herbert W., ed. *The Rhetorical Turn: Invention and Persuasion in the Conduct of Inquiry.* Chicago: University of Chicago Press, 1990.

Solomon, Martha. "The Rhetoric of STOP ERA: Fatalistic Reaffirmation." *Southern Speech Communication Journal* 44 (1978): 42-59.

Thonssen, Lester, A. Craig Baird, and Waldo W. Braden. *Speech Criticism*. 2d ed. Malabar, FL: Krieger, 1981.

Wander, Philip. "The Ideological Turn in Modern Criticism." *Central States Speech Journal* 34 (1983): 1-18.

____. "The Rhetoric of American Foreign Policy." *Quarterly Journal of Speech* 70 (1984): 339-361.

Warnick, Barbara. "The Rhetoric of Conservative Resistance." *Southern Speech Communication Journal* 42 (1977): 256-273.

Weaver, Richard. *The Ethics of Rhetoric*. Chicago: Henry Regnery, 1953.

White, Eugene E. *The Context of Human Discourse: A Configurational Criticism of Rhetoric*. Rhetoric/Communication. Columbia, SC: South Carolina University Press, 1992.

____. *Puritan Rhetoric: The Issue of Emotion in Religion*. Carbondale, IL: Southern Illinois University Press, 1972.

Wills, Garry. *Lincoln at Gettysburg: The Words that Remade America*. New York: Simon & Schuster, 1992.

Windt, Theodore Otto , Jr. "The Diatribe: Last Resort for Protest." *Quarterly Journal of Speech* 58 (1972): 1-14.

Zarefsky, David. *Lincoln, Douglas, and Slavery: In the Crucible of Public Debate*. Chicago: University of Chicago Press, 1990.

____. *President Johnson's War on Poverty: Rhetoric and History*. University, AL: University of Alabama Press, 1986.

Zyskind, Harold. "A Case Study in Philosophic Rhetoric: Theodore Roosevelt." *Philosophy and Rhetoric* 1 (1968): 228-254.

Index

A

action, 85
active construction, 118
ad hominem, 101, 177, 181, 183
Adams, John, 203
adaptation, 15, 29, 133
Addison, Joseph, 30
advisory speaking, 102
Agassiz, Louis, 147, 157
Allen, Woody, 224
allusion, 98, 101
Althusser, Louis, 213-214, 218, 220, 225, 227
amplification, 13, 101
analogies, 131
analogy, 183
anecdotes, 178
Anne, Queen, 209
Anthony, Susan, 190
anti-Semitism, 37
Antifederalists, 204-205, 210
antithesis, 177, 184
antithetical language, 186
appeasement, 135
archetype, 172
argument, xxi, 27, 85, 88, 95, 100, 104, 152, 155, 175-177, 179, 184-185, 233
argumentation, 83, 198
arguments, 132, 186
Aristotelianism, xiii
Aristotle, xix, 26, 28, 31, 97, 134-135, 163
Aristotle, Poetics, 28, 162
Aristotle, Rhetoric, 28, 162
Arnold, Carroll C., xv, 105
arrangement, 28, 79, 182
art of communication, 27
Aryan doctrine, 43
audience, xv-xvi, xix-xx, 15-16, 18, 21-22, 27-30, 72-73, 79, 83, 86-87, 133-134, 164, 177, 180-181, 184, 186, 191-193, 195, 198, 213, 219-220, 225-226, 231-232
author, 162
authority, 95-96

B

Baillie, Captain, 90, 104
Baldwin, C. S., 27-28
Bard, Morton, 170
Barthes, Roland, 221, 224
Basler, Roy P., 173
beauty, xv, 26, 77, 86, 104
belles-lettres, 31
Benjamin, Judah, 53
Bentley, Elizabeth, 171
Benton, Thomas Hart, 5
Best, Sergeant William Draper, 97
Bingham, Richard, 91, 93, 103
Birrell, Augustine, 3

Bitzer, Lloyd, xvi
Black, Edwin, xx, 105, 108, 219-220, 227, 232
Blair, Hugh, 97, 103
Boddington, Benjamin, 91
Booth, Wayne, xx, 163
Bossuet, Jacques-Benigne, 1
Bridgewater, 153
Bright, John, 1, 21, 23
Brown, John, 52, 182
Browning, Elizabeth Barrett, 191
Browning, O. H., 70-72, 82
Bryant, Donald C., 129
Bryant, William Cullen, 58
Bryce, James, 21-25
Buchan, Earl of, 89
Buchanan, James, 51, 57, 68, 70, 75
burden of proof, 181
Burke, Edmund, 1-8, 11-14, 18-19, 22, 25-26, 30
Burke, Kenneth, xvi, xix-xxi, 107, 110, 194, 213-214, 219, 222-225, 227, 233
Burnham, John, 171
Burtt, E. A., 145
Butler, H. M., 18-19, 22, 24
Byron, George Gordon, 11

C

Calhoun, 4
campaign oration, 175
Campbell, George, 103
Campbell, John Angus, xviii
Campbell, Karlyn Kohrs, xix, xxi
cancer, 169-171
cancer of communism, 166, 168, 172
Cannon, W. F., 148
capitalism, 35
Caplan, Harry, 92
Carnegie, Andrew, 128
catastrophism, 146-148, 157
catastrophists, 151, 158
cause, 37, 39-41, 123
causes, xv
certainty, 45
chain of being, 143
Chambers, Robert, 155-156
Chambers, Whitaker, 171
change, 199
Chapman, John, 191
character, xix, 4, 19, 22, 28, 78, 162-163, 166, 175, 184
Charland, Maurice, xx
Chatham, 14, 18, 22
Cheever, George, 168
Christian Anti-Communist Crusade, 141
Christian Anti-Communist Crusade University, 133
Church of England, 203
Cicero, xix, 1, 8, 91
civic action, xix

Jew as scapegoat, 35
John Birch Society, 166-167
Johnson, Samuel, 1-2, 8
judgment, 94
judicial critics, 25
justice, 92, 94, 97

K

Kauffeld, Fred, 128
Kierkegaard, Soren, 196
Kingsley, Charles, 145, 154
Kuhn, Thomas S., 137

L

Lamarck, 149
Lamb, Charles, 30
landmark, xi-xii
Langer, Susanne K., 194
language, 25, 27, 30, 72, 75-77, 84, 92, 101,
     103, 105-108, 112, 114, 117, 125, 233
Larson, Arthur, xvii, 127
law, 97
Law Center, 132
Law, Edward, 98
leader, 202
leader-people identification, 42
Lecky, W. E. H., 18-19
Leuchtenburg, William E., 108
Lincoln, Abraham, xvi, 1, 3, 6-7, 10, 12, 15,
     51-88, 173
Lincoln, purpose, 79
Lincoln's Inn, 90
literary art, 11
literary critic, 25-26, 30, 77
literary criticism, xv, 29-30, 102
literary form, 17, 194
literary quality, 6
literature, 1, 97
Locke, David, 58
Locke, John, 31
Lodge, Henry Cabot, 11-12
logic, 177
logical, 180
Longinus, 5
Louis A. Warren, 71
Lovejoy, Arthur O., 147, 156
Lucas, Stephen E., xix
Lyell, Charles, 148-151, 155
Lynd, Robert, 3
lyric, 191-192, 194, 196, 199
lyrical, 192

M

Macintosh, James, 98, 101
Madison, James, 74, 210
males, 197
Mansfield, Lord, 89-90
Markham, George, 98, 100
Markham v Fawcett, 98

Marquis of Headfort, 98, 101
marriage, 94, 96
Marx, Karl, 164
mass media, 110
Massy, Charles, 98-101
materialization, 34-35
McGee, Michael Calvin, xvi, xxi, 214, 217-
     218, 221-222, 227, 232
McGuire, Michael, 219
Mead, G. H., 221
Mein Kampf, 33
Memorial Sloan-Kettering Cancer Center, 170
Mencken, H. L., 11
metaphor, xviii, 166-172, 184, 191
Michelangelo, 57
Miller, Perry, 167-168
Minorca, 89
Missouri Compromise, 52
mistrust of persuasion, 139
Mitford, Sir John, 94-97
Montaigne, Michel, 30
moral judgment, 161-162, 166, 172
Morin, Claude, 217
Morley, John, 1, 5, 19-25, 29-30
Morris, Williams, 178
Morton Prince, 38
motives, 29
Mouvement Souveraineté-Association (MSA),
     215
MSA, 217
myth, xviii, 135
mythology, 187

N

narrative, 191, 221-225, 227-229, 231-232,
     234
narrative consistency, 232
narrative fidelity, 233
narrative ideological effects, 214
narrative probability, 224
National American Woman Suffrage
     Association, 189, 197
natural causes, 158
Natural Law, 43
natural selection, 143, 150, 154, 158
natural theology, 151, 153-154, 157
nature, 127-128
Nevins, Allan, 173
New Deal, 108, 167
New England, 203-204
Nichols, Marie Hochmuth, xvi, 105-106, 108
Nicolay, John G., 173
noneconomic interpretation, 39, 40

O

Objectivity, 45
occasion, 27-28, 78, 202
occasional speaking, 102
Ong, Walter J., xxi
opinion, 75